Looking
in
classrooms

Looking
in
classrooms

Thomas L. Good
University of Missouri, Columbia

Jere E. Brophy
University of Texas, Austin

Harper & Row, Publishers
New York,   Evanston,   San Francisco,   London

To Our Parents

Contents

Preface

The first purpose of this book is to provide a focus, a way of looking, at what teachers and pupils do in classrooms. The maze of interacting behaviors occurring in classrooms is rich and complex, and can be understood only if the observer can see and assess a wide variety of classroom factors. Many important events go unnoticed unless the observer is looking for them. For example, as John Holt (1964) points out in *How Children Fail*, untrained observers often focus their undivided attention on the teacher. They seldom look at students except when they are responding to teacher questions, and at these times the students are on their best behavior. Observers often fail to notice clues that describe the interest and involvement of the students in the task at hand. This book describes a number of things to look for in classrooms, and provides forms for observers to use to measure their presence through systematic observation methods. The book will provide the teacher, then, with concrete skills enabling him to become more aware of what he does in the classroom and to interpret causes and remedies for his observed weaknesses. By learning to use the observation forms, the student of classroom behavior, whether or not he is a teacher, will increase his skills for assessing classrooms on specific, observable criteria.

The second purpose of the book is to make some positive prescriptive statements about the classroom behavior of teachers. Detailed suggestions are supplied, for example, about how teachers can increase pupil involvement with school tasks and decrease the time students spend in "neutral" or engaged in disruptive activities. These suggestions are not made in the form of global, gratuitous advice; instead, advice is given in the form of specific, objective behaviors. Books written for the teacher typically provide only general information that often does not help the teacher in any direct way. For example, the teacher is often told to individualize instruction, but is not given specific information about how to do this. We have tried to say not only what to do, but also how to do it. This aspect of the book will be especially useful for the in-service and preservice teacher, since the information presented is highly concrete and specific.

Most of the prescriptive, detailed comments included in the book are established or at least suggested by research. However, they typically go beyond available data, in order to provide teachers with concrete suggestions presented in a form they can understand and apply. Implications and applications are usually spelled out rather than left for the reader to find for himself. Some of the comments and suggestions are based upon our observations in classrooms and our work with classroom teachers and students in classroom settings. While they are consistent with research findings, they do go beyond existing data. Therefore, our suggestions should be viewed not as research findings, but as good advice that has been drawn from a variety of sources.

Although principals, supervisors, and graduate students enrolled in classes in school psychology, school learning, or classroom interaction will find this book useful, the primary audience to which the book is addressed is the classroom teacher and the teacher candidate. Students enrolled in observation courses or student teaching seminars should find this book particularly useful. Teaching is a very important and exceedingly difficult job. This book is written to help teachers learn to perform this difficult task better, by making them more aware of how they behave in classrooms and by providing suggestions for improving observed weaknesses. In summary, then, this book is intended to help teachers and teacher candidates to acquire a *classroom language* for describing important classroom events and to learn new instructional patterns for improving their classroom effectiveness.

Much has been written about the replacement of teachers in the schools with computers and other technological devices. Even with continued technical progress, however, we believe that the teacher's role in the classroom will continue to be an important and vital one. This book is dedicated to classroom teachers and their efforts in supervising and aiding the development of their students.

We wish to acknowledge the secretarial assistance given by the Center for Research in Social Behavior, University of Missouri, Bruce J. Biddle, Director. Special thanks are expressed to Sue Gunn, Pat Hollowell, and Sherry Watts for typing the manuscript. We also sincerely appreciate the encouragement and stimulation that we received from colleagues at the Research and Development Center for Teacher Education at the University of Texas, Oliver H. Bown and Robert F. Peck, co-directors, and from our colleagues in the colleges of education at the University of Missouri and the University of Texas.

Numerous graduate students, research assistants, classroom teachers and colleagues have worked with the authors and helped us to think and learn about life in classrooms. We shall not attempt to credit all who have influenced us, because there are simply too many of them to mention. But for their contributions to the development of this book, and for their consistent encouragement, we gratefully acknowledge the following persons: Dr. Carolyn Evertson, Susan Florence, Suzi Good, Dr. Teresa Harris, Sue Jones, Dr. Vern Jones, Karen Mays, Sonia Mendoza, Dr. Shari Nedler, Kathey Paredes, Jo Ellen Rivers, Dr. Jev Sikes, Dr. Sherry Willis, Dave Wilson, and Dianne Wilson.

Special appreciation and thanks are extended to our wives, Suzi and Arlene, for the way they have sustained us in this effort through their unfailing patience, support, and enthusiasm. Finally, we dedicate this book to all who teach and who attempt to structure exciting learning environments for students, but especially to our first and most important teachers: our parents.

Looking
in
classrooms

CHAPTER 1

Classroom
life

This book has two major purposes. Our first goal is to help classroom teachers and students of classroom behavior to develop ways of looking at and describing what goes on in the classroom. Second, we want to provide teachers with concrete suggestions about ways in which they can behave for a positive influence on the interests, learning, and social development of their students. Chapters 1 and 2 define the problem by suggesting that teachers are often unaware of certain classroom behaviors, and that this lack of perception sometimes results in unwise, self-defeating behavior. Our intent is not just to deliver negative statements or to criticize teachers; rather, the spirit of the introductory chapters is to show that the development of skills for observing and describing classroom behavior is a prerequisite for improving classroom teaching.

A major purpose of the first two chapters is to sensitize the reader to the fact that it is difficult to perceive what takes place in the classroom. Life in classrooms proceeds at such a complex and rapid pace that it is difficult for the teacher or observer to monitor teacher and student behavior accurately. Certainly if one is to make valid suggestions about how to improve classroom behavior, he must be able to see and to assess what is happening in classrooms. The introductory chapters indicate the difficulties that reduce one's ability to see and to comprehend classroom life and discuss how such partial vision interferes with classroom progress.

The remainder of the book is designed to provide teachers, observers, and researchers with suggestions about what to look for in classrooms. Following the introductory chapters are several chapters that deal at length with certain aspects of the content of classroom life. Chapters 4 through 9 contain a number of suggestions about how teachers can interact more profitably with their students. To help teachers and observers learn to separate and make sense out of the thousands of events that occur hourly in classrooms, observation forms for coding classroom behavior have been placed at the end of each of these chapters. The reader can use the forms to measure some of the behaviors that are discussed in the chapters. Thus the chapters on classroom content have a twin focus: (1) to describe key classroom behaviors and make suggestions about effective teaching and (2) to provide ways to measure the presence or absence of some of these behaviors.

The emphasis of this book is on classroom behavior. We want the reader to become actively involved in the process of looking at how teachers and students actually behave in the classroom, so that he can generate alternatives for improving classroom learning when his present instructional procedures fail to produce desirable effects. To facilitate this goal, we have included many extended examples of classroom behavior in the text and have added practice exercises to help the reader learn how to describe and to cope with classroom behavior. Consistent with this philosophy of active involvement, we will begin with simulated dialogue from a classroom.

Mrs. Turner: an example

Before turning to a discussion of the problems that teachers face, it will be useful to sample a few moments of life in an elementary classroom. As you read the example, try to pinpoint those teaching behaviors that you feel are effective and those that you feel are ineffective. You might profitably think about what you would have done *differently* if you had been the teacher. *Jot down your ideas and reactions as you read the material* and try to note as many teaching strengths and weaknesses as you can find. This will give you a chance to describe and to react to classroom behavior. Find out how much you can see in the classroom dialogue that appears in the example.

Mrs. Turner is an attractive fourth-grade teacher at Maplewood elementary school in a large university town in the South. She has 30 students in her class. Students at Maplewood come primarily from lower middle-class and working-class homes. Most of the students are white (78 percent), and the rest (22 percent) are black.

Sally Turner has taught at Maplewood since graduating from the university three years ago. Her husband, Jim, is in his last year of law school and they plan to leave the city when Jim finishes school.

The classroom scene we will witness below takes place in March. The students have been reading about Columbus and his voyage, and Sally's lesson plan involved two goals: (1) to review the basic facts surrounding Columbus' voyage to the New World and (2) to have students compare the uncertainties, dangers, and fears that faced Columbus and his sailors to those that astronauts face on their journeys to the moon. The classroom scene begins as Sally passes out mimeographed copies of a map showing the sea routes that Columbus followed on each of his trips.

BILLY: (*almost shouting*) I didn't get no map.

TEACHER: (*calmly and deliberately*) Billy, share Rosie's map. Tim, you can look with either Margaret or Larry.

TIM: Can I look with Jill?

TEACHER: (*slightly agitated*) Okay, but don't play around. You and Jill always get into trouble. (*Most of the students turn to look at Jill and Tim.*) I don't want you two fooling around today!

(*smiling with warmth*) Okay, class, now does everybody have a map? I wanted to pass out these maps before I started the lesson. You can see that the route of each voyage is traced on this map. It might help you to understand that there were different trips and different routes. Now today pay special attention in the discussion because you'll need to know the information for tomorrow's quiz. If the discussion goes well today, I have a special treat for you— two filmstrips.

(*The class breaks out in a spontaneous, exuberant roar.*) Yea!

TEACHER: Who can tell me something about Columbus' background?

KAY: (*calling out*) He was born in 1451 in Italy.

TEACHER: Good answer, Kay, I can tell you have been reading the material. Class, can anyone tell me who influenced Columbus' urge to explore unknown seas? (*She looks around and calls on Jerry, one of several students who have raised their hands.*)

JERRY: He had read Marco Polo's story about his voyage to Cathay and all about the fantastic money he found there.

TEACHER: Okay. Jan, when did Columbus land in America?

JAN: 1492.

TEACHER: Terrific! I know you have been reading your lesson, good girl! Where did Columbus stop for supplies on the way to the New World?

JIM: (*laughingly*) But Mrs. Turner, the date was on the map you passed out.

TEACHER: (*with irritation*) Jim, don't call out comments without raising your hand!

BILL: (*calling out*) The Canary Islands.

TEACHER: Okay, Bill. Now, what were the names of the three ships? (*She looks around the room and calls on Biff who has his hand up.*) Biff, you tell us. (*Biff's face turns red and he stares at the floor.*) Biff Taylor! Don't raise your hand unless you know the answer. Okay, class, who can tell me the names of the three ships? (*She calls on Andrew who has his hand up.*)

ANDREW: (*hesitantly*) The Santa Maria, the Nina, and the . . .

TEACHER: (*supplying the answer*) Pinta. Nancy, tell us how long did the voyage to the New World take?

NANCY: (*shrugging her shoulders*) I don't know.

TEACHER: Think about it for a minute. It took a long time, Nancy. Was it less or more than 100 days? (*silence*) The answer was on the first page of the reading material. Class, can anyone tell me how long the voyage took? (*No hands are raised.*) Class, you better learn that point because it will be on the exam! Now, who can tell me why Columbus came to the New World? (*Mary and two other students raise their hands.*) Mary?

MARY: (*firmly and loudly*) Because they wanted to discover new riches like explorers in the East.

TEACHER: (*She pauses and looks at Max and Helen who are talking and at Jim who is headed for the pencil sharpener. Max and Helen immediately cease their conversation.*) Jim, sit down this minute. (*Jim heads for his seat.*) What are you doing on the floor?

JIM: (*smiling sheepishly*) Jan wanted me to sharpen her pencil.

JAN: (*red-faced and alarmed*) Mrs. Turner, that's not true! (*Class laughs.*)

TEACHER: Quiet, both of you. You don't need a sharp pencil, sit down. (*resuming discussion*) Good answer, Mary. You were really alert. Why else, Mary? Can you think of any other reason?

NANCY: (*calling out*) Because they wanted to find a short cut to the Eastern treasures. The only other way was over land,

and it was thousands of miles over deserts and moun-
tains.

TEACHER: (*proudly*) Good, Nancy! Now, who are "they"? Who
was interested in the riches?

BILLY: (*calling out*) Some Queen Isabella and some King Ferdi-
nand, I think. She paid for the trip because she thought
Columbus would make her rich.

TEACHER: Okay, Billy, but remember to raise your hand before
speaking. Why do you think Columbus was interested in
making the trip? Just to find money?

CLASS: (*calling out*) No!

TEACHER: Well, what problems did the sailors have in making the
trip? (*She looks around and calls on Jim who has his hand
up.*)

JIM: Well, they were away from home and couldn't write. Sort
of like when I go to summer camp. I don't write. I was
lonely the first few days, but . . .

TEACHER: (*somewhat confused and irritated*) Well, that's not
exactly what I had in mind. Did they get sick a lot? Class,
does anyone know? (*She looks around the room and sees
Claire with a raised hand.*)

CLAIR: Well, I don't remember reading about sailors getting sick
with Columbus, but I know that sailors then used to get
sick with scurvy and they had to be careful.

HANK: (*Approaches the teacher with great embarrassment and
asks in hushed tones if he can go to the bathroom. Permission is granted.*)

TEACHER: Yes, good answer, Claire. Claire, can you tell me how
they tried to prevent scurvy?

CLAIRE: They carried lots of fruit with them. (*pause*) You know,
like lemons.

TEACHER: Okay, Claire, but what is the name for the kind of
fruit they took with them?

CLAIRE: (*blushes*)

TEACHER: (*silently forms "c" sound with her mouth*)

CLAIRE: Citrus.

TEACHER: Very good! What other problems did the sailors have?
(*She calls on Matt who has his hand up.*)

MATT: Well, they didn't have any maps and they didn't know
much about the wind or anything, so they were afraid of
the unknown and scared of sailing off the earth. (*laughter*)

TEACHER: (*Noticing that many students are gazing at the floor or
looking out the window, she begins to speak louder and*

more quickly.) No, educated men knew that the earth was round. Don't you read very carefully?

ALICE: (*calling out*) But even though educated men knew the earth was round, Columbus' sailors didn't believe it. They called the Atlantic Ocean the "Sea of Darkness," and Columbus had to keep two diaries. He showed the sailors one that had less miles listed so they wouldn't get scared. But the men threatened mutiny anyway.

TEACHER: (*with elation*) Excellent answer, Alice. Yes, the men were afraid of the unknown; however, I think most of them knew that the earth was round. Okay, Matt, you made me drift away from my question: Why did Columbus want to go—what were the reasons for his trip other than money? James, what do you think? (*James shrugs his shoulders.*) Well, when you read your lesson, class, look for that answer. It's important and I might test you on it. (*with exasperation*) Tim! Jill! Stop pushing each other this instant! I told you two not to play around. Why didn't you listen to me?

TIM: (*with anger*) But Jill threw the map in her desk. I wanted to use it so I could trace my own map.

JILL: But it's my map and . . .

TEACHER: (*firmly*) That's enough! I don't want to hear any more about it. Give me the map and the three of us will discuss this during recess.

PRINCIPAL: (*talking over the PA system*) Teachers, I'm sorry to break in on your classes, but I have an important announcement to make. The high school band will not be with us this afternoon. So from 2:00 to 2:30 classes will go on in your regular rooms. Since I have interrupted your class, I would also like to remind you that tonight is PTA. Teachers, be sure that the boys and girls remind . . . (*During the announcement many pupils begin private conversations with their neighbors.*)

TEACHER: (*without much emotion or enthusiasm*) It's not recess time yet. Listen, we still have work to do. Tell you what we're going to do now. I've got two filmstrips; one describes the trip made by the astronauts. Watch closely when we show these films because after we see the filmstrips, I'm going to ask you to tell me the similarities between the two trips. Ralph, turn off the lights.

HANK: (*returning from his trip to the restroom*) Hey, Mrs. Turner, why are the lights out in here? It's spooky in here!

ALICE: (*impishly*) It's the Sea of Darkness!
(*Class breaks out in a spontaneous roar.*)
TEACHER: Quiet down, class! It's time to see the filmstrip.

The example of this fourth-grade class illustrates many points, but perhaps the two most basic facts shown are that teachers are often very busy and that teaching is frequently very complex. The hurried pace of classroom life is well illustrated here. Note that Sally had a constant stream of student behavior to react to in the few minutes of classroom life we witness. Also note that Sally had to react with a number of decisions instantaneously. Several decisions were quite complex and on occasion no doubt you expressed some bewilderment. "If I were the teacher, how would I have responded?"

If you did not take notes as you read the material, you should quickly reread the above example and write out your reactions to the teaching incident. What were the teacher's weaknesses and strengths? If you were to discuss this observation with the teacher, what would you tell her? You may want to repeat this exercise when you finish reading the book, in order to determine how much information you have gained between now and then. Complete the exercise now, then read our reactions to this teaching incident, which follow.

Reactions to the example
Sally Turner, like most teachers, has some strong qualities and some weak ones. Let us begin by talking about some of the good things that she does or attempts to do. First, Sally's attempt to breathe life into Columbus and ancient history by linking it to something significant in the students' lives is noticeable. Clearly, she has thought about the lesson. She has gone to the trouble to order filmstrips both of Columbus's voyage (a simulated description) and of the astronauts' trip to the moon.

She does a fair job of giving feedback to students about the correctness or incorrectness of their responses. After most student responses she provided the student with information about the adequacy of his answer. Although this may seem to be a small point, it is often a highly significant one. For example, the authors have been in classrooms where teachers often fail to provide students with this information. They do not respond at all to student answers, or they respond in such a way as to make it difficult for some students to know if their response is correct. An instance of such ambiguous teacher feedback is: "So, you think it's 1492?" Although many students know whether the response is right or wrong, many low-achievement students will not know unless the teacher specifically confirms or negates their response. If students are to learn basic facts and concepts they must know if their answers are adequate or incomplete.

Teacher questions

Many discussions are parrot-like sessions, with teachers asking a question, receiving a student response, asking a question of a new student, and so forth. Such discussions typically are boring exercises that accomplish very little other than to assess whether students have factual knowledge. Assessment of factual knowledge is important, but if that is all that is done in discussion-recitation periods, students come to perceive that the teacher is interested only in finding out who knows the answers. Learning becomes a fragmented ritual rather than a meaningful, enjoyable process.

There are two major ways in which teachers can influence student answers: (1) by the type of questions the teacher originally asks the student and (2) by follow-up questions the teacher may pose to students after they respond. First, we shall discuss the original questions that the teacher asked in this discussion. Sally Turner's initial questions were primarily factual questions. The students might have been more interested if they had been involved more directly in the discussion. This could have been accomplished with more questions of value and opinion. The following questions are representative of the types of discussion questions that could have been raised: Would you like to be an astronaut? Why would you want to go to the moon? Why is it important to go to the moon? How would you like to be isolated from your parents and friends for several days? How would you feel being in a 5-by-7-foot room and unable to leave it? Would you like to be a sailor on a ship and stay on that ship week after week, not knowing where you were going or what you would see? Would you volunteer for such a voyage? Why? What is mutiny? Is it justified? Would you have felt like mutiny if you had been a crew member on Columbus' voyage? Was it important to discover the New World? Why? How do you feel when you are afraid or apprehensive?

Some of these questions (like "Was it important to discover the New World?") could be considered factual questions, since the book probably gives an "answer." How students react to such questions depends upon the teacher. Too often teachers' questions say "tell me what the book said" to their students. Students should be encouraged to provide their own assessment of facts rather than always to simply accept the reasons listed in the text. Even when factual questions are used, they can be used to stimulate pupil thinking. For example, the teacher might ask "The book states two reasons why the Spaniards thought it important to discover the New World. What were these two reasons, and what information and values underlay their reasoning?" Or instead of asking "When did Columbus discover the New World?" the teacher might ask why the trip wasn't made before 1492. In the teaching example, Sally made excessive use of factual questions and used too few questions of value and opinion that might have stimulated student interest in the discussion.

In addition, her students were never encouraged to ask their own questions or to evaluate the responses of their classmates. For example, Sally might have encouraged students in this way: "Today I have several questions that I want to find answers for. You have been reading the material for a week now, and you probably have some questions that weren't answered in the reading material. Maybe the class and I can help you answer these questions. Any questions that we can't answer we'll look up in the World Book or in the school library. I wonder why Queen Isabella picked Columbus to head the voyage? Why not some other sailor? I think that's an interesting question! Now, let's have *your* questions. We'll list them on the board and see if we have answered them at the end of the discussion."

Although it is not necessary to solicit for every discussion period, it is a good instructional practice to do so frequently. *Such teacher behavior tells pupils that the purpose of discussion is to satisfy their needs and interests as well as the teacher's.* Furthermore, the teacher's behavior in asking for questions says (1) I have important questions I want to discuss with you; (2) you certainly must have some important questions; (3) we'll have an interesting discussion answering each other's questions; and (4) if we need more information we'll get it. This discussion stance by the teacher, if he uses it consistently, will in time teach students that discussion is not a quiz but a profitable and enjoyable process of sharing information to satisfy personal curiosity.

It is especially important that the teacher communicate enthusiasm and respect for students who do ask questions. Some teachers call for student questions but their reactions to them guarantee that students will not ask questions about issues that really interest them. Such teacher comments as "Well, that is not directly related to our discussion" or "That was answered in the book" may convince a student that he is the only one in class who doesn't know the answer.

Teacher questions after student responses
Sally seldom encouraged the students to evaluate their own thinking (e.g., "Well, that's one way; what are some other ways that

Columbus could have boosted his crew's morale?" "That's an accurate statement of how the crew members felt, but what about Columbus? Do you think he was fearful?"). Nor did she ask questions to evaluate the thinking of their classmates (e.g., "Sam gave his opinion about sailing with Columbus. Bill, do you agree with him? How do you feel?" "What are some other reasons in addition to the good reasons that Tim gave?"). Such opportunities to explore a particular question in depth help to make the discussion more enjoyable to students, make it less "right answer" centered, and help teacher and students alike to see if they really understand the material.

In the above paragraph we were, of course, talking about what the teacher does *after* a student responds. As mentioned previously, Sally did do a good job of giving students feedback about the correctness of their answers, and on occasion she did *probe* students for additional information. The word "probe" means that the teacher seeks an additional response from the student after his first response, by asking him to clarify his statements. Probing is designed to stimulate the pupil to provide for information or to demonstrate more awareness than he originally gave. Smith (1969) points out several ways in which teachers can probe student answers:

1. *Teacher Seeks Further Clarification by the Pupil ("What do you mean?" "Can you explain more fully?")—asking the pupil for more information or meaning.*

2. *Teacher Seeks Increased Pupil Critical Awareness ("Why do you think that is so?")—asking the student to justify his response rationally.*

3. *Teacher Seeks to Focus the Pupil's Response ("How does this relate to . . . ?" "Isn't this closely related to what Hank was saying?")—after a good response teachers may want to focus attention on a related issue.*

4. *Teacher Prompts Pupil (Teacher: "Ralph, give me the missing puzzle piece." Ralph: "I don't know which one it is." Teacher: "Well, is it a big one or a small one . . . ?")— the teacher gives the student a hint, making it easier for him to respond.*

Unfortunately, the word probe often conjures up a negative image to the teacher. He may react to it as though the word meant "pick the student's answer apart." No such use of the word probe is intended; rather, the meaning is to help students in a thoughtful manner to consider the implications of what they do and say—to think about the material. Probing techniques are gentle ways to focus a student's attention and to help him to think. For example, an automatic response to "When did Columbus discover America?" is an unthinking "1492." However, the question "Why not 1400 or 1450?" forces us to consider what the world was like in 1400. In the same way, the question "Why not 1965 for a moon walk?" focuses discussion on a variety of factors (national priorities, safety, etc.).

This is not to imply that factual questions are unimportant or that they should not be used in discussions. The point here is that factual questions should frequently be paired with other question types so that students are led to consider the implications of the facts or the circumstances that produce the facts. Probing questions are especially useful following factual questions, as a way to help students think more fully about the material. A useful exercise for the reader would be to review Smith's probing techniques and to find points in the example dialogue in Mrs. Turner's classroom where probing techniques could have been useful. *Write out the actual probes you would have used.*

How does teacher control classroom interaction?

An especially interesting fact in the teaching incident was that the teacher seldom (there was but *one* instance) called on students who had not indicated their willingness to participate. If you reread the example carefully, you will note that either students call out the answer or Sally calls on a student who has his hand up. Teachers often find it useful to call on students who do not raise their hands for a variety of reasons: (1) Shy students seldom raise their hands, and they need opportunities to speak in public and develop their communicative skills and self-assertion. (2) Low-achieving students often learn that to answer a question incorrectly is to receive public ridicule and rebuke. Students who avoid public response opportunities need to be sought out and be given opportunities to learn that they can successfully participate in classroom discussion. (3) When students learn that their teacher only calls on students who raise their hands, they may begin to tune out discussions they do not want to think about. In this situation, calling on students who do not have their hands up may increase student attention. Some teachers fall into the equally bad habit of calling on the student before they ask a question (although Sally does not exhibit this problem). "Ellen, what do you think about . . .?" "Heather, state Boyle's law." This procedure tells students that they do not have to listen unless they are named.

We do not know why Sally fails to call upon students who do not raise their hands, but if we can assume that this example of her teaching behavior is typical we know that the non-hand-raiser is seldom called upon in her class. A clue is provided in one incident suggesting why Sally may behave as she does. Recall that in the exchange with Biff, the teacher scolded him for having the audacity to raise his hand without knowing the answer. This suggests that Sally only wants to hear the "right" answer, that she is more interested in establishing her point and moving on with her lesson than she is in the learning of individual students. If a teacher typically responds this way to students, they will learn that they are not to raise their hand unless they are absolutely sure that their answer is correct. (Often calling on students who know the right answer is an unconscious teacher strategy for providing "self-reinforcement.") Teachers may delude themselves into believing that they are doing a good job because some of the same students consistently respond with good answers. Naturally, there will always be some students who are bigger risk-takers than others (such as those in the example who called out answers). However, if the teacher consistently shows that he only wants to hear "right" answers, many students, especially the timid non-gamblers, will be afraid to participate in class discussions.

Admittedly, the one example in Mrs. Turner's classroom behavior is not enough information upon which to base any but the most speculative conclusion; however, such behavior should encourage the observer to look for more information to confirm or negate the notion that the teacher does not want students to respond unless they know the answer. Some teachers, especially young beginning teachers, do unwittingly fall into the trap of discouraging youngsters from responding unless they know the answer "cold." This is because student silence or incorrect answers are difficult to respond to and are often embarrassing or threatening.

The incident with Biff illustrates two important points: (1) teachers may encourage students not to listen by falling into ineffective but consistent questioning styles; (2) often we can get enough evidence from what we see in classrooms to be able to make decisions and give firm suggestions to teachers, but at other times (e.g., the exchange with Biff) we may only note clues about teacher behavior or teacher assumptions. These need to be checked out by talking with the teacher or making additional observations.

Different teacher behavior for male and female students?

Interestingly, Sally Turner does not praise any response made by boys but frequently praises the responses of the girls. Again, it is not possible to say firmly that the teacher favors the girls in all situations, but it is reasonable to say that in this instance, the teacher was more responsive and supportive to female students. It is notable that no male student received teacher praise. Also, while there is very little attempt by the teacher to work with any of the students when they make inappropriate responses, we see that Sally is more likely to work with girls than with boys when she does do so. When boys gave an inappropriate response, she accepted the performance and either provided the answer herself or called upon another student to provide the answer. However, on two different occasions, she stays with a girl who is having difficulty responding. For example, when Nancy is having difficulty responding to the question, "How long did the voyage take?", Sally attempted to make the job easier for her by first providing a clue ("It took a long time") and then by reducing the complexity of the question from a memory question to a choice question ("Was it less or more than 100 days?"). Similarly, when Claire could not remember the word "citrus," Sally provided her with a nonverbal clue.

Although we would want to collect more information describing Sally Turner's behavior toward male and female students, apparently she may be more likely to praise the correct answers of girls and more likely to stay with them and work with them when they do not answer correctly. This occurs even though the frequency of questions that Sally asks boys and girls is similar; the *quality* of her feedback to these groups of students differs, even though the *quantity* of response opportunities is equivalent. The term quality refers to the way in which a teacher interacts with a pupil. Does the teacher ask him hard or easy questions? How long does the teacher wait for him to respond? Does the teacher praise his answers? Does the teacher probe for more information?

Classroom management

In the area of classroom management (creating learning environments, maintaining student interest in the discussion, etc.) Sally appears to be an average teacher. For the most part the students are attentive to her and to the discussion. Although the students do not appear enthusiastically engaged in the discussion, they do pay attention and there are few interruptions. However, there are several areas in which Sally Turner could improve.

To begin with, she does not have enough maps for all the students. Equipment and material shortages inevitably lead to trouble, especially when the students get to keep the material. A more careful count of the materials when Sally prepared them might have prevented both the minor delay at the beginning of the discussion and the major disruption (students fighting over a map) that occurred later in the discussion. Upon finding the shortage, and after hearing

Tim's request to sit with Jill, Sally could have responded: "Okay, that's fine. Sit with Jill, because I know you and Jill can share cooperatively. Billy and Tim, I'm sorry you didn't get maps. I failed to make enough copies, but I'll draw each of you a *special* map this afternoon." This would have accomplished two important things: (1) It would have assured Billy and Tim that they would get maps and make it less likely that they would "take the law into their own hands." (As will be pointed out in Chapter 6 on management, what the teacher does to prevent misbehavior from happening is substantially more important than what he does after misbehavior occurs.) (2) A different response would have encouraged a better self-concept, and perhaps better cooperation, in Jill and Tim. The teacher's original remarks ("You and Jill always get into trouble . . .") placed Jill and Tim in the spotlight. Such remarks may have caused them to develop an inappropriate attitude about their own misbehavior (i.e., it could not be too bad, because the teacher expects us to misbehave; so why not?). The implications of the teacher attributing negative rather than positive motives to student behavior will be discussed in Chapter 4. Let us simply say here that such teacher behavior subtly condoned the misbehavior by implying that it was expected, thus making such misbehavior more likely.

Credibility

Sally has developed the bad habit of not following up on what she says. In this class situation we hear her say on several occasions: "Don't call out answers, raise your hand." However, she repeatedly accepts answers that are called out and responds to these answers on several occasions with acceptance. Recall this instance:

> TEACHER: (*with irritation*) Jim, don't call out comments without raising your hand.
> BILL: (*calling out*) The Canary Islands.
> TEACHER: Okay, Bill . . .

There were several times when the teacher clearly accepted such responses. As we will see in future chapters, these discrepant teacher behaviors tell students that the teacher does not mean what he says. Such discrepancies, if they are consistent, may lead to a plethora of discipline problems.

Whether or not students call out answers is not the point here, of course. In the authors' opinion, there are certain times when students, particularly older students, should be encouraged to respond directly to one another without teacher permission. The point is, rather, that the teacher should be consistent in his demands on the students. If he does not want call-out responses (and there are many times when teachers will not), he should be consistent about his behavior. For example, when a student calls out an answer, the teacher should either ignore the student's response and call on someone else, or acknowledge the response indirectly ("Raise your hand if you want to respond. We don't want call-out answers today.") and then call on another student (who may or may not have his hand up).

We mentioned call-out responses as being particularly desirable when the teacher is trying to get students to respond to one another and trying to encourage students to evaluate the adequacy of responses on their own. You may be prompted to ask, then, why are call-out answers sometimes bad? The undesirable nature of call-outs stems from two basic points: (1) students who are verbally aggressive dominate the discussion and (2) low-achieving students who take more time to process information may not even think about questions because other students answer them too quickly. Obviously, the purpose of discussion is not to yield quick, automatic responses but to allow students to think about the topic.

There is at least one other area in which Sally could improve her classroom-management style. In two different discipline situations, she made use of rhetorical questions that caused her needless difficulty. For example, Jim has already started to his seat (which is, of course, exactly what the teacher wanted) when she needlessly asked, "What are you doing on the floor?" This question then touched off a more serious disruption. Similarly, in the Jill and Tim exchange, the teacher queries pointlessly ("Why didn't you listen to me?") and again the situation deteriorates and the whole class is distracted. The use of questions in discipline situations will be discussed fully in Chapters 6 and 7 but here we can say that such rhetorical, aggressive questions typically lead to clowning or aggressive student behavior. For example, how do you feel when someone says to you: "Why don't you listen?" "Can't you do anything right?" "Why are you always the difficult one?" These questions make most people feel irritated or aggressive. When we are treated aggressively, we respond aggressively.

Introducing the lesson
Previous discussion mentioned the teacher's negative expectations about student behavior ("You and Jill always get into trouble."). Sally also communicates undesirable expectations in other ways. Perhaps the most striking is her tendency to communicate to the pupils the idea that their discussion is important only because they will be

tested on the material. There is little suggestion that learning is fun or that the teacher herself enjoys learning. Note especially Sally's poor introduction to the lesson. She places great stress on the fact that the students will be tested on the material, but she provides little additional rationale as to why they are discussing Columbus' voyage. Too often teachers use only the threat of poor grades to motivate students. Contrast Sally's introduction with this alternate:

> TEACHER: Today we are going to talk about the astronauts' trip to the moon. How many of you saw the exciting TV film of the walk on the moon? (*after pausing*) I could hardly wait to see it. Ever since I was a student in the fourth grade, men have been debating the possibility of space flight and a trip to the moon. Several years ago many people didn't think such a trip would be possible, and there were fears that the men would be lost in space due to some unknown causes. In fact, the unknowns faced by the astronauts were very similar to the fears that Columbus and his men faced when they made the voyage to the New World.
>
> Yesterday I passed out a list of questions that we were going to discuss about Columbus' voyages. Take out your discussion guides now. I am interested in hearing your responses to the questions, and I'll enjoy listening to you identify and compare the common problems that Columbus and the astronauts faced. After the discussion, we'll see two filmstrips that are interesting descriptions . . . (*Class sounds its approval in a spontaneous cheer.*)

Here, the introduction more clearly suggests to the pupil what he is to do and why he is doing it. It also conveys the notion that the activity is both enjoyable and important. Furthermore, the lesson begins with the astronauts' voyage. Since students are more familiar with the astronauts than with Columbus, this introduction may make it easier to involve them in the discussion. Thus Sally's introduction could have been more focused and less tied to the assertion that "you'll need to know the information for tomorrow's quiz." In addition to the introduction, at other times in the discussion she makes reference to the fact that listening is important because the students are going to be tested on the lesson. Such references do much to convince students that learning and school are arbitrary, irrelevant exercises that are done only to please adults and to receive high grades. This point will be expanded later in Chapter 4.

Spontaneous reaction to student comments

Notable in Sally's discussion was the failure to pick up on themes that students initiated spontaneously, even when they were related to the purpose of the discussion. For example, part of Sally's intent was to get the students to appreciate the mutual sense of adventure and apprehension that explorers face. On two different occasions students indirectly brought up their sense of fear, but Sally failed to pick up on the theme. Jim, for instance, mentioned the loneliness of the first few days of summer camp. Here Sally could have asked a variety of questions. The following are examples: "Why are the first few days of summer camp strange? How did you feel on your first day at school? How do you think you will feel on your first day at Junior High? Why are we uncomfortable when we do something for the first time?" After such discussion, the fact that the newness of the situation faced by the explorers was both stressful and exciting would be more clearly appreciated by the class. A similar opportunity appears again at the end of the discussion when Hank verbalizes the spookiness of the room and Alice cleverly labels it as the Sea of Darkness. Sally could have profitably paused and pointed out that Alice's remark was a good one and perhaps added: "Okay, now listen (*speaking in a very quiet voice*). For one minute no one will make a noise. Let's pretend that we are on the Pinta. We have been at sea for two months. It is now completely dark and there is no sound on the ship. The only noise is the roar of the sea and the creaking of the boat as it is tossed from wave to wave. We are all scared because no one has ever sailed this sea! What will we run into in the darkness? What is our destination? What will it be like when we reach it? Will the residents there be hostile?"

If successfully used, such techniques may increase student awareness of the fears and other feelings of explorers and may involve the students more focally in the discussion. Teachers often stimulate very profitable and enjoyable discussions when they use student examples that are spontaneously expressed during discussion.

Summary

These are some of our reactions to the teaching incident. We hope that the teaching episode and our comments have caused you to think about teaching behavior. We hope the chapter has raised a number of questions about how teachers should behave in classrooms. Perhaps you noted strengths or weaknesses that were not touched on in our comments, or perhaps you take exception to some of the comments. If so, that's fine! The purpose of the chapter was to involve you directly in the process of looking at classroom behavior.

In Appendix A, you will find five additional classroom scenes that provide teacher-child dialogue in elementary and secondary classrooms. You may want to read these cases now, in order to raise more questions about teaching behavior. However, the greatest use of these materials will most likely come after you have completed reading the text, because the cases will allow you to practice the skills and put to use the information you glean from reading the book.

In conclusion, this chapter provided an opportunity to "visit" and react to a classroom that was neither inordinately bad nor good. Sally, like most teachers, had a number of strengths and weaknesses. We think it likely that Sally is unaware of many of her teaching weaknesses, and that she will not improve her teaching behavior unless she becomes aware of her ineffective techniques.

Are teachers really unaware of certain aspects of their classroom behavior, and of its consequences? If so, why are they unaware? How can they become aware of what they do in the classroom and more knowledgeable about how their behavior affects students? We turn to these questions in the next two chapters.

SUGGESTED ACTIVITIES AND QUESTIONS

1. Watch a video tape or film of classroom behavior with a group of fellow students or teachers. List the major strengths and weaknesses that you see and compare your list with what others see as the strengths and weaknesses.

2. If films are not available, select one of the case studies in Appendix A; as you read the class description, list the teaching strengths and weaknesses that you perceive. Compare your list with those made by others. How similar or dissimilar is the group's reaction to the teaching behavior?

3. Watch four or five 5-minute teaching segments that are drawn from different teachers. When you view such teaching segments, do so with at least three other observers. After watching the filmed teaching, rank order the teachers on the following criteria:

(a) I would feel most comfortable in this class.
(b) I would learn the most in this class.
(c) This teacher would be least likely to criticize me.

See if the teachers in the film were given the same rank order with fellow observers. Try to identify the teaching characteristics that made you respond as you did. What, for example, led each of you to think that you would feel comfortable in a particular teacher's classroom? If the group felt differently about the teachers (and they may) try to identify the characteristics that attracted some observers but that repelled other observers.

4. Think about the grade level that you teach (or plan to teach) and identify the ten most important skills, attitudes, and/or behaviors that a teacher must possess if he is effectively to instruct students at this grade level. Keep this initial list so that you can compare it with the list you make after you have read the entire book.

5. Reread the example of Mrs. Turner's fourth-grade class and identify four situations in which she could have probed for student responses. Write out the actual probes you would have used if you had been the teacher. Read some of the case studies presented in Appendix A and identify places where teachers could have asked probing questions.

6. The authors provided a critique of Mrs. Turner's teaching. What additional teaching behaviors (strengths or weaknesses) did you find that we have not mentioned? Explain why you feel these behaviors represent strengths or weaknesses.

7. Assume that you were an observer in Mrs. Turner's classroom. During recess she asks, "Well, you watched the explorer unit today. What are my two major teaching strengths and my two major weaknesses?" How would you respond? Why do you feel that the strengths and weaknesses you suggest are the most important or basic?

8. The authors rewrote Mrs. Turner's introduction to have a more desirable effect upon students. Improve upon the introduction by writing your own. In general, what steps should a good introduction include?

9. Why is it that teachers have a difficult time being aware of everything that occurs in the classroom?

10. The authors suggested that before conducting class discussion it is often a good idea to solicit from students the questions that they want to answer during the discussion period. Why is this a good idea? Under what circumstances might this plan be a poor approach?

CHAPTER

2

Teacher
awareness

Our brief glimpse into Sally Turner's classroom revealed that her classroom was exceedingly busy and that she was probably unaware of certain aspects of her behavior and its impact upon students. Obviously, if teachers are unaware of the effects of their behavior on students, then at times they are likely to interact with students in ineffective ways.

In this chapter we will present data to support the assertion that classrooms are busy places and that the fast pace observed in Sally Turner's class is a rather common occurrence. Data will also be presented to suggest that teachers are sometimes unaware of their classroom behavior and that sometimes teachers do behave in self-defeating ways. Furthermore, we will argue that teachers do not perceive many classroom events because (1) classroom interaction proceeds at a rapid pace; (2) teachers have not been trained to monitor and study their own behavior; and (3) teachers rarely receive systematic or useful feedback from supervisors. Finally, we will emphasize that neither teachers nor observers are likely to make sense out of classroom behavior unless they have a *definite* list of important behaviors to look for in the midst of classroom life.

Classrooms are busy places

Teachers lead busy lives. It has been pointed out that in a single day a teacher may engage in more than one thousand interpersonal exchanges with students (Jackson, 1968). In a study of four sixth-grade teachers it was found that teachers on the average initiated 80 individual interchanges with students each hour (Jackson and Lahaderne, 1967). In addition to initiating contacts with students, these teachers were also responding to student questions and moving from location to location. Teachers engaging in so many daily contacts will be hard pressed to keep track of the number and the substance of contacts that they share with each pupil. It may not be important for the teacher to remember all classroom contacts; however, recalling certain information (remembering the ten students who didn't get a chance to present their class reports, remembering that John had trouble with vowel sounds during reading, and so forth) may be very important teacher tasks.

Teachers must constantly respond to immediate classroom needs. While they are teaching, they have little time to reflect upon what they are doing or planning to do, because they are busy reacting to the present situation. Thus unless teachers are looking for signs of student disinterest or difficulty, for example, they may not see these and other important barometers of classroom life. This is to say that the teacher's world is literally consumed by immediate demands. The teacher is so absorbed in his present work that it is difficult for him to get a total perspective on what happens in his classroom. Gloria Channon (1970), an elementary teacher in New York City, describes how difficult it is for a teacher to monitor his own behavior.

> *The teacher, like the doctor in the midst of an epidemic, is so busy with the daily doings that she finds it hard to get some distance between herself and her functions, to see what is happening. As a result she is vulnerable to each day's experience in a special transient way.*

Philip Jackson's book *Life in Classrooms* also shows that teachers are so completely involved in classroom activities that they are hard pressed to explain specifically what they do or what they plan to do. The self-report data provided by these teachers suggest that the role demands of teaching leave little time for self-observation and analysis. *If teachers cannot conceptualize classroom life before they enter the teaching profession, they will have little time to develop this ability after entering the classroom.*

The teacher's world is not only filled with teaching demands, but also with a plethora of supervisory and administrative functions such that he has little or no time in school to think about his teaching behavior. Teachers perform such diverse duties as: supervising student behavior on the playgrounds and in lunchrooms; talking with parents about the progress of their children; grading homework; duplicating assignment sheets; collecting money for insurance premiums; and filling out forms for researchers. Channon (1970) specifies additional duties that many teachers must perform:

> *She works like a dog. She fills out reading cards and duplicates*
> *office records, book inventories, lunch lists, class photo lists,*
> *state census forms, report cards, reports by the hundreds . . .*
> *she writes lengthy anecdotal records and case history forms for*
> *the guidance counselors.*

Thus, research data and the records of certain teachers suggest that classrooms are busy places. Further, we have asserted that the hectic pace of classroom life interferes with the teacher's ability to see classroom behavior—his own and that of the students. A number of books written by former and current school teachers have appeared in print during the past few years. Although these books often emphasize the negative aspects of classroom life without citing the good teaching that exists, they do present excellent analyses of problems that exist in some classrooms. Interestingly, many of these authors suggest that they were not trained to see and respond to what actually was happening in the classroom; instead, they were responding to stereotypes or acting the way they felt they were supposed to act. In particular, Herbert Kohl's book *36 Children* and John Holt's book *How Children Fail* have dramatically indicated that the first step in changing their teaching tactics was becoming aware of what they were really doing in the classroom. We shall return to this point later in the chapter to show that researchers have reached a similar conclusion.

Classroom awareness

We have indicated that the classroom is a complex, busy place. It is so busy that teachers are unaware of much of what they and their students do in the classroom. Some data have been presented to indicate that classes are, indeed, busy places, but what proof do we have that teachers are unaware of or misinterpret their behavior in classrooms?

Some particularly revealing information about the lack of overlap between what teachers do and what they think they do is provided from the minicourse training experiences at the Far West Educational Development Laboratory (Borg et al., 1970). That laboratory has prepared a number of in-service courses designed to help teachers develop specific teaching skills. For example, their minicourse on independent work activity is designed to help teachers develop appropriate skills for (1) discussing with pupils the meaning of working alone; (2) discussing the assigned independent learning task; (3) eliciting potential problems and solutions from pupils; (4) establishing standards for what to do when finished; (5) providing delayed teacher response to the completed student work; and (6) evaluating pupils' success in working independently. These points are clearly specific and at first glance it would appear that teachers would know if they had performed such behaviors in their teaching. Such was not the case. Borg et al. (1970) write

> *The questionnaire data revealed that the majority of teachers thought they had used most of the skills presented in mini-course 8 in the precourse lesson. The observational data does not support this belief. The same phenomena have been observed in the evaluation of other minicourses: teachers often believe that they use a particular set of skills prior to taking the course, but an objective analysis of the data shows that this is not usually true.*

The report provides direct information that teachers, to some extent, were unaware of their teaching behavior. If teachers are unaware of their performance when teaching small groups of students in minicourse laboratory sessions, it is unlikely that they could accurately describe their behavior when teaching an entire class. Evidence that classroom teachers misinterpret their teaching behavior has been presented by Emmer (1967). He reports that teachers were unable to describe accurately even simple classroom behaviors such as the percentage of time that they and their students talked in the classroom. In most cases, teachers grossly underestimated the amount of time they talked in the classroom. Two additional classroom observational studies have shown teachers to be unaware of certain aspects of their classroom teaching behavior (Brophy and Good, 1970*b*; Good and Brophy, 1972).

More information to show that teachers misperceive their behavior at times is provided by Ehman (1970). In this study, ratings of teacher behavior made by students and by classroom observers were highly similar; however, ratings of the same behavior made by the teachers themselves differed sharply from the other two sets of ratings. The teachers could not accurately describe what they did in the classroom.

Discrepancies between teacher and student perception concerning the number of opportunities that students have for decision-making in the classroom have been reported by Wolfson and Nash (1968). Teachers consistently perceived students to be making many more decisions than students saw themselves making.

The six studies reported here demonstrate that teachers sometimes behave in ways that they are unaware of. In the following section we will present a few studies that describe how teachers behave in classrooms. We do not have proof that teachers are unaware of the behavior described in these studies. Nevertheless, given the goals that teachers verbally express and the current training philosophy at teacher education colleges, it seems likely that teachers are not behaving in accordance with their intentions.

Teacher domination

Researchers have noted that teachers monopolize verbal communication channels in the classroom. Adams and Biddle (1970), from a sample of first-, sixth-, and eleventh-grade teachers, concluded that teachers were the principal actors in 84 percent of classroom communication episodes, and that less than one-half percent of classroom verbal behavior was spent in discussion of feelings and interpersonal relations. Hudgins and Ahlbrand (1969) studied seventh- and ninth-grade English classes and reported figures very similar to those obtained by Adams and Biddle. Thus, this research suggests that teachers monopolize classroom discussion, even though most teachers do not want to do this nor are aware that they do. Perhaps teachers behave this way because they simply do not know how to solicit extended pupil talk.

There is evidence indicating that students are not as free to act as teachers believe them to be. Jackson and Wolfson (1968) vividly demonstrate the number of constraints that interfere with the wants and needs of nursery-school children. Not all of the constraints they report are due to teacher behavior, however. Many of the constraints they describe resulted when one child interfered with the goal of another child (they both wanted the same toy). Nevertheless, the number of constraints placed upon the behavior of nursery-school children are amazing. Jackson and Wolfson concluded that about 20 constraining episodes occurred each minute in the group of 97 children.

Dr. Oliver Bown, codirector of the Research and Development Center for Teacher Education at the University of Texas, speaking at the National Symposium of Evaluation in Education (Burkhart, 1969), had this to say about data that Jackson had collected in nursery schools.

> ... *he found that the kids were actually free to initiate and carry through an action only 5% of the time ... 95% of the youngsters' actions were essentially dictated. Now this is astounding and kind of unbelievable. I don't think a teacher could believe that she was doing this. I'm sure it would not correspond with the intellectual intent.*

Bown, at the same conference, reported some of his own data drawn from the video tapes of experienced teachers. He found that the average student in the sample made an independent, self-initiated statement about once every three weeks!

The extent to which this sample of teaching is representative of teaching in general is unknown; however, there is much data to indicate that teacher emphasis has been placed on obtaining student response to short factual questions, and that this pattern has not changed much over time. For example, Stevens (1912) looked in high-school classes and found that two-thirds of the questions asked by teachers were factual recall. Haynes (1935) looked at sixth-grade history classes and reported that 77 percent of teacher questions requested a factual response from students. Gallagher (1965) studied teachers of gifted students but found that they also asked many factual questions. He reported more than 50 percent of their questions were cognitive memory questions. Davis and Tinsley (1967) studied student teachers teaching high-school social studies classes and reported that roughly 50 percent of the questions required factual answers. Guszak (1967) found that 14 percent of the teacher questions in reading groups merely asked students to locate information in the book, and another 57 percent of the questions were short-answer fact questions.

Borg et al. (1970) summarized this literature and suggested that the types of questions teachers ask pupils have not changed in more than half a century, despite an increased emphasis upon the need for teachers to ask a variety of questions (Groisser, 1964; Sanders, 1966). This is not to suggest that teachers should not ask questions of fact. Factual questions are the best way to see if students have the basic information that is necessary before useful discussion can take place. However, the point here is to suggest that teachers use many more fact questions than they are probably aware of in their day-to-day classroom behavior.

The studies in this section were not presented to persuade readers that teachers should not be direct, for as we shall emphasize later in the book, there are many times when such behavior is very useful. To reiterate, these studies were reviewed to suggest that teachers are probably more directive than they realize.

In the following section, we will present data that shows teachers' classroom behavior to be uneven, with different students receiving differential teacher treatment. In part, we feel that such differential and often discriminatory teacher behavior occurs because teachers are not aware of their behavior, or because they do not realize the consequences of their behavior. Thus in the following pages we will show that teachers do treat students differently and assert that at times such differential teacher behavior interferes with student progress. This theme will receive more detailed treatment later in the book (especially in Chapter 4, Teacher Expectations). At present, our purpose is to review a few studies indicating that teachers sometimes do act in self-defeating ways.

Other teacher behavior

Previously, mention was made of the teacher as the principal actor in the classroom. When teachers do allow students to speak, however, which ones do they call upon? Jackson and Lahaderne (1967) indicated that child contact with the classroom teacher varies widely within the same classroom. Looking in four sixth-grade classrooms for roughly ten hours each, they found that teachers interacted with some students as few as 5 times and with others as often as 120 times. In addition, Jackson and Lahaderne noted that the sex of the student affects the quantity and quality of the communication patterns students share with teachers in each classroom. In summary, they found that boys have proportionately more interaction with teachers than girls do, but that the magnitude of this ratio varies with the nature of the communication, being greatest for disciplinary exchanges and smallest for instructional messages. That sex of students is a major factor in both elementary and secondary classrooms has been demonstrated by a number of researchers who have found males to be more salient to the teacher and to receive much more criticism than females (Meyer and Thompson, 1956; Lippitt and Gold, 1959; Jackson and Lahaderne, 1967).

More evidence on who talks in classrooms is available. For example, Hudgins and Ahlbrand (1969) noted: "The chief properties of formal pupil communication in the classroom are its brevity and the inequality of its distribution. There are additional interesting aspects of these communications, but they are variable from class to class and cannot be identified as properties."

Apparently, the achievement level of the student, as well as his sex, figures heavily in whether or not the student responds frequently. Good (1970) and Kranz et al. (1970) found that high-achieving, elementary-school students received more teacher questions and teacher praise than did low-achieving students. Similarly, Mendoza, Good, and Brophy (1972), and Horn (1914) have reported high-achieving students in secondary schools to receive more response opportunities than low-achieving students. Jones (1971), studying student teachers in secondary schools, also reported that high-achieving students received more teacher questions than did low-achieving students. Good, Sikes, and Brophy (1972) report that in comparison to other students, low-achieving males in sixteen junior high classrooms received inferior treatment, while high-achieving males received more frequent and more favorable contact with the teachers.

In addition to differences in the frequency of teacher contacts with students, there are some studies suggesting that the quality of teacher-child interaction varies with the achievement level of the student. Rowe (1969) found that teachers waited significantly longer for more capable students than for less apt students before giving the answer or calling on another student. Slower students had to respond more quickly to avoid losing their turn. Rowe also reports that these results surprised the teachers, who were not aware they were behaving in this fashion. One of the teachers, after being told of the results of the study, said, "I guess we just don't expect an answer, so we move on to someone else."

Brophy and Good (1970*b*) studied the classroom behavior of four first-grade teachers toward high- and low-achieving students. They reported only minor differences in the *frequency* of teacher contact with students of differing achievement levels, but found important variations in the quality of teacher contact with students of different achievement levels. For example, teachers were much more likely to praise high-achieving students than they were to praise low-achieving students. This was true even when differences among the students in success and failure were taken into account.

When high-achieving students gave a right answer in these classrooms, they were praised 12 percent of the time. Low-achieving students were praised only 6 percent of the time following a right answer. Even though they gave fewer right answers, low-achieving students received proportionately less praise when they did give a right answer. Similarly, low-achieving students were found to be more likely to receive teacher criticism for a wrong answer than were high-achieving students. After an incorrect response, low-achieving students were criticized 18 percent of the time, and high achievers were criticized 6 percent of the time. An additional finding of interest was that teachers were more likely to *stay with* high-achieving students (repeat the question, provide a clue, ask a new question) when they made no response, said "I don't know," or answered incorrectly. In contrast, they were more likely to *give up* on low-achieving students (give the answer or call on another student) under similar circumstances. The teachers were twice as likely to stay with high-achieving as they were to stay with low-achieving students. These results, in combination with Rowe's data, suggest that some teachers will expect and demand performance from high-achieving students but tend to give up on low-achieving students and accept only minimal performance.

In subsequent work by Good and Brophy (1972), with a different sample of teachers drawn from several different schools, the teachers were surprised and shocked when told what they had been doing in the classroom. They were not aware of their behavior. Interestingly, these investigators have also noted that teachers in some classes consistently gave up on some high-achievers more often than on other high-achievers. Again, teachers were not aware of their behavior and had no idea as to why they gave up on some high-achievers more readily than others. Teachers, then, may have an especially difficult time in monitoring the quality of their interactions with students (as opposed to the frequency or quantity of interactions). Remember that by quality we simply mean the way in which the teacher interacts with a student. (What type of question does he ask, a hard one or a simple one? How long does he wait for the student to respond? Does he praise the student when he responds? Does he probe for more information or give the answer?)

Sometimes the way a teacher groups his students influences the flow of communication in the classroom. For example, in their study of classroom behavior, Adams and Biddle (1970) discovered the existence of an action zone. This action zone included the students who sat in the middle-front row seats and those in seats extending directly up the middle aisle. These students received more opportunity to talk than the others. Possibly because the teachers tended to stand in front of their classes, their attention was focused on the students in immediate view. In any case, the fact remains that students seated in this section of the classroom received more teacher attention.

Other seating patterns often influence the flow of communication and affect peer status relations. For instance, teachers often group students by ability in order to reduce the range of individual differences within each group and to instruct more effectively. Often, however, teachers completely segregate classroom seating patterns on the basis of student ability. The top readers sit at the same table, the next best group sit together, and so on. Some teachers carry this process to such rigid extremes that there is very little contact between high-achievement and low-achievement students. When this occurs, it is likely to set up status differences among students and engender an attitude of inferiority in lows that will alienate them from the mainstream of classroom life.

Rist (1970) presents an interesting but distressing longitudinal case study of children progressing from kindergarten through second grade. He explains how teachers created a caste system within this group of students, and he discusses ways in which high-status children mirrored the behavior of their teachers and how they communicated disrespect for the low-status children. Interestingly, students who needed the most teacher help, the children who were shy and not very verbal, were seated in the rear of the room when they began kindergarten. Of course, this arrangement made it more difficult for these children to have contact with the teacher. Certainly the teacher was not aware that the placement of these children in the rear of the room would reduce their contacts with her and slow their classroom progress. Yet, these unfortunate circumstances did result from the teacher's decision to separate children who were perceived to have little learning potential. Such rigid grouping patterns also prevent low-achieving students from learning from their classmates. There is reason to believe that students will learn from their classmates when given the opportunity to do so (Coleman et al., 1966).

Many of the studies reviewed above suggest that the classroom teacher could improve his contact pattern with low-achievement students. If the low-achiever is relatively ignored and is treated with second-class status, schools will continue to see the low-achiever progressively fall further and further behind his peers the longer he stays in school. Physical separation of such students into rigid groups increases the probability that the teacher will treat them differently, with lows being treated less appropriately. Much of this will be done unwittingly by teachers, but it will be done nevertheless.

Susskind (undated) aptly summarizes the gap between what teachers do and what they think they do, ". . . in this not atypical school, the children do not ask questions, while the teachers ask an incredibly large number of questions. Further, the teachers and administrators are strongly opposed to this situation in theory, but are unaware that it exists in their classrooms." The point of this example is to show again that there is a gap between what teachers do and what they think they do or want to do. This is not to suggest that teachers should not use direct teaching methods. Obviously, students, particularly young students, will benefit from direct teaching methods, and, as we will point out later, there is no such thing as *the* appropriate teaching style. The correctness of an indirect or direct teaching style depends upon the objectives of the learning exercise and to some extent the personality of the teacher and the characteristics of the students themselves.

Why are teachers unaware?

We have discussed certain things that teachers do without awareness, and we will present additional examples later in the book. However, we will now discuss why teachers act in these ways. Certainly they do not act this way intentionally. We know this because, when interviewed, teachers express unawareness of their classroom behavior and are upset by it. This is true even when good teachers are interviewed in order to find out how and why they behave as they do in class (Jackson, 1968).

The first and greatest factor that makes it difficult for the teacher to assess his classroom behavior is that so much happens and happens so rapidly that the teacher is not aware of everything he does in the classroom. This problem can be solved in part, but not completely, through training. Even after teachers develop skills for conceptualizing what they are doing, awareness of everything that occurs or even everything that only the teacher does is still impossible. However, with practice teachers can become more aware of their classroom behavior.

A second factor diminishing the teacher's perception in the classroom is that teacher-training programs have seldom equipped teachers with specific teaching techniques or provided them with specific skills for analyzing and labeling classroom behavior. Much of teachers' lack of awareness in observing and monitoring their own behavior stems from the fact that they have not been taught any systematic technique for conceptualizing teacher behavior. Conceptual labels are powerful tools for helping us to be aware of what we do. For example, the Brophy and Good (1970b) study reported that teachers gave up on low-achieving students who had difficulty responding to questions. However, the teachers at the time they gave up on the students did not think of this as giving up. They were embarrassed by the resulting silence, they thought that the student was embarrassed, and/or they wanted to keep the discussion rolling. Similarly, teachers in the Rowe (1969) study were not aware that they were giving low-achieving students less time to respond and thereby were making response more difficult.

These findings suggest that teacher training institutions had not given the teachers ways of labeling what they were doing. This is not to say that teachers should never give up on students in recitation sequences, for there are times when it is appropriate to move on. However, teachers should be *aware* that they are giving up and should be aware of how often they do this with low-achieving students; otherwise, they will teach such students that the easiest way of reacting to a teacher's question is to make no response.

Similarly, teachers should be aware of the alternatives they have when students make no response or respond incorrectly: providing clues, probing, asking a simpler question, repeating the question, and so forth. This awareness can be learned if teachers are trained to identify and label specific teaching goals and specific skills to be used in reaching them. Being able to label specific teaching skills helps one both to be more aware of what he does in the classroom and to know how to respond when students act in specified ways.

Teacher education programs traditionally have not trained teachers to recognize and use specific behaviors. Instead, they have given teachers global advice (e.g., treat the whole child, individualize instruction) without linking it to specific behaviors. Smith (1969), in his book *Teachers for the Real World*, says it this way: "It does little good for a teacher to understand that he should accept the child and build on what he is if the teacher does not know how to assess what the child brings and lacks the skills necessary to work with him." Smith further notes: "Teachers often appear to have no interest in children or even to fear them, because they simply lack the conceptual equipment to understand them. No matter how idealistic the teacher may be, he will soon find his hopes crushed if he is unable to understand and cope with disturbing pupil behavior." We share the belief that teachers must be provided with specific, concrete skills if they are to be successful in the classroom.

Although many teacher education programs have begun to stress teacher training (the development of specific teaching skills and the ability to conceptualize and talk about the specific behaviors that teachers can use in specific situations), many still do not, and most in-service teachers do not have a rich vocabulary for describing what goes on in classrooms. Thus a second factor that helps account for teachers' poor self-awareness is lack of training for conceptualizing and performing specific teaching behaviors.

The third obstacle hindering the teacher's ability to perceive the classroom is that there is no formal, useful system of providing teachers with information about what they do in classrooms. Teachers are highly suspicious and often hostile toward the suggestions and evaluations provided by curriculum supervisors who visit them only two or three times a year at most and who provide gratuitous advice without knowing (and seldom asking) the nature of the classroom activity in progress. Because teachers usually know that supervisors' ratings are highly unreliable, and because teachers' and supervisors' most frequent disagreements are over appropriate classroom goals (McNeil, 1971), it is no wonder that teachers view current supervisory practices as inadequate. McNeil points out that teachers are most likely to change their classroom performance when they are provided with information that shows a discrepancy between what they want to do and what they are doing. Teachers are unlikely to get this information unless teachers and supervisors meet several times during the year. However, teachers rarely see their supervisors. A survey by the National Education Association reveals that only 34 percent of secondary teachers in the United States are ever observed even once during the year for a period of five minutes or longer. The median number of observational visits in secondary schools is one and the median in elementary schools is two, and only half of these visits are followed by a conference (McNeil, 1971). Unless they have a rare principal, teachers seldom receive direct, useful feedback about their teaching.

Empirical data suggest that, under the present supervisory structure, teachers may view feedback from supervisors suspiciously. For instance Tuckman and Oliver (1969) found that teacher behavior was not substantially changed by feedback from supervisors. In fact, they report that when supervisor feedback was the only information teachers received, it resulted in a significant but negative shift in teacher behavior. Teachers changed their behavior in the opposite direction to that suggested by the supervisor. However, these investigators reported that feedback from the students of these classroom teachers had a positive effect on teacher behavior. Apparently, the *source* of the advice and the *basis* on which it is given are of some concern to teachers. If they feel that supervisors do not spend enough time in the classroom to assess their behavior adequately, or that supervisors employ vague or irrelevant criteria, teachers can, and in some cases do, reject their supervisor's advice.

Lack of specific feedback also characterizes the fate of student teachers in university training programs. They seldom receive direct, useful feedback about their behavior. Medley (Burkhart, 1969) describes the following account of one supervisor's technique for providing a student teacher with information about her behavior. Although the example may be a bit extreme, it does suggest what the authors suspect to be a frequent problem in training programs: candidates do not learn specific teaching skills or a conceptual language for describing classroom behavior.

> ... *This particular woman said, "Well, I didn't say anything to the student teacher because this is a very sensitive area. But when she did something that was particularly bad, I looked at her, and she understood."* ... *we also interviewed the students, and believe it or not, one of the students said, "Well, Mrs. So-and-so didn't talk much. We just looked at this film, and when there was something that I had done particularly well, she looked at me, and I knew."*

Medley, in this same source, also reported the findings from his comprehensive study of the classroom behavior of student teachers. His major conclusion was that supervision and television feedback, as implemented in his study, had no effect on student teachers' behavior. Students and supervisors did not talk about *specific* behavior of mutual interest. He concluded that, "The most important substantive finding is that the seminal problem in improving teaching may be perceptual in nature; that the key to helping teachers change their behavior may lie in helping them see behavior—see what they themselves—and others as well, are doing." We share Medley's feelings. The next section discusses ways in which the teacher can get feedback about his behavior.

Feedback to teachers about classroom behavior

Typically, there are only three ways teachers can obtain systematic and reasonably reliable information about their classroom behavior. (1) Certain information can be collected from students. This alternative is not very useful for elementary-school teachers teaching primary-grade children, however, because young children are not capable of providing complex feedback. Intermediate-level students in elementary schools and secondary students can provide useful feedback, and teachers should actively seek out their opinions. (2) Fellow teachers can be asked to observe and code behavior during a free period. This source of feedback presupposes, of course, that fellow teachers have a free period and have the necessary observation skills. *A strategy for creating reciprocal visits and exchanging information is provided in Chapter 10.* (3) The teacher can develop a conceptual system for labeling his own behavior.

One's ability to describe his own classroom behavior heightens his awareness of his behavior as it unfolds in the classroom. Thus a conceptual system allows you to classify with reasonable precision what you are doing as you do it, making it possible for you to be aware of what you do and to remember how you have behaved. Many school districts now have video equipment so that teachers can see themselves in action. At first glance, video taping seemed like a real learning aid for the classroom teacher—what better way for a teacher to improve his teaching than to see himself as others do? However, studies reporting the changes in teacher behavior after viewing tapes have not been very impressive.

Of course, seeing a film of oneself teaching is like sitting in a classroom watching another teacher. The behavior on the film is still rapid and complex. If you don't know how to look, you don't see very much. Later research has demonstrated that when teachers viewed their film with a consultant *who could provide specific feedback* or with materials describing what to look for, positive change occurred. This indicates that video tapes, if used appropriately, can help teachers to analyze and improve their own behavior. Summarized reviews of the literature on the use of video and audio tape in helping teachers to improve their classroom behavior conclude that such materials are effective only if specific teaching behaviors are highlighted and discussed (Peck, 1971; Baker, 1970). If a teacher works in a school situation where he can be video taped several times a year, he is fortunate, but he will need the conceptual and observational tools for examining his own behavior. Developing these tools is our purpose here.

The terms *conceptual* and *observational tools* are simply another way of saying that we have a descriptive vocabulary. Every social organization, game, or any other system has a language of its own. Some are simple; others, like the classroom, are complex. For example, bridge has a unique descriptive vocabulary, as does football. If you cannot respond to such terms as three no-trump or first down, then you cannot really understand the games. Such terms were developed to effectively increase one's understanding of one's partner's hand or of what took place on an athletic field. We want to make you more familiar with the language of the classroom so that you will be able to describe more effectively and understand what you do in the classroom. Furthermore, we want to discuss positive behaviors that teachers can and should use in the classroom.

Summary

In this chapter we have shown that teachers are not aware of everything that goes on in the classroom, and that this lack of awareness at times interferes with their classroom effectiveness. We have suggested that this problem exists for at least three basic reasons: (1) Teacher training programs spend little time training teachers to perform specific behavior or to describe specific teaching behavior—too much college training is at an abstract level. (2) Classrooms are busy places, and teachers (and students as well) are so busy responding that they have little time to think about what they are doing. (3) Teachers operate in self-contained classrooms and are seldom observed on any systematic basis; consequently they seldom get valuable information about ways to increase their personal effectiveness.

We have posited that teachers need to develop skills for looking at classroom behavior. Preservice teachers also need insight into their own behavior when they do their practice observation and student teaching. A major goal of this book is to alert both the preservice and in-service teacher to important classroom behaviors. Our aim is to help teachers to acquire a classroom language for describing behavior and to develop new ways of structuring classroom learning experiences.

SUGGESTED ACTIVITIES AND QUESTIONS

1. The chapter has stressed that teachers sometimes are not aware of all of their classroom behaviors. When you teach (whether micro, simulated, or real), attempt to monitor your teaching behavior (e.g., the ratio of fact to thought questions) and see how your mental record compares with the actual record taken by a coder or that you hear when you play back your tape-recorded lesson. Practice monitoring your behavior, listening to what you say as you teach, and comparing your mental list with objectively recorded lists. Most of us will find that it is exceedingly difficult to monitor our teaching behavior, initially (we are so busy thinking about what we will ask next that we do not hear completely what we say), but that marked improvement comes with a little practice.

2. Give two concrete and specific examples to illustrate how a teacher's lack of awareness about what he does in the classroom might result in inefficient or self-defeating behavior.

3. How, specifically, could a teacher attempt to improve his ability to see behavior in classrooms?

4. When an observer enters the classroom, why is it important that he have a conceptual system for describing classroom behavior and things to look for in the classroom?

5. Describe the potential ill effects of placing students in learning groups on the basis of achievement or intelligence scores. What possible advantages can be gained by grouping students?

6. Teachers obviously want low-achieving students to do well in the classroom, but some of the data reviewed in this chapter suggest that low-achievement students receive less teacher contact and help than do high-achieving students. How could teachers improve their interaction patterns with low-achievement students without reducing their effectiveness with other students?

7. Why is the use of video equipment (allowing teachers to see themselves teach) relatively ineffective unless it is combined with specific directions concerning what to look for or specific descriptions of what did take place?

8. After reading this chapter do you have any questions about the ideas, facts, or concepts that were presented? Are there topics that you would like more information about? If so, write two or three of your own questions and turn them in to your instructor for feedback or trade questions with fellow teachers or students.

CHAPTER 3

Seeing
in
classrooms

We have discussed problems that teachers have in perceiving classroom behavior, and the difficulty of monitoring their behavior in classrooms that feature both rapidly occurring and complex patterns of behavior has been underlined repeatedly. We have stressed that, typically, teachers who have not been trained to observe specific important behaviors must nevertheless depend entirely upon their own perceptions of classroom life, because they do not receive significant aid from fellow teachers or supervisors.

We have also discussed research showing that teacher perception of classroom behavior differs, at least in certain respects, from that of students and observers (Ehman, 1970; Wolfson and Nash, 1968). So far, we have not tried to explain this. Why should teacher perception be at odds with the views of other observers? After all, students and observers also have seldom been trained to rate specific behaviors, and they must also observe rapidly occurring events. Why should observers see one thing and teachers another?

Part of the answer is that teachers or observers may miss parts of classroom life because events move so quickly. The purpose of this chapter is to highlight another reason: teachers and observers can and do *misinterpret* classroom behavior. That is, the problem of seeing in classrooms is a bit more complex and pervasive than we have described so far. While it is true that a fast classroom pace and not knowing what to look for reduce one's ability to perceive behavior in the classroom, another problem is that on occasion what we think we see is not congruent with reality. Our past experiences, biases, and prejudices can lead us to *interpret* what we see rather than to objectively see, describe, and analyze what really happened.

Anyone who wishes an accurate view of behavior may have to examine and become aware of the perceptual blinders through which he sees the world. For instance, a classroom observer who has been irritated by aggressive, highly verbal teachers may see such teachers as punitive and rigid, while another observer may see them as well organized and articulate. Similarly, a classroom teacher may see two students perform the same physical behavior but yet perceive the behavior differently. Imagine the following situation. Mr. Fulton, who teaches tenth-grade American history, has been talking with the class about a topic for five minutes when Bill Rink calls out, "Why are we talking about this?" Mr. Fulton, knowing Bill to be a troublemaker and class clown, assumes that Bill wants to waste time or provoke an argument. Therefore, he responds aggressively, "If you would pay attention, you'd know what we are doing and why. Pay attention!" However, compare the response Mr. Fulton made above with the interaction that he shares with Jim Thomas. Jim calls out the same words with the same tonal quality, "Why are we talking about this?" But Mr. Fulton, knowing Jim to be a good, dependable student, hears his words not as a threat but as a serious question. He reasons that if Jim does not understand why the class is discussing the topic, nobody does. He responds, "Jim, I probably haven't made this clear. Last Friday we discussed . . ."

The point here is that teachers on occasion react not to what they physically hear but to their *interpretation* of what the student said. The teacher's past experience with a student often influences his interpretation of what the student seems to be saying. This is not to suggest that teachers should not interpret student comments but to argue that they should be *aware* that they are interpreting and classifying student behavior. Some teachers fall into the unconscious trap of expecting a student to behave a certain way and then systematically coloring their interpretations of his behavior so that he appears to fulfill the teacher's expectation. In that reaction, the distinction between observed behavior and the teacher's interpretation of that behavior has been lost.

In brief, this chapter will suggest that anyone who tries to observe behavior will have to guard against the tendency of his own biases to color what he sees. An exercise to help the reader to identify his classroom biases is provided at the end of the chapter. After you have become more aware of the various teacher and student behaviors that incite your interest or disinterest, you will be able to interpret classroom behavior more objectively. General suggestions are also presented to help observers gather classroom data without unduly influencing the behavior of teachers and students.

Selective perception: an example

Teachers often perceive classroom behavior according to their own experience. The following illustration taken from the book *Problem Situations in Teaching* (Greenwood, Good, and Siegel, 1971) shows how the process might operate in the classroom. As you read the example, note how Mr. Smith's background influences his interpretation of classroom behavior.

> *... consider Mr. Smith, who has frequently observed two students, Jean and Shirley, in his senior civics class whispering together in the back of the room. He has always ignored this behavior, hoping it would disappear. The two girls are very physically attractive to Mr. Smith, and very popular among their classmates. He wanted to befriend them, but they seemed to make fun of him at times. Once when he tripped over a wastebasket, they seemed to laugh louder and longer at him than anyone else in the room. At other times, they would whisper together, look in his direction, and begin to giggle.*
>
> *Mr. Smith was not very popular when he was a student in high school. He was shy around girls, dated very little, and did not participate in varsity athletics, although he wanted to be admired and popular. He became a teacher, although he wanted to be a medical doctor, primarily because he felt that the local teacher's college was the only place that he could financially afford to attend and feel reasonably sure of being able to do the academic work required of him.*
>
> *On the day in question, another teacher had hurt his feelings by criticizing the tie that he had worn to school. The other teacher had said, "Man, you are never going to be a swinger as long as you wear square ties like that." During second period civics class, Jean and Shirley once again whispered together in the back of the room, looked in Mr. Smith's direction, and began to laugh. Mr. Smith inferred from their behavior that they were talking about him. He told them to go to the Dean of Girls' office.*
>
> *The Dean of Girls later told Mr. Smith that the girls had been telling one another jokes. Mr. Smith didn't really believe this "story" of the girls and told them in no uncertain terms*

that he was going to move them away from one another and that the next time they talked he would cut their grades. Both girls had confused and bewildered expressions on their faces and Jean began to cry. Shirley said, "Why are you treating us this way, Mr. Smith? We really thought that you were the one teacher that we have who really understands us!"

You can probably think of a great number of things that you would like to find out about Jean, Shirley, Mr. Smith, and others, before you begin to diagnose this case. A good starting point is to consider Mr. Smith's objectivity. Was he objective in examining the data? From a measurement stand-point, objectivity of this kind refers to the amount of agreement between observers. If two other teachers had observed the same behavior as Mr. Smith observed, would they have made the same inferences from the behavior of Jean and Shirley?

If Mr. Smith could remove his perceptual blinders for a moment, what would he have actually observed about Jean and Shirley's behavior and what would he have inferred? He had definitely seen the two girls whispering together, glancing at him and laughing at him from time to time. He could probably even guess how many times they have engaged in this behavior, if it were important. He did hear and see them laugh loud and long when he tripped over the wastebasket. Further, the Dean of Girls said the girls explained that they were telling jokes on the day that he sent them out of the class. Finally, we know precisely what the girls said to Mr. Smith when he talked to them later because we have an exact quote. We can't see the girls' faces or hear the way in which Shirley said what she did to Mr. Smith. Our data have many limitations, but it does provide some clues and suggests the need to collect additional information.

What kinds of inferences did Mr. Smith make from the behavioral data? Are there other interpretations that could be made? First, he seemed to feel that the girls saw him as an inadequate male. Second, he inferred that they were whispering and giggling about him and his inadequacies. After the incident was reported, Mr. Smith later said he refused to accept Shirley's statement concerning his adequacy as an understanding teacher. Are other inferences concerning the girls' behavior possible? Did Mr. Smith respond to the behavior that he observed, or did he respond to inferences that he drew from this behavior? Imagine Mr. Smith at some future time with some other teachers *in the lounge during their "planning period." Imagine another teacher saying, "I have Jean Sinders and Shirley Merrick in my class this semester. Boy, what lookers! Hey, George, didn't you have some trouble with them last semester?" Mr. Smith: "Did I ever! They were always disrupting the class. Every time I turned my back they were whispering and giggling and making all kinds of noise."**

This incident shows how a teacher can "see" more than just the behavior that occurs. Inferences about classroom behavior are useful, but such inferences should be made *after* we have collected objective information. A person's background, particularly his own experiences as a student and his personal definitions of a good teacher, can lead him to draw erroneous conclusions about classroom behavior. If the teacher does something we especially like (e.g., asks questions before calling on students), we may rate him high in all areas. Similarly, if the teacher does something we particularly dislike (e.g., humiliates a student who provides a wrong answer), we may evaluate him low on all dimensions of classroom behavior even if other aspects are positive. Thus when viewing teacher behavior it is important not to evaluate behavior as positive or negative independent of its effects upon students. For example, the teacher we see as hypercritical may be seen by his students as a person who sets high standards because he cares about them. As a case in point, see Kleinfeld (1972).

Observe behavior—don't interpret

It is exceedingly difficult for an observer to sit in a classroom and note the behavior that occurs without attempting to *interpret* what the behavior means. However, it is very important that observers concentrate on observing and coding classroom behavior, because time spent speculating about the possible motivation behind a student's or teacher's behavior increases the chances that the observer will miss significant aspects of classroom interaction. It is preferable to hypothesize about the causes of classroom behavior *after* an objective description of that behavior has been collected. Premature hypotheses about classroom behavior, particularly hypotheses that are made while we are still observing in the classroom, lock us into a narrow viewpoint. When we are looking for something,

*From Gordon E. Greenwood, Thomas L. Good, and Betty L. Siegel, *Problem Situations in Teaching*, pp. 8–10. Copyright © 1971 by Harper & Row, Publishers, Inc. By permission of the publisher.

we are likely to find it. Remember the example of Mr. Smith and recall how his perceptual blinders caused him to interpret behavior to make it conform to his view.

Looking for specific behaviors in the classroom is one way to minimize the degree to which our attitudes and biases will color what we see. For example, if we believe a teacher to be caustic and ineffectual, it is less likely that such an attitude will interfere with our description of classroom life when we pay attention to behavior (e.g., how often the teacher calls on low-achieving male students) than it will when we attempt to describe the teacher in global inferential terms (how good-looking, warm, friendly, fair, etc., is the teacher).

To help the reader to see more objectively in classrooms, the chapters that follow present *concrete* suggestions about what to look for and how to assess what is seen. However, a focus on behavior does not in itself guarantee that one will see accurately. Behavior will be seen accurately only if the observer wants to do so and is willing to practice and to compare his observations with those of others. Nevertheless, a focus on behavior is a useful starting point for trying to see and describe classroom life.

One useful way to begin to train yourself to see accurately is through case studies in which you focus attention on one or only a few students. This is particularly true when the case study involves reporting *observed behaviors*. Most readers of this book will have conducted a case study previously or will presently be completing one as a course assignment. Such assignments facilitate one's ability to observe and describe behavior accurately, and these skills are necessary to the generation of effective, concrete plans for dealing with students. Traditional case studies are excellent analytical tools for expanding one's ability to see and to interpret student behavior.

Since the case study is such a common educational assignment, it will not be discussed here. Readers who are unfamiliar with case-study techniques are encouraged to examine other references. Useful descriptions of how to conduct case studies can be found in Perkins (1969) and Shaffer and Shoben (1956). Gordon (1966) and Almy (1969) describe a variety of techniques for looking at student *behavior* in the classroom, and these sources are useful for students who want to learn more about child study.

Discovering bias

We have noted that observers and teachers often misinterpret behavior because their own background and biases lead them to color classroom behavior and because they attempt to interpret behavior prematurely. The first step in changing this undesirable behavior is to become aware of its presence and consequences. That is, the teacher needs to become aware of both his *behavior* (e.g., he criticizes some students almost every time they give a wrong answer) and its *consequences* (e.g., the student volunteers less, begins to avoid the teacher, and hands in fewer homework assignments).

When we become aware of our attitude we can often control or adapt our personal behavior more optimally. For example, the teacher who unhesitantly says, "I am a fair grader. I am never influenced by the student as a person, and I grade only the paper," is often an extremely unfair grader. The fact is that knowing who wrote the paper does influence most graders. With certain students, teachers tend to *read more into the answer* than is really there (especially with students with whom they have worked closely). We demand more proof from other students; although a student's first paragraph in an essay is excellent, a teacher suspects this student does not really know the material.

Similarly, other factors such as the quality of handwriting may influence the way we grade an essay exam (Chase, 1968). Once a teacher realizes that he does have *biases* that interfere with grading fairly, he can take steps to reduce the effects of this bias. For example, teachers can mask the identity of the student who wrote the paper before grading it, can grade all papers on the first question before going to the next question, and can score only content and not penmanship.

In the same way, one can improve other weak spots in his teaching behavior if he becomes aware of them. But self-study and examination that increase self-understanding are difficult to conduct. Part of the problem is that we take so little time to assess ourselves as persons. But a different and more pervasive problem is that it is difficult to admit certain feelings and reactions because we feel that they are unprofessional or inappropriate. For example, we tend not to accept the fact that we react differently to different students.

Greenberg (1969) presents interesting descriptions of the various myths that frequently produce teacher problems. He describes the myth of "liking all students equally," and notes that such magnanimous behavior is impossible. We believe that teachers will treat students in equally fair and facilitating ways if and when they are aware of their feelings about the students. However, this does not mean identical teacher behavior, because some students need more teacher contact, others need more opportunity to work on their own, and so forth. As human beings, teachers experience the full range of human emotions: they will distrust some students; they will be proud of certain ones; some will delight them; and yet others they will want to avoid. Similarly, observers will have different reactions toward different teachers. If we are not careful, these feelings will interfere with our ability to see teachers accurately.

Once we identify how we feel about certain student and teacher characteristics, it is often possible to monitor classroom behavior more objectively. For example, if we realize that a student makes us uneasy because of his physical ugliness, filth or smell, embarrassing questions, or shyness, we can take steps to make the student more attractive to us. However, if we can only think "I love all students," we are unlikely to identify our differential behavior toward students whom we dislike. The assignment outlined below will help you to identify some of your attitudes and preferences toward students.

Case study: for self-study

Earlier we suggested that conducting case studies may sharpen your ability to observe classroom behavior. In this section you will be exposed to a case-study assignment that provides you with an opportunity to study student behavior to gain more insight into your personal values, preferences, and attitudes. This case study forces you to consider the types of students (or teachers) that you find fun and exciting to work with and to identify the types of students who annoy, bore, or disgust you. The case study outlined here will help you increase your awareness of student and teacher traits that have positive or negative effects upon you and will improve your classroom insight.

From the following list, select two contrast groups for study—any two except the pair (1) and (4). If you are not in an observation course, pick peers who are in your class or pick two different college instructors and analyze their differential behavior. Better yet, arrange to observe in a class similar to the one you teach or will be teaching.

1. Select the two students with whom you most enjoy working; that is, if you were the classroom teacher, which two students in the class would you select first to be in your own room? (Positive feelings)
2. Select two students whom you dislike the most in the classroom. (Negative feelings)
3. Select two students for whom you have *no strong feeling* whatsoever. Use the class roster here so that you will not forget about anyone. (Apathy, indifference, do not notice when they are absent)
4. Select two students (one boy, one girl) who best represent

the child you would want your daughter or son to be like at this age. (Identification)

After selecting the four students, begin to observe them more closely during class activities. If you are observing in public schools and you choose to take notes during class, be sure to obtain the teacher's permission and let him know that the notes are about students and not him. Some of you will be busy teaching during the day, so your notes will have to be made after class ends. Some of you may want to consult the references on the case study approach (see p. 45) to improve your observational skills. In any case, the notes are for your own use, and the form you utilize is completely open. Bear in mind that any information you record in classrooms is confidential; students should never be identified by name. Even notes that you take in class should include no *actual* student names (notes are often lost). For this case study, it is *not* necessary to collect data from the school files (which might influence the observation anyway). Normal classroom behavior is sufficient.

Analyze the similarities and differences among the four students. This analysis between students should provide you with clues regarding the types of student behavior that are likely to touch off positive or negative responses in your own behavior. You will then be in a better position to understand why you behave as you do and be able to change your behavior in certain ways in order to interact more positively with students who irritate you. You will want to raise some of the following questions when you compare and contrast the students:

1. What are the students like physically? How do they look? Do they have nice clothes? Are they attractive? Clean? Are they large or small for their age? Are they male or female?
2. What are their favorite subjects—what lessons bore them? What are their strong and weak points as students? As persons?
3. What are their most prominent behavioral characteristics? Do they smile a lot? Do they thank you for your attention? Do they seek you out in the classroom—more or less than the average student? Do they raise their hands to answer often? Can they be depended upon to do their own work? How mature are they? Are they awkward or clumsy?
4. What are their social characteristics and what level of socio-economic-status homes do they come from? What is their ethnicity?

The goal of this exercise is not to put you through an intensive, total, self-analysis. It is to start you thinking about the possible linkages between your feelings about students and how these feelings relate to the way students treat you and the way you treat them in the classroom. A valuable parallel exercise would be to list the teacher behaviors that provoke your interest or boredom. The purpose of such activities is, of course, to make you more aware of what you like and dislike, so that these attitudes will not interfere with your classroom observation and teaching.

Simplifying the observational task

In this chapter, emphasis has been placed on the need to study observer and teacher biases to prevent them from interfering with an objective view of classroom life. However, another major obstacle hinders perception in classrooms: the sheer physical complexity of the classroom can, at times, prevent us from seeing certain events. While the teacher instructs a reading group, for example, four students may be at the science table, three listening to tapes at the listening post, four reading at their desks, and three writing at the blackboard. No observer can monitor everything that takes place in the classroom. Even relatively simple tasks may be impossible to code simultaneously. For instance, if an observer wants to code the number of hands raised when a teacher asks a question and whether or not the student called on by the teacher has his hand up, he may find himself still counting hands when the teacher calls on the student and will thus be unable to determine whether or not the student had his hand up.

One useful way to break down the physical complexity of the classroom is to study the behavior of a few students. Such students can be studied intensively, and their behavior will mirror what is taking place in the entire classroom around them. For example, the observer can choose to focus on a few students (perhaps two high, two middle, and two low achievers—one female and one male at each achievement level), or on a particular group of students (low achievers). Then a record can be made of everything these students do. For example, it might be useful to look at these differences between high, middle, and low achievers:

1. How often do low, middle, and high achievers raise their hands?
2. Do all students approach the teacher to receive help, or do some students seldom approach the teacher?

3. How long does the reading group last for each group of achievers?
4. Are the students involved in their work? How long do they work independently at their desks?
5. How often are students in different groups praised?

These questions represent a few of the many you can examine. Here, our purpose is not to suggest what to look for (this will come later), but to examine ways and procedures that will facilitate looking. Studies of representative students are an excellent way of reducing the complexity of looking in classrooms. These studies allow one to focus attention upon the teacher and only a few students, rather than trying to code everything that takes place in a large classroom. This focus on a few students is especially useful when you first begin to observe in classrooms.

Another strategy for aiding ability to observe in classrooms is simply to *limit* the number of behaviors that you look for at one time. The student observer, or teachers participating in self-evaluation or in-service programs, will do well to restrict their attention to only five to ten behaviors at any one time. When one attempts to measure too many things, he becomes confused and cannot measure objectively. It would be better for an observer to concentrate on certain behaviors for a couple of days and then start to code a new set of behaviors.

Reliability

In addition to realizing his own biases and limiting the number of students and behaviors observed, an observer should learn to estimate his ability to code classroom behavior accurately by comparing his observations with those of other observers. Perhaps the easiest way to determine if you are observing what happens and not allowing your personal biases to interfere with your observing is to check your observations with those collected by someone else. (A fuller description of reliability is appended at the end of the chapter. The reader desiring more information on reliability is referred to this material.)

In general, the observation forms presented in this book can be used reliably with very little practice. After discussing observation scales for a short time period (5 to 20 minutes, depending upon the scale), students should be able to achieve general agreement (60 percent to 90 percent agreement) and thus be able to use the scale reliably to code classroom behavior. Let us discuss agreement further. If observers are watching a video tape and coding the number of academic questions that a teacher asks, we may find that one observer tallied 16 instances of academic questions while another observer tallied only 10. The agreement between observers can be estimated using a simple formula suggested by Emmer and Millett (1970):

$$\text{agreement} = 1 - \frac{A-B}{A+B}.$$

The formula tells us to subtract the difference between the two observers' counts and to divide them by the sum of the two observers' counts. The A term is always the larger number. Thus the agreement in this example would be:

$$1 - \frac{16-10}{16+10} = 1 - \frac{6}{26} = 1 - 0.23 = 0.77\%.$$

General plan for looking in classrooms

What you look at in a classroom will vary from situation to situation and from individual to individual. Some observers will be able to focus on six behaviors, another may be able to code ten. Some observers may be in the classroom eight hours a week, some only four. Some observers may see two or three different teachers, while others will remain in the same room. Despite such situational differences, there are some general principles to bear in mind when looking in classrooms.

First, observers often try to reduce the complexity of classroom coding by focusing their attention exclusively upon the behavior of the teacher. This is particularly true of teachers in training who are still trying to determine what teachers do in the classroom. This is misplaced emphasis. *The key to looking in classrooms is student response.* If students are actively engaged in and enjoying learning activities, it makes little difference if the teacher is lecturing, using discovery techniques, or using small group activity for independent study.

Earlier, mention was made of the fact that some observers may see a teacher as punitive and rigid, while others see the same teacher as well organized and articulate. A good way to reduce your own bias in viewing teacher behavior is to supplement your observations with attention to the effects of teacher behavior upon student behavior. When you code in the classroom, reduce the number of things you look at to a small, manageable set, but look at both teacher and student behaviors.

The classroom teacher who wants to receive relevant feedback about his behavior and that of his pupils, and the observer who wants to see what life in a classroom is like, must be careful not to disturb the natural flow of behavior in the classroom. By "natural" we simply mean the behavior that would take place in the classroom if the observer were not present. Students, especially young ones, will adjust quickly to the presence of an observer if teachers prepare them properly and if observers follow through with appropriate behavior. The teacher should make a brief announcement to explain the observer's presence, so that the students will not have to wonder about him or try to question him to find out for themselves. For example, a second-grade class might be told: "Mr. Ramon will be with us today and the rest of the week. He is learning about being a teacher. Mr. Ramon will not disturb us because we have many things we want to finish, and he knows how busy we are. Please do not disturb him because he too is busy and has his own work to do."

The observer can help the teacher by avoiding eye contact with the students and by refusing to be drawn into long conversations with them or aiding them in their seatwork—unless, of course, the observer is also a participant in classroom life. (Some university courses call for students to serve as teacher aides before they do their student teaching.)

Observers should not initiate contact with students, nor do anything to draw special attention to themselves (e.g., frequently ripping pages out of a notebook). It is especially important when two observers are in the same room that they do not talk with one another, exchange notes, and so forth. Such behavior bothers both the teacher and the students, and causes attention to be focused on the observers so that natural behavior is disturbed.

When students approach the observer, he should appear to be busy and avoid eye contact unless the student speaks to him. In most situations the observer can politely but firmly remind the student that he should be in his seat working, and he can tell the student that he is very busy with his own work. Requests for help should simply be referred to the teacher: "I'm sorry, I can't help you. Ask your teacher, Mrs. Brown."

If children bring pictures that they have drawn especially for you, react to such gifts pleasantly, but with minimal response, and then send the child back to his seat.

Occasionally the student may ask a question that the observer cannot redirect to the teacher. For instance, if the student asks: "Are you writing about me?" you need only make a minimal response ("I'm very busy writing about everything in the room and I have to keep at my work") and then direct the student back to his seat.

In advance of coming into the classroom, the observer should talk with the teacher about where he will sit in the room, how he should be introduced to the students, and how he should respond when individual students approach him. Without such preparation, both teachers and observers frequently are paralyzed when students approach the observer. The teacher is embarrassed because students are out of their seats, and he is indecisive about what to do because he does not know whether the observer wants to inspect their work or would prefer not to be bothered. Observers are often unskilled at dealing with students. They are not sure how to act when approached, except that they don't want to be a rude guest. These difficult moments in coding will be reduced if the observer meets with the teacher before the coding begins to discuss what he wants to do and how he should be introduced. Mutual agreement should be reached about how to deal with students who are bent upon making themselves known to the coder. At such meetings, observers can also obtain curriculum materials and information about the students (seating chart, achievement ranking). Such information is necessary if the observer plans to conduct an intensive study of only a few children at different achievement levels.

Summary

This chapter has stressed the fact that objective coding of behavior is the way to guard against our biases and gain the most benefit from classroom observations. In particular, stress has been placed upon reducing personal bias in observing by (1) becoming aware of our biases; (2) looking for specific behavior, to break down the physical complexity of the classroom; and (3) checking our observation data against the observations of others. Exercises have been suggested for helping you observe your own or another's behavior objectively. Procedures for minimizing the observer's effect on the classroom have been discussed, along with techniques for observing unobtrusively in the classroom. These considerations should be borne in mind when you use the observation schedules following Chapters 4 through 9 to observe in classrooms.

This chapter in combination with the previous two chapters has identified many of the factors that block our perception of classroom behavior. In these introductory chapters we have also discussed ways in which we can reduce problems of bias and complexity as well as ways in which we can observe more objectively in the classroom. In the following chapters we will develop the theme of looking in classrooms by providing detailed comment about *what* to look for in classrooms. The following chapters provide a focus on what could and should be occurring in classrooms. Furthermore, at the end of each chapter you will find forms for rating scales that can be used to code or look for the presence or absence of the teaching behaviors that were discussed in each chapter.

SUGGESTED ACTIVITIES AND QUESTIONS

1. Visit a classroom or watch a video tape of a classroom discussion and try to tally the number of times that the teacher: (1) asks a question, (2) responds to a student's answer, and (3) praises a student. Compare your tallies with a fellow observer by calculating the percent of agreement between your observations.

2. Try some simple observation with one or two others and attempt to code behavior reliably. For example, attempt to keep track of three goldfish. After five minutes of observation can you agree on which is fish one, two, or three? Can you agree upon which fish moves the most? Which is the fastest when it does move? Which fish is the most aggressive or most playful? Most observers will find this seemingly simple task to be quite complex when they first attempt it. Do a similar exercise for a group of five nursery school children or five older students. Which child is the most aggressive? Which child is busiest? (Add other questions of your own.)

3. Think back over all the teachers you have ever had and list the major characteristics of your favorite teacher. What was he like as a person? What were the chief elements of his teaching style?

4. Similarly, list the distinguishing factors of your least liked or least effective teacher. Why were you more comfortable, more stimulated in one class than the other? Was it because of the teacher, the subject matter, students in the class, or a combination of factors?

5. Identify the ten student characteristics or behaviors that will delight you most when you are a teacher. What does this list tell you about your personal likes and your teaching personality?

6. List the ten student characteristics or behaviors that are most likely to irritate you or make you anxious. Why do these behaviors bother you? How can you deal fairly with students who exhibit behaviors that are bothersome to you?

7. Why should classroom observers attune to student behavior as well as to teacher behavior?

8. What can an observer do to minimize his disruption of the natural flow of classroom events?

APPENDIX

A coding exercise

Subsequent chapters in this book are followed by appendixes containing observation forms that you can use to observe and record classroom behavior objectively. Before you can do so profitably, however, you will need to acquire certain basic coding habits and skills and to learn to check your coding reliability. These skills are not difficult to learn, but they do require a little concentration and practice.

A good way for you to begin is to carefully study the following example. The example provides coding instructions and coding sheets adapted from the authors' dyadic interaction observation system (Brophy and Good, 1970a), and shows the coding of Arlene and Suzi, two observers who coded in the same classroom at the same time. By using the same system to code classroom interaction with one or more friends and by computing agreement percentages as shown for Arlene and Suzi in the example, you can practice using this typical coding scheme and can assess your reliability as a coder.

The coding system shown in Figure 1 (p. 62) is typical of those presented later in the book, in that it applies only to certain kinds of teacher-student interactions; it is not used continually. You may have seen or used a different type of coding system that involved continual coding, recording information every 30 seconds, for example, regardless of what was going on at that time. The coding approach taken in this book is different. Instead of presenting a general system to be used continually, we provide a variety of forms tailored for use in specific situations. Certain forms are used when the teacher is lecturing, for example, while others are used when he is giving seatwork directions, and still others when he is dealing with management problems.

Thus you do not code continually with these forms. You use a given observation form only when the appropriate behavior is present (i.e., when *codable instances* are observed). When no codable instances are present you do not code anything, or else you use a different observation form appropriate to the present situation.

Coding question-answer-feedback sequences

In this example, teacher and student behavior are coded during question and answer interchanges. Whenever the teacher asks a question and calls on a student to respond, the observers code information about whether the student is male or female, about the quality of the student's response, and about the nature of the teacher's feedback reaction to the student. If you have not done so already, study the coding instructions in Figure 1 before continuing.

Coding sheets are prepared so that this information can be quickly recorded by entering check marks in appropriate places on the coding sheet. No writing or note taking is required. The coding sheet is organized to follow the time sequence involved in coder decision-making, so that in coding a given interchange the coders move from left to right across the page (see Figures 2, 3, and 4). As soon as they recognize that a codable interchange is occurring (i.e., the teacher has asked a question and is calling on a student to respond), the coders begin recording the information. When the teacher selects a student to respond, coders record his sex by entering a check mark under M or F. Then, after noting the student's response and the teacher's reaction to it, they code the quality of the response by entering a check mark under $+$, $\pm$, $-$, or 0. Finally, they code the teacher's feedback reaction by entering one or more check marks in the appropriate teacher reaction columns. For example, if the teacher simply affirmed that a correct response was correct, and then went on to another question and another student, coders would enter a check mark in the $+$ column. However, if the teacher had praised the response and then asked the same student another question, coders would have entered check marks in both the $++$ and the New Ques. columns.

To see if you understand, try to code the following sequence:

TEACHER: Which is heavier, a pound of lead or a pound of feathers? George?
GEORGE: Neither one—they're both a pound!
TEACHER: That's right—good thinking, George!

To code this sequence correctly, you would:

1. Enter a check under M—George is a male student

2. Enter a check under $+$—he answered the question correctly

3. Enter a check under $+$—the teacher affirmed the answer ("That's right")

4. Enter a check under $\pm$ —the teacher also praised the student ("Good thinking")

Once the teacher's response to the student's answer (or failure to answer) has been coded, the information for that particular question-answer-feedback sequence is complete, and coders drop down to the next row and move back to the left side of the coding sheet to be prepared for coding the next sequence. The next sequence may be with the same student (if the teacher has repeated the question, rephrased or given a clue, or asked a new question, thus giving the student a second opportunity to respond), or it may be with a new student.

Thus each row contains information about a single question-answer-feedback sequence, and this interaction can be reconstructed from the coding sheets. In the example, both Arlene's and Suzi's sheets (Figures 2 and 3, respectively) show that in the first observed codable interchange: (1) the teacher called on a female student to respond; (2) the student responded correctly; (3) the teacher affirmed that her response was correct. Inspection of the second row on each sheet shows that Arlene and Suzi agree that the teacher directed the second question to a male student and that he also answered correctly. However, the coders are in disagreement about the teacher's feedback reaction. Arlene felt that the teacher's reaction was simply affirmation of the correctness of the student's answer, but Suzi saw the teacher's reaction as more intense or positive, and so she coded it as praise. This is the first of several coding disagreements between Arlene and Suzi.

How serious are these disagreements? Can their coding be trusted? To answer such questions, objective methods of assessing coders' reliability are required. An objective analysis of Arlene's and Suzi's reliability is presented below.

Establishing reliability

To establish reliability, you will need to code in the company of at least one other person. This will allow you to assess reliability by comparing your codes with theirs and will provide the basis for clearing up ambiguities and misunderstandings through discussion of disagreements. Once good reliability is established, you can code semi-independently. However, it is wise to continue to check reliability periodically, even after initial proficiency has been established. This will help guard against the tendency to gradually drift into undesirable observation and coding habits over time. Even the use of structured, standardized observation instruments cannot guarantee against coding inaccuracies. Thus even the most experienced coders need to recheck their reliability occasionally if they want to be sure that their observations can be trusted. This is especially important, of course, in research situations.

Two or more coders can check their reliability either by visiting in a classroom together or by coding the same film or video tape of classroom interaction. When films or video tapes are available it is often advisable to use them in the initial stages of learning to code. Any number of coders can all code the same films or video tapes, and they can be replayed to refresh everyone's memory when disagreements are discussed.

At first, the major source of disagreement between coders usually is speed. That is, if one or both coders fall behind while trying to make up their minds about a code or trying to find the correct place on the coding sheet to record it, they may fail to observe or record one or more instances of codable interaction that occurred while this was going on. Such problems disappear rapidly with practice, however, and coders soon learn to keep up with the pace of classroom interaction.

At first, the major source of disagreement between coders usually will occur not because one coder coded an interaction that the other one missed, but because both coders coded the interaction but coded it differently. That is, the two coders disagree in their observation of the instance in question. By analyzing and discussing these instances of disagreement, coders can usually identify common or repeated causes. For example, one coder may always code "good" as praise, while another coder might not consider "good" to be praise. Thus the first coder would code many more instances of praise in the classroom of a teacher who frequently said "good." By identifying and coming to agreement about how to resolve those reported sources of disagreement, coders can eliminate most unreliability.

Computing coder agreement percentages

Arlene and Suzi show general agreement in the coding example, but there are several disagreements. To assess their agreement precisely, they would compute agreement percentages. The computations involved are shown below.

Assessment of coder agreement in using this type of observation scheme requires getting answers to two questions: (1) When a codable interchange appeared, did both coders code it? (2) When both coders did code an interchange, did their coding agree? The first question deals with coding speed, the ability of the coders to keep up with the pace of classroom interaction. The second deals with coder agreement on how particular interchanges should have been coded.

Coder speed can be assessed with the formula given in the chapter. This formula can be used whenever agreements on frequency, or number of codes, is being measured. In our example, Suzi coded 11 interchanges, while Arlene coded 10. Applying the formula, agreement would be:

$$1 - \frac{A - B}{A + B} = 1 - \frac{11 - 10}{11 + 10} = 1 - \frac{1}{21} = 1 - 0.05 = 95\%$$

Thus Arlene and Suzi showed good, but not perfect, agreement. Arlene missed 1 of 11 codable interchanges, while Suzi coded all 11. (It is possible that both coders missed one or more other codable interchanges, but we cannot tell from the data. If the coders knew that they both had missed additional coding, they would have to take this into account in interpreting their agreement data. In this case the 95 percent figure would be deceptively high.)

To assess coder agreement on how particular interchanges should be coded, we turn our attention to those interchanges that both Arlene and Suzi coded. Suzi's extra coding (the seventh row on her coding sheet) is not used in this analysis, because we do not know how Arlene would have coded this interchange and, therefore, we have nothing to compare with Suzi's coding. To facilitate comparison, Figure 4 shows Arlene's codes superimposed on Suzi's coding sheet (skipping Suzi's seventh row, because Arlene does not have a parallel set of codes; Arlene's seventh row belongs with Suzi's eighth row, and so on).

Coder agreement is computed separately for the three separate decisions that each coder had to make concerning each interchange: (1) the sex of the student; (2) the quality of the student's response; and (3) the nature of the teacher's feedback reaction. The method to be used in computing agreement is (1) establish the number of *coding decisions* that were made and (2) compute the percentage of these decisions upon which the two coders agreed.

Since 10 interchanges were coded by both coders, the coders each had to note the student's sex 10 times. Agreement between Arlene and Suzi on these decisions about student sex was perfect (10/10 = 100 percent agreement).

There were also 10 student responses to be coded as right, part-right, wrong, or no response. Arlene and Suzi also agreed on all 10 of these coding decisions (100 percent agreement).

Disagreements appear in the coding of the teacher's feedback reactions to students. Twice Arlene coded "affirm" while Suzi coded "praise"; otherwise, the two coders agreed in coding a total of 10 teacher feedback reactions. Thus they agreed in 10 out of 12 (83 percent) of the instances in which they both coded an aspect of the teacher's feedback (there are 12 codes here, rather than 10, because the teacher showed two different categories of feedback on each of two occasions).

Overall, Arlene's and Suzi's agreement is quite good. One clear pattern of disagreement does show up: Suzi tends to code "praise" at times when Arlene codes "affirm." This occurred twice out of the five times that this particular distinction had to be made (i.e., their agreement for the praise vs. affirm decision is only 60 percent). We cannot tell from the data which coder is correct, if either is. Arlene and Suzi would have to discuss these instances of disagreement to discover the reason for them.

Interpreting classroom coding

The example is too short to allow firm conclusions, but we can make some tentative hypotheses about the teacher on the basis of it. First, note that the majority of questions are answered by boys. If this proves to be a reliable finding, it suggests that the teacher is not calling on girls as much as he should be. This could be brought to his attention for discussion and possible action.

The students' answers show an appropriate success rate. The difficulty level of teachers' questions should be such that most, but not all, are answered correctly. This way the difficulty level is adjusted to student ability. Students can follow the lesson and respond without great difficulty, but at the same time the questions are not so old or easy that they present no challenge.

When the students in this example did not respond correctly, they tended not to respond at all. If this happens often, it may mean that the teacher is not waiting long enough to allow students to formulate a response, or that he is overly critical in response to wrong answers, so that his students hesitate to answer unless they are sure they are right. In any case, it usually is better that students make some response rather than remain silent when stuck. If they remain silent, it is likely that inappropriate teacher behavior is the reason.

A tendency to criticize students when they do not respond correctly shows up in this teacher's codes and may be part of the explanation for the students' tendency to remain silent when stuck. *Criticism is almost never appropriate* in these instances. However, note that the teacher also tends to praise frequently. Taken together, these codes suggest that he may be generally overreacting to student performance here. He might do better to be more problem centered and less personal in his feedback reactions.

The pattern of praise and criticism suggests that the teacher may be playing favorites and/or may prefer boys to girls, although much more data would be needed to find out for sure.

Conclusion

The extended example above shows how you would establish coder agreement and use coded information to draw inferences about teaching. The principles involved are applicable to any coding in the classroom. To check agreement on frequency or *number* of codes, use the formula:

$$\text{agreement} = 1 - \frac{A - B}{A + B}.$$

To check agreement on *how* interchanges should have been coded, compute a percentage by dividing the number agreed upon by itself plus the number not agreed upon (i.e., agreements divided by total decisions).

To interpret coded information, look for suggestive patterns that give clues about appropriate and inappropriate teacher behavior (this will be discussed at length in the following chapters). Remember, though, that interpretations based on one or just a few observations are tentative and suggestive. Do not make judgments on the basis of insufficient evidence.

FIGURE 1. Coding Categories for Question–Answer–Feedback Sequences

STUDENT SEX

SYMBOL	*LABEL*	*DEFINITION*
M	Male	The student answering the question is male.
F	Female	The student answering the question is female.

STUDENT RESPONSE

+	Right	The teacher accepts the student's response as correct or satisfactory.
±	Part right	The teacher considers the student's response to be only partially correct or to be correct but incomplete.
−	Wrong	The teacher considers the student's response to be incorrect.
0	No answer	The student makes no response or says he doesn't know (code student's answer here if teacher gives a feedback reaction before he is able to respond).

TEACHER FEEDBACK REACTION

++	Praise	Teacher praises student either in words ("fine," "good," "wonderful," "good thinking") or by expressing verbal affirmation in a notably warm, joyous, or excited manner.
+	Affirm	Teacher simply affirms that the student's response is correct (nods, repeats answer, says "Yes," "OK," etc.).
0	No reaction	Teacher makes no response whatever to student's response—he simply goes on to something else.
−	Negate	Teacher simply indicates that the student's response is incorrect (shakes head, says "No," "That's not right," "Hm-mm," etc.).
−	Criticize	Teacher criticizes student, either in words ("You should know better than that," "That doesn't make any sense—you better play close attention," etc.) or by expressing verbal negation in a frustrated, angry, or disgusted manner.
Gives Ans.	Teacher gives answer	Teacher provides the correct answer for the student.
Ask Other	Teacher asks another student	Teacher redirects the question, asking a different student to try to answer it.
Other Calls	Another student calls out answer	Another student calls out the correct answer, and the teacher acknowledges that it is correct.
Repeat	Repeats question	Teacher repeats the original question, either in its entirety or with a prompt ("Well?" "Do you know?" "What's the answer?").
Clue	Rephrase or clue	Teacher makes original question easier for student to answer by rephrasing it or by giving a clue.
New Ques.	New question	Teacher asks a new question (i.e., a question that calls for a different answer than the original question called for).

FIGURE 2. Arlene's Codes

FIGURE 3. Suzi's Codes

	STUDENT SEX		STUDENT RESPONSE									TEACHER FEEDBACK REACTION					
NO.	M	F	+	±	−	0	++	+	0	−	---	GIVES ANS.	ASK OTHER	OTHER CALLS	RE-PEAT	CLUE	NEW QUES.
1		✓	✓				✓	✓									
2	✓		✓				✓										
3	✓		✓			✓	✓									✓	
4	✓		✓				✓										
5	✓						✓										
6		✓			✓						✓						✓
7		✓	✓		✓		✓							✓			
8	✓		✓						✓								
9	✓		✓						✓			✓					
10	✓					✓					✓						
11	✓																
12																	
13																	
14																	
15																	

FIGURE 4. Arlene's Codes Superimposed over Suzi's Codes

CHAPTER 4

Teacher
expectations

In Chapter 2 we mentioned studies by Rowe (1969) and by Brophy and Good (1970b) in discussing how achievement patterns can affect the ways teachers deal with different children in their classrooms. Rowe found that teachers would wait longer for an answer from a high-achieving student than they would from a low-achieving student. Brophy and Good found that teachers were more likely to give highs a second chance to respond in failure situations and that they praised highs more frequently for success and criticized them less frequently for failure. Both of these studies provide examples of how teachers treat high-achieving students in ways that are likely to insure their continued success, while treating low achievers in ways that are likely to slow their progress even further. Let us look at some related examples from other research.

Palardy (1969) studied the reading achievement produced by two groups of first-grade teachers. Using a questionnaire, Palardy identified a group of 10 teachers who thought that boys could learn to read just as successfully as girls in the first grade and another group of 14 teachers who thought that boys could not learn to read as successfully as girls. This information was gathered from a single item that was just one part of a larger questionnaire, so that the teachers were not aware of the nature of the study.

Five teachers from each group were then selected for further study. These teachers were all Caucasian females with bachelor's degrees and at least three years of teaching experience in the first grade. All taught in middle-class schools and used the same basal reading series to work with three reading groups in heterogeneously grouped, self-contained classrooms. Reading readiness and reading achievement scores were then obtained from the ten classrooms involved, and the two groups were compared.

The students were exactly comparable on the reading readiness scores taken in September, so that there was no initial group difference. However, differences were apparent among the boys in reading achievement scores obtained in March. Boys in classes in which the teacher believed they could achieve as well as girls averaged 96.5 on these reading achievement tests, while those in classes of teachers who did not believe that they could do as well as girls averaged only 89.2. The girls in these classes averaged 96.2 and 96.7 respectively. Thus in the classes where teachers did not think boys could achieve as well as girls, the boys did, indeed, have a lower level of achievement.

Another study in this vein was conducted by Doyle, Hancock, and Kifer (1971). These investigators asked first-grade teachers to estimate the IQs of their children, shortly before an IQ test was given. The teachers' IQ estimates were then compared to the IQs obtained from the tests. The comparisons showed that the teachers tended to overestimate the IQs of girls and to underestimate the IQs of boys. Also, these estimates were related to the reading achievement of the children. Even though there was no IQ difference between the boys and the girls, the girls showed higher reading achievement. Furthermore, within both sexes, the children whose IQs had been overestimated by the teachers had higher reading achievement than those whom the teachers had underestimated. All of this might simply mean that the teachers were heavily influenced by the children's reading abilities in making judgments about their general intelligence. However, it is likely that the teachers' expectations affected their teaching of reading. In addition to the previous findings, it was discovered that the classes of teachers who generally overestimated their children's IQs achieved more than the classes of teachers who generally underestimated, regardless of sex.

These studies show that school achievement is not simply a matter of the child's native ability; teachers' expectations are also involved. Several other studies have shown this same result with different types of students in different types of settings. Douglas (1964), in a massive study of the tracking system used in the British schools, found that children who were clean and well clothed and who came from better-kept homes, tended to be placed in higher tracks than their measured ability would predict. Once in these tracks they tended to stay there and to perform acceptably. Mackler (1969), studying a school in Harlem, also found that children tended to stay in the tracks in which they were placed, even though initial placement was affected by many factors other than measured ability. The findings of Douglas and of Mackler show that: (1) teachers' expectations about a child's achievement can be affected by factors having little or nothing to do with his ability; yet (2) these expectations can determine his level of achievement by confining his learning opportunities to those available in his track. A student placed needlessly in a low track is unlikely to reach his potential, because his teachers do not expect much from him and because his self-concept and achievement motivation are likely to deteriorate over time.

Studies in three very different settings show that student learning was affected by the expectations induced in their instructors. Beez (1968), working with adult tutors who were teaching Head Start children, Burnham (1968), working with swimming instructors teaching preadolescents how to swim, and Schrank (1968), working with Air Force mathematics instructors teaching airmen mathematics all found the same results. In each study, teachers' expectations were manipulated by the experimenter. Sometimes the teachers were led to believe that the children or classes they would work with had high learning potentials; sometimes they were led to believe they had low learning potentials. There was no factual basis for these expectations, since the groups had been matched or randomly selected. Nevertheless, in each case students of instructors who had been led to hold high expectations learned more than the students of instructors who had been led to expect little. Beez (1968) monitored the teaching behavior in his study, and found that the achievement differences were a direct result of differences in the teaching to which the children were exposed. Tutors who had high expectations attempted to teach more than those with low expectations and succeeded in doing so.

Teachers' expectations as self-fulfilling prophecies
The studies presented above each illustrated how teachers' expectations can function as self-fulfilling prophecies. That is, teachers' expectations affect the ways they treat their students, and, over time, the ways they treat the students affect the amount that the students learn. In this sense, then, expectations are self-fulfilling: teachers with high expectations attempt to teach more, and teachers with low expectations tend to teach less. As a result, both groups of teachers tend to end up with what they expected, although not with what they might have achieved with different expectations in the first place.

Robert Rosenthal and Lenore Jacobson's *Pygmalion in the Classroom* (1968) created wide interest and controversy about this topic. Their book described research in which they deliberately tried to manipulate teachers' expectations for their students' achievement, to see if these expectations would be fulfilled. Their study involved several classes in each of the first six grades of school. Teacher expectations were created by claiming that a test (actually a general achievement test) had been developed to identify late intellectual bloomers. The teachers were told that this test would select children who were about to bloom intellectually and, therefore, could be expected to show unusually large achievement gains during the coming school year. A few children in each classroom were identified to the teachers as late bloomers. These children had actually been selected randomly, not on the basis of any test. Thus there was no real reason to expect unusual gains from them. No factual basis existed for the expectations induced in the teachers.

However, achievement test data from the end of the school year offered some evidence that these children did show better performance (although the effects were confined mostly to the first two grades). Rosenthal and Jacobson explained their results in terms of the self-fulfilling prophecy effects of teacher expectations. They reasoned that the expectations they created about these special children somehow caused the teachers to treat them differently, so that they really did do better by the end of the year.

Controversy has raged over this topic ever since. The findings of *Pygmalion in the Classroom* were widely publicized and discussed and for a time were accepted enthusiastically. Later, however, after critics (Snow, 1969; Taylor, 1970) had attacked the Rosenthal and Jacobson study and after a replication failed to produce the same results (Claiborn, 1969), the idea that teacher expectations could function as self-fulfilling prophecies began to be rejected.

We think the evidence now available supports the idea that teacher expectations are sometimes self-fulfilling. However, this statement requires some explanation, both about the research available and about the way the process is defined and described.

Regarding research, one must make a distinction between two types of studies in this area. The first type, which includes Rosenthal and Jacobson's work as well as those of others who have tried to replicate that study, involves attempts to manipulate or induce teacher expectations. That is, the investigators tried to create expectations by identifying "late bloomers," using phony IQ scores, or providing some other fictitious information about the students' ability. The second type of study, exemplified by the first four studies discussed in this chapter, uses the teachers' own expectations as they exist naturally. No attempt is made to induce expectations. Instead, the teacher is simply asked to make predictions or to rank or group students according to achievement or ability.

Studies involving induced expectations have produced mixed, mostly negative results. Two recent studies suggest that the failures in some studies involving induced expectancies occurred because the teachers did not acquire the expectancy that the experimenter wanted them to have. The most obvious case is where teachers know that the expectancy is not true. This was shown by Schrank (1970) in an adaptation of his earlier study of Air Force mathematics courses. For this second study, Schrank merely simulated the manipulation of teacher expectations; the teachers actually knew that the students had been grouped randomly rather than by ability levels. Under these conditions, even with instructions to teach the groups as if they had been tracked by ability level, no expectation effects were observed. Similar results were found by Fleming and Anttonen (1971), who tried to falsify IQ information on children. They found that the teachers did not accept the phony IQs as real and, therefore, did not allow them to affect their treatment of students. When faced with too great a discrepancy between what they saw in their everyday contacts with their students and what a test purported to reveal about them, the teachers rejected the test data.

These results suggest that attempts to induce expectations in teachers will fail if the expectations are too obviously and sharply discrepant from the students' observable characteristics. Credibility of the source is probably another important factor. Teachers are much more likely to accept the opinions of the principal or the teacher who worked with the students the previous year than the opinions of a researcher who comes in, administers a test, and leaves without acquiring any more personal knowledge of the students.

Thus the negative results in studies using induced teacher expectations should not necessarily be taken as disproof of the self-fulfilling prophecy idea. The negative results are more likely due to failure to induce the desired expectations in the teachers than to failure of teacher expectations to affect teacher behavior. Naturalistic studies using teachers' real expectations about their students have usually yielded positive findings. These studies show that teachers' expectations do tend to have self-fulfilling prophecy effects, causing the teachers to behave in ways that tend to make their expectations come true. It is likely that many students in most classrooms are not reaching their potential because their teachers do not expect much from them and are satisfied with poor or mediocre performance when they could obtain something better (Brophy and Good, 1973).

Overenthusiastic popular accounts of *Pygmalion in the Class-room* have sometimes misled people about the self-fulfilling prophecy idea. Sometimes they imply that the mere existence of an expectation will automatically guarantee its fulfillment or that a magical and mysterious process is involved (just make a prediction and it will come true). Most teachers rightfully reject this idea as utter nonsense. However, this is not what we mean when we say that teachers' expectations can act as self-fulfilling prophecies. We refer here to something resulting naturally from a chain of observable causes, not to something akin to magic or ESP.

How the process works

The fact that teachers' expectation can be self-fulfilling is simply a special case of the principle that any expectations can be self-fulfilling. The process is not confined to classrooms. Although it is not true that "wishing can make it so," *our expectations do affect the way we behave in situations, and the way we behave affects how other people respond.* In some instances our expectations about people cause us to treat them in a way that makes them respond just as we expected they would.

For example, look ahead to the time when you accept your first teaching job and receive notice about which school you are being assigned to (or look back on this experience if you have gone through it already). Unless they already have information, most teachers in this situation want to find out as much as possible about the school and the principal with whom they will be working. Often, information can be gathered from a friend already teaching at the school. Suppose the friend says, "Mr. Jackson is a wonderful man. You'll love working for him. He's very warm and pleasant, and he really takes an interest in you. Feel free to come to him with your problems; he's always glad to help." If you heard this about Mr. Jackson, how do you think you would respond to him when you met him? Think about this situation for a few moments. Now let's think about another situation. Suppose that your friend said, "Mr. Jackson? Well, uh, he's sort of hard to describe. I guess he's all right, but I don't feel comfortable around him; he makes me nervous. I don't know what it is exactly, it's just that I get the feeling that he doesn't want to talk to me, that I'm wasting his time or irritating him." How do you think you would act when meeting Mr. Jackson after you had heard this?

If you are like most people, your behavior would be quite different in these two contrasting situations. Given the first set of information about Mr. Jackson, you would probably look forward to meeting him and would approach him with confidence and a friendly smile. Among other things, you would probably tell him that you heard good things about him and that you are happy to be working with him and are looking forward to getting started. Given the other set of expectations, however, you would probably behave quite differently. You would be unlikely to look forward to the meeting in a positive sense, and you might well become nervous, inhibited, or overly concerned about making a good impression. You would probably approach with hesitation, wearing a serious expression or a forced smile, and speak to him in rather reserved, formal tones. Even if you said the same words to him, the chances are that they would sound more like a prepared speech than a genuine personal reaction.

Now, put yourself in Mr. Jackson's place. Assume he knows nothing about you as a person. Take a few moments to think about how he might respond to these two, very different approaches.

Chances are that Mr. Jackson would respond quite differently. In the first instance, faced with warmth, friendliness, and genuine-sounding compliments, he is likely to respond in kind. Your behavior would put him at ease and cause him to see you as a likeable, attractive person. When he smiles and says he will be looking forward to working with you, too, he will really mean it.

But what if Mr. Jackson is faced with a new teacher who approaches him somewhat nervously and formally? Again, he is likely to respond in kind. Such behavior is likely to make him nervous and formal, if he is not already. He is likely to respond in an equally bland and formal manner. This is likely to be followed by an awkward silence that makes both you and Mr. Jackson increasingly nervous. As the authority figure and host, Mr. Jackson will probably feel compelled to make the next move. In view of your behavior, attempts at small talk would be risky, so he probably will get down to business and begin to speak in his capacity as principal, talking to you in your capacity as one of his teachers.

These examples show how expectations can influence behavior and how the behavior in turn can help produce the originally expected results. Teachers who expect Mr. Jackson to be friendly and who approach him in a warm manner make it easier for him to feel at ease and to be friendly. On the other hand, teachers who expect him to be cold and who approach him formally tend to make him nervous so that he responds in a way that does appear cold.

The examples also show that it is not just the existence of an expectation that causes self-fulfillment, it is the behavior that this expectation produces. This behavior then affects the other person, making him more likely to act in the expected ways. In the classroom the process works like this:

1. The teacher expects specific behavior and achievement from particular students.
2. Because of these different expectations, the teacher behaves differently toward the different students.
3. This teacher treatment tells each student what behavior and achievement the teacher expects from him and affects his self-concept, achievement motivation, and level of aspiration.
4. If this teacher treatment is consistent over time, and if the student does not actively resist or change it in some way, it will tend to shape his achievement and behavior. High-expectation students will be led to achieve at high levels, while the achievement of low-expectation students will decline.
5. With time, the student's achievement and behavior will conform more and more closely to that originally expected of him.

The model clearly shows that teacher expectations are not automatically self-fulfilling. To become so, they must be translated into behavior that will communicate expectations to the student and will shape his behavior toward expected patterns. This does not always happen. The teacher may not have clear-cut expectations about a particular student, or his expectations may continually change. Even when he has consistent expectations, he may not necessarily communicate them to the student through consistent behavior. In this case, the expectation would not be self-fulfilling even if it turned out to be correct. Finally, the student himself might prevent expectations from becoming self-fulfilling by overcoming them or by resisting them in a way that makes the teacher change them. Thus a teacher expectation requires more than its own mere existence in order to become self-fulfilling. It must lead to behavior that will communicate the expectation to the student, and this behavior must be effective in moving the student in the expected direction.

Practice Examples

We have provided some practice examples you can use to sharpen your own understanding of the self-fulfilling prophecy concept. Read each example and see if you think a self-fulfilling prophecy was involved. If so, you should be able to identify: (a) the original expectation, (b) behaviors that consistently communicate this expectation in ways that make it more likely to be fulfilled, and (c) evidence that the original expectation has been confirmed. If the example does not contain all three elements, it does not illustrate a self-fulfilling prophecy.

1. Coach Winn knows that Thumper Brown is the son of a former All-American football star. Although he has never even seen Thumper carry the ball, he predicts, "That boy will help our team in his sophomore year." In practice sessions, Winn treats Thumper like all the other players. He carries the ball the same number of times in the drills as the other runners, and the coach praises him only when his performance deserves it. Thumper wins a starting position in his sophomore year, becoming an outstanding player and being named to the all-conference team.

2. Judy, a junior education major, tells her roommate, "I'll bet Ralph brings me flowers for our pinning anniversary." On their Monday night date, Judy remarks, "Ralph, the funniest thing happened. Ann knitted a sweater for her pin-mate for their pinning anniversary and it practically reached his knees." During another conversation the same evening, she says, "Yes, the initiation went perfectly. It was lovely, absolutely lovely. I love the sorority house at initiation time. The flowers are so nice, especially the roses. They are so special. They make me feel warm and happy." When Ralph arrives Saturday night for their anniversary date, he presents Judy with a lovely bouquet of roses.

3. Mrs. Explicit is giving directions to John Greene, a second grader who is frequently in trouble. Mrs. Explicit has no confidence in John's responsibility, so she gives him detailed instructions: "John, take this note to Mrs. Turner, whose room is at the end of the hall, across from the room where our fire drill exit is. This is a big responsibility, and I want you to remember . . . you will not make noise in the hall . . . don't stop to look in any other classrooms . . . and above all, don't go outside." John responds, with an obviously pained look, "Mrs. Explicit, don't you trust me?"

4. Dean Helpful counsels a few students in addition to his normal administrative duties. He does so because he is very interested in current student problems, and he enjoys the opportunity to stay in tune with student life. In September, the dean begins to counsel Tom Bloom. The dean knows that Tom will probably flunk out of school at the end of the semester. His entrance scores are very low, and his writing skills are particularly poor. He is also socially withdrawn and shy, making it unlikely that he will get to know his instructors very well or receive much special help from them. The dean tells Tom that he may encounter academic difficulty, and urges him to enroll in the reading clinic and to devote extra time on Saturdays to his studies. In addition, he has Tom report to his office once a week. Tom realizes that the dean expects him to have trouble unless he works hard. He begins to work as hard as he can, and keeps it up for the whole semester. When the grade slips are mailed in January, Tom finds he has made a B average.

5. Mrs. Graney knew that Bill Burton would be a problem. She had his older brother the year before, and he was uncontrollable. Trying to keep Bill out of trouble, Mrs. Graney seats him at a table far away from the other third graders in the room. Before long, though, Bill begins to throw things at the other children to attract their attention.

6. Jim Flywood, a pilot, is taking his sister Sandy on her first plane trip. Jim really wants to put a scare into Sandy, hoping that she will stop her daily begging for rides. Jim puts the plane through a rapid series of tight loops and then ends with a vertical dive, leveling off only at the last moment. Jim was so successful that he even frightened himself when he momentarily lost control of the plane. However, Sandy loved the ride and wants to know when she can have another.

7. Mal Chauvin is a young physics professor teaching undergraduates for the first time. He is especially concerned about reaching the girls in his class, because he expects them to have a difficult time. He thinks that most of the girls at the college are there just to get a husband, and he does not think they have much interest or aptitude for physics. To avoid embarrassing them, he never calls on them to answer a mathematical question or to explain difficult concepts. He also shows his concern by looking at one of the girls after he introduces a new point and asking, "Do you understand?" However, the girls usually find this more embarrassing than helpful, and in general they do not do very well in his course.

8. Miss Ball is concerned about the peer-group adjustment of Dick Stewart, one of the boys in her second-grade class. Although Dick had participated all year long in the races and group games conducted during recess, he began to withdraw from the group in the spring when she started the boys playing baseball. Although Dick was coordinated well enough, he had not played much baseball and had difficulty in both hitting and catching the ball. As a result, he was usually one of the last boys chosen when teams were selected. After this happened a few times Dick began to withdraw, claiming that he did not want to play because he had a headache, a stomachache, or a sore foot. This did not fool Miss Ball, who recognized that Dick's embarrassment was the real reason.

To help Dick compensate for his deficiencies and to see that he did not lose peer status, Miss Ball began allowing him to serve as umpire for ball games. This way he had an important and active role. She reinforced this by praising and calling the other children's attention to his umpire work. In private contacts she reassured Dick that he should not feel badly because he was not playing, and that there could not be a ball game without an umpire.

In the last few days of school Miss Ball decided to let Dick play again, now that his confidence was built up. She was gratified to see that he was picked earlier than usual by the team captain. However, his batting and catching were just as bad as they had been before. The next day he was the last one chosen, and he begged off, complaining of a headache.

Answers

Let us see how well you were able to identify self-fulfilling prophecies. If we have been successful in describing the process, you should have correctly classified each example.

In case 1, Coach Winn's original expectancy about Thumper is fulfilled. However, there is no evidence that Winn behaved in some manner to influence Thumper's performance. Thus it would not be correct to say that the coach's prediction acted as a self-fulfilling prophecy, even though his prediction was accurate.

Case 2 is an example of a self-fulfilling prophecy. Judy expected to receive flowers, and consciously or subconsciously communicated this expectation to Ralph. Ralph took the hint and fulfilled her original expectation.

In case 3, Mrs. Explicit's original expectancy is "if I don't give Johnny explicit instructions, he will take advantage of the situation and misbehave." She subconsciously communicates this expectation in her behavior toward Johnny. However, even though Johnny gets her "real message," his behavior does not change in the direction of her expectation. Therefore, this is not an example of a self-fulfilling prophecy. However, if Mrs. Explicit were to continue to treat Johnny this way, he might begin to behave as she expects. At this point, her expectations would have become self-fulfilling.

Case 4 is an especially interesting and instructive example. The dean fears that Tom will flunk out, and he communicates this expectation to Tom. Tom gets the message, but reacts by working as hard as he can to prove himself. He ends up doing very well, despite the dean's original expectation. Similar examples occur every day in doctors' offices. A doctor who fears that his patient is about to have a heart attack will quickly place him on a strict diet and exercise program. He also schedules the patient for regular appointments so he can check his progress. In this way a heart attack is avoided and the person's general health improves. Both the doctor and the dean communicate serious concern, but they follow this up with attempts to deal with the problem. If, instead, they communicated hopelessness and did nothing to change the situation, their expectations probably would have been fulfilled.

Case 5 is a classic illustration of a self-fulfilling teacher expectation. Mrs. Graney expects the boy to be a problem and, therefore, begins to treat him like one. However, her treatment involves separating him from his peers and forcing him to misbehave to get peer attention, so that her expectations become fulfilled.

Case 6 is a tricky example. Jim fully expects to scare his sister by dangerously maneuvering his plane. Ordinarily his behavior would have been effective, since Jim scared even himself by flirting with tragedy. However, Sandy had not been in a plane before and assumed that her brother's behavior was routine. She did not perceive the clues, or did not interpret them correctly, so that his behavior did not communicate fright. In this case Jim's expectation was not fulfilled, even though he consciously and deliberately tried to fulfill it. This can happen in the classroom if the student does not perceive the teacher's behavior as the teacher intends it. For example, a comment like, "That's not quite right," would be discouraging to a high-achieving student who thought he had answered correctly but might be encouraging to a low-achieving student who doubted that he was even partially correct.

Case 7 is another example of teacher expectations as self-fulfilling prophecies. Despite his good intentions, the teacher's treatment of the girls in his class tends to erode their confidence and reduce their opportunities to learn through participation in class discussions. The result is low motivation and low performance, just as the teacher expected.

Case 8 also illustrates how a teacher's expectation can be self-fulfilling, even though the expectation itself might be unformulated and unrecognized by the teacher. Miss Ball's conscious intention is to build Dick's confidence so that he will participate in ball games. However, her approach takes into account only his attitude and not his need for practice in hitting and catching the ball. Although she may never have thought about it this way, her approach follows from the basic expectation that Dick cannot hit or catch and, therefore, needs some alternate role. This is very different from the idea that Dick cannot hit or catch and therefore needs to be taught to do so. Miss Ball's attempt at solution of the problem involves many good things for Dick, but not the things he most needs: practice at hitting and catching the ball. As a result, by the end of the year he is even further behind his classmates in these skills than he was earlier.

This last example is one of many that could have been given about how teachers will adopt inappropriate strategies if they define a problem improperly. This is often done by teachers who are concerned about their students' self-concepts. They sometimes confuse the relationship between self-concept and abilities, thinking that they have to improve self-concept before abilities will improve. Usually, the opposite is true. Low self-concept results from low abilities, and improvement in abilities will produce improvement in self-concept. When students show handicaps, inhibitions, or lack of skill, the appropriate teacher strategy is to provide remedial instruction and extra practice or opportunities to learn. Although well-meant, attempts to provide compensation in other areas to make the student feel better about his problem without changing it are not what he needs.

Appropriate teacher expectations

How can knowledge about the self-fulfilling prophecy effects of teacher expectations be applied by the classroom teacher? Several suggestions offered in an attempt to answer this question are presented in later sections of this chapter. Before getting to them, however, we wish to discuss two frequently made suggestions that we do *not* think are appropriate. Either suggestion would effectively eliminate undesirable self-fulfilling prophecies if teachers could follow it. The first is that teachers should have only positive expectations; the second is that they should have no expectations at all.

The suggestion that teachers should have only positive expectations is appealing on the surface. Confidence and determination are important teacher qualities, and a "can do" attitude helps cut large problems down to workable size. However, this must not be carried to the point of distorting reality. Students show large individual differences in learning abilities and interests, and these cannot be eliminated through wishful thinking. Some students are capable of more than others, and a teacher will only frustrate both himself and his students if he sets unrealistically high standards that some or all cannot reach.

Expectations should be appropriate rather than necessarily high, and they must be followed up with appropriate behavior. This means planned learning experiences that take the student at the level he is now and move him along at a pace he can handle. The pace that will allow continued success and improvement is the correct pace and will vary with different students. The teacher should not feel guilty or feel that he is stigmatizing the student by moving him along at a slower pace because he is a slower learner. As long as the child is working up to his potential and progressing at a steady rate, the teacher has reason to be satisfied. There will be cause for criticism only if the slower child is moved along at a slower pace than he can handle, because the teacher's expectations for him are too low, are never tested out or reevaluated and, consequently, are not changed.

Some authors have suggested that teachers try to avoid self-fulfilling prophecy effects by avoiding forming expectations altogether. This means refusing to discuss students with their previous teachers and avoiding or ignoring cumulative records or test information. This is not a good suggestion, however, for two reasons. First, expectations cannot be suppressed or avoided. Experiences tend to stay with us and make an impression on us. When events occur repeatedly they gradually are seen as expected and normal, and expectations are reinforced every time repetition occurs. Thus teachers build up expectations about their students simply from interacting with them, even if they try to avoid other sources of information. Second, the question of whether other sources of information are solicited is not as important as the question of how information is used. Information about students will create expectations about them, but it will also be useful in planning individualized instruction to meet their specific needs. The teacher should try to get information and use it in this way, rather than to avoid obtaining information. Suggestions about how teachers can profitably use information in school records and test data are presented in Brubaker (1968).

Expectations built up through repetition can be very compelling. If John has turned in completed homework every day this year, he probably will do so again tomorrow. If Susan has been among the bottom five in class on every math test this year, she probably will be on the next one too, unless her teacher provides extra math instruction and practice and takes steps such as giving shorter but more frequent tests to Susan and other students like her.

Regular repetition of student behavior will build up strong expectations in all teachers, including (and perhaps especially) teachers who try to deny or suppress them. Inevitably, some of these expectations will be pessimistic. However, teachers can avoid undesirable self-fulfilling prophecy effects if they remain alert to their own expectations forming and changing, and if they monitor their own behavior to see that negative expectations are not communicated. To the extent that such expectations do exist, they should be of the helpful variety, combining expressions of concern with behavior geared to remediate the difficulty. Saying that a student needs help is bad only if the teacher does not provide that help in a positive, supportive way.

Forming and changing expectations

Teachers form some expectations about their students before they even see them. The individual cumulative record files provide IQ data, achievement scores, grades, and teacher comments that create expectations about achievement and conduct. Other expectations are picked up in chats with colleagues who taught the students in earlier grades. The reputation of the family, or the teacher's prior experience with an older brother or sister, may also condition what he expects from a particular student.

Some teachers deliberately try to avoid being influenced by the past. They do not look at records or seek information about their students until they have had a chance to see them and form their own impressions. This is not necessarily an improvement, however, since a lack of data from the files does not prevent most teachers from forming strong and general impressions very quickly. In one study, for example, first-grade teachers were able to rank their children in order of expected achievement after the very first week of school. Furthermore, these rankings, made without benefit of any test data, were highly correlated with achievement ranks from tests given at the end of the year (Willis, 1972). Thus first impressions lead to specific and largely accurate expectations about students, even in teachers who are aware of the phenomenon. Rather than trying to eliminate expectations, teachers must remain aware of them and see that they do not lead to inappropriate treatment of certain students. If low expectations lead to inappropriate teacher behavior, they may well become self-fulfilling. For example, a first-grade teacher who expects a particular child to have great trouble in learning to read may begin to treat the child differently from the way he treats other children. To avoid pressuring or embarrassing the child, he may call on him infrequently and only to read easy passages. Over the year this will mean that the child will receive fewer opportunities to practice, and whenever he has trouble reading the teacher will give him the word and quickly move on to another student. So long as this keeps up, the child will gradually fall further and further behind his classmates in reading ability.

His reading ability will not improve even if the teacher attempts to compensate by allowing the child to be first in the lunch line, to sit near him, or to take notes to the office frequently. Like the efforts of Miss Ball in our example of the student inept at baseball, these are misdirected and inappropriate intervention strategies for the low-achieving reader. The child may enjoy these activities and may become more receptive to the teacher and his instruction efforts, but he will not improve in reading unless he gets the instruction and practice he needs.

A teacher who behaves this way is reacting to a label (low achiever, low potential, slow learner) instead of to the student as he is. A subtle shift has taken place in which the teacher has lost his focus on instructing the student, on taking him from where he is to some higher level of progress, and has become fixated on the status quo. This somehow makes the lack of progress acceptable and, at the same time, reinforces the teacher's low expectations.

To avoid falling into this rut, teachers need to keep their expectations open and to bear in mind their role as instructor. If expectations are allowed to become too strong or too settled, they can begin to distort perception and behavior. The teacher may begin to notice only those things that fit his expectations, and may start deviating from good teaching practice.

Once formed, expectations tend to be self-perpetuating. This is because expectations guide both perceptions and behavior. When we expect to find something, we are much more likely to see it than when we are not looking for it. For example, most people do not notice counterfeit money or slight irregularities in clothing patterns. However, treasury department officials and inspectors for clothing manufacturers, who have been trained to look for such deviations, will notice them. Similarly, valuable rare coins and unusual abilities and aptitudes usually are not noticed except by those who are on the lookout for them. This is part of the reason why teachers often fail to notice good behavior in students who are frequent discipline problems in the classroom. They are used to misbehavior from these students and are on the lookout for it, so they tend to notice most of the misbehavior that occurs. With a set toward misbehavior, however, they miss a lot of the good behavior that someone else might have noticed and reinforced.

Expectations not only cause us to notice some things and fail to notice other things, they also affect the way that we interpret what we do notice. The optimist, for example, notices that the glass is half full, while the pessimist observes that it is half empty. Mistaken beliefs and attitudes about other people are self-perpetuating and difficult to correct because of their tendency to influence how we interpret what we see. If we are convinced that a person has particular qualities, we often see these qualities in him when we observe him.

Consider the teacher who asks a complex, difficult question and then gives his students some time to think about the answer. After a while he calls on Johnny Bright, whom he sees as an intelligent and well-motivated student. Johnny remains silent, pursing his lips, knitting his brow, and scratching his head. The teacher knows that he is working out the problem, so he patiently gives him more time. He has an attentive and eager expression as Johnny begins to speak. Finally, Johnny responds with a question, "Would you repeat that last part again?" The teacher is happy to do so, because this indicates that Johnny has partially solved the problem and may be able to do it by himself with a little more time. He asks Johnny what part he wants repeated and then obliges. He then waits eagerly, but patiently, for Johnny to respond again. If someone interrupted the teacher at this point to ask him what he was doing, he might respond that he was "challenging the class to use creativity and logical thinking to solve problems."

Suppose, however, that the teacher had called on Sammy Slow instead of Johnny Bright. The teacher knows that Sammy is a low achiever, and he does not think Sammy is very well motivated, either. When called on, Sammy remains silent, although the teacher notes his pursed lips, his furrowed brow, and the fact that he is scratching his head. This probably means that Sammy is hopelessly lost, although it may mean that he is merely acting, trying to give the impression that he is thinking about the problem. After a few seconds, the teacher says, "Well, Sammy?" Now Sammy responds, but with a question instead of an answer, "Would you repeat that last part again?" This confirms the teacher's suspicions, making it clear that any more time spent with Sammy on this question would be wasted. After admonishing Sammy to listen more carefully, he calls on someone else. If interrupted at this point and asked what he was doing, the teacher might respond that he was "making it clear that the class is expected to pay close attention to the discussion, so that they can respond intelligently when questioned."

In this example the teacher's expectations for these two students caused him to see much more than was objectively observable to a more neutral observer. The observable behavior of the two boys was the same, and they made the same responses to the initial question. Yet the teacher interpreted the behavior quite differently by reading additional meaning into it. His interpretations about the two boys may have been correct, but we (and he) cannot tell for sure because he did not check them out. Instead, he acted on them as if they were observable facts, so that his treatment of Sammy was grossly inappropriate.

Although the need to continually check out and adjust expectations may seem obvious, it can be difficult to do, in everyday life as well as in the classroom. (For example, the widely advertised brand is not always better than the unknown brand, the more expensive item is not necessarily better than the cheaper one, nor is the large economy size always a better bargain than the regular size. Yet every day most people automatically accept such things without checking them out.)

Similarly, the fact that a student could not do something yesterday does not mean that he cannot do it today, but the teacher will not find out unless he gives the student a chance. Expectations stress the stable or unchanging aspects of the world. The teacher, however, is a change agent who is trying to make his students something different from what they are today. Therefore, he must keep his expectations in perspective. To the extent that they are negative, expectations represent problems to be solved, not definitions of reality to which he must adapt.

Basic teacher expectations

The following sections in this chapter will present certain basic attitudes and expectations teachers must have if they are to do their jobs successfully. Descriptions and examples of how these expectations are communicated to students through observable behavior are also provided. When these types of inappropriate behavior are observed in a teacher, the problems may be due, in part, to inappropriate expectations about teaching in general or about a particular student in the classroom.

The teacher should enjoy teaching

Teaching brings many rewards and satisfactions, but it is a demanding, exhausting, and sometimes frustrating job. It is hard to do well unless you enjoy doing it. Teachers who do enjoy their work will show this in their classroom behavior. They will come to class prepared for the day's lessons, and will present lessons in a way that suggests interest and excitement in promoting learning. They will appear eager for contact with students, will keep track of their individual needs and progress, and will take pride and satisfaction in helping them overcome learning difficulties. Difficulties and confusion in students will be perceived as challenges to be met with professional skills and not as irritations. When the student does achieve success, the teacher shares in his joy. In general, the teacher who enjoys his work sees himself as a benevolent resource person to his students and not as a warden or authority figure.

Teachers who really don't enjoy teaching also show it in their classroom behavior. They appear apathetic or negativistic, and act as if they are "putting in their time" on the job. They seem eager to escape the students or the classroom when opportunities arise and may frequently assign work just to keep students busy or resort to needless student recitations because they are unprepared or unwilling to teach. They seem unconcerned about students who are not learning the material, being content to rationalize rather than accept the challenge of finding another way to teach them. They may seem mildly pleased when a student achieves success after struggling with a concept, but they do not light up with joy or excitement.

What about yourself? If you are a teacher, how do you feel in the classroom? Do you feel at home and enjoy yourself there, or would you really rather be somewhere else? If you are a student observer, how do you feel about the work of a teacher? Is this work that you would enjoy as a career?

If your personal response to these questions has been negative, some careful thought and reassessment is in order. If you think you cannot and will not really enjoy teaching, you should avoid going into it, or should get out of it if you can. If you do not enjoy it but are open to change, do not give up. You may have been operating with inappropriate attitudes and expectations about teaching, which may have prevented you from enjoying the satisfactions that the job offers. Or, you may have serious but remediable faults in teaching technique. In either case, after you have read this book and practiced systematic observation of your own and other teachers' classroom behavior, you may become aware of facts about yourself that you never realized before. Once awareness exists, change is possible, and you may be able to reorient your approach to the teaching role and to sharpen your specific teaching skills. This in turn can enable you to find the enjoyment that you can and should expect from work as a teacher.

The teacher's main responsibility is to teach

The teacher's job involves many roles besides that of instructing students. At times the teacher will serve as a parent surrogate, an entertainer, an authority figure, a psychotherapist, and a record keeper, among other things. All of these are necessary aspects of the teacher's role. However, they are subordinate to and in support of the major role of teaching. Important as they are, they must not be allowed to overshadow the teacher's basic instructional role.

It sometimes happens that teachers working with young children will become more concerned with mothering or entertaining the children than teaching them. In these classes, much of the day is spent in reading stories, playing games, working on arts and crafts projects, singing and listening to records, Show-and-Tell, and enrichment activities. Often the teachers basically do not like to spend time teaching the curriculum, and feel they must apologize to or bribe the children when lessons are conducted. This type of teacher is meeting his own needs, not those of the children. By the end of the year the pupils will have acquired negative attitudes toward the school curriculum, and they will have failed to achieve near their potential.

Research by Thomas (1970) suggests that this problem is peculiar to adults. Thomas studied the tutoring behavior of college tutors and fifth- and sixth-grade tutors working with second-grade students in reading. Even though the college students were senior education majors enrolled in a reading methods course, the fifth- and sixth-grade tutors were just as effective for producing reading gains in the second graders. Thomas noted interesting differences, however, in the behavior of the two groups of tutors. The college students spent much time trying to coax the children into liking them, into enjoying the reading materials, and into practicing the reading skills. In contrast, the fifth and sixth graders were more direct and businesslike. They accepted the fact that the second graders were having reading difficulties and that the tutoring sessions were for teaching them with the materials in front of them and not for discussing matters outside the lesson. Apparently, adults have negative expectations about children's interests in learning activities and inhibitions about remedial work with slow learners that children do not have. Children tend to see teaching and learning as normal, expected activities that do not require explanation or apology.

At the higher grades, failure to teach is sometimes seen in teachers who have low expectations about their own classroom management abilities or about the learning abilities of a particular class. Where homogeneous grouping is practiced in a junior high or high school, for example, teachers assigned to a period with a low-achieving class may sometimes abandon serious attempts to teach their subject. They may, perhaps, attempt to entertain the class, or else merely act as a sort of proctor who is interested only in seeing that the noise does not get out of hand. Such behavior indicates a serious lack of confidence in the teacher, either in his own ability to motivate and control the class or in the students' ability to learn or to become interested in the subject matter. It represents a total surrender to failure expectations, in which emphasis has been switched from teaching the class to merely keeping the class happy.

Teachers must understand that the crucial aspects of teaching are task presentation, diagnosis, remediation, and enrichment

Failure to be clear about crucial aspects of teaching characterizes teachers who favor high achievers over low achievers or who pay more attention to answers than to the thinking processes that a student goes through in reaching an answer. Such teachers sometimes act as if the students are expected to learn on their own with no help from them. If a student does not catch on immediately after one demonstration, or does not do his work correctly after hearing the instructions one time, they react with impatience and frustration.

Such behavior represents a fundamental failure to appreciate the teacher's basic role. The teacher is in the classroom to instruct. This involves more than just giving demonstrations or presenting learning experiences. Instruction also means giving additional help to those who are having difficulty, diagnosing the source of their problem, and providing remedial assistance to correct it. It means conducting evaluation with an eye toward identifying and correcting difficulties and not merely as a prelude to passing out praise or criticism. It means keeping track of each student's individual progress, so that he can be instructed in terms of what he learned yesterday and what he should learn tomorrow. It means finding satisfaction in the progress of the slower students as well as the brighter ones.

There are many aspects of teacher behavior that help indicate whether or not the teacher clearly understands what he is supposed to be doing with his students. The handling of seatwork and homework assignments is one good indicator. The purpose of such assignments is to provide students with practice on the skills they are learning and to provide the teacher with information about their progress.

Teachers should monitor the students' performance on seatwork and homework, noting the particular error patterns that occur. This will suggest the nature of individual students' learning problems and the nature of the remedial actions the teachers should take. However, some teachers fail to use seatwork and homework in this way. They simply pass out the work and then collect and score it, without following up the scoring with remedial teaching. Students who succeed are praised, while those who need help receive only criticism or low marks. Seatwork thus does not lead to diagnosis and remediation.

Teachers can create negative attitudes toward seatwork assignments if the assignments are inappropriate or if they are not adjusted to individual differences within the classroom. Seatwork assignments should be made with specific instructional objectives in mind. This may mean separate assignments for different groups of students in a class. Assignments that are too difficult or too easy for a given student will not fulfill their instructional purpose. In particular, overly simple and repetitious seatwork will rightly be regarded as annoying busywork by the students. Teachers sometimes create this attitude in otherwise well motivated and bright students who tend to do the seatwork quickly and correctly. If the teacher's method of handling students who finish quickly is to assign them more of the same kind of exercises, the students will learn to slow down their pace or hide the fact that they have finished. Teachers would do much better to assign alternate activities of the students' choice, or to allow them to move on to more challenging problems of a similar type.

Another important indicator is the way the teacher responds to right and wrong answers. When the teacher has the appropriate attitude, he accepts either type of response for the information it gives about the student. He neither becomes overly elated about correct answers nor overly depressed about incorrect answers. He uses questions as a way to stimulate thinking and to acquire information about the student's progress. Questions should come in sequences designed to see that both the students who answer them and the rest of the class who are listening develop a deeper understanding of the concepts being discussed. The questions should not be a series of disjointed verbal tests or spot checks on the students' memories.

Inappropriate expectations can even be communicated through praise. Although praise and encouragement are important, they should not interfere with basic teaching goals. If the teacher responds with overly dramatic praise every time a student answers a simple question, the class will likely be distracted from the content of the lesson. A contest in which the more confident and outgoing students compete for teacher recognition and approval will probably result. The better strategy is to follow a simple correct answer with simple feedback to acknowledge that it is correct. The teacher should then advance the discussion by asking another question or adding information to expand on the previous one. Praise can be saved for times when it can be given more effectively and meaningfully, especially during contacts with individual students. Criticism, of course, should be omitted entirely. In general, the teacher's behavior during question and answer sessions should say, "We're going to discuss and deepen our understanding of the material," and not, "We're going to find out who knows the material and who doesn't."

When praise is given to students, it should be specific praise that reinforces their feelings of progress in learning new knowledge and skills. Empty phrases like "how nice" or "that's good" should be avoided in favor of more specific statements. Praise should stress appreciation of the student's efforts and the progress he is making, and usually should be focused on his more general progress rather than on single isolated successes. All of this helps to reinforce the teacher's role as a resource person who facilitates learning, as opposed to a judge who decides who has learned and who has not.

Teachers should expect all students to meet at least the minimum specified objectives

Although all students cannot reasonably be expected to do equally well, reasonable minimal objectives can be established for each teacher's class. Naturally, most students will be capable of going considerably beyond minimal objectives, and the teacher should try to stimulate this development as far as their interests and abilities allow. However, in doing so, teachers must not lose sight of basic priorities. Remedial work with students who have not yet met minimal objectives should not be delayed in favor of enrichment activities with those who have. Ways that teachers can use grouping, peer tutoring, and other techniques to make time for such remediation are discussed in Chapter 8.

Teachers with appropriate attitudes will spend extra time working with the students who are having difficulty. Their behavior when interacting with these students will be characterized by supportiveness, patience, and confidence. In contrast, teachers with inappropriate attitudes will often spend less time with the students who most need extra help. When they do work with these students they will tend to do so in a half-hearted way that communicates disappointment and frustration. Such teachers are often overly dependent on achieving easy success and eliciting many right answers. They will need to change this attitude if they are to acquire the patience and confidence needed to do effective remedial teaching with slower learners.

Teachers should expect students to enjoy learning

Teachers can and should expect students to enjoy learning activities, including practice exercises, and they should back these expectations with appropriate behavior. This is one of the most common areas where teacher expectations become self-fulfilling. When teachers do have the appropriate attitude toward schoolwork, they present it in ways that make their students see it as enjoyable and interesting. Tasks and assignments are presented without apology, as activities valuable in their own right. There is no attempt to build up artificial enthusiasm or interest; the interest is assumed to be already there. Comments about upcoming assignments stress the specific ways in which they extend or build upon present knowledge and skills. Comments about present work reinforce the students' sense of progress and mastery. The teacher does not try to give learning a "hard sell," or to picture it as "fun." He does not expect the students to enjoy it in the same way they enjoy a trip to the circus or a ride on a roller coaster. Instead, he expects the quieter but consistent satisfactions and feelings of mastery that come with the accumulation of knowledge and skills.

The teacher with a negative attitude toward school learning behaves very differently. He sees learning activities as unpleasant but necessary drudgery. If he believes in a positive approach toward motivation, he will be apologetic and defensive about assignments and will frequently resort to bribery, attempting to generate enthusiasm artificially through overemphasis on contests, rewards, and other external incentives. If he is more authoritarian and punitive, he will present assignments as bitter pills that the students must swallow or else. In either case, the students will quickly acquire a distaste for school activities, thus providing reinforcement for the teacher's expectations.

Other evidence of inappropriate teacher attitudes toward school activities include: a heavy stress on the separation between work and play, with work pictured as unpleasant activity one does in order to get to play; a tendency to introduce assignments as something the class *has* to do, rather than merely as something they are going to do; the use of extra assignments as punishments; and practices such as checking to make sure that everyone has signed out one or more books from the library. Teachers with negative attitudes also have a tendency to discuss academic subjects in a way that presents them as dull and devoid of content. For example, they tend to say, "We're going to have history," instead of, "We're going to discuss the voyage of Columbus," or "Read pages 17 to 22," instead of, "Read the author's critique of Twain's novel." All these behaviors tell the students that the teacher does not see school activities as very interesting or very pleasant.

The teacher should expect to deal with individuals, not groups or stereotypes

As a rule, teachers should think, talk, and act in terms of individual students. This does not mean that they should not practice grouping, or that terms such as "low achievers" should not be used. It does mean that teachers must keep a proper perspective about priorities. Grouping must be practiced as a means toward the goal of meeting the individual needs of each student. Similarly, labels and stereotypes are often helpful in thinking about ways to teach individuals better. Ultimately, however, the teacher is teaching John Smith and Mary Jones, not Group A or "low achievers." The way teachers talk about students in their classes is an indication of how they think about them. If there is continual mention of groups to the exclusion of individuals, the teacher may well have begun to lose sight of individual differences within groups and to overemphasize the differences between groups. If this has happened, observers will note that the teacher has too many choral responses and not enough individual responses in group situations, that he has not changed the group membership in a long time, that groups are seated together and spend most of the day together, or that the teacher spends more time with the high group and less with the low group.

Similarly, observers should be alert to teachers' use of oversimplified, stereotyped labels in describing certain students (immature, discipline problem, slow learner, etc.). The teacher may be reacting more to these stereotypes than to the student's individual qualities, and may well fail to notice behavior that doesn't fit the stereotype. This will show up in behavior such as labeling or criticizing the student directly, describing problems without trying to do anything about them, or treating the student on the basis of untested assumptions rather than observed behavior. These behaviors suggest that the stereotyped label has begun to structure the teacher's perception of the student.

The teacher should assume good intentions and a positive self-concept

Teachers must communicate to all of their students the expectation that the students want to be, and are trying to be, fair, cooperative, reasonable, and responsible. This includes even those who consistently present the same behavior problems. The rationale here is that the teacher's basic faith in the student's ability to change is a necessary (but often not sufficient by itself) condition for such change. If the student sees that the teacher does not have this faith in him, he will probably lose whatever motivation he has to keep trying. Thus teachers should be very careful to avoid suggesting that students deliberately hurt others or enjoy doing so, that they cannot and probably will not ever be able to control their own behavior, or that they simply do not care and are making no effort to do so. Even in cases where this might actually be true, there is nothing to be gained and much to be lost by saying so to the student. Such statements will only establish or help reinforce a negative self-concept, and will lead to even more destructive behavior ("If they think I'm bad now, wait until they get a load of this").

Serious failures on the teacher's part should be brought to his attention immediately by an observer, since the teacher still may be able to salvage the situation somewhat by convincing the student that he spoke in anger and really did not mean what he said. However, if the student is convinced that the teacher did mean what he said, the teacher's chances of establishing a productive relationship with him are seriously and perhaps permanently damaged.

The teacher should expect to be obeyed

Some teachers have serious discipline problems of their own making. Usually the cause is failure to observe one of the principles for establishing classroom rules that are discussed in Chapter 5. Obedience is usually obtained rather easily by teachers who establish fair and appropriate rules, who are consistent in what they say, who say only what they really mean, and who regularly follow up with appropriate action whenever this is necessary. This produces credibility and respect; the students are clear about what the teacher expects of them and know that they are accountable for meeting these expectations.

There are many observable teacher behaviors that damage or undermine teachers' credibility and, therefore, their ability to command obedience. Among these behaviors are: inconsistency about rules; playing favorites or picking on certain students; making threats or promises that are not kept; making vague threats or promises that clearly do not have any meaning or implications for the future; failure to explain general rules or principles, so that reactions appear to be arbitrary and inconsistent to the students; indecisiveness or hesitancy in giving instructions; failure to listen to the whole story or get all the facts, so that hasty and ill-conceived solutions have to be retracted and changed; failure to take any action in response to obvious and serious defiance that cannot be simply ignored. These behaviors will convince students that the teacher does not know what he really wants and does not mean what he says; that he does not really expect to be taken seriously and obeyed. This will tend to make them question and test the teacher's instructions, rather than accept and obey them. This can be prevented if the teacher can show the students that he is quite serious about what he says, well aware of what he is saying when he says it, and seriously intent upon seeing it carried out. These points will be developed more fully in the following chapters.

The teacher should expect some difficulties

Despite what has been said in this chapter and in other parts of this book about confidence and positive expectations, there inevitably will be difficulties, and teachers must expect them and be prepared to deal with them. This may, at first, appear contradictory to what has been said previously, but a careful analysis will show that it is not. Granted, while positive expectations may go a long way toward solving and preventing problems, they will not prevent or solve all problems. Expectations are not automatically self-fulfilling. However, positive expectations are necessary and important. Without them, the situation would be considerably changed. To the extent that positive expectations initiate behavior that does lead to self-fulfilling prophecy effects, they help prevent and solve problems that otherwise would appear. The benefits of self-fulfilling prophecy effects related to these positive expectations simply would not be gained if these expectations were not there in the first place.

In addition, the self-fulfilling prophecy effects of negative expectations must be considered. Where no negative expectations exist, undesirable self-fulfilling prophecy effects cannot occur. Where negative expectations do exist, however, some are likely to result in behavior that will produce undesirable self-fulfilling prophecy effects, thus adding to the teacher's burden. In addition to problems that would have been there anyway, there are added problems caused by the teacher's own negative expectations.

An additional benefit of consistent positive expectations is that they cause the teacher to examine his own behavior and to ask what he might be doing differently to help the situation. This is an important function, since teachers, like everyone else, are strongly tempted to take credit for success but to blame failure on things other than themselves. This was shown, for example, in a study by Good,

Schmidt, Peck, and Williams (1969). They asked 14 fifth-grade teachers and 14 eighth-grade teachers to describe the students in their classrooms who presented the biggest problems to them and to explain why the students presented problems. In responding to these questions, teachers mentioned themselves as part of the problem in only 4 of 74 cases. The other 70 were seen as problems of limited student ability, poor student attitude, or a home life that did not support the school. Most of these cases were described as if they were permanent, unchangeable situations.

Similar results were found in a study by Quirk (1967). Without informing the teachers who were actually the subjects in his experiment, Quirk arranged for some to think they had succeeded (their students learned) and for others to think they had failed (their students did not learn). He then asked the teachers to assess their performance. He found a strong tendency for teachers who had experienced success to take credit for it by attributing it to their own presentation. In contrast, teachers who had been led to experience failure usually blamed it on the students or on factors other than their own teaching presentation.

Such rationalizing is not particularly malicious and not confined to teachers. We all want to see ourselves as likable, competent, and successful, and we all tend to repress or explain away the things that do not fit this self-image. Such defensiveness is not necessary in teachers who adopt positive, but appropriate, expectations for their students. Because the expectations are appropriate, the teacher does not need to feel guilty or dissatisfied if slower students do not do as well as better students. Success is defined as progress in terms of the students' capabilities. Since the expectations are also positive, they remind the teacher continually to think in terms of forward progress and to analyze the problem and question his teaching approach when progress is not evident. This helps him to stay on top of the situation and to adapt quickly to changes as they appear. The teacher will recognize and exploit breakthroughs as they occur and will respond to failure with a search for another way to do the job rather than for an excuse or explanation.

Even though appropriately positive attitudes and expectations are not automatically or totally effective by themselves, they are necessary and important teacher qualities. Teachers will not always succeed with them, but they will not get very far at all without them. Attitudes and expectations usually cannot be observed directly, of course, but teacher behavior can be observed and measured. Observation instruments for recording teacher behavior related to the basic teaching attitudes and expectations discussed are presented in the appendix for this chapter. By measuring such behavior in other teachers and by becoming conscious of it in your own teaching, you can learn to detect and eliminate the undesirable self-fulfilling prophecy effects that result when inappropriate attitudes and expectations are present.

Summary

In this chapter, we have shown how teachers' attitudes and expectations about different students can lead them to treat students differently, so that teachers' attitudes and expectations sometimes become self-fulfilling. A particular danger is that low expectations combined with an attitude of futility will be communicated to certain students, leading to erosion of their confidence and motivation for school learning. This will confirm or deepen the students' sense of hopelessness and cause them to fail even where they could have succeeded under different circumstances.

Expectations tend to be self-sustaining. They affect both perception, by causing the teacher to be alert for what he expects and to be less likely to notice what he does not expect, and interpretation, by causing the teacher to interpret (and perhaps distort) what he sees so that it is consistent with his expectations. In this way, some expectations can persist even though they do not fit the facts (as seen by a more neutral observer).

Sometimes low expectations or defeatist attitudes exist because the teacher has given up on certain students and accepts failure in teaching rather than trying to do anything further with them. In these instances, inappropriate attitudes and expectations help the teacher to take his mind off the problem or to explain it away. Such an attitude or expectation explains ("Johnny's limited intelligence, poor attitude, and cumulative failure in school have left him unable to handle eighth-grade work; he belongs in a special education class") and, therefore, seems to justify the teacher's failure with this student. The attitude psychologically frees him from continuing to worry about the student's progress and from seeking new and more successful ways to teach him.

Once a teacher and student become locked into such a circle of futility, they tend to stay there. The teacher's behavior causes the student to fall even more behind than he might have otherwise, and this failure in turn deepens and reinforces the teacher's already low expectations.

Teachers can avoid such problems by adopting appropriate general expectations about teaching and by learning to recognize their specific attitudes and expectations about individual students and to monitor their treatment of individual students. In particular it is essential that teachers remember that their primary responsibility is to teach, to help each student reach his potential as a learner. It is natural that teachers form differential attitudes and expectations about different students, because each student is an individual. To the extent that these are accurate and appropriate, they are helpful for planning ways to meet each student's needs. However, they must constantly be monitored and evaluated, to insure that they change appropriately in response to changes in the student. When teachers fail to monitor and evaluate their attitudes, expectations, and behavior toward students, they can easily get caught in the vicious circle of failure and futility described above.

By keeping a general focus on instruction as his main task, and by training himself to observe students systematically with an eye toward their present progress and needs, the teacher can maintain a generally appropriate orientation to the classroom. He can reinforce this by learning to recognize and evaluate the attitudes and expectations that he forms spontaneously in daily interactions with students. This will enable him to correct inaccuracies and to use accurate information in planning individualized treatment.

Remember, teaching attitudes and expectancies can be your allies and tools if properly maintained and used. However, if unquestioningly accepted and allowed to solidify, they can become defense mechanisms that lead you to ignore or explain away problems rather than solve them. Therefore, learn to control your attitudes and expectations—don't let them control you!

SUGGESTED ACTIVITIES AND QUESTIONS

1. Which students in your preservice teacher education courses (or teachers at your school) are the brightest? What behavioral evidence and information have you used to form your expectation? How accurate do you think your estimates are?

2. When teachers form their expectations about how students will perform in their classes, do you think that teachers tend to underestimate or overestimate the following types of learners: loud, aggressive males; quiet, passive males; loud, aggressive females; quiet, passive females; students who are neat and who follow directions carefully; students with speech impediments; and students who com-

plain that schoolwork is dull and uninteresting? Why do you feel that teachers would tend to overestimate or underestimate the ability of these student types?

3. Analyze your own attitudes about classroom learning. As a student did you see learning assignments as typically enjoyable? If you did, why was learning fun for you? Was it because you did well or because learning *per se* was fun or exciting? When learning was not fun, was it due to particular teachers or subjects?

4. What can you do as a teacher to make learning more enjoyable for your students?

5. Write an original example of a self-fulfilling prophecy. Illustrate an example that happened to you, a relative, or a classmate. Be sure that you include each of these three steps: an original expectation; behaviors that consistently communicate this expectation; and evidence that the original expectation has been confirmed.

6. Select scales that are designed to measure teacher expectations and use them to rate real teachers or video taped teaching situations.

7. Role-play (you be the teacher and let classmates play pupils at a specific grade level) the beginnings and endings of lessons. Try to communicate appropriate expectations.

8. Read one or two of the case studies in Appendix A (p. 363) and list all instances when teachers communicate positive or negative expectations. Compare your lists with those made by others.

9. How can a teacher's overemphasis on praise and right answers interfere with student learning?

10. Should teachers hold expectations for student performance?

11. Why do the authors stress that expectations should be appropriate rather than necessarily positive, and that they must be followed up with appropriate behavior?

12. How do teachers form their expectations about students?

13. Explain in your own words why expectations, once formed, tend to be self-perpetuating.

14. Discuss ways in which inappropriate teacher expectations may lead to inappropriate teacher behavior.

15. In particular, how might a teacher's use of homework and seatwork assignments communicate undesirable expectations to students?

APPENDIX

Observation forms for measuring teacher behavior related to the basic teacher attitudes and expectations discussed in the chapter are presented in this appendix. Each form has a numbered title, a definition of the classroom situations in which it should be used, and a description of its purpose. Although all the forms share these common properties, they differ from one another in several ways. Some are confined to strictly behavioral categories and require simple counting of observed events, while others require the coder to make inferences or judgments and score the teacher on more global rating scales. Also, some call for only a single coding for a single event, while others involve coding several items of information about series of events that occur in sequences.

A skilled coder can use many of the observation forms during a single observation, so long as he does not require himself to code two things at the same time. At the beginning, however, it is best to start with one or two forms while you acquire basic observation and coding skills.

The observation forms define the applicable classroom situation and then list several alternative ways that the teacher could respond in the situation. The different teacher behaviors listed are mutually exclusive, but sometimes more than one could occur in a given situation. To use the observation forms correctly you must be able to: (1) recognize when relevant situations are occurring that call for use of the form; (2) accurately observe the teacher's handling of the situation; and (3) accurately record this information on the form. If the teacher shows more than one codable behavior in the situation, simply number consecutively the different behaviors that the teacher shows. This will preserve not only the information about which different techniques were used but also the sequence in which they were used.

Using coding sheets

An example of how the coding sheet would be used and how the information recorded on it can be recovered later is presented on p. 104. This example shows the coding sheet for teacher's behavior when introducing lessons or activities or making assignments (Form 4.1). This form is used to measure the teacher's motivation attempt (if any), as opposed to his specificity or completeness in presenting the assignment (the latter is covered on a different form). Form 4.1 is used whenever the teacher introduces a lesson or activity or makes an assignment to the class or to a group within the class.

On this form, the observer would note carefully what attempt the teacher made to build up interest or *motivate* the students to look forward to or to work carefully on the lesson or assignment; this information is numbered by categories and those numbers are used to record the behavior in the coding columns.

In the example, the coding sheet shows that 3 such instances were observed by the coder (the coding sheet has room for 50 instances). Note that the coder has entered a "4" as his first code. This indicates that the teacher began a lesson or gave an assignment with no attempt at all to motivate or build up interest. He may have given some directions to get the group started, but he did not attempt to build up to the activity—"Yesterday we finished page 53. Open your books to page 54. Mark, begin reading with the first paragraph." He also did not promise rewards or threaten punishment for good or bad performance in the activity.

The teacher's behavior the second time he introduced a lesson or activity is coded in the next row. Here the coder has entered both a "1" and a "3." This indicates that the teacher began with a gushy buildup, but later also mentioned the information or skills that would be learned in the activity.

The third row also shows a "1" followed by a "3," indicating again that the teacher introduced a lesson or activity with an excessive buildup, followed by mention of the information or skills to be learned.

Although not enough instances are recorded to make interpretations with great confidence, a pattern is noticeable in the three instances coded. The teacher appears to be basically positive in his presentation of lessons and activities. No negative motivation attempts (apology, threat of test, or punishment) appear. However, in his attempts to motivate positively the teacher may be overdoing it, in that the observer coded two instances of overdramatic buildup.

If this did indeed develop as the teacher's stable pattern, some guidelines for additional questions and observations would emerge. What would be the effects of this overdramatizing on the class? Would it tend to amuse them or cause them to lose respect for the teacher? Would it train them to begin to complain or suspect unenjoyable activities if the teacher failed to give the coming activity a big buildup? If there were evidence that the teacher's overacting was having these kinds of effects on the class, he might be advised to try to tone down his motivation attempts. If there appeared to be no adverse effects on the class, it might be advisable for the teacher to continue his present style of motivating the class and instead work on changing problem behaviors that appear to have negative consequences.

The observation forms in this appendix, as well as all of the forms following subsequent chapters, will be partially filled in, to show how they look after being used in the classroom. However, we will no longer add our interpretations of the data shown on these example coding sheets. Studying the partially filled in coding will help you quickly grasp what is involved in using each observation form. In addition, it will provide a basis for practicing interpretation of coded data. If possible, arrange to compare your interpretations of these data with the interpretations of a friend or colleague. Discuss any disagreements in detail, to discover the reasons for them and to determine what additional information (if any) would be needed in order to resolve the matter with confidence. Your instructor or in-service leader can help you to resolve coding difficulties.

The observation forms are divided up so that each measures just one or only a small number of related teacher behaviors. Thus each form is a self-contained observation instrument that can be used independently of the others. Once you have acquired some skill as a coder, however, you will want to observe several aspects of teacher behavior, using several different forms. To do this, you may find it convenient to combine several forms onto a single coding sheet. There are many ways to do this, and personal preferences and convenience are the primary criteria for deciding whether or not a given method is desirable. To show how this can be done, we have provided a sample coding sheet in Figure 5 that combines Forms 4.1, 4.2, 4.3, 4.4.

The four forms were compressed onto a single coding sheet by using only key terms rather than the full behavior category descriptions that appear on the originals. Use and purpose descriptions are omitted entirely, since it is assumed that the coder is already familiar with the four original forms. The result is a sheet with spaces to code up to 50 instances of each of the four teacher behaviors. A coder would use this sheet until he used all 50 spaces for one of the four behaviors; then he would switch to a new sheet.

Figure 5 shows only one of many ways that these four forms could have been combined onto a single coding sheet. For your own coding, feel free to create coding sheets that meet your preferences and needs. There is no single right coding sheet; the one that you like and that does the job is the one you should use.

Generally all the information you need to code is on the sheet. For example, in Figure 5, column one, you can see that most of the ways a teacher can motivate students when introducing a lesson have been summarized into nine categories, and if the teacher's behavior cannot be described in one of these nine categories, use the tenth category. Occasionally the user will have to supply some information of his own. Notice scales representing Forms 4.3 and 4.4 (individual praise and individual criticism) in Figure 5. When individual students must be identified, as in these examples, the user will have to supply his own identification codes. In the first instance, under *individual praise*, we see that student 14 received teacher praise for a successful accomplishment (category 3).

Thus, depending on his coding goals, the user will have to supply appropriate code numbers. For example, if the coder is interested in how teachers praise male and female students, respectively, then he need only use a 1 when girls are praised and a 2 when boys are praised. Obviously, in Figure 5 the coder is coding the entire class, because, in the second instance of a teacher praising an individual student, the student's number is 23. If you are interested in coding the behavior of an entire class, simply assign each student a unique number and use this number whenever interactions involving him are coded.

Predictions, expectations, and untested assumptions

The following list of predictions and interpretations indicates some that teachers have made about students. In each case observed, the interpretation was simply assumed to be true—it was not tested out or verified. Even if verified, however, such interpretations should not be verbalized to the students, because of the undesirable incidental learning that may result. Read the list to help establish what is meant by an *untested assumption* about a student. As you observe additional examples in classrooms, add them to the list for future reference. The key is that the teacher behaves as if the assumption is true, without first testing it out.

1. The student is not ready for a particular book or problem.

2. The student can't be trusted or believed. Unless proven innocent, he's guilty.

3. The student can't be allowed to use special equipment because he'll only break it.

4. The student must be isolated from others because he can't control himself.

5. The student will cheat unless you take precautions to prevent it.

6. The student can't talk quietly, so he's not allowed to talk at all.

7. The student won't like (or understand) the activity coming up next.

8. The student obviously knows the answer because he is smart (or obedient, or his hand is up).

9. The student will need help in finding the page (or other things he can easily do himself).

10. The student will cause trouble unless he sits next to the teacher.

11. The student will need a "crutch" to be able to do this exercise, so he is given one.

12. The student is daydreaming, not thinking about schoolwork.

13. If Johnny Bright doesn't know the answer, no one will.

14. The student will fail next week's test.

15. It's Friday afternoon, so the class will be rowdy.

16. The student just doesn't care about his schoolwork.

17. All you can do for this student is see that he gets lots of sunlight, water, and air.

FORM 4.1. Introducing Lessons, Activities and Assignments

USE: When the teacher is introducing new activities or making assignments
PURPOSE: To see whether or not the teacher pictures schoolwork as worth-
    while or enjoyable
        Observe teacher behavior when introducing activities and making assign-
ments. For each codable instance observed, record the numbers (consecutive-
ly) of each category applicable to the teacher's behavior.

BEHAVIOR CATEGORIES   CODES
  1. Gushes, gives overdramatic build-up   1. __4__   26. ____
  2. Predicts that group will enjoy the activity   2. _1,3_   27. ____
  3. Mentions information or skills the group will   3. _1,3_   28. ____
     learn   4. ____   29. ____
  4. Makes no attempt to motivate; starts right   5. ____   30. ____
     into activity
  5. Apologizes or expresses sympathy to group   6. ____   31. ____
     ("Sorry, but you have to. . .")   7. ____   32. ____
  6. Bribes, promises external reward for good   8. ____   33. ____
     attention or work   9. ____   34. ____
  7. Warns group, or reminds them, about test to be   10. ____   35. ____
     given later
  8. Threatens punishment for poor attention or work   11. ____   36. ____
  9. Presents the activity itself as a penalty or   12. ____   37. ____
     punishment   13. ____   38. ____
 10. Other (specify)   14. ____   39. ____
                                                          15. ____   40. ____

NOTES: 16. ____   41. ____
                                                          17. ____   42. ____
                                                          18. ____   43. ____
                                                          19. ____   44. ____
                                                          20. ____   45. ____

                                                          21. ____   46. ____
                                                          22. ____   47. ____
                                                          23. ____   48. ____
                                                          24. ____   49. ____
                                                          25. ____   50. ____

FORM 4.2. Evaluations After Lessons and Activities

USE: When teacher ends a lesson or group activity
PURPOSE: To see whether the teacher stresses learning or compliance in making evaluations
    When the teacher ends a lesson or group activity, code any summary
evaluations he makes about the group's performance during the activity.

BEHAVIOR CATEGORIES
1. Praises progress in specific terms; labels knowledge or skills learned
2. Criticizes performance or indicates weaknesses in specific terms
3. Praises for generally good performance, for doing well or knowing answers
4. Criticizes for generally poor performance (doesn't detail the specifics)
5. Ambiguous general praise ("You were very good today.")
6. Ambiguous general criticism ("You weren't very good today.")
7. Praises good attention or good behavior
8. Criticizes poor attention or misbehavior
9. No general evaluations of performance were made

NOTES:
    Teacher uses stock phrase ("You were really good today; I'm very pleased").

    #13 cut off by bell; might have praised him otherwise.

CODES

1.	5	26.	
2.	5	27.	
3.	6	28.	
4.	5	29.	
5.	9	30.	
6.	5	31.	
7.	3	32.	
8.	5	33.	
9.	9	34.	
10.	5	35.	
11.	5	36.	
12.	5	37.	
13.		38.	
14.		39.	
15.		40.	
16.		41.	
17.		42.	
18.		43.	
19.		44.	
20.		45.	
21.		46.	
22.		47.	
23.		48.	
24.		49.	
25.		50.	

FORM 4.3. Individual Praise

USE: Whenever the teacher praises an individual student
PURPOSE: To see what behaviors the teacher reinforces through praise, and
to see how the teacher's praise is distributed among the students

BEHAVIOR CATEGORIES	STUDENT NUMBER	CODES
1. Perseverance or effort; worked long or hard	14	1. 3
	23	2. 3,4
2. Progress (relative to the past) toward achievement	6	3. 3
	18	4. 3
3. Success (right answer, high score) achievement	8	5. 1
4. Good thinking, good suggestion, good guess or nice try	8	6. 1
	8	7. 1
5. Imagination, creativity, originality		8. —
6. Neatness, careful work		9. —
7. Good or compliant behavior, follows rules, pays attention		10. —
		11. —
8. Thoughtfulness, courtesy, offering to share; prosocial behavior		12. —
		13. —
9. Other (specify)		14. —
		15. —
NOTES:		16. —
All answers occurred during		17. —
social studies discussion.		18. —
		19. —
		20. —
Was particularly concerned about		21. —
#8, a low-achieving male		22. —
		23. —
		24. —
		25. —

FORM 4.4. Individual Criticism

USE: *Whenever the teacher criticizes an individual student*
PURPOSE: *To see what behaviors the teacher singles out for criticism, and to see how the teacher's criticism is distributed among the students*
Whenever the teacher criticizes an individual student, note the student's name or number and code the behavior that is criticized.

BEHAVIOR CATEGORIES	STUDENT NUMBER	CODES
1. Lack of effort or persistance, doesn't try, gives up easily	16	1. 3
	21	2. 3
2. Poor progress (relative to expecta-tions), could do better, falling behind	5	3. 3,4
	12	4. 3
3. Failure (can't answer, low score), lack of achievement	5	5. 1
4. Faulty thinking, wild guess, failure to think before responding	————	6. ——
	————	7. ——
5. Trite, stereotyped responses, lack of originality or imagination	————	8. ——
	————	9. ——
6. Sloppiness or carelessness	————	10. ——
7. Misbehaves, breaks rules, inattentive	————	11. ——
8. Selfish, discourteous, won't share; antisocial behavior	————	12. ——
	————	13. ——
9. Other (specify)	————	14. ——
	————	15. ——
NOTES:	————	16. ——
	————	17. ——
	————	18. ——
	————	19. ——
	————	20. ——
	————	21. ——
	————	22. ——
	————	23. ——
	————	24. ——
	————	25. ——

NOTES:
All answers during social studies discussion.

Teacher sharply critical of student #5; seems irritated with him generally.

FIGURE 5. Sample Coding Sheet Combining Four Observation Forms

MOTIVATION ATTEMPT, INTRODUCING ACTIVITIES	EVALUATIONS AFTER ACTIVITIES	INDIVIDUAL PRAISE	INDIVIDUAL CRITICISM
1. Gushy build-up	1. Praises specific progress	1. Perseverance, effort	1. Poor persistence, effort
2. Enjoyment	2. Criticizes specifically	2. Progress	2. Poor progress
3. New information, skills	3. Praises general progress	3. Success	3. Failure
4. No motivation attempt	4. Criticizes general performance	4. Good thinking	4. Faulty thinking, guessing
5. Apologizes	5. Ambiguous praise	5. Imagination, originality	5. Triteness
6. Promises reward	6. Ambiguous criticism	6. Neatness, care	6. Sloppiness, carelessness
7. Warns of test	7. Praises good behavior	7. Obedience, attention	7. Breaks rules, inattentive
8. Threatens to punish	8. Criticizes misbehavior	8. Prosocial behavior	8. Antisocial behavior
9. Gives as punishment	9. No group evaluation	9. Other (specify)	9. Other (specify)
10. Other (specify)			

CODES	CODES	STUDENT NUMBERS AND CODES	STUDENT NUMBERS AND CODES
_4_ 1. __ 26.	_5_ 1. __ 26.	_14_ 1. 3 __ 26.	_16_ 1. 3 __ 26.
_4,3_ 2. __ 27.	_5_ 2. __ 27.	_23_ 2. 3,4 __ 27.	_21_ 2. 3 __ 27.
_4,3_ 3. __ 28.	_6_ 3. __ 28.	_6_ 3. 3 __ 28.	_5_ 3. 3,4 __ 28.
__ 4. __ 29.	_5_ 4. __ 29.	_18_ 4. 3 __ 29.	_12_ 4. 3 __ 29.
__ 5. __ 30.	_9_ 5. __ 30.	__ 5. __ 30.	__ 5. __ 30.
__ 6. __ 31.	_5_ 6. __ 31.	__ 6. __ 31.	__ 6. __ 31.
__ 7. __ 32.	_3_ 7. __ 32.	__ 7. __ 32.	__ 7. __ 32.
__ 8. __ 33.	_5_ 8. __ 33.	__ 8. __ 33.	__ 8. __ 33.
__ 9. __ 34.	_9_ 9. __ 34.	__ 9. __ 34.	__ 9. __ 34.
__ 10. __ 35.	__ 10. __ 35.	__ 10. __ 35.	__ 10. __ 35.
__ 11. __ 36.	__ 11. __ 36.	__ 11. __ 36.	__ 11. __ 36.
__ 12. __ 37.	__ 12. __ 37.	__ 12. __ 37.	__ 12. __ 37.
__ 13. __ 38.	__ 13. __ 38.	__ 13. __ 38.	__ 13. __ 38.
__ 14. __ 39.	__ 14. __ 39.	__ 14. __ 39.	__ 14. __ 39.
__ 15. __ 40.	__ 15. __ 40.	__ 15. __ 40.	__ 15. __ 40.
__ 16. __ 41.	__ 16. __ 41.	__ 16. __ 41.	__ 16. __ 41.
__ 17. __ 42.	__ 17. __ 42.	__ 17. __ 42.	__ 17. __ 42.
__ 18. __ 43.	__ 18. __ 43.	__ 18. __ 43.	__ 18. __ 43.
__ 19. __ 44.	__ 19. __ 44.	__ 19. __ 44.	__ 19. __ 44.
__ 20. __ 45.	__ 20. __ 45.	__ 20. __ 45.	__ 20. __ 45.
═ 21. __ 46.	__ 21. __ 46.	__ 21. __ 46.	__ 21. __ 46.
__ 22. __ 47.	__ 22. __ 47.	__ 22. __ 47.	__ 22. __ 47.
__ 23. __ 48.	__ 23. __ 48.	__ 23. __ 48.	__ 23. __ 48.
__ 24. __ 49.	__ 24. __ 49.	__ 24. __ 49.	__ 24. __ 49.
__ 25. __ 50.	__ 25. __ 50.	__ 25. __ 50.	__ 25. __ 50.

FORM 4.5. Teacher's Use of Tests

USE: *When the teacher gives a quiz or test*
PURPOSE: *To see if the teacher uses tests appropriately as diagnostic tools
and teaching aids, rather than merely as evaluation devices*
*Code items A, B, and C when the teacher gives the test. If possible,
code items D, E, and F after observing how test results are used*

BEHAVIOR CATEGORIES
A. Test content
   1. Test mostly requires integration or application of knowledge or skills
   2. Test is balanced between memory and integration or application
   3. Test is mostly rote or factual memory; no thinking or application
      involved
B. How is test presented to students?
   1. Test presented as a diagnostic aid to the teacher—assesses strengths and
      weaknesses
   2. Test presented without explanation, rationale, or discussion of follow
      up
   3. Test presented as a threat or hurdle to the class—to find out who
      knows the answers and who doesn't
C. What expectations are communicated in the teacher's directions to students?
   1. Teacher gives positive directions (eyes on your paper, guess if you're
      not sure)
   2. Teacher gives negative directions (no cheating or else, no guesswork)
D. Is the test reviewed with the class?
   1. Test is reviewed and discussed with class
   2. Test scored by teacher, not reviewed with class
E. How does the teacher follow up with students who scored poorly?
   1. Teacher arranges for remediation with those who do not meet minimal
      standards and retests to see that they reach those standards
   2. Some remediation attempted, but teacher doesn't retest to insure
      mastery
   3. No evidence of remedial efforts with those who perform poorly
F. How does the teacher follow up if the whole class scores poorly? (code
   NA if Not Applicable)
   1. Teacher reviews or reteaches material that was not mastered and retests
      to insure mastery
   2. Some remediation attempted, but teacher doesn't retest to insure
      mastery
   3. No evidence of remedial efforts when material was not mastered

CODES

TEST		A	B	C	D	E	F
Spelling	1.	3	2	1	2	3	NA
History	2.	2	3	1	1	2	NA
	3.						
	4.						
	5.						
	6.						
	7.						
	8.						
	9.						
	10.						

FORM 4.6. Teacher's Use of Ability Grouping

USE: *In classrooms in which the teacher has grouped the students for small group instruction*

PURPOSE: *To see if the teacher is using grouping appropriately as a means of individualizing instruction*

GROUP COMPOSITION AND INSTRUCTION TIME

GROUP NAME	NUMBER OF BOYS	NUMBER OF GIRLS	START OF LESSON (TIME)	END OF LESSON (TIME)	LENGTH OF LESSON
Astronauts	3	5	8:31	9:00	29
Magicians	4	5	9:08	9:35	27
Champions	4	3	9:45	10:00	15
			:	:	

Note any information relevant to the following questions:
1. Is the class arranged so that each group is seated together as a group? *No*
2. How long have these particular groups been operating? *Since October 15*
3. Does the teacher plan to regroup? When? *Beginning of second semester*
4. Does the teacher teach the groups in the same order each day? *Yes*
5. If time for a group lesson runs short, does the teacher make it up later? *Usually not*
6. Do the groups have differential privileges regarding what they are allowed to do without special permission? *Astronauts have access to supplementary readers (considered too difficult for other two groups).*
7. If the teacher groups for more than one subject, are the groups the same or are they different? *Groups only for Reading*
8. Does the teacher show differential enthusiasm or emotion when working with the different groups? *Seemed more subdued, less involved when working with the Magicians.*

Record any descriptive or evaluative statements the teacher makes about a group.

GROUP	TEACHER'S COMMENT
Astronauts	*I'm proud of your progress - Keep up the good work*
Champions	*We're almost to the end of the reader; keep up the good work and we'll finish it by Friday.*
Champions	*Let's stop reading and get ready for recess. It's time to have fun and relax.*
Astronauts	*This is the best reading group.*
Magicians	*This the middle achievement group in reading.*
Champions	*This is the lowest reading group.*

FORM 4.7. Teacher's Use of Time

USE: *Whenever activities are introduced or changed*
PURPOSE: *To see if the teacher spends time primarily on activities related to teaching and learning*
Record starting time and elapsed time for the following teacher activities (When more than one activity is going on, record the one in which the teacher is involved). Totals for the day are entered in the blanks in the lower left corner of the page.

BEHAVIOR CATEGORIES
1. Daily rituals (pledge, prayer, song, collection, roll, washroom, etc.)
2. Transitions between activities
3. Whole class lessons or tests (academic curriculum)
4. Small group lessons or tests (academic curriculum)
5. Going around the room checking seatwork or small group assignments
6. Doing preparation or paperwork while class does something else
7. Arts and crafts, music
8. Exercises, physical and social games (nonacademic)
9. Intellectual games and contests
10. Nonacademic pastimes (reading to class, Show-and-Tell, puzzles and toys)
11. Unfocused small talk
12. Other (specify)

NOTES:
 # 3, 5, 7 = *Reading Groups*
 # 11, 13 = *Math lesson & seatwork*
 # 9 = *outside recess (free play)*

TOTAL TIME PER CATEGORY

BEHAVIOR CODE	TOTAL MINUTES
1.	20
2.	24
3.	38
4.	88
5.	30
6.	
7.	
8.	15
9.	
10.	
11.	
12.	

CODES FOR EACH NEW ACTIVITY

	STARTING TIME	BEHAVIOR CODE	ELAPSED TIME
1.	8 : 15	1	15
2.	8 : 30	2	3
3.	8 : 33	4	27
4.	9 : 00	2	5
5.	9 : 05	4	25
6.	9 : 30	2	4
7.	9 : 34	4	36
8.	10 : 10	2	5
9.	10 : 15	8	15
10.	10 : 30	2	2
11.	10 : 32	3	38
12.	11 : 10	2	5
13.	11 : 15	5	30
14.	11 : 45	1	5
15.	11 : 50	Lunch	
16.	:		
17.	:		
18.	:		
19.	:		
20.	:		
21.	:		
22.	:		
23.	:		
24.	:		
25.	:		
26.	:		
27.	:		
28.	:		
29.	:		
30.	:		
31.	:		
32.	:		
33.	:		
34.	:		
35.	:		
36.	:		
37.	:		
38.	:		
39.	:		
40.	:		
41.	:		
42.	:		
43.	:		
44.	:		
45.	:		
36.	:		
47.	:		
48.	:		
49.	:		
50.	:		

FORM 4.8. Teacher's Predictions and Untested Assumptions about Students

USE: *Whenever the teacher makes a prediction about an individual or group*
PURPOSE: *To see what kinds of expectations the teacher communicates*
    directly
    Record what the teacher says when he makes a prediction or directly
communicates an expectation about an individual or group, or when he acts
upon an untested assumption. What does he predict (about whether they can
or cannot succeed, for example)? What untested assumption does he act
upon? See the list of predictions, expectations, and untested assumptions for
more examples.

GROUP OR INDIVIDUAL	PREDICTION, EXPECTATION, OR UNTESTED ASSUMPTION
# 5	Can't read Astronaut's supplementary reader.
# 14	"Won't know this one" on Friday's test

CHAPTER

5

Modeling

Janice Taylor is an attractive senior at Compton College majoring in social studies. She plans to teach for a while after graduating and then marry and raise a family. Presently she is doing her student teaching at Oak Junior High School. The students at Oak come from middle-class homes, and this pleases Janice because as a student she attended a similar school and came from a middle-class home. However, at times she feels quite apprehensive. She has not been in a junior high school for several years, and although she gained some useful information in her college classes, she has not taught. Will students obey her? Can she make them enjoy schoolwork? Doubts about her ability as a teacher become more prevalent as the time for her to assume teaching responsibility nears. She has been observing in Mrs. Woodward's class for two weeks. One more week to observe, and then Janice is to become the teacher for the second-period (a slow class) and sixth-period (an average class) civics classes.

Janice watches Mrs. Woodward intensively because this is the first opportunity she has had to observe a junior high school teacher, and she wants to learn how to get the children to respond and to obey. Janice likes Mrs. Woodward and feels that she is a good teacher who treats the students fairly and is respected by them. However, Janice is basically a shy and soft-spoken person, and frequently becomes nervous when she is around loud, aggressive people. Consequently, she is often upset by the forceful way in which

Mrs. Woodward runs the class. She speaks in a loud, booming voice, and if students are misbehaving she does not hesitate to give them a "tongue lashing" or to send them out of the room. Mrs. Woodward's favorite tactic when students are disruptive is to boom out, "I'm telling you once and for the last time (Alice and Ted or whoever), listen to your classmates when they talk." Students typically stop after Mrs. Woodward pinpoints their misbehavior.

One week later, when Janice is teaching the class, she loudly addresses some misbehaving students in the same way, "I'm telling you once and for the last time, listen to your classmates. . . ." Think about these two questions:

1. Why did Janice imitate Mrs. Woodward's teaching style?

2. How might Janice have taught if she had taught with a different cooperating teacher?

In the previous example, the student teacher learned many things from observing a supervising teacher. (Indeed, this example is a rather common one; several research studies have shown that the cooperating teacher greatly influences the teaching style of the student teacher.) Not all of the things Janice learned were directly connected with teaching, and relatively few of them were deliberately taught by Mrs. Woodward. Janice "picked up" beliefs, attitudes, and habits simply by observing them.

How does this happen? Research has shown that many things are learned without deliberate instruction by the teacher or deliberate practice by the learner. The learner only needs to see the behavior demonstrated by someone else, and he can then imitate it for himself. A person who demonstrates the behavior is called the *model*, and this form of learning is often called *modeling* (Bandura, 1969).

When used purposefully, modeling can be a powerful teaching tool. Many things can be learned much more easily through observation and imitation than by trying to understand and respond to verbal explanations and instructions. This is especially true for younger students, whose abilities to follow complex verbal instructions are limited.

Awareness of modeling
Most teachers recognize the power of prepared demonstrations as teaching tools. However, they are usually less aware of the more general modeling effects that occur in the classroom, and less likely to take advantage of them through deliberate, planned modeling

behavior. We all know how bad examples can lead to misbehavior, but we are less aware of the power of a good model's example to influence positive behavior. Children learn many things by imitating models rather than by being instructed in a systematic fashion. They learn to speak their native tongue this way, as well as most of their attitudes, values, problem-solving strategies, and social behavior. In fact, these things not only can be taught through behavioral example, behavioral example is usually a more powerful influence than verbal instruction.

If there is discrepancy between our preaching and our practice, students will tend to do what we do, not what we say. This was shown in a recent experiment with childrens' altruism (Bryan and Walbek, 1970). Each child in the study played a game with an adult model. The game was designed so that each model and child could win money by succeeding at it. Unknown to the children, the experimenter controlled these winnings so that each model and each child won a specific amount. As part of the experiment, a box requesting donations for poor children was placed in the room where the game was conducted. Each adult model made mention of this donation box. Some of the adult models spoke in favor of donating, saying that it was a good thing to help the poor and that people should donate. With other children, the adult model complained about the donation box. He stated that his winnings should be his own, and that nobody should ask him to donate part of his winnings to someone else. Half the time when the model preached in favor of donating he followed up by donating part of his winnings. The other half of the time he did not donate, despite his words. Similarly, half the time the adult model who spoke against donating did not donate; the other half of the time, however, the adult model went ahead and donated some of his winnings even after speaking against it and saying that he resented it.

The results of the experiment showed clearly that the children's donating behavior was affected much more by what the adult *did* than by what he *said*. Children who observed the model donate part of his winnings tended to do the same themselves, regardless of whether the model spoke for or against donating. Similarly, children who saw that the adult did not donate tended not to donate themselves, even if the model had spoken in favor of donation. The children clearly took their cue from what they saw the models do, not what they heard the models say.

The same thing happens in the classroom. If students perceive discrepancies between what the teacher says and what he practices, they will ignore what he says. Also, if they see discrepancies between what he says he demands and what he actually allows, they will guide their behavior according to what he allows. For example, students will obey the teacher for the first few days if he tells them to do their seatwork quietly and on their own. However, if it gradually becomes clear that the teacher does not intervene in any way when students do not work quietly or when they copy from one another, they will come to see that he does not mean what he says.

This points up the need for teachers to be aware of their behavior in the classroom. Modeling effects can occur at any time, not just at those times when the teacher is deliberately trying to serve as a model. Remember, all that is required is that the students *see* the behavior modeled before them. The potential for modeling effects exists at all times; it is not something the teacher can turn on or off at will. What students learn from watching the teacher as a model may be either desirable or undesirable. The teacher is responsible for living up to his own ideals, and he must remain aware of his role as a model in order to assure that most of what the students learn from observing him is positive and desirable.

What is learned from models

Exposure to a model can result in either or both of two responses by the learner: imitation and incidental learning. *Imitation* is the simplest: the learner observes the model's behavior and then imitates it to make it his own. Often this is used as a teaching technique, as when students observe their teacher perform a zoology dissection or a chemistry or physics experiment and then repeat the process on their own. However, unplanned and sometimes undesirable imitation also occurs. Students will often pick up distinctive expressions, speech patterns, or gestures that their teachers use, whether or not they are used consciously. They will also take their cue from the teacher in learning how to react in ambiguous situations. If the teacher responds to student embarrassment with tact and sympathy, the class will tend to follow suit. However, if he reacts with insensitive sarcasm or ridicule, they will probably laugh and call out taunts of their own.

Besides imitation, observation of a model produces *incidental learning*, sometimes called inferential learning. The learner observes the model's behavior and on the basis of these observations makes inferences about the model's beliefs, attitudes, values, and personality characteristics. Here the learner is making inferences about why the model is behaving as he is or about what type of person would behave the way the model behaves. This is often called incidental learning because it involves acquisition of information in addition to or instead of what the model was trying to convey.

For example, suppose a teacher calls on a student to go to the blackboard and work out a mathematical equation. The teacher will serve as a model in the way he reacts to a mistake made by the student. One teacher might inform the student that he has made a mistake and ask him to look the problem over again to see if he can find where he went wrong. Another teacher might inform the student that he made a mistake and then call on someone else to replace him at the board and do the problem correctly. Both teachers would be teaching the mathematical content, specifically, the question of how to solve the particular problem involved. However, the incidental learning acquired by the student called to the board and by the rest of the class in this situation would differ with the two teachers.

In the first case, the students learn: "The teacher is friendly and helpful. It is safe to make a mistake. He'll give you a chance to correct yourself if you can do so, or will give you some help if you can't." In the second teacher's class, the students learn: "You had better be ready to perform when you get called to the board. The teacher wants to see the problem done correctly and has short patience for anybody who can't do it right. If you know the answer, raise your hand and try to get called on to go to the board. If you're not sure, try to escape the teacher's attention so that you don't get embarrassed."

Incidental learning of this type goes on whenever students observe their teacher reacting to errors. The teacher probably is not trying to teach the information that is learned incidentally; in fact, some of it is undesirable information that he would like to avoid if he knew about it. Nevertheless, the students will learn these things through observing him. How to do mathematics is only one of the things they will learn in these situations.

By making inferences from the teacher's behavior in other situations, the students will also learn about such things as the teacher's moral, political, and social values, his likes and dislikes, and his feelings about the class in general and themselves in particular.

Factors affecting what is learned from observing a model

The potential for modeling effects exists whenever a model is being observed by learners. However, the amount and kind of learning that results from such observation depends on several other factors. These factors influence whether or not the learners are likely to imitate the model, and whether the information they learn incidentally is desirable or undesirable from the model's viewpoint. These factors and their effects on modeling are summarized here. (For a more detailed treatment, see Bandura, 1969).

One important factor is the situation. Modeling effects are more likely to occur in new situations or situations where the expected behavior of the learner is unclear. Like Janice Taylor in the example at the beginning of this chapter, when we enter a new situation and are unsure about what to do, we tend to "do as the Romans do," by observing and imitating models. In a sense, the behavior of the models we observe in such situations defines the situation for us. It tells us what is normal or expected. This was shown in a fascinating series of experiments on emotional reactions by Schachter (1964). He administered stimulating drugs to subjects in his experiments, but he did not tell the subjects what kinds of reactions they might expect from the drugs. He then put the subjects in rooms with models (confederates of the experimenter) to see how they would be affected by the models' behavior. Some models displayed anger and aggression, others showed a giggling euphoria. Most subjects assumed that the effect of the drug was to make them feel like the model that they saw appeared to feel, so that subjects exposed to aggressive models tended to become angry and aggressive, while those exposed to euphoric models tended to become euphoric themselves.

Because modeling effects are strongest in ambiguous situations where people do not know what to expect and tend to observe models in order to find out, modeling effects in the classroom are likely to be especially strong at the beginning of the year. Based on early contacts with their new teacher, students will make inferences about the teacher and decide whether or not they like him, what kind of person he is, whether he invites or discourages questions and comments, whether or not he really means what he says, whether he is interested in individual problems, whether he is patient and helpful or frustrated and discouraged in dealing with slow learners, whether he seems reasonable and open minded or opinionated and unapproachable, and many other things. Also, the teacher's early behavior tends to set the tone for classroom climate variables such as the degree of competitiveness in the classroom, the degree of pressure and tension felt by the students, the degree of organization and order, and the degree to which students are responsible for their own behavior.

It is vital that teachers model appropriate behavior from the first day of school. Opportunities to teach through modeling will be greater at this time, because many things are still fluid or ambiguous. Later, when both the teacher and the class settle into predictable routines, it will be more difficult to effect change. Once patterns are established they tend to persist, and firmly established expectations tend to lead to self-fulfilling prophecy effects such as those discussed in the previous chapter.

In addition to situational factors, modeling effects vary with the personality and behavior of the model himself. A warm, enthusiastic teacher whom the students like will be imitated by them. The students are likely to adopt many of his attitudes and beliefs and to imitate his behavior. Students are less likely to imitate a teacher whom they dislike or do not respect, especially in the sense of adopting or conforming to his ideals. Much undesirable incidental learning will occur from observation of such teachers, but relatively few desirable modeling effects are likely.

The model's actual behavior and the consequences of that behavior are also important. Behavior that is seen as relevant or effective, or which has been rewarded, is likely to be imitated. Behavior that has been ineffective or has been punished is not likely to be imitated. Reward and punishment can be powerful factors, and will sometimes lead students to imitate undesirable behavior even in teachers that they do not like or respect. Thus hostile, sarcastic, or hypercritical teachers usually produce a destructive classroom climate. The students imitate such teachers, even though they dislike them, because the teacher not only models but rewards such behavior.

Teacher rewards and punishments will also influence student reactions to one another. When students observe the teacher praise or reward a classmate for a particular behavior, or when they discover through incidental learning that the teacher holds the classmate in high regard, they are likely to adopt the classmate as a model and imitate him. On the other hand, if they see their teacher reject or mistreat a classmate, they may imitate the teacher and begin to mistreat him themselves.

Other factors, such as the degree to which the student's attention is focused on the relevant behavior and the degree to which he is given instructions and time to practice the relevant behavior, also affect the kind and amount of learning that takes place through modeling. These will be discussed in later sections of this chapter, which list several positive attitudes and behaviors that teachers can present through modeling. Some of these things are preached but not always practiced consistently by teachers. Others are things not often thought of as being taught in the classroom but which can be taught by teachers who are aware of their modeling role. Suggestions are made for how teachers can increase desirable outcomes through deliberate modeling. Also, behaviors are pointed out that should be avoided because they tend to produce undesirable incidental learning effects.

Teaching through modeling

The most obvious use of modeling as a teaching device occurs in deliberate demonstrations that are given as parts of lessons. To teach many skills, especially to younger children, demonstration is the method of choice. Teachers differ in their skills as demonstrators, however, so that some demonstrations are more successful than others. Guidelines for effective demonstrations are presented in the following section.

In addition to formal demonstrations of skills, there are many other ways teachers can instruct or stimulate cognitive development through modeling. Especially important, for example, is teacher modeling of logical thinking and problem solving for students. Students cannot observe their teachers performing such operations unless the teachers share them by thinking out loud. Suggestions on how teachers can use modeling to stimulate development of these abilities in their students are given below, following the section on demonstrations.

Effective demonstrations

Some things can be demonstrated with little or no verbalization. Demonstrations are usually much more effective, though, if they are accompanied by verbal explanations. This is especially true for the kinds of things that are demonstrated by teachers. Usually these demonstrations provide examples of more general principles or rules that the teacher wants the students to learn. Thus the teacher should not focus simply on getting the student to be able to do the immediate problem; his focus should be on helping the student to learn the more general rule. Thus a demonstration should not only show the student the physical movements involved in solving a problem, it should also include explanations of the thinking that lies behind the movements.

To say that demonstrations need explanations may seem obvious, but research shows that people usually leave out important pieces of information when explaining or demonstrating something to someone else (Flavell, 1968; Hess, Shipman, Brophy, and Bear, 1971). People tend to assume that the listener sees the situation the same way they do, so they often forget that certain things need to be explained. You have probably discovered this for yourself if you ever sought out a friend or relative for driving lessons, swimming lessons, or instructions about how to cook a complicated dish. Professional instructors can teach these skills to beginners with ease and efficiency. Most other people cannot do this, however, even though they may be able to drive, swim, or cook very well.

What's the trick? The expert instructor has broken the process down into step-by-step operations. He assumes no knowledge in the learner. Instead, he defines each term that he introduces and points to each part as he labels it. He describes what he is going to do before each step and describes what he is doing as he does it. He has the learner master one step at a time, rather than trying to have him do the whole job at once. He takes his time and gives corrections in a very patient tone, so the learner can concentrate on the task at hand and not worry about working quickly enough.

The things that teachers demonstrate in school are not usually so complex as the examples above, but the principles for effective demonstrations remain the same. Teachers will need to bear this in mind when demonstrating new skills (e.g., word attack, mathematics operations, art projects, and science experiments) and when giving instructions for seatwork or homework. Such strategies are especially important when doing remedial work with students who clearly do not understand how to perform the steps involved in solving problems. A good demonstration should proceed as follows:

1. Focus attention. Be sure everyone is attentive before beginning, and see that their attention is focused in the right place. Hold up the object or point to the place you want them to look at.
2. Give a general orientation or overview. Explain what you are going to do, so that students will have a general idea of what is going to happen. This will get them mentally set to observe the key steps as you go along.
3. If new objects or concepts are introduced, be sure to label them and have the students repeat the labels until you are sure they understand. A student cannot follow an explanation if he does not know what some of the words mean.
4. Go through the process step-by-step. Begin each new step with an explanation of what you are going to do next, and then follow through by describing your actions as you do them. Think out loud throughout the demonstration.
5. Perform each action slowly and with exaggerated motions to help insure that the students follow.
6. Have a student repeat the demonstration so you can observe

him and give corrective feedback. If the demonstration is very short you can have him do the whole thing and wait until the end to give feedback. If the demonstration is longer or more complex, break it into parts and have the student do one part at a time.

7. In correcting mistakes, do not dwell on the mistake and the reasons for it, but instead redemonstrate the correct steps and have the student try again.

These principles form guidelines for observing demonstrations. When a demonstration does not succeed, it is likely that one or more of these principles have not been followed.

Thinking out loud at each step is crucial, especially when the task is primarily cognitive and the physical motions involved are relatively minor or nonessential. If you only demonstrate procedures such as pouring into a test tube, placing a number on the board, or making an incision during a dissection, the student will not be able to follow you (unless he already knew what to do and therefore did not need a demonstration in the first place!). While he watches you, he will need to hear you describe how you are filling the test tube exactly to the 10 ml. line, how you get the sum by carrying two ten units and adding them to the rest of the numbers in the tens column, or how you begin your incision at the breastbone and stop just short of the hip bones. Unless you verbalize the thinking processes going on in your mind as you work through a problem or demonstration, the processes will be hidden from the student. And, unless the student knows enough to figure out each step by himself, watching your demonstration may give him no more information about what you are doing and how you are doing it than you would get from watching a magician perform a baffling trick.

Modeling logical thinking and problem-solving behavior

Teachers should regularly think out loud when trying to solve problems, so that students can see them model the thought processes involved. Much of the school curriculum, especially in the first few years, is devoted to teaching simple facts and basic skills that are learned through rote memory and practice. Partly because of this, many children begin to assume that everything is learned this way—that you either know an answer or you don't. The possibility that they might arrive at an answer by thinking about the problem and working it out for themselves is not always recognized. This leads to a preoccupation with finding out what the right answer is at the expense of learning how to cope with particular types of problems. Instead of developing effective problem-solving strategies to use in these situations, some students develop strategies for covering up their ignorance. Many of these are discussed in John Holt's (1964) *How Children Fail*. Teachers can help avoid these problems by modeling good problem-solving strategies themselves and by encouraging the development of them in their students.

The basic method of modeling for this purpose is to think out loud when problem solving. Often this can be done in connection with lessons in the curriculum. In giving directions about how to do seatwork or homework, for example, and in doing remedial work with students who are having difficulty, teachers should verbalize each step in their thinking processes from beginning to end. Verbalizing will help the student see the way the problem is approached and help him see that the answer is a logical conclusion following a chain of reasoning, rather than something that the teacher just knew and that he must commit to memory.

Although this may seem obvious, we have observed many teachers who do not teach this way. Instead, they tend to ask "Who knows the answer?" rather than "How can we find the answer?" They fail to give enough stress to the thinking and problem-solving processes that the problem is supposed to teach. Among other things, such teachers spend more time with and are more rewarding toward students who are succeeding, and they are less accessible and less supportive toward those who most need their help. Other tell-tale behavior occurs in instances when students give answers that are acceptable but are not the ones the teacher was looking for. Instead of modeling respect for process by complimenting the student on his answer, "That's right, I hadn't thought of that," such teachers tend to reject these answers as if they were totally wrong. Unless the students are mature and secure enough to see this teacher behavior as unreasonable, it will tend to make them distrust their own problem-solving abilities, and they will begin to think in terms of guessing what the teacher has in mind rather than attempting to rationally work through a problem. It will also tend to depress student curiosity, creativity, and initiative.

Perhaps the best place to observe the degree to which a teacher models concern for process is in watching the way he handles errors in reading, seatwork, and homework exercises. Except for the relatively few things that are purely and simply matters of rote memory, errors in reading and in working out assigned problems are evidence that the student has not mastered the principles involved. The appropriate teacher response in such situations is to help the learner master these principles, not merely to give him the right answer to a particular problem. Yet many teachers typically respond to reading failures by simply giving the student the correct word (or calling on someone else), and they grade work assignments merely by marking answers correct or incorrect. Neither of these responses is usually of much help to the student.

Merely providing the correct answers to these single examples will not help the student to learn to cope with similar problems involving the same principles. He needs to know why the answer is correct, not merely to know what the answer is. The teacher needs to model the application of the principles by describing the process out loud, being sure to include each step in the problem-solving process.

Teachers can also model problem-solving processes in areas outside the regular curriculum. Opportunities to do so are presented whenever plans have to be changed, repairs or substitutions have to be made, or immediate problems have to be solved. These may include stuck drawers, equipment that will not function properly, science demonstrations that do not work, broken items that need fixing, and special events that require changes in plans or schedules. When things like this happen, teachers should share their thinking with the students. They should first define the problem, since it may not be obvious to the students. Then they should verbalize their thoughts about solutions, or better yet, solicit suggestions from the group if time permits. This will come as a genuine revelation to certain students who on their own would not think of fixing something that is broken or substituting for something that is missing.

Many students, especially those from disadvantaged backgrounds, fail to develop adequately what Rotter (1966) has called an "internal locus of control"—an appreciation of their own potential for affecting the world through goal-oriented thinking and problem solving. Such students tend to feel helpless in the face of frustrations and adversity, so that they often accept them passively instead of trying to cope with them more actively and effectively. They have learned to think in terms of accepting their fate rather than shaping it. Teachers can help combat this by modeling rational problem solving in their own behavior and by encouraging and rewarding it in their students.

Another way to model thinking and problem-solving strategies is through the use of games such as Password or Twenty Questions. The following example shows how:

TEACHER: Today we are going to play a game called Twenty Questions. John, you can help us get started. In a minute I'm going to go over to the window and turn my back while you point to something in the room. When everybody has seen what you are pointing to, go back to your seat and call me. Then I'll come back and start asking you questions to see if I can figure out what you pointed to. I'll have to ask you questions that you can answer either yes or no. If I'm smart enough to figure out what you pointed to in twenty questions or less, I win. Now, let's see if you can stump me. Remember, you can point to anything in the room that you want, as long as it is visible —something I can see.

(Teacher goes over to the window and looks out.) Okay, I'm not looking now. Point to something you don't think I'll be able to figure out.

JOHN: Okay, we're ready.

TEACHER: All right, I'm going to turn around now. Don't give me any hints by looking at what John pointed to. *(Teacher turns around.)* Well, let's see. There's no point in guessing, because there are too many things it could be. I think I'd better try to narrow it down some. Now, what's a question that would narrow it down for me? I know—I'll find out where it is in the room. *(Teacher walks to center of room and points to the left side.)* I'm in the center of the room now. Is it somewhere on this side of where I'm standing?

JOHN: No, it isn't.

TEACHER: Good, now I know that it is somewhere on the right side of the room. I'll have to narrow it down some more. Let's see, Ralph is seated about halfway back there. Is it in front of where Ralph is sitting?

JOHN: No.

TEACHER: Okay, now I know that it is on the right side of the room somewhere in back of Ralph. Let's see, it could be something on the walls, it could be one of you, it could be something on a desk, it could be something that you're wearing . . . I'd better narrow it down some more. Is it a person or a part of the body?

JOHN: No.

TEACHER: Well, now I know it must be an object of some kind. Is it something that someone is wearing or that they have on their desk?

JOHN: Yes.

TEACHER: Good, that eliminates all those things along the wall. Well, let's find out if it's something somebody's wearing or if it's on a desk. Is it something on a desk?

JOHN: No.

TEACHER: Hummm, then it has to be something that one of these six students is wearing. Is it worn by a boy?

JOHN: No.

TEACHER: Well! Now we know that it is something that either Janice or Mary is wearing. Let's see . . . is it an article of clothing?

JOHN: No.

TEACHER: Good, that really narrows it down. It must be their jewelry or accessories. Let's see, is it worn on the head or the neck?

JOHN: No.

TEACHER: Ah! Now we're getting close. It looks like it has to be either Janice's ring or Mary's wrist watch. Now I'm ready to make a guess. Is it Mary's wrist watch?

JOHN: Yes.

TEACHER: Well! I win! I did it in only nine or ten questions. I thought I'd probably win, because I had it pretty well narrowed down after five or six questions.

By thinking out loud this way, the teacher models his problem-solving strategies for the students. In addition, his reactions to "no" answers help reinforce the idea that such answers gave him valuable information and did not make him feel disappointed. Overemphasis on getting answers and underemphasis on thinking processes have caused many students to become conditioned to think that they have failed or have asked a dumb question simply because the answer to a question is "no." Holt (1964) even noticed this tendency in children playing Twenty Questions.

After modeling as in the above example, the teacher could follow through by having the students play the game themselves. Besides games such as Twenty Questions and Password, riddles and brain teasers can be used to model and practice problem solving, as well as exercise in which the problem and answer are given and the students are asked to show how the answer is reached. In all such activities the teacher can model methods of approaching the problem efficiently and systematically and can acknowledge and reinforce these methods when they are used by the students.

Modeling curiosity and interest in learning for its own sake

By the very nature of their jobs, teachers are, or should be, committed to learning. This commitment should come across in the teacher's classroom behavior. He should not only model interest in curriculum subject matter, but also commitment to learning and knowledge in general.

One important place teachers can model this is in responding to their students' questions, especially questions that are not covered in a textbook. Questions from the class are a sign of interest in the topic. They indicate that the students are participating actively in the discussion and thinking about problems rather than just passively listening. These are the teachable moments when the students are most receptive to new learning.

At these times, teachers should be sure to respond in a way that shows that questions are welcome and valued. First, the question itself should be acknowledged or praised: "That's a good question, John. It does seem strange that the Boston people would want to throw that tea in the water, doesn't it?" Then the teacher should attempt to answer the question, or refer it to the class for discussion: "How about it, class? Why would they throw the tea in the water instead of taking it home with them?"

If the question is one that neither the teacher nor the class is prepared to answer, some strategy should be adopted to find the answer. Relevant questions should not be simply dropped, or brushed aside as unwelcome intrusions. The teacher should promise to get the answer himself, or better yet, assign the student who asked it to go to the library (or other resource) to find the answer and then report on it to the class the following day. If necessary, he should give the student guidance about how to get the desired information. This behavior helps to reinforce the idea that learning is important for its own interest value and worth pursuing for its own sake. It communicates the implicit assumption that students will want to know everything they can about American history, not just the particular facts in their textbooks. This helps place the book in context as a means to an end rather than an end unto itself.

Teachers do not have to wait until a student asks a question in order to model curiosity and interest in learning. This can be done in many different ways. Interest in reading can be modeled directly when the class goes to the library. The teacher can check books out at this time, too, and follow up later by giving his reactions to these books in class. During class discussions, the teacher can model curiosity in the way he responds to questions for which he does not have a ready answer. Here he should not only respond warmly to the question itself but also should follow up by sharing his thinking through verbalizing his thoughts about it: "I never thought about that before. Why didn't they just take the tea home with them? I doubt that they just didn't think about it. That tea was very valuable, and they must have considered stealing it. So they must have decided not to steal it, but throw it in the water instead. How come?" The teacher could continue in this vein or else invite the class to make suggestions at this point.

Curiosity and interest in learning can also be modeled in the information the teacher gives the class about his private life. Although an interest in books, newspapers, magazines, and other educational resources can be stimulated through class assignments and projects, it can also be generated, perhaps more effectively, and with greater generalizability, through teacher modeling. When the teacher reads a book, magazine article, or newspaper item of interest, he should mention it to the class so they can read it themselves if they wish. Ideally, he should have the item available to pass around so that students can note the reference or borrow the item if they wish to follow up on it. The teacher should also distribute announcements of coming television programs, museum exhibits, entertainment events, and other special events of educational or cultural value. Here again, a written announcement can help when passed around the class for individual reference.

It is important that references to out-of-school educational and cultural events be made in a way that leaves the decision about whether or not to respond completely up to the student. There should be no hint that the teacher is pressuring the students to take part or is planning to check up on them later to see if they did. (When assignments of the latter sort are made, they should be labeled as such, whether they are required of everyone or are voluntary projects for extra credit. Such assignments are valuable and useful, but they should not be confused with the kinds of totally voluntary suggestions advocated here.)

The teacher should make many of these totally voluntary suggestions, in addition to whatever projects or assignments are made. This is because it is important to model an interest in learning for its own sake (completely free of any connection with school tests or school credit) and to show that the teacher assumes that students, too, will have these interests. There will usually be a strong temptation after the announced event to check up on the students and see how many participated, but this temptation should be resisted. Comments volunteered by students should be acknowledged and encouraged, but there should be no head count to see who participated and who did not. The teacher can give his own impressions if he participated—specific statements about the aspects that most intrigued or interested him, not general reports about how worthwhile the whole experience was. If the teacher did not participate, he should say so if asked: "Unfortunately, I had to miss it, but I'd like to hear about it."

The teacher can also reinforce curiosity and interest in learning through the asides and comments made in passing during class conversations. Without belaboring the point unnecessarily, he can get across to the class that he regularly reads the newspaper ("I read in the paper last night that . . ."), watches the news ("Last night on the six o'clock news they showed . . ."), and participates in other outside educational and cultural pursuits. The students should also be aware that their teacher thinks carefully about elections and participates in them, keeps abreast of major news developments, and otherwise shows evidence of an active and inquiring mind.

Socialization through modeling

The previous sections described how teachers can use their role as a model to teach curriculum content and to stimulate thinking and curiosity. These uses of modeling are closely related to the teacher's role as an instructor to his students.

However, the teacher also socializes his students through modeling. That is, he shapes the values, attitudes, and behavioral standards that his students adopt. Students' ideas about appropriate and inappropriate behavior and about how they should look upon themselves and others are affected by what they see when they observe their teachers.

Research on moral development (reviewed in Hoffman, 1970) shows that children progress to successively higher levels of moral knowledge as they grow older. Young children tend to have a hedonistic or punishment-avoidance orientation. Their behavior responds more to their own desires and fears of punishment than to an intellectual moral system. By the time they reach elementary school, children have developed moral codes. However, these tend to be in the form of overgeneralized rules acquired from adults—a list of dos and don'ts without any real understanding. Some children never really develop much past this stage, so that even as adults their moral thinking is mostly confined to a set of overgeneralized rigid rules.

Where conditions for moral development have been more favorable, school children gradually develop a higher level of moral knowledge. Rules become less rigid as the child learns to take into account situational factors and to separate motives, intentions, and actions. By adolescence, these rules usually are organized into a coherent, general moral system, so that the student not only can identify the most just or moral way of behaving in a given situation, but can also explain his choice by relating it to general principles of morality.

Although the situations producing good inner self-control and a highly developed moral sense are complex and not completely understood, at least two things appear to be important. The child must see ideal behavior patterns modeled by the adults around him, and he must come to see that rules are supported by rationales based on logic and consideration of the general welfare of people. Rules should not be seen as arbitrary demands to be followed only because they may be enforced by a powerful authority figure.

The teacher is in a good position to foster this development through the thinking and behavior he models in the classroom. He may be the primary influence in this area for many students, since many parents rarely use the child-rearing techniques that foster good moral development (Hess, 1970). Students who have been raised by arbitrary and punitive parents, who make and enforce but do not explain their demands, are likely to remain at an immature stage of moral development unless they are sufficiently exposed to other, more effective, adult models. When another adult does succeed in breaking the child away from a moral code featuring rigid rules and punishment avoidance, that adult is likely to be a teacher.

Some of the major ways teachers can use their positions as models to socialize their students are discussed in the following sections.

The teacher's credibility with his students

Credibility is vital in all human relationships. We tend to like and accept another person if we see him as honest and reliable. Conversely, we are uncomfortable if we feel that the person does not know what he is talking about, does not tell the truth, or fails to keep his promise. Only a few instances of this type can create mistrust, since most people believe that someone who has lied or otherwise shown himself to be unreliable in the past will do so again in the future.

The need for teachers to protect their credibility is even more important when working with young children than with older students or adults. Children tend to take things literally and to see things in a polarized, either-or fashion. They have difficulty making fine distinctions and taking into account extenuating circumstances. Thus they will take teachers' threats and promises literally, even though these may contain exaggerations or figures of speech that the teacher does not literally mean. Promises or threats that are not followed through tend to be seen as lies or at least as evidence that the teacher does not mean what he says. Once a child begins to perceive his teacher this way, he will tend not to believe threats or promises until he sees them come true. He will also tend to test any teacher rule or control statement (this is discussed at greater length in the following chapter).

Problems in this area can be prevented if the teacher carefully monitors what he says to his class. Nothing should be promised or threatened that the teacher does not have every intention of carrying out. When unforeseen circumstances cause a change in plans, the reasons for the change should be fully explained to the class so that the teacher's credibility is maintained.

All teachers can expect problems in this area early in the year. Because of their experience with teachers during the previous year, or because of a history of unfortunate experiences with adults generally, some students automatically will doubt or even discount what a new teacher tells them. They will tend to be skeptical about threats and promises and may tend to interpret teacher behavior as being something other than what it is. Praise, for example, may be seen as an attempt by the teacher to "butter them up," or to "con" them for some ulterior motive. A few may even believe that only a fool would trust a teacher or take what he says at face value.

With these students, teacher credibility must be established, not merely maintained. The teacher may not only have to model appropriately by practicing what he preaches, he may have to call the students' attention to his own credibility. This may mean discussing the subject directly and pointing to the record: "George, you've got to understand that I mean what I say. I'm not playing games or talking just to hear myself talk. Think—have I misled you or made a promise I didn't keep? . . . Well, try to remember that. It's frustrating for me to know that you always think I'm trying to fool you or put something over on you. Maybe other people have let you down in the past, but I'm not them, and you've got to try to remember that. I try to give you and everybody else in the class a square deal, and in return I expect all of you to respect me and trust me. If I ever do anything to let you down, you let me know about it right away so that we can straighten it out."

It is sometimes helpful to use the local slang or street language in talking to students, especially adolescents. This should be done, however, only if the teacher knows this language and feels comfortable using it. Students will understand more formal English, even though they might not use it themselves if they were trying to say the same thing. Furthermore, they will be aware that the teacher is struggling to communicate something very important in his own way of speaking. All of this helps reinforce the teacher's credibility. On the other hand, if the teacher were to affect the local slang or use it inappropriately, the students would probably pick this up and interpret it as more evidence that the teacher was trying to "con" them. Thus, the degree to which communication is honest and direct is much more important than the particular language in which it is phrased.

Rational control of behavior

Another area to be stressed through modeling, especially by teachers working with younger students, is the importance of a rational approach to coping with the world and its problems. Piaget (1970), among others, has shown that young children often assume people's actions to be conscious and deliberate, to think that they do things "because they want to." They have difficulty with concepts such as accidents and random events, tending to assume that someone deliberately made them happen for his own reasons. Because they are often treated authoritatively by the school and by their parents, they often do not see the reasons behind rules and may ascribe them to the whims of the rule makers. This attitude often will persist through adolescence in students raised in authoritarian home backgrounds. Furthermore, almost all adolescents tend to resent and resist rules to some degree, as part of the process of becoming independent and self-regulating.

Thus teachers at all levels should regularly spell out the rationales underlying their decisions and rules. There will be good reasons for a rule or decision if it is rational in the first place, and these reasons should be explained to the class. This sort of modeling has a double payoff. First, it stimulates the students intellectually, helping them to link causes to their consequences and to see rules as means of achieving larger goals rather than as goals in their own right. Second, it tends to motivate them, to make them more willing to accept the rule or decision. Like anyone else, students are more willing to accept and internalize rules they can understand.

Teachers cannot assume that students will figure out the rationales underlying rules by themselves. They need to be told. Without such explanation, many students will assume the teacher is acting arbitrarily, perhaps just to flaunt his authority or indulge a personal whim. By carefully explaining the rationales, teachers can help the class to see rules and decisions as carefully thought-out attempts to solve observable problems. Once the class learns to think this way, they will be capable of establishing their own rules on such matters as how limited resources can be shared fairly and how noise and disruptions can be minimized without undue restrictions on everyone.

For example, consider a third-grade teacher who has just acquired a View-master for use in his classroom:

TEACHER: Now that you all know how to use the View-master, I'm going to keep it here in the cabinet where you can get it and use it by yourselves. I think we need to talk about this, though, because there is only one View-master and I know most of you will want to use it. We need to work out ways to see that everyone gets a chance.

JOHN: Why not let us sign up so we could take it home with us one day at a time.

TEACHER: No, we can't do that, because it has to stay at school. The principal feels there is too much danger of damage if we let people take it home with them. Also, I'd hoped to develop a plan so that many of you could use it on the same day. If only one of you had it each day, some would have to wait almost a month before getting a chance.

MARY: We could look at it together.

TEACHER: Well, I hadn't thought about that, but I guess you could if it didn't get too noisy. Remember, there will be a group lesson and seatwork going on while the View-master is being used.

GEORGE: Well, it wouldn't be too noisy if just a few of us used it and if we went back in the corner.

TEACHER: Yes, I agree. I think that would work. But how will we decide who uses it at a given time?

SALLY: The first ones to finish their seatwork should use it.

TEACHER: I don't know about that, Sally. I wouldn't want you all to start racing through your work so you could be first to get at the View-master. I want you to think about your work and do it carefully without being distracted or trying to work very quickly. Also, I want to make sure that everyone gets his chance.

JOHN: We could just make a list and take turns.

TEACHER: Well, maybe we could make three lists, John. One for each reading group. How about if we divide each reading group into three groups of three or four students each, and then have each group take turns with the View-master? The first group could use it one day, the second group the next day, and the third group the third day. Then the first group would get its turn again.

MARY: Who decides what pictures to look at?

JOHN: Just take turns, naturally.

CHUCK: Yeah.

TEACHER: Yes, you and the other people in your group could decide on your order. When it's your turn, you would decide what pictures to look at. Does this plan sound good to you then? (*Class agrees.*) Okay, let's see if we've got this straight now. Each reading group will divide up into three groups, with three or four in each group. Every day, one of the three groups will use the View-master during self-chosen activity time. The groups will meet at the small table back in the corner. One person at a time will decide what pictures to look at next. Is that it? (*Class agrees.*) Okay, remember to handle the View-master carefully. Also, feel free to talk about the pictures, but keep the conversation quiet enough so that it doesn't disturb the rest of the class.

As a footnote to the above example, we might add one additional point: to model rationality successfully, teachers must apply the same standards to themselves as they do to the students. This means being ready to abandon a rule if no good reason can be shown for it or if the reasons that led to its inception have since disappeared. In our example, it is likely that the rule about using the View-master will be needed for only a few weeks. By this time many of the students would no longer be interested in using the View-master every time their turn came up. As this point, it would make sense to take into account this change in demand and modify the rule. The students should be allowed to work out the new rule themselves within whatever restrictions are needed to maintain classroom order.

Respect for others

Good teachers model respect for others by treating their students politely and pleasantly and by avoiding behavior that would cause anyone to suffer indignities or "lose face" before the group. Many well-intentioned attempts to help students learn politeness and good manners are undermined by teachers' failures to model the behavior they preach.

Respect for others must be presented effectively in the first place. Guidelines for social behavior should be presented as aspects of the Golden Rule ("Do unto others as you would have them do unto you"), not as rituals to be practiced for their own sake. Teachers should stress that in using politeness and good manners one shows concern for the feelings of others and respect for their personal dignity. Students will find this more meaningful and will be more willing to cooperate than when they are asked to show good manners merely to please the teacher or to "be nice."

The teacher must then back up his verbal explanation and rationale with appropriate modeling. This often can be difficult, since teachers have responsibility for their classrooms and are continually exerting authority. Because of this, it is easy for them to slip into the habit of giving orders brusquely or of criticizing in nagging, strident tones. This is especially likely with younger students, who are sometimes treated by teachers and other adults as if they had no feelings or could not understand what was said to or about them. Usually they do understand, of course, and they feel hurt or resentful when treated badly. This is why it is usually not only appropriate but desirable that teachers treat even the youngest students with the same respectful manner and tone of voice that they would use when dealing with another teacher. This holds also for interaction with hall guards, monitors, secretaries, janitors, bus drivers, and other school personnel.

As much as possible, directions should be given in the form of requests rather than orders. The words "please" and "thank you" should be used regularly. Tone and manner are also important. When directions are shouted or delivered in a nagging voice, the teacher's manner tends to distract from the verbal content and may cause anxiety or resentment.

What is said *about* students can be just as beneficial or destructive as what is said *to* them. Many teachers will regularly criticize a student in front of the class, or publicly comment about him to classroom visitors. For example, on our visits to classrooms teachers have pointed at specific students while they explained the sordid details of a problem family background, listed the student's typical forms of misbehavior, or stated that they were having him tested so he could be moved to a classroom for mentally retarded children. Sometimes such statements were made loudly in front of the entire class, while at other times the teacher spoke in more hushed tones intended only for our ears. Even in the latter cases, however, the student involved heard what was said and the rest of the class usually did, too. Naturally, all of the students were watching and listening carefully to what the teacher was telling us. Instead of modeling concern and respect for their students, these teachers were setting themselves up as "the enemy."

The potentially destructive effects of such behavior will be obvious to most readers. Yet, it is remarkably common, having occurred in about half of the classrooms we have visited. Others, notably

Jonathan Kozol (1967) in *Death at an Early Age,* have made similar observations. For whatever reason, adults will apparently make all sorts of statements when speaking to another adult about children and adolescents that they would never make to the student directly. In an extreme case known to the authors, a teacher who was leaving at midterm introduced her successor to the class by having each student stand in turn while she gave a lengthy description of his personal idiosyncrasies. Although such callous disregard for students' feelings is fortunately rare, instances like those mentioned above are commonplace. Apparently the inhibiting factors that prevent us from treating people callously when we speak directly to them do not work as efficiently when we are speaking about them, even if they are clearly within earshot. In view of this, the safest policy probably is to avoid discussing individual students at all with visitors to the class. Visitors should be requested to save their questions until the students have gone home or at least are outside the classroom.

When the teacher does choose to speak to classroom visitors during class time, he should take advantage of the opportunity to model and reinforce desirable behavior. In describing class activities, for example, he can take care to stress the skills that students are learning and the progress they are making. This should be done with reference to the class as a whole or to a subgroup within it rather than to an individual singled out for specific attention. The teacher could also take the opportunity to state publicly that he holds his class in high regard and is proud of them. Rather than describe to the visitors what individuals are doing, the teacher could invite the visitors to question the students themselves. This invitation will reinforce the idea that the teacher has pride and confidence in his students and will avoid putting them in the uncomfortable position of being talked about in a conversation between the teacher and the visitors. If a student is asked to do something or make some sort of presentation for the visitors, he should be asked politely rather than directed, and he should be thanked when he finishes. He also should be introduced by name to the visitor.

Comments made about individuals should be restricted to their positive individual traits and their present activities or the goals they are presently working toward. ("Richard is a talented artist. He's making a poster for the class bulletin board right now.") Public comparisons with other students should be avoided. ("John is one of our brighter students.") These are some of the ways teachers can show their respect for the dignity and individuality of their students when visitors come to the classroom. Basically, this involves extending to the students the same degree of courtesy and respect that would be extended to fellow teachers if the visitor was being taken on a tour of the school instead of just one classroom. Courtesy and respect should be modeled at all times, of course, not just when visitors come.

Fostering a good group climate

Ideally, the group climate in the classroom is one of friendliness and cooperation. Some classes, however, are notable for jealousy, hostility, and unhealthy aggressive competition. When this occurs, the teacher is almost always contributing to the situation both through direct modeling and through teacher behaviors that indirectly foster ill will among the students.

Direct modeling includes sarcasm, vindictiveness, scapegoating, and other overreactions to misbehavior. If students see their teacher regularly react this way to frustrations or annoyances, they are likely to begin to do so themselves. The teacher's behavior will raise frustration levels in the students, and at the same time will provide them with a model for dealing with it by taking it out on others.

Extreme forms of this classroom climate have been observed by Henry (1957), who speaks of "the witch hunt syndrome." Henry describes classrooms that are notable for destructive and hostile criticism of students by the teacher and by fellow students; for negative competitiveness, in which one student's loss is another's gain; for frequent accusations and attempts to elicit public confessions of wrongdoing; and for evidence of docility and powerlessness in the victims, who tend to accept such treatment rather than rebel against it.

Most of this negative classroom behavior was directly traceable to the behavior of the teachers. For example, they would initiate and maintain public witch hunts, in which students would be asked to publicly tattle on or criticize other students. The tattling would be followed by public criticism and punishment of the victim. Group hostility was further developed through practices such as emphasizing destructive criticism in the comments made about students' responses or work, and making it clear that similar comments were expected when students were asked to comment about one another's work. One teacher even organized a witch hunt formally by conducting a weekly hearing in which each student's behavior for the week was publicly reviewed and criticized.

Less extreme, but more common, is teacher behavior that promotes ill will in the group. Foremost among these are playing favorites and rewarding activities such as tattling that pit one student against another. Students should be praised and rewarded for their good work, but not in ways that make one gain at the expense of another (or even make it seem that way). At times praise of individual students or of parts of the group is useful and appropriate as a means of motivating other students. These comments should be confined to praise, however ("Good job, Johnny—that looks neat as could be"). There should be no blaming of others and no invidious comparisons ("John's desk is nice and clean, but look at the rest of yours. Why can't you be more like him?")

Behavior of this sort will only cause resentment, both against the teacher and against the student being praised. Encouraging students to tell on one another, or rewarding them for doing so, can have the same effect. So can putting a particular student in charge while the teacher leaves the room, telling him to write down the names of anyone who misbehaves. So can passing out papers so that students grade one another's and then call out the score of the person they are grading (public reporting focuses too much attention on individuals' grades and invites problems such as ridicule and resentment). In general, anything that places a student in the position of being against a classmate or of profiting from his problems can cause harm to everyone involved. The class will resent this teacher behavior, and the victim will probably resent the behavior of the other students. "Teacher's pet" is in a bad position also, since he probably will be isolated from his peers.

When a teacher inherits a class that is highly competitive and hostile (usually because their previous teacher acted like the teacher described above), he should do as much as possible to eliminate this by fostering friendly, cooperative relations. Peer tutoring and group project assignments can help, along with making very clear how much he values individual integrity and success and how he is not going to be interested in assessing guilt or punishment. It will also help to verbalize and model individualized standards ("Did I do my best?") and recognition of individual differences coupled with positive ex-pectations ("Some people will take more time to learn this than others, but you will all learn it if you keep at it").

Showing interest in the students

The behavior of many teachers says "don't bother me" to their class. Sometimes this is communicated directly, as when a teacher greets a student who has come to him with a question by saying, "Now what do you want?" This is especially common with younger children. Teachers often expect these children to have the same social sophistication as adults, including the ability to discriminate about when to approach the teacher and when to wait. Young children are less inhibited than older ones, and are less aware of how an adult might react when interrupted while talking or doing paper work. They are quite sensitive to hostility, however. Unless the teacher is very careful, a message intended to say, "Please don't bother me now, I'll be with you in a minute," can be perceived as, "Don't bother me—go away." Usually only a few repetitions of this are required before the student follows the directions as he sees them.

To avoid this undesirable incidental learning, teachers must be emotionally prepared to deal with student questions and concerns as they arise. If there are times when the teacher does not want to be interrupted (such as when conducting small group lessons), this should be stated clearly and explained to the class. Whenever students do come to the teacher, he should respond with concern and interest. Even if the student must be put off because something more pressing has to be handled immediately, this can be done in a way that reflects such concern. Tone and manner are more important here than the exact words used. The teacher should speak in a soft, friendly tone, use the student's name, and include a positive statement about when this problem will be handled, "Not right now, Johnny, come back when reading group is over." This short statement recognizes the student individually, shows concern for his problem, and states willingness to deal with it at a specific time. Compare this with, "Not now—we don't bother teacher during reading group." This reminds Johnny of the rule, but does not show concern for him or reassure him that he is welcome to come back later.

A similar type of incidental learning often occurs when students come to the teacher to show their work or creations, or to tell something personal that they want the teacher to hear. Even if the student is not put off in a negative fashion, he often is dismissed quickly with an empty comment such as "Really?" or "How nice." Although these may be meant as positive responses, only the most dependent and attention-starved students will accept them as such. Show-and-Tell and similar activities often produce this type of response in teachers who are not really listening to the students or watching what they do. Such teachers will occasionally give themselves away by saying something like, "That's nice" after a student has told a sad story. If the student is relating a story or showing and describing an object, the teacher should pay careful attention and ask relevant questions or make relevant comments.

Teachers can respond appropriately in these situations without getting into a long and detailed discussion with the student. A brief response will usually do just as well, provided it is a meaningful statement that is relevant to what the student has said or done.

This means, of course, that the teacher must pay attention to what the student is saying or doing in order to respond appropriately. The response, then, should be meaningful and specific. When the student shows an artistic creation, for example, the teacher can ask him to describe it (or can label it himself if he knows what it is) or make some specific comments about it. When the student shows seatwork or homework, the teacher should point out any mistakes and review them with him, or ask him to try to correct them himself. If there are no mistakes, the teacher should compliment the student not merely for the paper itself but for the skill it represents, "That's good work, Pete. You're really learning how to multiply."

Even deliberate, well-meant behavior by the teacher can sometimes cause unintended negative reactions. Inappropriate praise is probably the most frequent of these. Praise that is delivered in a straightforward, direct manner and is specific to the accomplishment being praised will be perceived as genuine by students and will be valued by them. Other sorts of praise, while well-intended, may have a different reception. One type is the vacuous or empty, "That's good" or "How nice," especially when delivered with an insincere or disinterested manner. This is not truly praise, since the teacher has not really paid much attention to what the student has said or done. It is essentially a way of rushing him off, and it will be perceived this way by most students.

Overdramatized praise is equally undesirable. Students tend to be realistic about their accomplishments, since their peers are their severest critics. They monitor one another's schoolwork and creations, and they know roughly where they stand in each area. Therefore, when a teacher sucks in his breath and gushes "Isn't that wonderful!" they will react with healthy skepticism. The praise may be accepted as genuine, but perceived as overdone and perhaps embarrassing. Furthermore, consistent praise of this sort will usually cause the teacher one of two kinds of trouble. First, if he tends to favor a minority of the class with such praise, he will engender jealousy and hostility among the others. A different sort of problem will arise if he praises everyone this way: he will create a demand for it. The students will see overdramatized praise as simply the way this teacher praises and will no longer be satisfied with ordinary praise. Credibility will be damaged because the students will begin to wonder if the teacher really means what he says when he says it without gushing. Respect will be undermined because even kindergarten children know that such behavior is appropriate only for infants, if at all. Thus while they may view the teacher as warm and loving, they will also tend to see him as a comic figure to be laughed at or manipulated rather than respected. Suggestions on how to praise appropriately are given in the following chapter.

Modeling listening and communication habits

The phrase "teacher talk" conjures up in many people an image of long-winded, righteous nagging. The word "lecture" has a similar meaning for some people. These images usually are one result of experience with a teacher who talked *at* them rather than *to* them. Some teachers talk at their students regularly, and too many teachers do so more often than they realize.

Ideally, the teacher should use a normal conversational tone in most situations. His manner in giving explanations or asking questions in class should be the same as it would be if he were in the company of a group of friends. While a little acting is valuable at times, it should not replace the teacher's natural style of behavior. He should not have one way of speaking with his students and a different way of speaking with adults, nor should he try to cultivate either a syrupy or a severe tone. These are phony and even very young children know it.

Questions should be genuine questions requiring answers and not merely rhetorical ones seeking merely compliance or agreement. Most questions should require substantive answers, not merely "yes" or "no." Discussions should be true interchanges of knowledge and opinions and not merely monologues in which the teacher asks and then answers his own questions. When questions are asked, the teacher should wait for the student to respond in his own words and not try to put words in his mouth for him. When a student makes a response or contributes to a discussion, the teacher should model careful listening and hear him out, not cut him off as soon as he mentions a key phrase the teacher wanted to hear.

In general, the teacher must be a good listener and follow the same rules for polite discussion that he would follow in the company of other adults. If he does not, the students will quickly get the message and will begin to respond to his behavior by trying to figure out what he wants and then giving it to him, instead of by listening to his questions and thinking about them. They may also imitate his rudeness by butting in on one another or calling out answers when a classmate pauses to think.

Modeling emotional control

One of the major problems facing growing children is achievement of an optimal relationship between emotions, feelings, and impulses on the one hand, and conscience, or feelings about correct and appropriate behavior, on the other. Infants start with little emotional control, but they acquire it gradually as they develop and learn about parental and societal expectations. When socialization is incomplete or unsuccessful, the result is an immature adult who lacks effective emotional control. Depending upon the prominent emotions he displays, he may appear happy but overly loud and socially inept; he may be very dependent on someone else to reassure him and tell him what to do; he may respond to frustration or anxiety by withdrawing or turning to alcohol or drugs; or he may act out anger and hostility by attacking other people. These are just a few of the behavior patterns observed in adults who have not learned to express their emotions in mature and socially acceptable ways.

A different type of adult emerges from a socialization pattern that has been too "successful," a pattern that has led the person to reject his emotions or to keep them under rigid control. Such people tend to be stern, sober, overcontrolled, and inhibited about their own emotions and feelings.

The optimum is somewhere between these two extremes of emotional immaturity and emotional overcontrol. To the extent that problems exist in a given individual, they are likely to be mostly in one direction or the other. Teachers, and educated people generally, are more likely to have problems with overcontrol of their emotions. Young children and many older students, especially those who come from disadvantaged areas, often have poor emotional control. This in itself can cause problems, especially if an overcontrolled teacher is teaching in a lower-class school.

To the extent that the teacher is comfortable and in control of his emotions, he can be a valuable model to his students. This is especially true in regard to negative emotions, such as anger, hostility, fear, or frustration. By showing or reporting these emotions, the teacher helps communicate that they are normal and understandable. This will be reassuring to some students who may feel compelled to try to deny or repress their own similar emotions because they think they are dishonorable, sinful, or seriously abnormal. Because of the way they have been reared, these students have difficulty distinguishing between the feeling or experience of emotion and the way it is expressed in behavior. For example, instead of realizing that anger and aggression are normal emotions that must be controlled and expressed in acceptable ways, they may feel that they are never justified in becoming angry or that aggressive feelings must be repressed or denied. Fear is another emotion that is often denied. Many boys especially would feel ashamed and dishonored to admit that they were afraid in a situation, because they see fear as something unacceptable rather than as a normal reaction to be controlled and overcome.

Teachers can help break down tendencies to deny natural emotional reactions by freely discussing their own feelings and by taking advantage of opportunities to point out that unpleasant emotions are normal in some situations. Discussions in history and current events, for example, provide many such opportunities. By discussing the feelings of Columbus and his sailors or better yet, by role-playing these individuals, students can learn much about experiencing and dealing with strong negative emotions. If these reactions do not come out spontaneously, the teacher can point out that such emotions were natural and understandable under the circumstances.

This same thing can be done at a more direct level in discussions about appropriate and inappropriate social behavior. This is especially valuable for junior-high and high-school students who tend to develop inhibitions and fears about social acceptability with their peers. Fear of ridicule before the group becomes very strong at these ages, and students often inhibit impulses or actions or decline to ask questions because they are afraid of being laughed at. They will take pains to cover up inhibitions and areas of ignorance rather than admit to them. This can lead to what Sullivan (1953) has called "delusions of uniqueness," in which the student comes to believe that he may be the only one of his peers who has the fears, doubts, or inhibitions that he has.

Teachers can be a big help here by discussing and role-playing some of the situations their students deal with in the peer group every day: reacting to half-serious jokes and jibes about personal appearance or habits, dealing with conflicts between what the group is urging and what conscience dictates, responding to flirtations from the opposite sex, fears of losing face before the group, and so forth. These activities will help place the fears and self-doubts in these situations out in the open, and will help students see that they are not alone in having such experiences.

To set up this kind of role-playing exercise, the teacher should define each role in a hypothetical situation and briefly sketch the interactions that are to take place. Then he should assign a student to each role, perhaps taking a role himself:

> TEACHER: Janice and Matt, let's role-play a situation where one of the guys gives you a bad time. Pretend we're part of a big group at a pizza place. Matt, you're a guy who's interested in Janice and trying to make conversation with

her to get to know her better. I'll be a friend of yours who keeps butting in with smart remarks. Janice, you pretend that we're two guys that you know well enough to say hello to, but that's all.

Role-play exercises like these will provide many opportunities for students to learn about emotional reactions. By leading discussions about how people feel in the situations that are role-played and about how the participants could or should react, teachers can help students develop insight into their emotions and confidence in their abilities to cope with stressful situations.

Teachers need to show that emotions are not only acceptable, but also controllable. This can be modeled directly, for example, in situations where the teacher has become angry himself: "Look, I've had about as much of this as I can take. I've tried to be patient and give you time to straighten yourself out, but you've kept bugging me for several days now and I'm starting to get angry. If you don't cut it out and begin to treat me with more respect, I'm going to be forced to resort to punishment. I don't want to do this, but you're not leaving me much choice." In this example the teacher communicates anger, but in a nondestructive and controlled way.

Anger and misunderstandings between students can be dealt with by encouraging the students to verbalize their anger and the reasons for it, rather than to express it physically. The technique of role reversal (Johnson, 1970) is especially useful here. Each student involved can be asked to take the role of the other student as a means of helping him to see the other student's point of view, "Now if you were George, how would you feel after everybody laughed?" This promotes better understanding of the situation, and gives the students practice at verbalizing and controlling hostility instead of expressing it directly. Suggestions for handling disputes between students are given in greater detail in the following chapter.

Teachers must be comfortable with their own emotions if they are to discuss certain taboo subjects productively. Many students never ask the questions they would like to ask about sex or drugs, for example, because they know their teachers cannot tolerate objective discussions of these matters. Discussion is closed off because the teacher has made it clear that no decent person would even consider masturbation, fornication, or pornography, and that anybody who uses drugs is a dope fiend. Other teachers inhibit discussion by overreacting to what they consider to be obscene language. In these classes the student can ask what he wants to ask only if he is capable of using terms such as "penis," "vagina," or "copulation."

If he knows only the slang or street language substitutes for these words, and if he knows that the teacher will not allow use of his terminology, he will not ask his question.

Teachers should try to evaluate objectively their own emotional tolerance in taboo areas. If they can handle discussions in these areas without becoming flustered or upset, they can be a valuable resource to their students. If they cannot, it is probably better to avoid getting into such discussions, since it is not likely that flustered teachers would do much good, and they may well spread some of their inhibitions to their students.

If it is possible to do without penalty, teachers should also avoid situations in which they are trying to inculcate values or standards that they do not believe or accept themselves. Teachers are often put in this position when asked to implement a school's sex or drug "education" program, when the program is more propaganda than education. Generally, it is better for teachers to leave out those parts of the program that they cannot accept or to ask the principal to provide a substitute who can argue for them convincingly (if the principal or school board absolutely insists that these ideas be presented). If the teacher tries to present the ideas himself, his students will almost certainly detect that he does not believe them, and his credibility will be damaged.

Observers may notice teachers communicating negative emotions without realizing they are doing so. Noticeable anxiety may appear, for example, when the principal or some visitor enters the room or when a particular child acts up. Disgust may be registered by shrinking away from physical contact with a student or by a horrified expression following mention of a tabooed subject.

Observers can be of help to teachers by calling their attention to this evidence of negative emotion. This must be done with caution, however, because the teacher's behavior is an instinctive reaction that may be very difficult for him to change or even discuss. Fear or rejection of specific individuals can usually be dealt with effectively by calling the teacher's attention to it, discussing the problem, and suggesting some remedial steps. Changing the teacher's behavior in relation to taboo topics can sometimes be more difficult, however, since this behavior may be connected with a larger pattern of inhibition or neurosis. When this is true, the teacher may strongly resist getting into a discussion of his feelings on the subject. Even here, though, some discussion of how the teacher should behave in these situations in the future should be carried out. This is because certain students will be fascinated or amused by the teacher's negative reaction and may regularly do things calculated to produce it.

At the same time, other students pick up the teacher's unhealthy negative emotions on the subject through imitation of him as a model. Thus some remedial plan of action is needed to prevent things from getting worse.

Summary

In this chapter we have pointed out that students learn from their teacher simply by observing him as a model. Two types of observational learning that result from exposure to a teacher-model were described: imitation, in which the students copy what they see their teacher saying or doing; and incidental learning, in which they observe what he says and does and then use this information to make inferences about his beliefs, attitudes, values, and personal qualities.

When students like and respect their teacher, they will begin to imitate him, as a way to be more like him and to earn his respect and affection. If the students do not like or do not respect their teacher they are less likely to want to imitate him, although they will develop a picture (mostly negative) of his personality by observing him.

Unfortunately, students are also likely to imitate a rejecting and punitive teacher, if they fear his wrath. This is not the positive kind of imitation that a liked and respected teacher induces; it is a frantic attempt to "get on the teacher's good side" and escape or minimize punishment. The students, at least at first, imitate this teacher's behavior not because they think it is good or effective, but because they think the teacher will reward them if they do or will punish them if they do not. However, if bad habits originally learned this way become well established, they can persist long after the students escape the teacher who caused them in the first place.

The students may learn from observing their teacher model at any time, since all that is necessary for such learning to occur is the chance to observe the model. Teachers cannot choose to model at some times but not others; they cannot turn the process on or off at will. However, by learning to monitor their behavior more closely, and to consciously and systematically model when opportunities arise, teachers can use modeling as a teaching tool and can help insure that most of what their students learn from observing them is beneficial.

The most obvious use of deliberate modeling is in a lecture and demonstration. By learning to give clear and effective demonstrations, teachers can minimize their students' learning problems, as well as the time they need to spend repeating and reteaching.

There are other ways, however, for teachers to educate through deliberate modeling. Thinking and problem solving skills can be taught this way if the teacher shares his thinking by verbalizing aloud each step involved in the process of solving a problem. This modeling should illustrate not only the logic and actions involved, but also the use of good scientific practices such as thinking about alternatives before responding and checking each step in a long process before going on to the next.

Intellectual curiosity and a value on learning can be modeled through comments and behavior showing that the teacher is interested in the subject generally and not just the textbook, that he values and will help find answers to students' questions, and that he reads, keeps abreast of current events, and shows other evidence of intellectual activities outside the school setting.

Teachers not only educate (in a more narrow sense) through modeling; they also socialize their students by infusing attitudes and values about behavior. A teacher who models rationality, emotional maturity, politeness and good manners, and personal respect in his classroom behavior will tend to induce these qualities in his students. In contrast, a hostile, sarcastic, or hypercritical teacher will produce a class atmosphere marked by these undesirable qualities.

In general, the teacher has little hope of inducing positive qualities in his students if he does not model them himself. Students rightfully become cynical and resentful when they see a double standard of behavior (one for the teacher, another for them), or when they see clear discrepancy between what the teacher says and does. A basic factor determining where a teacher stands with students is his personal credibility, a quality that often is hard won and easily lost.

Remember, if you want to command positive respect (not fear) from students, you'll have to model what you teach. Students looking for a model who embodies the qualities that you hold up as ideals should find that model in you.

SUGGESTED ACTIVITIES AND QUESTIONS

1. Assume that you are a teacher beginning a new year with a group of students. Outline the points that you plan to make in order to convey your interest in the subject and in the students.

2. Define the situation you plan to teach in (subject content, type of student, grade level, etc.) and role-play activity 1 above with classmates or other teachers. Seek feedback from observers concern-

ing how sincere they felt you were and how interested they were in what you had to say.

3. Use the rating scales at the end of the chapter to observe the modeling behavior of real teachers or apply them to video tapes. Identify positive and negative instances of teacher modeling and attempt to pinpoint any incidental learning that may be taking place. If films are not available, read the case studies in Appendix A (p. 363) and list positive and negative instances of modeling. Compare your list with those that others make.

4. Why does the cooperating teacher often exert a powerful influence upon the student teacher's classroom style?

5. In the example at the beginning of the chapter, Janice Taylor was student teaching in a school that was composed of students who came from homes that were similar (same socioeconomic level, etc.) to Janice's. To be a good model should a teacher necessarily have the same socioeconomic origin or be of the same race as his pupils? What are possible advantages or disadvantages in matching teachers and students this way? Should students be exposed to teachers who have personalities similar to themselves, or will they learn more by being with teachers whose personalities differ markedly from theirs?

6. Why is it relatively useless to tell people to "Do as I say, not as I do"?

7. Why is it that the most powerful effects of modeling are likely to occur at the beginning of the year?

8. Describe in your own words the steps that are included in effective demonstrations.

9. How can a teacher model his curiosity and interest in learning?

10. Explain the following statement: "What is said *about* students can be just as destructive as what is said *to* them."

11. Why do the authors suggest that when students make errors the teacher must do more than give them the correct answers?

12. In what ways can you as a teacher become more credible to your students? Be explicit.

13. Explain, in your own words, how you can help your students to learn that emotions are acceptable and controllable.

FORM 5.1. Getting Help from Students

USE: When teacher requests a student to run an errand or perform a duty
PURPOSE: To see if teacher models politeness and respect for students
*   For each codable instance, code whether or not the teacher shows each of the four behaviors.*

BEHAVIOR CATEGORIES

1. Calls student by name
2. Asks rather than tells. Uses interrogative rather than imperative language form
3. Says "please"
4. Says "thank you"

NOTES:

Doesn't say "please" but asks in polite manner.

Students appear eager to help her.

	CODES							
	1		2		3		4	
	YES	NO	YES	NO	YES	NO	YES	NO
1.	✓		✓			✓	✓	✓
2.	✓		✓			✓	✓	
3.	✓		✓			✓		✓
4.	✓		✓			✓	✓	
5.		✓	✓			✓		✓
6.	✓		✓			✓	✓	
7.	✓		✓			✓	✓	
8.								
9.								
10.								
11.								
12.								
13.								
14.								
15.								
16.								
17.								
18.								
19.								
20.								
21.								
22.								
23.								
24.								
25.								

FORM 5.2. Teacher's Response to Students' Questions

USE: When a student asks the teacher a reasonable question during a discussion or question–answer period
PURPOSE: To see if teacher models commitment to learning and concern for students' interests

Code each category that applies to the teacher's response to a reasonable student question. Do not code if student wasn't really asking a question or if he was baiting the teacher.

BEHAVIOR CATEGORIES
1. Compliments the question ("Good question")
2. Criticizes the question (unjustly) as irrelevant, dumb, out of place, etc.
3. Ignores the question, or brushes it aside quickly without answering it
4. Answers the question or redirects it to the class
5. If no one can answer, teacher arranges to get the answer himself or assigns a student to do so
6. If no one can answer, teacher leaves it unanswered and moves on
7. Other (specify)

NOTES:

#7 Explained that question would be covered in tomorrow's lesson.

CODES

1.	4	26.	
2.	4	27.	
3.	1,4	28.	
4.	4	29.	
5.	4	30.	
6.	3	31.	
7.	4	32.	
8.	4	33.	
9.	7	34.	
10.	4	35.	
11.	4	36.	
12.		37.	
13.		38.	
14.		39.	
15.		40.	
16.		41.	
17.		42.	
18.		43.	
19.		44.	
20.		45.	
21.		46.	
22.		47.	
23.		48.	
24.		49.	
25.		50.	

FORM 5.3. Teacher's Response to Unexpected Answers

USE: When a student answers the teacher's question in a way that is reason-
able but unexpected
PURPOSE: To see if teacher models respect for good thinking when a ques-
tion doesn't lead to the expected response
For each codable instance, code each applicable behavior category
shown by the teacher in reacting to a reasonable but unexpected answer.

BEHAVIOR CATEGORIES
1. Compliments ("Why, that's right! I hadn't thought of that!")
2. Acknowledges that the answer is correct or partially correct
3. Gives vague or ambiguous feedback ("I guess you *could* say that...")
4. Responds as if the answer were simply incorrect
5. Criticizes the answer as irrelevant, dumb, out of place, etc.
6. Other (specify)

NOTES:

*Tends to respond minimally – looking
ahead to the expected answer. Teacher
actually reading Teacher's Manual a
couple of times while children are
responding.*

CODES

1.	3	26.	___
2.	4	27.	___
3.	3	28.	___
4.	3	29.	___
5.	4	30.	___
6.	3	31.	___
7.	3	32.	___
8.	3	33.	___
9.	4	34.	___
10.	3	35.	___
11.	4	36.	___
12.	4	37.	___
13.	3	38.	___
14.	___	39.	___
15.	___	40.	___
16.	___	41.	___
17.	___	42.	___
18.	___	43.	___
19.	___	44.	___
20.	___	45.	___
21.	___	46.	___
22.	___	47.	___
23.	___	48.	___
24.	___	49.	___
25.	___	50.	___

FORM 5.4. Personal Relationships with Students

USE: When teacher has been observed frequently enough so that reliable information is available
PURPOSE: To see if teacher models an interest in individual students
Note any information relevant to the following questions:

1. Do students seek out this teacher for personal contact? Do they show things, make small talk, seek advice? *No. They usually come to him only when they need something (permission, help, supplies).*

2. Does the teacher actively seek out individual students for informal personal contacts or must they come to him? *No informal contacts observed.*

3. Is he accessible to students before, during, and after school hours? *Yes but see #1*

4. When students tell him things, does he listen carefully and ask questions, or does he respond minimally and cut short the conversation? *He often responds curtly or cuts short the conversation by giving a direction.*

5. When the teacher questions students in informal contacts, does he ask open-ended questions seeking their opinions, or does he ask leading or rhetorical questions that elicit only cliché responses or compliance? *No informal questions observed.*

6. How does the teacher react when students mention taboo topics? Can he tolerate discussion, or does he quickly close it off? *Not observed.*

7. In general, does the teacher talk *to* students, or *at* them? Does he use a natural voice, or a special "teacher tone"?

   Teacher is cold, standoffish. Students avoid him. He is "strictly business" in dealing with them. Much "teacher talk".

FORM 5.5. Success Explanations

USE: Whenever teacher makes a comment to explain a student's success
PURPOSE: To see if teacher models appropriate reactions to success, or if
he fosters undesirable incidental learning instead
For each codable instance, code each behavior category that applies.
How does the teacher explain good performance by students?

BEHAVIOR CATEGORIES

1. Native intelligence or ability ("You're smart")
2. Effort or perseverance ("You worked hard, stuck to it")
3. Luck ("Looks like I picked the ones you knew")
4. Easy questions ("You should get those; everybody knows them")
5. Compliance ("You listened carefully, did as you were told")
6. Irrelevant attributes ("You're a big boy")
7. Cheating ("You copied"; "Did someone tell you the answer?")
8. Other (specify)

NOTES:

#8: Sarcasm (what — have you reformed?")

CODES

1.	5	26.	__
2.	4	27.	__
3.	1	28.	__
4.	5	29.	__
5.	1	30.	__
6.	1	31.	__
7.	5	32.	__
8.	8	33.	__
9.	5	34.	__
10.	5	35.	__
11.	__	36.	__
12.	__	37.	__
13.	__	38.	__
14.	__	39.	__
15.	__	40.	__
16.	__	41.	__
17.	__	42.	__
18.	__	43.	__
19.	__	44.	__
20.	__	45.	__
21.	__	46.	__
22.	__	47.	__
23.	__	48.	__
24.	__	49.	__
25.	__	50.	__

FORM 5.6. Failure Explanations

USE: Whenever teacher makes a comment to explain a student's failure
PURPOSE: To see if teacher models appropriate reactions to failure, or
if he fosters undesirable incidental learning instead
For each codable instance, code each behavior category that applies.
How does the teacher "explain" students' failure?

BEHAVIOR CATEGORIES
1. Low intelligence or ability ("You can't keep up")
2. Laziness or lack of perseverance ("You didn't work at it, gave up too easily")
3. Bad luck ("Looks like I picked the ones you didn't know")
4; Difficult questions ("That's a hard one, you're not ready for it yet")
5. Non-compliance ("You didn't listen, didn't do as you were told")
6. Irrelevant attributes
7. No cheating ("See, you can't do it by yourself"; I see no one gave you the answer this time")
8. Other (specify)

CODES

1.	5	26.	
2.	5	27.	
3.	4	28.	
4.	5	29.	
5.	5	30.	
6.	4	31.	
7.	4	32.	
8.	5	33.	
9.	4	34.	
10.		35.	
11.		36.	
12.		37.	
13.		38.	
14.		39.	
15.		40.	
16.		41.	
17.		42.	
18.		43.	
19.		44.	
20.		45.	
21.		46.	
22.		47.	
23.		48.	
24.		49.	
25.		50.	

NOTES:

All "4's" were addressed to the low - level reading group.

#2 and #8: Errors here seemed to be because students were unable to do the work, not because they hadn't listened to directions or tried to follow them.

FORM 5.7. Overemphasis on Misbehavior

USE: *When teacher has been observed frequently enough so that reliable information can be coded*
PURPOSE: *To see if the teacher is fostering undesirable incidental learning about how he expects students to behave*
   Check any of the following observations that are evident in this teacher's class :

_____ 1. Students not allowed to use resource or reference books because they might harm them

_____ 2. Audiovisual self-teaching devices cannot be used without teacher supervision because students might harm the devices otherwise

_____ 3. Students must spend at least a specified minimum time on seatwork, because they won't do neat work if allowed to do something else when they finish early

__✓_____ 4. Students never allowed to correct their own tests

_____ 5. When teacher leaves room, a student is assigned to take down names of anyone who misbehaves

__✓_____ 6. Teacher overdwells on cheating and takes elaborate precautions to prevent it

_____ 7. Teacher spies on students, searches for forbidden objects, etc.

Note any other observations concerning rigid rules and restrictions or other overemphasis on misbehavior:

Allows no talking during seatwork (because students might "cheat"). During a short quiz the teacher told students, "Move your desks apart so you won't be tempted to cheat."

FORM 5.8. Group Climate

USE: When teacher has been observed frequently enough so that reliable information can be coded
PURPOSE: To see if teacher models respect for individuals and avoids practices that foster destructive group climates
   Check any behavior categories that apply to this teacher's classroom behavior.

BEHAVIOR CATEGORIES

POSITIVE

✓ 1. Makes a point of forbidding ridicule or hostile criticism; insists on respect for others

    2. Uses peer tutoring, team learning, or other methods involving cooperation among students

    3. Speaks well of class to visitors

✓ 4. Publicly acknowledges and praises prosocial behavior (sharing, helping others, showing sympathy and good will)

✓ 5. Other (specify) *Frequently uses subtle means of promoting good atmosphere (speaks of "sharing" answers and ideas," "helping" others solve problems, "working together" on projects, etc.)*

NEGATIVE

    1. Encourages or rewards tattling

    2. Publicly compares students or groups, causing embarrassment to one or both

    3. Encourages or rewards destructive, hostile criticism of fellow students

    4. Uses types of competitive practices that allow some students to gain at others' expense

    5. Punishes boys by making them stay with girls (and vice versa)

    6. Allows students to call out answers or insulting remarks when someone can't respond

✓ 7. Has "pets" that get preferential treatment (rewards, privileges, helper roles, etc.)

    8. Picks on certain students, or uses them as scapegoats

    9. Other (specify) *While generally positive, tends to hold up students #6 and #10 as examples to others.*

FORM 5.9. Positive Modeling

USE: When the teacher has been observed frequently enough so that reliable information can be coded
PURPOSE: To see if teacher takes advantage of opportunities to teach through deliberate modeling
Record any information relevant to the following questions:

MODELING THINKING
When the teacher must solve a problem or think through a question, does he think out loud? Does he allow students to hear the steps he goes through, or explain them after giving the answer?

Does this well when reviewing seat work and homework, but often doesn't explain rationale when she answers students questions during discussion.

Does he include activities that allow students to practice thinking and problem-solving (20 questions, brain teasers, solving hypothetical problems)?

Uses drill-like games and contests but none that promotes thinking and problem-solving

MODELING COMMITMENT TO LEARNING
Does the teacher give evidence of a continuing active interest in learning (discuss newspaper or magazine articles, books, TV programs, special events, educational activities of teacher)? *Only in response to a question or comment from class.*

FORM 5.10. The Teacher's Credibility

USE: When teacher has been observed frequently enough so that reliable information can be coded
PURPOSE: To see if teacher's behavior undermines his credibility with his students
    Below is a list of teacher behaviors that tend to undermine the teacher's credibility with students. Check those behaviors that are observable in this teacher.

            1. Teacher is gushy, overdramatic, unconvincingly "warm"

✓   2. Teacher's praise is unconvincing because he continually uses a stock phrase or fails to specify what he is praising

       3. Teacher insists on "nice" or "acceptable" motives and thoughts, or tends to deny or explain away taboo problems rather than deal with them

       4. Teacher will resort to obviously false or exaggerated "reasons" in defending rules, decisions, or opinions, rather than admit mistakes

       5. Teacher promises, when he doesn't yet know whether he can deliver or fails to follow through on announced intentions

       6. When students express fears or suspicions, teacher responds with vague or unconvincing reassurances rather than investigations or detailed explanations

       7. Teacher cannot tolerate differences of opinion on matters of taste or values; tends to foist his own values on the students

       8. Teacher will not admit areas of ignorance or acknowledge mistakes

       9. Teacher tends to talk down to students, sermonize, or repeatedly harp on pet topics or gripes, to the extent that students are alienated or amused

✓   10. Teacher clearly favors or picks on certain students

      11. Students have learned that they can get teacher to change rules, decisions, or assignments by badgering him or complaining

      12. Teacher's assumptions about his students' home backgrounds, values, interests, or life styles are grossly inaccurate

      13. Teacher brushes aside questions on complex or touchy issues by repeating platitudes or oversimplified "reasons" or "solutions"

✓   14. Teacher sometimes appears not to believe what he is saying (specify)

      15. Other (specify)

NOTES:

         Overuses, "Very good, John."

Management b
prevention
problem

CHAPTER

6

Management I: preventing problems

Classroom management is of major concern to almost everyone connected with education (under *classroom management* we include the teacher functions variously described as discipline, control, keeping order, motivation, and establishing a positive attitude toward learning, among others). New teachers often fear that they will not be able to control the class or that the class will not respect them, and even experienced teachers will usually say that establishing good control over the class is a major goal in the first few weeks of the year. Principals and other school administrators reinforce this concern, tending to give low ratings to teachers who cannot control the class or have discipline problems.

Differences in approach to classroom management are very noticeable to observers who get a chance to compare different teachers. Classrooms are often strikingly different from one another in this respect, depending upon each teacher's attitude toward learning and the sort of relationship that he has established with the students. Four of the more commonly observed types of classrooms are the following ones:

1. The class is in continual chaos and uproar. The teacher spends much of his day trying to establish or reestablish control, but he never succeeds for long. Directions and even threats are often ignored, and punishment does not seem to be effective for very long.

2. This class also is noisy, but the atmosphere tends to be more positive. This is largely because the teacher goes to great pains to make school fun for the students, introducing many games and recreational activities, reading stories, and favoring lots of arts and crafts and enrichment activities. There are still problems, however. Many students pay little attention during lessons and group activities, and seatwork is frequently not completed or not done carefully. Lack of attention occurs even though the teacher holds these activities to a minimum and tries to make them as pleasant as possible.

3. This class is quiet and well disciplined. The teacher has established many rules to insure this, and he monitors the students' behavior closely to see that the rules are followed. Infractions are noted quickly and are cut short with a stern warning or with punishment when necessary. The teacher spends a fair amount of time doing this, partly because he is so quick to notice any misbehavior. He appears to be a successful disciplinarian, because the students usually obey him. However, the class atmosphere is uneasy. The observer gets the feeling that trouble is always brewing just under the surface. Furthermore, whenever this teacher leaves the room, the class tends to burst into noise.

4. This class seems to run by itself. The teacher spends most of his time teaching, and very little time is spent in handling discipline problems. The students follow instructions and complete assigned tasks on their own, without close supervision by the teacher. Students involved in seatwork or enrichment activities interact with one another, so noises may be coming from several sources in the room at the same time. However, these tend to be controlled and harmonious sounds coming from students productively involved in activities, rather than disruptive noises that come from boisterous play or disputes. When noise does become disruptive, a simple reminder from the teacher is usually enough to handle the problem. An observer in this class usually senses a certain warmth in the atmosphere and goes away positively impressed.

How are these four very different rooms to be explained? Probably the simplest answer is that the students are different. Perhaps those in the first class are rebellious, while those in the fourth class are well socialized and highly motivated for learning. However, all four types of classes are found in every school, whatever its socioeconomic status. Thus all classroom differences cannot be attributed entirely to the types of schools or students involved. Also, the authors' experience around schools suggests that teachers usually have the same types of classroom atmospheres year after year.

Some teachers have chronic control problems, while others regularly gain respect and obedience with little apparent effort, even from students who were a problem for another teacher the year before. It is likely that teachers mentioned in the example of four types of classrooms would regularly, year after year, show the same consistent patterns of behavior. The first "can't cope," the second "bribes the students," the third "runs a tight ship," and the fourth "has few control problems."

Before reading on in this chapter, take some time to think about these four teachers and list some of the attitudes and behaviors that might help explain each teacher's unique situation. Assume that all four have roughly equivalent groups of students to work with at the beginning of the year. List three attitudes or behaviors for each teacher that might help explain why his classroom environment has evolved along the lines described. What expectations and assumptions might each of these four teachers make about the students and the learning process? What might his students learn from observing him as a model?

Management as motivational stimulation and problem prevention

An important purpose of the examples of classroom management was to help you focus on the teacher's role in shaping the learning environment or atmosphere in his classroom. There is no clear-cut atmosphere early in the year. It develops gradually through the interaction of the teacher with his students. Depending upon the expectations communicated by the teacher, the behavior he models, and the classroom management approach he uses, the same students might respond very differently. This varying behavior can often be seen in junior high and high schools where the same group of students is taught by more than one teacher. The same class that is interested and attentive for one teacher can be rebellious and bored with another.

Generally, the most important determinant of classroom atmosphere is the teacher's method of classroom management, especially his techniques for keeping the class actively attentive to lessons or actively involved in productive independent activities. This is why the present chapter is entitled classroom "management" rather than classroom discipline or control. These latter terms have a connotation that we wish to avoid: the idea that the problem of motivating students in classrooms is primarily one of dealing successfully with their misbehavior.

Although classroom management is often discussed in terms of dealing with misbehavior, research on classroom discipline (Kounin, 1970) and on behavior modification generally (Bandura, 1969) suggests that this approach puts the cart before the horse. Emphasis on behavior problems and on attempting to get rid of them through punishment tends to be an ineffective approach, often making the situation worse (the reasons for this will be explained later in the chapter). A generally much more effective tactic is to stress and reward desirable behavior and use classroom-management techniques that will prevent problems from emerging rather than to deal with problems after they emerge. Thus the key to classroom-management success lies in the things the teacher does ahead of time to create a good learning environment and a low potential for trouble. This enables the teacher to deal successfully with problems by minimizing them through prevention.

This fact was shown most clearly in a series of studies on classroom discipline by Kounin and his associates (Kounin, 1970). These investigators studied many different kinds of teachers and classrooms, using interviews, on-the-spot note taking, and coded video tapes of classroom interaction. They did not try to conduct an experiment or to influence the teachers in any particular way. Instead, they simply observed what went on in the classroom and developed ways to measure relevant teacher and student behavior. Their intent was to find out which teacher behaviors would be correlated with which measures of student behavior. The findings of several studies all pointed to the same result: the teachers' methods of dealing with discipline problems were simply unrelated to the frequency and seriousness of such problems. Measures of discipline techniques failed to differentiate teachers who could not cope with discipline problems from teachers who could handle them successfully and minimize them.

There *were* important and consistent differences between such teachers, however, and measures developed to capture these differences were not highly correlated with measures of "discipline," in the sense that this word is usually understood. Instead, they were measures of classroom-management techniques. They were measures of teacher behaviors that increased the amount of time students spent in profitable work activities and that led to successful resolution of minor inattention problems before they developed into major disruptions. *This is why we will stress repeatedly that successful classroom management is primarily a matter of preventing problems before they occur, rather than an ability to deal with them after they have emerged.*

This is not the whole story, of course. Problems emerge in all classrooms, and some students are disturbed enough to require extraordinary and individualized treatment. Suggestions for dealing with some of these special problems are made in the following chapter, after techniques for general classroom management are discussed.

Essential teacher attitudes

Everyone knows that something as complex as classroom management cannot be reduced to a simple cookbook that applies neatly to all situations. Some people overreact to this basic truth, however, and assume that there are no general rules, that each teacher must discover his own individual style by finding out what works best for him. This is not so. There are general principles that will apply to most situations, and these can be learned and practiced systematically. These principles will not eliminate or solve all problems, but they will handle most problems successfully and at the same time will leave the teacher in the best possible position for handling the remaining problems that require special solutions.

The following sections present specific suggestions for teachers to use in managing their classrooms. Before moving to these teacher behaviors, however, we wish to stress the importance of certain, key teacher attitudes. We discuss these attitudes first because they must be present if the techniques suggested later in the chapter are to be successful. *The various attitudes and behaviors to be described complement and reinforce one another to form an internally consistent and systematic approach to teaching and managing a class. Attempts to use isolated parts of this system as techniques or gimmicks will not succeed for long.* The success of this approach ultimately depends upon the teacher's ability to establish his credibility with students and to gain their respect. To do this, a teacher has to approach students as an individual person, not merely as an impersonal authority figure or "player of the teacher role." A teacher who tries to manipulate students by using aspects of this system as gimmicks or isolated techniques, without having established the personal relationships to back him up, will soon find himself resorting to threat and punishment.

Although many teacher attitudes and other qualities that provide the basis for successful management have been discussed in more detail in the previous two chapters, they will be reviewed briefly here insofar as they relate to classroom management. Basically, these are qualities that will make the teacher someone whom the students will respect and want to please, not merely to obey.

To begin with, the teacher must like the students and respect them as individuals. He need not be overdramatic or even particularly affectionate; if he enjoys being with the students and has genuine concern for their individual welfare, this will come through in his tone of voice, facial expressions, and other everyday behavior. Even young children will quickly adjust to a teacher's personality (Anderson, 1945). There is no need for a typically quiet or undemonstrative teacher to emote in an attempt to impress the students with his concern.

It is important, however, to get close to the student in situations calling for private interactions. A teacher who is standoffish will tend to be perceived as cold by his students and will seem to be talking at them rather than to them, regardless of his good intentions. Therefore, teachers should form the habit of bending down close to students when speaking with them privately. In the early elementary grades, gestures such as patting the head or back, or resting the hand on the shoulder are often effective (unless resented by the student). These are among the ways that teachers can and should nonverbally communicate concern or affection in situations when they are bending down to confer with a child, praising him, or encouraging him. Preschool and early elementary school teachers should use these techniques regularly.

Teachers working with older students ordinarily should not, however. These students will not need physical contact as much as younger ones, and some might resent it or become embarrassed. For adolescents striving toward independence and autonomy, physical contact by an adult can be threatening. However, secondary-level teachers should regularly bend close to students and deal with them at their level during private contacts, and they should also make an effort to know each individual through informal contacts. These associations will provide better understanding of the student's individual interests and needs, knowledge that will be helpful in individualizing instruction in the classroom. They will also provide a basis for showing concern and for establishing a warm relationship with the student.

The teacher who can get close to students and show concern for them is off to a good start. He must also establish and maintain credibility, however. Most students have been exposed to enough discrepancies between what adults preach and what they practice that they do not automatically believe what they are told by adults,

including teachers. Some, especially those from economically depressed areas, may even go so far as to automatically assume that
the adult is always trying to "con" them. They may find expressions
of concern hard to accept as genuine, and may instead see such
expressions as attempts to manipulate them for ulterior motives.
Thus, for some students, respect and belief in the teacher's credibility must actually be established, not merely maintained.

Credibility is established largely by making sure that teaching
and action coincide, and by pointing this modeling out to the class
when necessary. Once the teacher has established himself as a
respectable and likable person and as someone who can be believed,
he will be in a good position to practice classroom management
using the techniques described later. Because the students like and
respect him, they will want to please him and will be more likely
to imitate his behavior and adopt his attitudes. They will also be more
likely to sympathize with him when he is challenged or defied,
instead of allying with the defiant student against him.

Credibility will also provide the structure that the students
want and need. They will be able to depend on what the teacher
says and will be much less likely to test him constantly to see if he
means what he says. Such testing often consumes a great deal of
time in classrooms, especially in disadvantaged neighborhoods. Teachers who take time early in the year to listen to students and to
explain carefully the rationales underlying rules and assignments
are making a wise investment. This ultimately will establish teacher
credibility and reduce the students' tendencies to continue to test
the teacher throughout the year.

Credibility in the teacher also helps enable students to accept
responsibility for their own behavior. When a teacher has established
fair rules and has consistently enforced them, rule breakers can get
angry only at themselves. However, if the teacher lacks credibility
because he makes empty threats or enforces rules inconsistently,
rule breakers who are punished are likely to turn their resentment
against him or feel that he is picking on them ("Johnny did it
yesterday and you didn't do nothing").

The teacher must also possess appropriate expectations if he is
to achieve successful classroom management. Gaining the respect of
the class and establishing credibility will go a long way toward making students willing to conform. However, students will tend to
conform not so much to what the teacher says in words but to what
the teacher actually expects. By interpreting the teacher's behavior,
they will adjust to his habits and learn to identify what he really
means when it differs from what he says. Thus if the class has learned

that when the teacher looks up from a reading group and says, "No talking over there," he really means "Keep the noise down to a tolerable level," they will respond to the second message, not the first. The adaptation would be all right, except that some times the teacher really means "Keep quiet." At these times the students will tend to react to him in the usual way, and misunderstanding and possible resentment may result.

Because of such factors, it is vital for teachers to carefully think through what they really expect from their students and then to follow this up by trying to monitor their own behavior to see that it is consistent with these expectations. This will help eliminate empty, overgeneralized, or inconsistent verbal statements. Observers can be very helpful here, since teachers are often unaware of inappropriate expectations. The teacher described as "bribing" the students in the examples at the beginning of this chapter is a case in point. Even though he was liked and respected by the class, he tended to have discipline problems when trying to organize them for lessons.

Bribing students to learn usually results when a teacher has inappropriate attitudes toward learning. He tends to think of school-related tasks as unrewarding drudgery, and he assumes that students will not enjoy them. This attitude is quickly picked up by the class, who learn to wince, sigh, or protest whenever he mentions stopping a play activity and beginning a lesson. Their behavior will confirm and reinforce the teacher's expectation, and at the same time build up his guilt at the prospect of making them learn. In turn, his guilt will tend to make the teacher minimize the time spent in lessons and start to bribe the students by promising them rewards if they will tolerate the lesson for awhile.

This type of teacher is not really a positive influence on his students, even though he may have the students' affection and, to a degree, their respect. Until he can change his attitudes and expectations about learning and about enjoyment of school activities, the teacher will remain more of a buddy to the class than an educator. His students will very likely do poorly on their achievement tests, and their next teacher the following year will be faced with a rehabilitation job in motivating them for school.

To establish the groundwork for successful classroom management, teachers must have the following personal qualities: (1) they must have the respect and affection of the students; (2) they must be consistent and, therefore, credible and dependable; (3) they must assume responsibility for the students' learning, seeing their own function as primarily one of teaching (as opposed to mothering, babysitting, entertaining, etc.); (4) they must value and enjoy learning and expect the students to have or acquire these same values. Furthermore, the teacher not only must have these basic attitudes and expectations but also be able to communicate them to his students and model them in his behavior.

General management principles

If we assume a teacher has the personal qualities described in the previous section, what specific steps can he take to establish good classroom management? The rest of this chapter and the one that follows will attempt to answer this question, moving from more general to more specific situations, and from techniques that help prevent problems to techniques that must be used in remediating problems after they have appeared.

The recommendations in this section all concern general principles of classroom organization. These principles are based on one or more of the following assumptions: (1) students will be more likely to follow classroom rules when they clearly understand and accept these rules; (2) management should be approached with an eye toward maximizing the time students spend in productive work, rather than from a more negative viewpoint stressing control of misbehavior; (3) the teacher's goal is to develop inner self-control in the students, rather than merely to devise ways of controlling them by exerting his authority; and (4) teachers will minimize discipline problems if their students are regularly engaged in meaningful work geared to their interests and aptitudes.

Establish clear rules where rules are needed

Certain aspects of classroom management recur on a regular basis because they are part of the daily routine. These include such matters as storage of clothing and personal belongings, use of the toilets and drinking fountains, access to paper and other everyday supplies, use of special equipment (supplementary readers, audio-visual aids, art supplies, etc.), and behavior during periods of independent work (e.g., what a student who finishes his seatwork should do while the teacher is still busy with a reading group).

In these or any other situations where a rule is required, the rule should be made very explicit to the students, and the rationale for it should be explained in detail. Explanation is especially important at the beginning of the year. With children in kindergarten or first grade who are new to the school situation, teachers will need to give demonstrations and lessons on the use and care of classroom equipment. Many children will never have used or perhaps never even have seen pencil sharpeners, audiovisual equipment, or certain arts and crafts equipment. Also, with younger children a simple verbal explanation may not be enough. A demonstration followed by an opportunity to practice the behavior on their own may be required before they can do what the teacher wants them to do.

Demonstrations and practice will be less necessary with students who have had school experience, but even these students will need thorough discussions of rules. Each new grade adds some new experiences that they have not been through before. More importantly, teachers differ in their classroom management expectations and demands. Sometimes last year's teacher will have demanded behavior that is directly contradictory to what this year's teacher wants, especially on the matter of what things the student must seek permission to do and what he may do himself without permission. Therefore, each teacher should specify rules clearly and demonstrate the desired behavior if necessary.

Rules should be kept to a minimum and should be clearly needed. If a rule is not supported by an obvious and convincing rationale, it should be discarded or revised. Is the rule an end in its own right or simply a means to an end? If it is a means, does it succeed in achieving the desired end?

Usually, rules are means to ends. Therefore, they should be presented as such to the class, and not overgeneralized or presented as ends in themselves. For example, the rationale underlying rules about how students should behave during periods of seatwork should be based on the idea that no one should disrupt a group lesson the teacher is conducting or disrupt other students who are still involved in seatwork.

There is a range of activities that a student who finishes seatwork could engage in without disturbing either the teacher or the other students still at work (read a supplementary reader, begin an art project, examine a science display, work on homework, talk quietly with another student who has also finished, etc.). This range will vary across teachers and students, of course, but it still should be a range. An overgeneralized rule to fit the situation, such as "When you finish your seatwork you will stay quietly in your seats and not talk to anyone or leave your seats for any reason," would not be justifiable. It is much more restrictive than it should be and will cause more problems than it solves. Instead, the teacher should present the basic goal of avoiding disturbances to the students involved in a group lesson or in seatwork. This could be followed up with a listing of examples of acceptable and unacceptable behavior in this situation.

Ideally, classroom rules should be elicited in guided discussion rather than simply presented as law by the teacher. When teachers clearly define problems that need solution, students are capable of developing rules that will do the job. Participation in the establishment of classroom rules helps the students see the reasonableness of the rules and accept responsibility for keeping them; also, helping to make the rules guides the students in learning to plan their lives rationally and to see themselves as actively controlling their destinies rather than simply responding to external pressures.

When rules are no longer needed or when they no longer do the job they were meant to do, they should be modified or dropped. When presenting any such change, the teacher should be sure to explain the reason for it and not just announce it. Better yet, he can open the problem to class discussion and invite the students to develop their own solution. Good classroom management involves establishing clear rules where rules are needed, avoiding unnecessary rules, reviewing rules periodically and changing or dropping them when appropriate, and involving the students as much as possible in establishing and changing rules.

Let the students assume independent responsibility

There is no reason for teachers to do things that students could be doing for themselves. With proper planning and instruction, even the youngest children can take out and replace equipment, sharpen pencils, open milk cartons, pass out supplies, carry chairs, and form orderly lines by themselves. Older students can also work independently or in small groups, and can check their own work. Yet teachers sometimes insist on doing these things themselves or on controlling them through such rituals as calling out the names of the students one by one. This serves only to create delays, divert the teacher from his teaching task, and retard the development of independent responsibility in the students.

Teachers will sometimes say, "I tried to get them to do it themselves, but they couldn't." In this case the appropriate response is to conduct a demonstration lesson on how to perform the behavior involved and to allow the class to practice it, rather than for the teacher to do it himself or develop a ritual. A little time spent in explanation early in the year and a little patience in tolerating slowness and mistakes while the students learn to act on their own will pay off great dividends later in the year.

Some teachers adopt overly rigid rules on the grounds that they are needed to prevent waste or vandalism. ("If I let them sharpen their pencils they'll sharpen them right down to the eraser." "If

I put out supplementary readers, they'll just steal them." "If I allow them to work in groups they'll just copy from one another or waste time." This attitude represents an avoidance of the problem rather than an attempt to solve it. It also communicates negative expectations to the students. Prevention of this sort is appropriate for infants, but not for even the youngest school children. When students understand the rationales underlying rules, and when they know their teacher expects them to follow these rules, they will do so.

Needless rituals and delays can be avoided by letting students assume all of the classroom management functions that they can handle on their own. This procedure will help minimize the disruptions that often begin when students are idle during lulls in activities and at the same time will help the students develop independence and responsibility.

Minimize disruptions and delays

Management problems start and spread much easier when students are idle or distracted by a disruption than when everyone is involved in productive activity. There are many things teachers can do to hold disruptions and distractions to a minimum.

Thorough daily planning is important here. Problems often begin when a teacher breaks the flow of a lesson or activity because he needs to prepare equipment that could have been prepared earlier or to look something up in his manual. Good preparation will eliminate waiting time whenever possible. Unless there is no alternative, the entire class should never be lined up to do something one at a time. These situations should be handled instead by breaking the class into subgroups or by appointing assistants to help.

For example, suppose the class is preparing to leave for lunch, and that this preparation involves tidying up the room, getting lunches that students have brought with them, and visiting the washroom. Thirty minutes or more can be spent on these activities by regimenting the entire class (holding up each lunch in turn and having the owner come and get it, having students come to the wastebasket one by one to throw away anything they have picked up around their desks, having the entire class form lines to go to the washroom all at the same time, etc.). This can be handled efficiently in a few minutes, however, through grouping. While part of the class get their lunches, another group can clean up their desks and throw away trash, and a third group can use the washroom. As groups finish one activity, they rotate into another. This way the same goals can be accomplished in less time and with much less regimentation by the teacher.

The time needed for distributing paper or other supplies can be cut down by having one student from each row or table pass out the items to his group. Distributing supplies can be facilitated by making sure that such items are stored where the students can get them unaided. In early elementary grades, supplies should be low enough so that the children can reach them, and stored neatly for easy identification and replacement. In general, items should also be stored as close as possible to where they typically are used to cut down traffic in the classroom and reduce spilling and dropping accidents.

Use of storage space should be determined by convenience. Store frequently used items in places where they can most conveniently be taken out and returned. Items that are rarely used or used only at a different time of the year can be stored in the harder to reach areas.

The room should be arranged to promote free and easy traffic flow. Heavily used traffic lanes (areas around the door, the drinking fountain, the coat rack, or lanes between the students' usual seats and special areas for group lessons) should not be obstructed. Traffic lanes should be wide enough for students to move freely without bumping into each other or into some of the furniture.

Delays and waiting time frequently result when there is high demand for something that is in short supply, as when the entire class must use paste from a single jar or get supplies from a single container. Much time can be saved here by storing small items (crayons, paste, pencils, etc.) in several containers instead of a single, large container.

Dead time in junior-high and high-school classes can often be prevented through advance preparation. Unless it is important for the teacher to model the motions involved, complicated diagrams, maps, or mathematical computations should be prepared on the blackboard before class begins or distributed on mimeographed sheets rather than constructed on the board during class. Similarly, many science experiments and other demonstrations can be partially prepared ahead of time when the preparations themselves do not need to be demonstrated to the class. Often the students might be usefully involved in these preparation activities, especially when they must be done during class time; the job will be speeded up and, at the same time, students will be given a chance to participate more actively in the demonstration or experiment.

Bear in mind that when students are asked to wait with nothing to do, four things can happen and three of them are bad: the student may remain interested and attentive; he may become bored or fatigued, losing his interest and ability to concentrate; he may become distracted or start daydreaming; or he may actively misbehave. Therefore, plan room arrangement, equipment storage, preparation of equipment or illustrations, and transitions between activities so that needless delays and confusion are avoided.

Plan independent activities as well as organized lessons

Usually students spend a good part of their school day working at their seats on assigned seatwork or on activities they have selected for themselves. Disruptions often originate with students who are not working on their assigned work or who have finished it and have nothing else to do. Sometimes teachers bring trouble on themselves by failing to provide worthwhile seatwork or by failing to have back-up plans prepared if seatwork is completed more quickly than anticipated. Kounin (1970) found that such teachers tended to have more classroom management problems than their better prepared colleagues.

Some teachers may need to be reminded that seatwork is (or should be) a basic part of the curriculum and not merely a time filler. It should provide the students with opportunities to practice the skills they are learning or to apply them in solving problems. If properly designed and used, the exercises also provide teachers with good information about how each student is progressing. Therefore, teachers should plan seatwork as carefully as they plan the rest of their lessons, and should make its importance clear to the students when assigning it. The students should know which skills or abilities they are to use and develop in doing the assignment.

The assignment should be specific (the teacher should assign particular exercises and not merely provide enough problems to keep everyone busy without particularly caring how many or which ones they do), and the work should be used for diagnosis and remediation (the teacher will check the work and follow up with students who do not understand). Checking seatwork will insure that students are held accountable for the assignment and will make it likely that the assignment will have its desired effects.

In addition to being specific about the seatwork assignment, the teacher should provide clear options for students who finish. At times these options may mean additional specific assignments (e.g., reviewing the story they are going to study in reading group later). Where no specific assignment is appropriate, the teacher may wish to make some suggestions. In any case, the students should know clearly what options are available to them if they finish their seatwork early. They should not have to repeatedly come and interrupt the teacher to ask if one thing or another is permissible. Nor should they be tied so closely to the teacher that he has to redirect their work every 15 or 20 minutes.

The teacher should also establish a clear-cut rule regarding getting help with seatwork. What is a student to do if he is not sure how to do the work or if he has not understood the directions clearly? Different teachers will prefer different answers to this question (ask another student, come up to the teacher but wait quietly until the teacher can conveniently turn his attention from the group, ask a designated tutor or assistant, etc.). Regardless of what rule is adopted, however, it should be made very clear to the students.

Students must be provided with appropriate seatwork and other independent activities so that they will be profitably occupied when the teacher is busy with small group instruction. Each student should know what his assignment is, what he should do if he cannot continue, and what he can or should do when he finishes. These will provide a basis for responsible self-guidance, and will minimize problems resulting from idleness or confusion about what to do.

Encourage procedural questions

Teachers should expect and desire the students to seek help when they need it and should provide ways for them to get it. Confusion and uncertainty about how to do work assignments are to be expected as daily occurrences. Discovering and helping to clear up these problems are part of the essence of the teacher's role. After all, if students could learn new skills quickly and easily after seeing a single demonstration, they would not need a specially trained teacher. Yet, some teachers regularly react with blame, frustration, or disgust when students indicate they do not understand. Even when they follow up this initial reaction with remedial teaching, the damage is done.

Students in the classes of such teachers learn to cover up their inadequacies by giving the appearance that they understand the work. They will copy from a neighbor rather than leave an answer blank or seek out the teacher for help. Whether or not they really do understand, they will nod their heads reassuringly if the teacher asks, "Do you understand?" after a demonstration or a seatwork assignment. In general, they will develop the mechanisms that John Holt (1964) describes in *How Children Fail* by attempting to please the teacher at all costs and to avoid any disclosure of confusion. Student defensiveness is almost certain to develop unless teachers view learning difficulties as legitimate and expected and see students' efforts to bring them to their attention as desirable.

Recognition of a student's difficulties does not mean that a teacher should drop whatever he is doing the minute a student expresses a problem or that he should end up doing the student's work for him. It does mean that the teacher should plan to meet these needs and to set up ways to arrange for communication of problems and remediation through reteaching. If he does not want students coming to him with seatwork problems while he is conducting a group lesson, he should make this clear to them. At the same time, he should make it clear that they are welcome to come to him when the lesson is over, or that he will go over the seatwork assignment and check each individual's progress before beginning another group lesson.

With students who appear convinced that they cannot do the work or who regularly try to get the teacher to do it for them, a fine line must be drawn between two extremes. First, the teacher should repeatedly encourage the student and express the belief that he will be able to succeed with continued efforts. The student's expression of inability should not be accepted or even indirectly legitimized through such comments as, "Well, at least try."

On the other hand, the teacher's availability and willingness to help must also be stressed. It must be made clear to the student that he will learn the most by doing as much as he can for as long as he can and, therefore, he should not come to the teacher at the first sign of problems. However, if he has tried at length to solve a problem and has not been able to do so, he should seek help. Consistent application of these principles, along with effective reinforcement as the student progresses, will help him both to master the skills and to acquire confidence and a healthier self-concept.

Here is how the situation might be handled appropriately:

STUDENT: I can't do number four.

TEACHER: What part don't you understand?

STUDENT: I just can't do it.

TEACHER: Well, I know you can do part of it, because I see that you've done the first three problems correctly here. The fourth problem is similar, but just a little harder. You start out the same way, but then you have to do one extra step. Review the first three problems, and then start number four again and see if you can figure it out on your own. I'll come by your desk in a few minutes and see how you're doing.

Compare this with the following inappropriate treatment:

STUDENT: I can't do number four.

TEACHER: You can't? Why not?

STUDENT: I just can't do it.

TEACHER: Don't say you can't do it—we never say we can't do it. Did you try hard?

STUDENT: Yes, but I can't do it.

TEACHER: Well, I see that you did the first three problems. Maybe if you went back and worked a little longer on the fourth problem you could do it too. Why don't you work at it a little more and see what happens?

In the first example, the teacher communicated positive expectations and provided help in the form of a specific suggestion about how the student should proceed. Yet, the teacher did not give him the answer or do the work for him. In the second example, the teacher communicated half-hearted and somewhat contradictory expectations and did nothing to move the child out of the impasse he had reached.

Teachers must not only provide appropriate seatwork and clear-cut procedures for students to follow when they need help, they must also follow up by providing appropriate help when students request it. All of this support will insure that students get the most out of their seatwork assignments and, at the same time, will minimize the potential for management problems that originate when students are idle or confused.

Cueing and reinforcing appropriate behavior

Previous sections have discussed how teachers can arrange the classroom to minimize management problems and can establish rules and procedures to insure that students are clear about what is expected of them. However, rules will not handle all situations, and teachers need to know how to efficiently and effectively give on-the-spot instructions when they are needed. Also, regardless of whether a general rule or a specific instruction is involved, teachers should clearly specify and reward desirable behavior in their students as a means of insuring that students know what to do and are positively motivated to do it.

Stress positive, desirable classroom behavior

Students, like everyone else, find learning easier and more pleasant when someone is showing them what *to* do rather than what *not to* do. This is why most lessons begin with a demonstration or explanation that the students watch and then imitate. Teachers would not think of teaching addition by naming all the sums that 2 + 2 do not equal. In general, learning a positive skill or concept directly is easier than to have to learn it by trial and error.

Teachers are usually aware of the value of the positive approach when applied to the teaching of school subjects, but they (and everyone else) often forget it when dealing with behavior. The result is a string of "don'ts," with too much emphasis on what the students should not be doing instead of on what they should be doing. Such an attitude is not helpful to the students, and it may create anxiety or resentment against the teacher. Therefore, teachers must train themselves to give behavioral prescriptions in positive terms, as in the following examples.

Positive Language	*Negative Language*
Close the door quietly.	Don't slam the door.
Try to work these out on your own without help.	Don't cheat by copying your neighbor.
Quiet down—you're getting too loud.	Don't make so much noise.
Sharpen your pencil like this (demonstration).	That's not how you use a pencil sharpener.
Carry your chair like this (demonstrate).	Don't make so much noise with your chair.
Sit up straight.	Don't slouch in your chair.
Raise your hand if you think you know the answer.	Don't yell out the answer.
When you finish, put the scissors back in the box and put the bits of paper on the floor into the wastebasket.	Don't leave a mess.
These crayons are for you to share—use one color at a time and put it back when you're finished so others can use it too.	Stop fighting over those crayons.
Your understanding is important here, so use your own ideas. When you do borrow ideas from another author, be sure to acknowledge them. Even here, though, try to put them in your own words.	Don't plagiarize.
Speak naturally when making	Don't just read your report to us.

your report. State the facts like
you would when talking to a
friend.

As you conduct the experiment,   Take your time when doing this
remember to note the caution   experiment, or you'll mess it
statements given in the instruc-   up.
tions. Be sure you have checked
out the things mentioned there
before proceeding to the next
step.

Be ready to explain how you ar-   Don't just guess.
rived at your answer—why
you think it is correct.

Sometimes negative statements are appropriate, as when a
student is doing something that must be stopped immediately (fighting, causing a major disruption); even here, however, negative remarks should be followed up with positive statements telling the
student what he should be doing instead. Teachers should phrase
their behavioral instructions in positive, specific language that clearly
indicates the desired behavior.

Praise desired behavior

In addition to stating desired behavior by phrasing rules in a
positive way, teachers should follow up by praising or otherwise
rewarding such behavior when it is observed. Research on behavior
modification (Bandura, 1969) has shown this to be a powerful tool,
both for reinforcing desirable behavior in students who show it and
for modifying the behavior of those who do not.

However, most teachers are much quicker to criticize misbehavior than they are to praise desirable behavior. In addition, much
of the praise that *is* given is simply for isolated right answers or for
relatively unimportant behavior ("Jack has his hands folded and is
ready to line up"). Praise for extended effort or for careful work is
not nearly as frequent as it should be.

Students will strive for attention and praise from a teacher they
respect. Therefore, their behavior can be shaped and controlled by a
teacher who makes his praise contingent upon showing desirable behavior. This opportunity will be lost, however, if the teacher fails to
praise often enough to be effective, or if he praises inappropriately.

Failure to praise sufficiently will lead to trouble with certain
students—those who most need approval and attention from the
teacher. When they are not getting enough payoff through ordinary

participation in class activities, these students will develop special ways to obtain teacher attention (many will settle for attention if they cannot get praise). They may find, for example, that they can regularly get a strong teacher response by whistling, going to the pencil sharpener, wadding up paper and tossing it in the wastebasket, falling out of their seats, or using some other attention-getting mechanism.

For certain students, even the negative teacher attention they elicit through mechanisms is better than no attention at all. Also, this behavior often leads to a reward, eventually. Teachers, either unconsciously or because they recognize the need for attention that such behavior signifies, frequently will follow up by coming to the student to talk with him privately about his behavior or to encourage him to get involved in work assignments. This will often lead to praise or expressions of warmth or concern, so that in effect the student ends up by getting rewarded for misbehaving.

Instead of focusing on attention-getting behavior when it appears, teachers should ignore it. If it is too disruptive to be ignored, they should respond in a way that minimizes attention to the behavior itself and instead leads the student back to the lesson or to productive involvement in his assignment. (Methods for minimizing attention-getting behavior are discussed in the next chapter.)

It may be better for the student to get teacher attention through provocative behavior than not to get it at all. However, the best course for both the teacher and the student would be for the teacher to pay closer attention to him when he is behaving desirably and to praise this behavior. Praising desirable behavior is especially necessary with slower students who find the work difficult and need encouragement from the teacher to help give them the confidence and incentive to persevere.

In addition to praising frequently enough, teachers need to praise appropriately. Some guidelines for praising appropriately follow.

1. Praise should be simple and direct. It should be delivered in a natural voice, without gushing or overdramatizing. Even very young children will see theatrics as insincere and phony.

2. Praise is usually more effective if it is given in straightforward declarative sentences, "That's very good, I never thought of that before," instead of gushy exclamations, "Wow!" or rhetorical questions, "Isn't that wonderful!" The latter are condescending and are more likely to embarrass the child than reward him.

3. The particular behavior or accomplishment being praised should be clearly specified. Any noteworthy effort, care, or perseverance should be recognized, "Good! You figured it out all by yourself. I like the way you stuck with it without giving up," instead of "Yes! That's right." Whenever a student acquires a new skill, this should be noted, both to praise the student and to reinforce the value of the skill: "I notice you've learned to use a variety of different kinds of sentences in your compositions. They're more interesting to read now. Keep up the good work."

4. Teachers should use a wide variety of words when praising students. Some teachers lean on a single stock phrase that is overused, and it soon becomes meaningless to the class. It begins to sound insincere and gives the impression that the teacher has not really paid much attention to the students.

5. Verbal praise should be backed with nonverbal communication of approval. Somehow, "That's good, Billy," just is not very rewarding when it is said with a deadpan expression, a flat tone of voice, and an air of distraction or apathy. The same phrase is much more effective when delivered with a smile, a tone communicating appreciation or warmth, or gestures such as a pat on the back. Statements like "You were really good today" are ambiguous. Students, especially the younger ones, may take them as praise for compliance rather than for learning. These statements are most frequently made at the ends of lessons or other structured activities. Instead of "You were very good today," teachers should praise in a way that unambiguously rewards learning efforts: "I'm very pleased with the way you read this morning. I was especially pleased with the way you pronounced the initial consonants and how you read with so much expression. You made the conversation between Billy and Mr. Taylor sound very real. Keep up the good work."

Students will be encouraged by a teacher and motivated to work for him if they know that he sees and appreciates their efforts and progress. Teachers can create this condition by making a concerted effort to praise student effort and progress, using natural, genuine language and describing the behavior being praised in specific terms.

Getting and holding attention
So far we have discussed general personal qualities and behavior of teachers that can help establish a good classroom atmosphere and maximize the time and effort students devote to learning. In this

section we will suggest techniques for dealing with everyday problems of minor inattention and disruption caused by boredom, fatigue, distraction, or other situational variables. Techniques for dealing with more serious and recurrent problems are discussed in the next chapter.

Kounin's (1970) research suggests that the most successful way to handle situational inattention and distraction is to prevent it from happening or, if it does occur, to check it before it spreads and becomes more serious. Several techniques for accomplishing this are discussed in this section. These techniques help focus the students' attention to a lesson and thereby minimize the frequency of disruptions that start as inattention or distraction. The basic principle involved is for the teacher to behave in ways that make the students attend at all times, not merely those times when he is dealing with them individually.

Focus attention when beginning lessons

Teachers should establish that they expect each student's full attention to lessons at all times, including times when another student is reciting or answering a question. There are several techniques teachers can use to do this.

First, the teacher should be sure to get the students' attention before beginning a lesson. Some teachers fail to do so or even deliberately use the technique of starting in a loud voice as a way of attempting to get inattentive students to pay attention. This is generally not recommended, since it is inconsistent with several ideas that the teacher should be trying to promote. Briefly, it connotes rudeness; it places the teacher in the position of talking *at* rather than *to* the students; it reinforces the idea that one gains attention by talking louder than others and breaking into their conversations; and it causes the teacher to begin a lesson without proper orientation and without having the entire class set to listen and focus their attention properly.

For these reasons, teachers should never launch into lessons without having gained the full attention of everyone. For this purpose, the teacher should have a standard signal that tells the class, "We are now ready to formally begin the lesson." The particulars of this signal will vary according to teacher preferences and probably will vary from lesson to lesson in the same teacher. One teacher might prefer, "All right, let's begin," while another might say, "Everyone turn to page 62." Whatever the particular method, the teacher should develop a predictable, standard way of introducing each type of lesson. This will tell the students that the transition between activities is over and the new activity is about to begin.

After giving this initial signal, the teacher should pause very briefly to allow the signal to take effect. Then, when he has attention, he should begin briskly. Ideally, he should start with a comment or two describing what is going to be done in this lesson. This will give the class an overview to help focus their attention and provide motivation for learning. The teacher should then go right into the first part of the lesson proper.

Teachers should review their expectations regarding responses to these signals early in the school year. With children in the early grades, this might take the form of a structured lesson, in which the teacher models the signal, explains what the children are to do when they hear it, and then has them practice it a few times. While signal responses can be introduced less formally with older students, nevertheless, the point should be made very clear that when the signal is given, everyone is expected to concentrate fully on the teacher and the lesson at hand.

The pause between the giving of the signal and the beginning of the lesson should be relatively brief, just long enough for the students to follow the direction and focus their attention. If the pause is too long, some students will begin to lose this sharp focus. Therefore, the teacher should intervene quickly and directly if one or a few students do not respond. If the students are looking at the teacher, he should communicate through expression and gesture that they should now follow the instructions and pay attention. If a student is not looking, the teacher should call his name. Usually this by itself will be enough; if not, a very brief focusing statement can be added, "Look here."

Once into the lesson, the teacher should follow the guidelines for dealing with inattention presented in a later section of this chapter. Teachers should know how to keep attention as well as how to get it initially. Several aspects of the teacher behaviors that help students maintain constant attention are discussed below.

Keep lessons moving at a good pace

Teachers often begin with good attention but lose it by spending too much time on minor points or by causing everyone to wait while students respond individually, while equipment is passed out individually, and so forth. Attention will wander when students are waiting or when something they clearly understand is being needlessly rehashed. Lessons in which material that all or most of the students know thoroughly is being reviewed are abused in this way by some teachers. When students clearly know the material, the review should be cut short. There is no need to ask the next 35 questions simply because they are in the teacher's manual. If certain students in the group do need further review, it would be better to work with them individually or to form them into a special group rather than to make all the others go through the review too.

Monitor attention during lessons

Throughout the lesson, the teacher should regularly scan the class or group he is teaching. The students are much more likely to keep their attention focused on the lesson if they know that the teacher regularly watches everyone (both to see if they are paying attention and to note signs of confusion or difficulty). In contrast, the teacher who buries his nose in the manual, rivets his eyes on the blackboard, or tends to look only at the student who is now reciting or answering the question is asking for trouble.

Show variety and unpredictability in asking questions

The teacher should hold all students accountable for paying attention to the entire lesson and for learning all of the material, not just the part they have been asked to recite or demonstrate. The best way to do this is to develop variety and unpredictability in asking questions. The students should know that they may be called on at any time, regardless of what has gone on before, and that they may be asked any sort of question (for example, after a response the teacher might ask, "Paul, what did Ted say? Do you agree with him?").

Such techniques are useful for keeping students accountable for attending to the entire lesson. For example, the teacher should occasionally ask a student to repeat an answer just given by another student, or perhaps to state whether the answer was correct or incorrect. Complete unpredictability in questioning style also helps. The teacher should occasionally ask more than one question of a given student, or question him again shortly after he has answered a previous question.

Teachers who are too predictable encourage their students to develop undesirable habits. The most obvious example is the teacher who regularly has students read one paragraph in a reader and regularly goes from one end of the group or row to the other. This behavior encourages the students to figure out which paragraph they are going to read and to practice on that paragraph rather than pay attention to each paragraph as it is read by someone else. Similarly, whenever the teacher assigns problems in a predictable pattern (according to seating, alphabetically, etc.) some students will respond by attending only to the material they are going to be accountable for.

Other predictable teacher questioning styles can also have

undesirable results. For example, when the teacher calls a student's name before asking the question, all of the other students in the class know that they are not going to be required to answer the question. This may cause some of them to turn their attention to something else rather than to thinking about the question and how they would answer it. Similarly, if the teacher calls for a show of hands and regularly calls on only those who raise their hands, he is encouraging certain students to "tune out."

Other potentially undesirable things that students can learn from observing predictable patterns are: "Teacher always asks the person sitting next to him to read first." "If I answer one question, I won't be called on again until everyone else has been questioned." "If I raise my hand and give the impression that I understand, the teacher won't check me out." "When we put practice examples on the board, the teacher always takes them in the same order that they are in the book."

Predictable teacher behavior of this sort is almost always picked up by the class. The result, with some students, is a search for ways to "beat the system." This means less attention and, in the long run, less learning.

Stimulate attention periodically

When things become too predictable and repetitive, the mind tends to wander. There are several things teachers can do to help insure continual attention as a lesson or activity progresses.

The teacher's own variability is one important factor. There is no need for theatrics, but lectures delivered in a dull monotone with a minimum of facial expressions and gestures soon produce yawns. Teachers should speak loud enough for everyone to hear and should see that the students do so, too. More importantly, they should modulate their tone and volume to help provide stimulation and break monotony. It also helps to use a variety of techniques within the lesson so that it does not settle into an overly repetitive or predictable pattern. Lectures should alternate with demonstrations, group responses, and reading, or short factual questions with thought-provoking discussion questions.

Even extended presentations usually can be broken into several parts. By changing voice inflection or by using transitional signals, "All right," "Now," and others, the teacher can help stimulate attention by cueing the students that they are now moving into a new aspect of the presentation.

In addition to these more subtle techniques, attention can and should be directly stimulated at times. For example, the teacher can set up careful attention to a question by challenging the class, "Now here's a really hard question—let's see who can figure it out," or by creating suspense, "Let's see, who will I call on next?" When the type of question changes, this can be noted in a statement that will call the students' attention to the change and at the same time stimulate interest: "All right, let's see if we understood the story." "All right, you seem to know the theory, now let's see if you can apply it to a practical problem."

In discussions, the teacher can model careful listening, and can stimulate it in students by sometimes asking them to show that they have listened to and understood what a classmate has just said before giving their own opinion.

In using these techniques to insure accountability, the teacher must be careful to present them in a way that avoids threatening the students. These techniques are to be used for challenging the class, stimulating interest, and avoiding predictability—not to catch inattentive students in order to embarrass or punish them. If misused this way, they will only cause resentment and will not have the desired positive effects.

In general, these techniques should be used in ways that do not call attention to the technique itself. Emphasis on the technique may cause anxiety or resentment, or at least distract attention from the content focus at hand. It usually would not be appropriate for a teacher to say, "Remember, I might call on you at any time to tell me what's happening, so pay attention." It would be better to simply use this technique without calling attention to it, meanwhile stimulating interest in the topic and communicating expectations for attention in more positive ways.

Teachers can help insure continual attention to lessons and discussions if they move at a brisk pace, monitor all of the students, stimulate attention periodically through both subtle and direct techniques, and enforce accountability through variety and unpredictability in questioning patterns.

Terminate lessons that have gone on too long

This is especially important for younger students, whose attention span for even the best lesson is limited. When the group clearly is having difficulty in maintaining attention, it is better to end the lesson early than to doggedly continue. When lessons go on after the point where they should have been terminated, more and more of the teacher's time is spent compelling attention, and less of the student's time is spent thinking about and learning the material being taught. Teachers are usually aware of this, but they sometimes pursue a lesson anyway because they do not want to get off their schedule.

This attitude is self-defeating. Maintaining the schedule is no victory if it has been won at the cost of rising tensions in the teacher and class. Also, the material will probably have to be retaught to some extent since students do not learn as efficiently under these conditions as they do under more favorable ones. Thus the wise teacher tailors his schedule to the needs of his students rather than trying to force the whole class into his mold.

Teachers sometimes needlessly prolong an activity because they want to give each student a chance to participate individually. This often happens in recitation lessons and in activities such as Show-and-Tell. While the teacher's purpose in wanting to give everyone their chance is laudable, it is not appropriate for this type of activity. When recitation becomes boringly repetitive or when Show-and-Tell becomes stilted and predictable, the teacher should move on to something else. However, it is important to see that students who didn't get their chance to participate one day can do so the next. Sometimes teachers allow the same small group of students to dominate Show-and-Tell activities continually (Rist, 1970).

Some teachers deliberately prolong repetitive activities in order to use them as a break or an opportunity to do paper work. For this reason, Show-and-Tell sometimes goes on for an hour in certain early elementary classrooms. Similarly, older students are sometimes asked to read aloud from readers or to make repetitive recitations when these activities are not really needed or useful. As a result, the students become bored and restless, and their respect and credibility for the teacher can be damaged.

Students know that if an activity is really important and if a teacher is really interested, he will be actively participating and paying careful attention to what is happening. Instead, if he is only paying minimal attention while doing paper work, even very young children will become bored. They know a disinterested babysitter when they see one.

Summary
In this chapter we have pointed out that the key to successful classroom management is prevention—teachers do not have to deal with misbehavior that never occurs. The chapter goes on to suggest prevention techniques that teachers can use to hold management problems to a minimum.

Many problems originate when students are crowded together, forced to wait, or idle because they have nothing to do or do not know what to do. Crowding can be minimized in several ways.

Classroom arrangement and equipment storage should be planned so that traffic is minimized and needed items are quickly and easily accessible. Problems that occur when everyone wants or needs the same item can be reduced by stocking several items rather than just one, or by storing in several small containers rather than one large one.

Waiting can be minimized by allowing students to handle most management tasks on their own, by eliminating needless rituals and formalities, by simultaneously assigning different subgroups to do different jobs rather than having the whole class tackle only one job at a time, and by establishing rules where needed.

Confusion and idleness can be minimized by preparing appropriate independent work assignments in sufficient quantity and variety, and by seeing that students know what to do if they finish their present assignment or if they get stuck and need help.

The preceding aspects of teacher planning and preparation will minimize problems, although they must be complemented by appropriate everyday classroom teaching behavior. In particular, it is important to specify desired behavior in positive terms, to notice and call attention to positive behavior when it appears, and to specifically praise students for producing it.

It is especially important to look for and praise students' efforts and progress in their work. The preventive planning mentioned previously will help make the classroom a good environment for learning; emphasis on positive behavior, appropriate attention, and praise from the teachers will help motivate students to make the best use of this environment.

Good planning and preparation and good motivating strategies will provide a solid basis for preventive classroom management. It is then up to the teacher to follow through by using teaching strategies that will maximize student attention to lessons and involvement in productive activities. Teachers should establish clear signals to gain students' attention and alert them to the fact that an activity is beginning.

Upon gaining attention, they should provide a brief overview or advance organizer to tell the students what is coming and help them mentally prepare for it. Then they should keep the activity moving at a brisk pace, avoiding unnecessary delays. If an activity has gone on too long, it should be terminated.

To help hold students accountable for the material and to stimulate their continuing attention, teachers should vary their questioning patterns and avoid falling into repeated, predictable patterns that tempt certain students to try to beat the system.

Teachers who learn and consistently apply the strategies presented in this chapter will maximize productive student activity and minimize the time students spend "in neutral" or misbehaving. Remember, though, that the classroom-management approach presented here is an integrated system. Each aspect of it is important, and all aspects must occur in combination and mutually reinforce one another to be maximally effective. Attempts to use isolated parts as techniques are unlikely to succeed, especially over a long period.

SUGGESTED ACTIVITIES AND QUESTIONS

1. Emphasis in this chapter and the two previous chapters has been placed on the need for teachers to attend to *positive,* not negative, student behavior. Why do you feel that many teachers spend too much time reacting to negative behavior, especially of a minor sort?

2. This chapter and previous chapters have also communicated the need for teachers to make learning an enjoyable process *per se* rather than indirectly or subconsciously teaching students that school assignments are done only to get a reward—adult approval, opportunity to play a game, a high grade, and so forth. Teachers sometimes do an excellent job in planning useful and enjoyable learning activities only to undermine their efforts to establish the attitude that learning is a viable end *per se* by telling students such things as, "You've done so well today that I am going to give you a free hour after lunch so you can do the things you really want to do." In general, what guidelines should a teacher follow when he summarizes learning activities? Apply your ideas by returning to the case study of Mrs. Turner that was presented in Chapter 1. What would be an effective way to end the lesson she presented? Write out in a few sentences your ending and compare your response to the endings written by others.

3. Describe in your own words how teachers can praise appropriately. What type of student will be most difficult for *you* to praise? Why?

4. Why is it suggested that teachers show variety and unpredictability in asking questions? Watch a video tape of a teacher conducting a class discussion and determine whether the teacher's questioning style is unpredictable.

5. Think about the grade level you teach or plan to teach and

specify the minimum set of rules that will be observed in your room. Be sure to state your rules in positive terms. Are your rules really essential for establishing a good learning climate? Why?

6. Describe how you will establish rules in your classroom and what criteria you will use for adding or deleting rules as the year progresses.

7. Describe in your own words the importance of preventing discipline problems before they occur, and describe preventive steps that teachers can take to reduce the number of discipline problems that they will face.

8. The teacher, while conducting a reading group, notices two students talking loudly at table 1 while three other students at table 1 are busily engaged in independent activities. Should the teacher stop the misbehavior? If so, how? Should the teacher focus on desirable or undesirable behavior? After you read Chapter 7 return to this question and see if you would answer it in the same way.

FORM 6.1. Transitions and Group Management

USE: During organizational and transition periods before, between, and after lessons and organized activities
PURPOSE: To see if teacher manages these periods efficiently and avoids needless delays and regimentation
How does the teacher handle early morning routines, transitions between activities, and clean-up and preparation time?

Record any information relevant to the following questions:

1. Does the teacher do things that students could do for themselves?

2. Are there delays caused because everyone must line up or wait his turn? Can these be reduced with a more efficient procedure?

3. Does the teacher give clear instructions about what to do next before breaking a group and entering a transition? *Students often aren't clear about assignment so they question her during transitions and while she is starting to teach next group.*

4. Does the teacher circulate during transitions, to handle individual needs? Does he take care of these before attempting to begin a new activity? *Mostly, problem is poor directions before transition, rather than failure to circulate here.*

5. Does the teacher signal the end of a transition and the beginning of a structured activity properly, and quickly gain everyone's attention? *Good signal but sometimes loses attention by failing to start briskly. Sometimes has 2 or 3 false starts.*

Check if applicable:

_____ 1. Transitions come too abruptly for students because teacher fails to give advance warning or finish up reminders when needed

_____ 2. The teacher insists on unnecessary rituals or formalisms that cause delays or disruptions (describe)

__✓__ 3. Teacher is often interrupted by individuals with the same problem or request; this could be handled by establishing a general rule or procedure (describe) *See #3 above.*

__✓__ 4. Delays occur because frequently used materials are stored in hard to reach places *Pencil sharpener too close to reading group area, causing frequent distractions.*

_____ 5. Poor traffic patterns result in pushing, bumping, or needless noise

_____ 6. Poor seating patterns screen some students from teacher's view or cause students needless distraction

_____ 7. Delays occur while teacher prepares equipment or illustrations that should have been prepared earlier

---

FORM 6.2. Poor Attention to Lessons

USE: When teacher is having difficulty keeping students attentive to a lesson
PURPOSE: To identify the probable cause of the poor attention
     When students are notably inattentive to a lesson or activity, what is
the apparent reason? (Check any that apply)

    _____ 1. Activity has gone on too long
    _____ 2. Activity is below students' level or is needless review
    _____ 3. Teacher is continually lecturing, not getting enough student
             participation
     ✓ 4. Teacher fails to monitor attention—poor eye contact
     ✓ 5. Teacher overdwells, needlessly repeating and rephrasing
    _____ 6. Teacher calls on students in an easily predictable pattern
    _____ 7. Teacher always names student before asking question
     ✓ 8. Activity lacks continuity because teacher keeps interrupting
             (specify cause for interruption)
    _____ 9. Activity lacks variety, has settled into an overly predictable or
             boring routine
    _____ 10. Other (indicate)

Frequent delays while teacher finds place in manual. This is also main reason for poor eye contact. #5 often asks teacher for attention (and gets it) but then instead of teaching the teacher elaborates for 30-40 seconds on why the students should listen and when he ends the sermon and begins the lesson several students have "drifted" away.

CHAPTER 7

Management II: coping with problems effectively

Consistent use of the classroom management techniques discussed in the previous chapter will hold inattention and misbehavior problems to a minimum, especially if the discussions, seatwork, and other activities and assignments are enjoyable and appropriate to the students' needs and interests. Some problems will still occur, however, and the teacher must be prepared to cope with them effectively. The present chapter contains suggestions on how teachers can train themselves to observe such problems when they occur, to accurately diagnose their causes, and to respond to them with appropriate action.

Dealing with minor inattention and misbehavior

This section explains how teachers can respond to minor incidents of inattention in ways that will check them before they become serious or begin to spread. (More serious misbehavior problems will be discussed later.) The techniques described in this section should be used when the teacher has to deal with relatively minor problems of inattention, distraction, or minor misbehavior. They all help the teacher to achieve a single goal: *eliminate the problem as quickly as possible and with as little distraction of other students as possible.* The techniques should be used whenever this goal applies to the situation. In situations where this goal is not appropriate, for example, where misbehavior problems are serious or need some investigation and decision-making, a different sort of response is required. These more difficult behavior problems will be discussed in subsequent sections. The suggestions in this section apply to the following situation: one or more students are engaged in minor mischief, and the teacher wants to eliminate this behavior and return their attention to work as quickly as possible. The following teacher behavior will help do this.

Monitor the entire classroom regularly

Kounin (1970) stresses the trait of monitoring as an important ability in successful classroom managers. He noted that these teachers showed "with-it-ness"—their students knew that these teachers always "knew what was going on" in their classrooms. When the teacher regularly scans the classroom to keep an eye on what's going on, he is able to nip potential problems in the bud. Also, he is in a better position to respond appropriately to the particular problem. If he fails to notice what's going on, however, he is prone to make such errors as failing to intervene until a problem becomes disruptive or spreads to other students, attending to a minor problem while failing to notice a more serious one, or rebuking a student who was drawn into a dispute instead of the one who was responsible for starting it.

If teachers make such errors regularly, they will convince their students that they do not know what is going on in the room. This, in turn, will make the students more likely to misbehave and to test the teacher by talking back or trying to confuse him. Thus, it is important for teachers to form the habit of regularly scanning their classrooms, even while conducting small group lessons.

Seating patterns should be arranged so that this is possible. The teacher should always be able to see all of the students in the room. For reading groups and other small group activities, the teacher should be facing the bulk of the class, who are involved in seatwork. The students in the small lesson group should be seated facing the teacher, with their backs to the rest of the class. This way the teacher will be able to monitor the entire class effectively, and distractions to students in the group will be minimized.

When the teacher is writing on the board or at his desk, or when he is talking with individual students, he should be sure to look up and scan the class frequently. Many conflicts between students begin when one student "starts something" while the teacher's back is turned.

It is not enough simply to communicate positive expectations about attention and work involvement and to provide meaningful activities; the teacher must *show* students that he is alert and aware of what is going on in the room. To do this, the teacher must monitor the classroom continually.

Ignore minor misbehavior

It is neither necessary nor advisable for teachers to intervene in a direct way every time they notice a management or control problem. Many times the disruptive effect of the teacher's intervention will be greater than that of the problem he is dealing with. When this is true, it is more appropriate for the teacher to delay action or simply to ignore the problem.

For example, a teacher may notice that a student has dropped a pencil or has neglected to replace some equipment that should have been put away. These and similar incidents will sometimes require teacher action, but they rarely require any *immediate* action. Therefore, the teacher should wait until a time when he can deal with them without disruption. Stopping a lesson or group activity to tell a student to pick up a pencil or put away a book will only cause more problems.

Much minor misbehavior can be simply ignored, especially when it is of the hit-and-run variety. For example, if the group is distracted because someone accidentally drops a book, or if two students briefly whisper to each other and then return their attention to the lesson, it is usually best to take no action at all. Intervention is not needed, since the students' attention is now back on the lesson. There is nothing to be gained by disrupting the lesson to call attention to minor misbehavior that is already completed. Even if the whispering were to resume, the teacher usually is still better off to avoid disruptive intervention. Instead, one of the techniques described in the following section would be preferable. The teacher's simplest and best response is to ignore minor management problems and fleeting instances of inattention or minor misbehavior that occur during ongoing activities.

Stop repeated minor misbehavior and inattention without disrupting the activity

When minor misbehavior is repeated or intensified or when it threatens to become disruptive or to spread to other students, the teacher cannot simply ignore it; he will need to take action to stop it. Unless the misbehavior is serious enough to call for some investigation or some sustained intervention by the teacher (and it seldom is), it should be dealt with in a way that eliminates it as quickly and as nondisruptively as possible. There are several techniques teachers can use to eliminate minor misbehavior quickly. These techniques should be used in preference to more disruptive procedures whenever the teacher's goal is simply to return inattentive students to work involvement and at the same time to avoid distracting the other students.

1. *Eye contact.* The simplest method is just to look at the student and establish eye contact with him. If this can be accomplished, it usually is enough by itself to return his attention to the lesson or the task at hand. To make sure the message is received, the teacher may want to add a head nod or other gesture such as looking at the book the student is supposed to be reading.

Eye contact becomes doubly effective for stopping minor problems when the teacher successfully forms the habit of regularly scanning the room. Because his students will know that he regularly scans the room, they will tend to look at him when they are misbehaving (to see if he is watching). This, in turn, makes it easier for the teacher to intervene through eye contact. Teachers who do not scan the room properly will have difficulty in using eye contact in these situations, because they usually will have to wait longer before the students will look at them.

2. *Touch and gesture.* When the offending students are close by, the teacher does not need to wait until he can establish eye contact. Instead, he can use a simple touch or gesture to get their attention. This is an especially effective technique in reading groups or other small group teaching situations. A light tap, perhaps followed with a gesture toward the book, will get the message across without need for any verbalization.

Gestures and physical signals are also helpful in dealing with events going on in different parts of the room. If eye contact can be established, the teacher may be able to communicate his message by shaking his head, placing his finger to his lips, or pointing. These gestures should be used when possible, since they are less disruptive than leaving the group or speaking in a loud voice to students across the room. In general, touch and gesture are most useful in the early grades, where much teaching is done in small groups and where distraction is a frequent problem. Also, some adolescents resent any attempt by a teacher to touch them, so that touching would be unwise here.

3. *Physical closeness.* When the teacher is checking seatwork or moving about the room at other times, he can often effectively

eliminate minor behavior problems simply by moving close to the students involved. If the student knows what he is supposed to be doing, the mere physical presence of the teacher will be enough to motivate him to get his attention on the appropriate task. This technique is especially useful with older elementary students.

4. *Asking for task responses.* During lessons or group activities, often the simplest method of returning a student's attention is to ask him a question or call on him for a response. This request automatically compels his attention, while avoiding mention of the misbehavior.

This technique should be used with care, however, because it can backfire. If used too often, it may be perceived by the students as an attempt to "catch" them. Also, the questions asked in these situations must be ones that the student can answer or at least can make a reasonable response to. If there is no way that the student can meaningfully respond to the question because he was not paying attention to the previous one, the question should not be asked. To do so would only embarrass the student and force him to admit that he was not paying attention (thereby violating an important principle by focusing on the misbehavior instead of the lesson) or, if he dares, to respond with a sarcastic or aggressive remark.

Although it might be appropriate to ask a clearly inattentive student, "John, Tom says that the villain in the story was motivated by jealousy—what do you think?" it would not be appropriate to ask, "John, what did Tom just say?" Acceptable alternatives would be to simply move toward the student, to call his name and gesture, or to ask him a question that he can reasonably respond to even if he has not heard the previous one.

5. *Praise desirable behavior.* This is something that teachers should do in general, of course. However, at times it can be used as a technique to eliminate specific misbehavior. Instead of calling attention to misbehavior, the teacher praises desirable behavior in another student, preferably one near the offender. This is not usually a good technique to use during lessons, since it disrupts the flow. However, it is often useful during times when the students are doing seatwork or other independent activities. It should be used when the opportunity arises, because it allows the teacher to reinforce desirable behavior rather than criticize and call attention to undesirable behavior. The teacher can praise a student for persistence rather than criticize his neighbor who has given up; note with pleasure that a student has already finished his assignment rather than criticize his neighbor who has been wasting his time; or praise the student who has carefully straightened his desk rather than criticize his neighbor who has not.

When using this technique, teachers should be sure to monitor the misbehaving students and follow up with appropriate action. When a student changes his behavior and begins to do the things that his neighbor was praised for, he too should be praised. *The technique will not be successful without such follow up,* since it will make the teacher appear to be playing favorites by praising only certain pet students. Also, teachers should reward not only students who are working on their seatwork, but also those who complete it appropriately. Comments such as, "Oh dear, what can you do now?" or reactions such as assigning more of the same type of work will tempt the students to string out independent work assignments as long as possible. By giving the student additional practice on skills that he already has overlearned, the teacher in effect punishes desirable behavior rather than rewards it. Instead, the student should be allowed to go on to more demanding problems or to switch to another activity of his own choosing.

These are several techniques that enable teachers to eliminate minor problems without disrupting the activity or calling attention to the misbehavior. Eye contact, touch and gesture, and physical closeness are the simplest, since no verbalization is needed. These methods are especially effective with younger elementary students. A fourth method is to call on the student to answer a question or make a response, a technique that will be effective if it is not done too often and if the response required is not unreasonable. A fifth method is to praise desirable behavior of a student seated near one or more classmates who are not showing this behavior. This method will remind the students about what they are supposed to be doing and will help motivate them to do so, provided that the teacher regularly praises them when they, too, behave desirably.

Dealing with prolonged or disruptive misbehavior

So far we have presented techniques for preventing inattention and for dealing with minor misbehavior. Consistent application of these techniques will hold behavior problems to a minimum. However, what should the teacher do when these techniques have not worked, or when the behavior is too serious to be dealt with without a more direct and disruptive intervention? Suggestions for dealing with these more serious matters are presented in this section.

Stopping misbehavior through direct intervention

When misbehavior is dangerous or seriously disruptive, the teacher will have to stop it directly by calling out the name of the student involved and correcting him. Since such direct intervention in itself is disruptive, it should be done only when necessary.

Like the techniques described in the previous section, *direct intervention should be used only when no information is needed.* Situations where no information is needed are those in which both the teacher and the students involved are very clear about what the students are supposed to be doing at the time. In addition, the particular misbehavior should be transparently obvious to the teacher. This would include such behavior as laughing and talking with a neighbor, shooting wads of paper or rubber bands, and copying a neighbor's work. In situations like these, where the teacher can see that the student is simply fooling around or has become distracted from a well-defined task, he does not need any special information to be able to act. He needs only to stop the misbehavior and return the student to the task.

In more ambiguous situations, where the student cannot reasonably be expected to know what he is supposed to be doing, or in situations where the teacher is not sure what is going on (e.g., if two students are talking, they may be discussing the problem as directed, or they may be being inattentive to the problem), the teacher may need to get more information and make some decisions before intervening with direct instructions to the students involved.

There are two basic ways for teachers to intervene directly. First, they can demand an end to the misbehavior and follow this up by indicating the appropriate behavior. Intervention should be short, direct, and to the point. It should name the students, identify the misbehavior that must be stopped, and indicate what should be done instead. The teacher should speak firmly and loud enough to be heard, but he should not shout or nag. Commands such as "John! Get back to your seat and get to work" and "Mary and Laura! Stop talking and pay attention to me," are not appropriate when the students clearly know that they are misbehaving; in those circumstances it is not necessary to label the misbehavior or call attention to it. Instead, a brief direction telling them what to do will be sufficient: "John, finish your work" and "Mary and Laura, look here."

A second direct intervention technique that teachers can use to stop misbehavior is to remind students of relevant rules and expected behavior. As we discussed earlier, clear-cut rules for classroom behavior should be established early in the year, after careful explanation or thorough discussion of the reasons for them. If this has been done properly, the teacher can then use brief reminders of the rules to prevent control problems or to stop them when they occur. Quick rule reminders can serve the teacher's purpose in control situations, without causing him to sermonize excessively, or to point out or embarrass individual students.

As with other forms of direct intervention, rule reminders should be given briefly and firmly. In some ways they are preferable to the method of demanding an end to misbehavior, because they help the students internalize behavioral control. When the student is clear about the rules and the reasons for them, rule reminders help him see his own responsibility for his misbehavior and help keep the situation from becoming one of conflict with the teacher.

Rule reminders are often the best way to handle misbehavior during independent work periods and to deal with loudness and disruption. When the class has become noisy during a reading group, for example, rather than attempt to name the offenders or leave the group, it may be simplest for the teacher to say, "Class, you're getting too loud. Remember to speak softly and not disturb the reading group," or "Frank, if you have finished your assignment you can work on vowel sounds at the listening post, but don't bother Johnny. Remember, we don't disturb people who are busy working."

Situations in which students know what to do but are not doing it because they are engaged in *disruptive* misbehavior call for direct intervention by the teacher. Such intervention should be brief and direct, and it should stress the expected appropriate behavior rather than the students' misbehavior. Sometimes this can be done through a simple rule reminder; at other times the teacher will have to indicate appropriate behavior in more specific detail.

Inappropriate intervention

We have presented suggestions for intervening directly to stop disruptive misbehavior that was easily interpretable. These suggestions concerned what teachers *should* do. We will now consider some cautions about what teachers *should not* do in these same situations. First, *the teacher should not ask questions in these situations*. There is no need for questions, since the situation is clear. The teacher's goal is simply to return the misbehaving students to productive work; there is no need to conduct an investigation. More importantly, the kinds of questions asked in such situations usually are not real questions but rhetorical questions. The essential meaninglessness of these questions and the tone in which they are asked show that they are not questions at all. Instead, they are attacks on the student: "What's the matter with you?" "Why haven't you finished the work?" "How many times do I have to tell you to get busy?" Such questions do no good and may start trouble if they cause embarrassment, fear, or resentment. Suggestions about how to question the students more appropriately are presented in the following section on getting information.

Teachers should also avoid threats and appeals to authority when stopping misbehavior through direct intervention. By simply stating how they want the student to behave, teachers communicate the expectation that they will be obeyed. However, if they add a threat ("Do it or else . . ."), they place themselves in a position of conflict with the student, and at the same time, they indirectly suggest that they are not sure he is going to obey.

If a student should ask why the teacher is telling him to behave as he is, the teacher should give the appropriate reason. If, instead, the teacher becomes defensive and appeals to authority, "You'll do it because I say so," he will produce only anger and resentment. This teacher behavior constitutes a direct challenge to the student and may cause the student to lose face before his peers, so that it will often result in an explosion against the teacher. Furthermore, if his classmates feel that the teacher is treating the student unfairly, the teacher's relationships with other members of the class will suffer.

Besides inappropriate questioning and arbitrary exertion of authority, there is a third problem that teachers must avoid when stopping misbehavior through direct intervention. This is overdwelling upon the misbehavior itself, commonly called nagging. In a direct intervention situation there is no need or reason to describe the misbehavior in detail or to catalogue the number of times the student has misbehaved in the same way during the last week, month, or year.

Here again, such behavior constitutes an attack on the student rather than a corrective measure. It places the teacher in conflict with him, and it can endanger teacher credibility and respect. When a teacher does this regularly, the students may come to see it as enjoyable or funny. Some may even begin to disobey deliberately, just to see if they can trigger a new or more spectacular response from the teacher.

Difficulties in this area often appear when teachers don't know that they should stress the positive or forget to do so in dealing with students' behavior. Gradually the teachers get into a rut in which they regularly describe a student's misbehavior instead of changing it. At this point the teacher in effect may be telling the student that he has given up any hope of change, "John, every day I have to speak to you for fooling around instead of doing your seatwork. It's the same story again today. How many times do I have to tell you? You never learn." Given this teacher behavior, chances are that it will also be the same story tomorrow and the day after. John will probably continue in this fashion unless the teacher realizes that his role is to change John's misbehavior and reinforce his appropriate behavior, not merely to describe his misbehavior and berate him for it.

Instead of merely nagging John, the teacher should attempt to isolate the cause of his misbehavior and to develop a solution for the problem. It may be, for example, that the seatwork is too easy, too difficult, or otherwise inappropriate for John. Or, John may have developed a troublesome "fooling around" relationship with one of his classmates, so that a conference, and possibly also a new seating arrangement, is required. In any case, rather than let the situation continue, the teacher should discuss it with John, come to an agreement with him about his future behavior, and follow through with appropriate treatment (these matters are discussed in detail in the following sections).

There are three kinds of behavior that teachers should avoid when dealing with disruptive behavior that is easily interpretable: unnecessary and meaningless questioning, use of threats and arbitrary exertion of authority, and overdwelling on the misbehavior (nagging). These reactions do no good, and they may cause needless anger, anxiety, or resentment in students.

Conducting investigations

The previous section cautioned against questioning students in situations where no information is needed. This section deals with those situations which are not clear enough for a teacher to act without getting additional information. Here the teacher will need to question one or more students, and it is important that he do so appropriately. Unfortunately, many teachers (and other adults) tend to question children and adolescents in ways that fail to get the required information or make the situation worse by producing negative side effects.

Questions should be genuine attempts to get information, not rhetorical questions of the type described in the preceding section. They should also be direct and to the point and should concern matters of *fact* that the student can answer. Questions about students' *intentions* should not be asked unless the teacher seriously wants and needs the information: "Why did you leave the room?" "Why haven't you turned in your homework?" Such questions about intentions help establish a clear picture of what the student was doing and why. However, pseudoquestions about intentions should be avoided. Too often teachers berate students with rhetorical questions, "Did you think you could get away with it?" or confuse them with questions about intentions that they cannot really answer, "Why didn't you remember to be more careful?"

When questioning students to establish the facts in a dispute or discipline situation, the best policy usually is to talk to each one privately, or at least to confine the discussion to the students directly involved. This avoids putting individuals on the spot in front of the group, thereby minimizing needs to save face by lying or confronting the teacher. If more than one student is in on the discussion, the teacher should be sure to question each one individually and insist that the others be quiet while the student being questioned gets a chance to answer. If the teacher instead allows others to jump in or if he addresses a question to the group rather than to an individual, the students are likely to begin arguing among themselves over who did what first to whom.

When discrepancies in the stories begin to appear, or when one student appears to be lying, the teacher needs to guard against making snap judgments or accusations. He should point out the discrepancies, and perhaps indicate that he finds certain statements hard to believe. This intervention must be done in a way that avoids rejecting anyone's statement out of hand and that leaves the door open for the offender to change his story.

The teacher should make it clear that he wants and expects the students to tell the truth. They will be motivated to do so if his words are backed with appropriate and credible actions that reveal him as someone who wants the best for all concerned, not as an authority figure who is going to assess guilt and punishment. There must be no reward for lying and no punishment for telling the truth.

The facts need not always be established in unambiguous detail. Since the teacher's goal is to promote long-run development of integrity and self-control, not merely to "settle" an individual incident, it is often desirable to leave contradictions unresolved or to accept a lie or exaggeration without labeling it as such. This is especially true in situations where the teacher is pretty certain that a student is not telling the truth but is unable to prove this.

Even if the student is guilty, he will resent it if the teacher tells him he is lying. He will conclude that the teacher is picking on him, or perhaps that the teacher has such a low opinion of him that he expects him to lie. More appropriately in these situations, the teacher should remind the students that he tries to treat the class fairly and honestly and expects them to reciprocate; state that he "just doesn't know what to think" about the present situation, in view of the discrepancies and contradictions; state that there is no point in discussing the incident further without any new information; remind the students about expectations regarding the behavioral area that is involved and give them specific instructions about what they are to do now. This technique will be most successful in achieving the long-run goals. It avoids accusations and punishment, and it increases the probability that students who lied will recognize their own lies and feel guilty about them.

When a problem is serious or disruptive, and when the teacher is unclear about the facts, an investigation will be needed. This must be handled carefully, because of the danger of putting students "on the spot" and setting off even more serious "face-saving" gestures. It is usually best to conduct investigations privately, away from the rest of the class. The teacher should hear out all students involved, but insist on questioning and getting information from only one at a time. Questions should elicit the relevant facts and (sometimes) intentions and motivations. The students should not be browbeaten with rhetorical or confusing questions that express the teacher's frustration rather than seek information.

Sometimes the investigation will not yield a clear picture, because someone has withheld or distorted information. When possible, it may be best to leave the matter unresolved in such situations, rather than to expose the guilty party. This will add to his shame and deny him the opportunity to feel picked on, so that he will be more likely to change his behavior.

Once the teacher has finished his investigation, he should resolve the issue. Usually this will require only a rule reminder, although it may require some special action or the working out of a new agreement about expected behavior. Resolution of the problem usually should *not* require punishment, although this will sometimes be necessary. The question of when to use punishment is taken up in the following section, along with suggestions about how to punish effectively.

Effective punishment
Punishment is sometimes useful in working with a student to help him control his misbehavior, but only in some situations and

only when used in combination with other techniques. A teacher who relies heavily on punishment (instead of using the management techniques we have so far described) cannot succeed, except in the most narrow and temporary sense. At best he will be like the teacher described in the previous chapter who "runs a tight ship." He may achieve a grudging compliance, but only at the cost of high group tension and frustration and of being continually in conflict with his students. The class will obey him out of fear when he is present but will be out of control when he is not in the room.

Thus, punishment can do more harm than good, especially if overused. Nevertheless, teachers should not hesitate to administer punishment when circumstances call for it. When properly used, it is a legitimate and helpful method of dealing with certain discipline problems. To use it properly, however, teachers should know when to use it, what sort of punishment to use, and how to apply it.

When to punish

As a general rule, punishment is appropriate only in dealing with *repeated* misbehavior. It is a treatment of last resort, to be used when students persist in the same kinds of misbehavior despite continued expressions of concern and explanations of the reasons for rules. It is a way of exerting control over a student who is unable to control himself.

Resorting to punishment is not a step that a teacher should take lightly, since it signifies that neither he nor the student can cope with the problem. It is an expression of lack of confidence in the student, telling him that the teacher thinks he is not trying to improve or perhaps that he thinks the misbehavior is deliberate. This can be damaging to the student's self-concept, as well as to the chances for solving the problem.

This is why punishment is simply inappropriate for dealing with isolated incidents, no matter how severe—because in a single occurrence of misbehavior there is no reason to believe that the student acted deliberately or, at least, that he will repeat it again in the future. Punishment especially should be avoided, even in cases of repeated misbehavior, when it appears that the student is trying to improve. In fact, any approximations of appropriate behavior should be rewarded. In these instances, teachers should give students the benefit of the doubt by assuming their good will in trying to improve and by expressing confidence in their ability to do so. Punishment should be used only as a last resort, when a student has repeatedly failed to respond to more positive treatment.

What punishment does

Although punishment may sometimes be needed, its effects are limited and specific. Teachers need to be aware of what punishment does and does not do, if they are to use it properly and avoid deluding themselves about its effectiveness. A great body of research evidence (reviewed in Bandura, 1969) shows that punishment is primarily useful only for controlling misbehavior, not for teaching desired behavior. Furthermore, punishment affects the expression of behavior but not the desire or need for that expression. *Punishment can reduce or control misbehavior, but by itself it will not teach the student desirable behavior or even reduce his desire to misbehave.* Thus, punishment is never a solution by itself; at best it is only part of a solution. It will temporarily stop misbehavior, however, and therefore it is appropriate when the misbehavior is repeated and serious enough to require its use.

Using punishment for the right reasons

Punishment should be used consciously and deliberately, as a part of the teacher's treatment of repeated misbehavior. Even though it is a last resort, it should not be used in an unthinking fashion. It must not be used as a way of getting even with a student, or of "teaching him a lesson." Students will learn plenty from hostile or vindictive punishment, but not the lesson that the teacher intends. When attacked personally they will respond, like anyone else, with anger, resentment, and a desire to strike back. Needless to say, this will not help solve the problem.

Even an uninvolved observer can tell when a teacher is using punishment to deal with his own frustrations or anger rather than using it as a deliberate control technique. This kind of punishment is usually accompanied by statements or thoughts like, "We'll fix your wagon," or "We'll see who's boss." Statements like those do not indicate use of punishment as a technique; they are emotional outbursts indicating poor self-control and emotional immaturity in the teacher.

Types of punishment

Different types of punishment are not all equally appropriate. Behavior restrictions, limitation of privileges, and exclusion from the group are recommended punishment methods. Severe personal criticism, physical punishment, and assignment of extra work are not recommended.

Personal attacks on the student are never appropriate. Severe personal criticism is not punishment and cannot be justified on the grounds that the student needs it. It has no corrective or control function. It will only deepen the problem by causing resentment of the teacher, both in the victim and in the rest of the class.

Physical punishment can sometimes be a useful and appropriate technique, especially for infants. We do not recommend its use in schools, however, for several reasons. First, it is difficult to administer objectively and unemotionally. By its very nature, it places the teacher in a position of attacking the students, physically if not personally. This could cause physical injury, and in any case it will tend to undermine the teacher's chances of dealing with the student effectively in the future. Second, physical punishment is usually over quickly, and it has an air of finality about it. Because of its intensity, attention tends to be focused on the punishment itself rather than on the misbehavior that led to it. Third, because of the above, physical punishment usually fails to induce guilt or personal responsibility for misbehavior in the offender. He is much more likely to be sorry for having gotten caught than for having mis- behaved. Fourth, physical punishment is only temporarily effective at best. The students who misbehave most insistently and defiantly in the classroom usually come from homes where their parents beat them regularly as a form of discipline. Criminals convicted of assault and other violent crimes almost always show backgrounds in which physical punishment was the primary socialization "technique." In general, it seems that physical punishment teaches people to attack others when angry; it does not teach them appropriate behavior, and a change in behavior is what is desired in the long run.

Some teachers punish by assigning extra work or by having the students write out something like, "I must not talk in class," a certain number of times. We do not recommend assigning extra school work as punishment because of what this may do to the student's attitudes toward school work. Both teachers and students should see work assignments as opportunities for the students to practice the skills they are learning. When work assignments are used as punishments, the students are more likely to see work assignments in general as drudgery.

What about writing assignments that do not pertain to school- work, such as copying behavioral rules or writing compositions about them? These assignments may or may not be effective punishment, depending on how they are handled. At first glance, writing out "I must not talk in class" a specified number of times might seem to be a good way of calling a student's attention to the rule. However, this method tends to call attention more to the punishment than to the rule. Unless the student must write out the rule only a few times (five or ten), he is likely to see this form of punishment as ineffectual behavior on the part of the teacher and to either resent it or think it is funny.

In some circumstances, an effective device may be to ask the student to write a composition about how he should behave. This will force him to think about the rationales underlying rules for behavior rather than to just simply repeat the rules in rote fashion. If the teacher does use this form of punishment, however, he should be sure to read the composition carefully and discuss it with the student. The punishment itself is only part of the treatment.

Personal criticism, physical punishment, and assignment of extra schoolwork should not be used as punishment techniques. Other more appropriate techniques should be used when punishment is called for. Compositions about classroom rules and the reasons for them may sometimes be appropriate. They should not be too long, however, and they should be followed up with a feedback conference. Methods of punishing effectively through withdrawal of privileges, behavioral restrictions, and exclusion from the group are discussed in the following sections.

How to punish effectively

More important than the type of punishment used is the way the teacher presents it to the student. It should be made clear to the student that punishment is being used as a last resort, and not because the teacher wants to get even with him or enjoys punishing him. The student should see that his own behavior has brought the punishment on himself, because he has left the teacher no other choice.

Tone and manner are very important here. The teacher should avoid dramatizing the situation, "All right, that's the last straw." "Now you've done it," or making statements that turn the situation into a power struggle, "I guess we'll have to show you who's boss." Instead, the need for punishment should be presented to the student in a quiet, almost sorrowful voice. The teacher's tone and manner should communicate a combination of deep concern, puzzlement, and regret over the student's behavior.

Whether or not it is fully stated in words, the teacher's implied message should be "You have continually misbehaved. I have tried to help by reminding you about how to behave and explaining why it is so important, but your misbehavior has continued. I don't understand this, but I am worried about it and I still want to help. I cannot allow this misbehavior to continue, however. If it does, I will have to punish you. I don't want to do this, but I have to if you leave me no other choice." This approach will help make the student see punishment as a thoroughly disagreeable experience that he will want to avoid. It will also make him more likely to see his predicament as his own fault, and less likely to think the teacher is picking on him or treating him unjustly. If necessary, the teacher should then follow up by assessing appropriate punishment and by providing for some sort of satisfactory resolution of the problem.

Ideally, the punishment should be closely related to the offense. If a student misuses materials, for example, it may be most appropriate to restrict or suspend his use of them for a while. If he continually gets into fights during recess, he can lose recess privileges or be required to stay by himself during this time. If he is continually disruptive, he can be excluded from the group.

Whatever the punishment, the teacher should be sure to make clear the reasons why the student is being punished and what he must do to restore his normal status. This involves making a clear distinction between the student's unacceptable behavior and his overall acceptance as a person. The student should know that he is being punished solely because of his unacceptable behavior, and that he can regain his status by changing his behavior.

Withdrawal of privileges and exclusion from the group should be tied closely to the remedial behavior whenever possible. This means telling the student not only why he is being punished, but what he may do in order to regain his privileges or rejoin the group. This explanation should stress that punishment is only temporary, and that he can redeem himself by showing clearly specified desirable behavior, "When you can share with the others without fighting," "When you can pay attention to the lesson," "When you can use the crayons properly without breaking them." The student should be left with only himself to blame for his punishment, but he should also be given a specified way that he can redeem himself. This will focus his attention on positive behavior and provide him with an incentive for changing.

This is in contrast to the "prison-sentence" approach, "You have to stay here for ten minutes," "No recess for three days"; and the "I am the boss" approach, "You stay here until I come and get you," "No more crayons unless I give you permission," which should be avoided. These techniques make no explicit improvement demands on the student, and they make it easy for him to get angry or feel picked on.

Punishment that places restrictions on the student will be most effective if the restrictions are closely related to the offense, if they follow closely after the offense, and if removal of restrictions is conditional upon student improvement. Punishment that is closely related to the offense is more easily seen as fair. The student has no one but himself to blame if he loses a privilege because he has abused it. On the other hand, if the teacher punishes by imposing restrictions in an entirely unrelated area, the student may feel that he is being picked on or attacked. An especially bad practice of this type is to lower students' grades as punishment for misbehavior. Except where the punishment is *directly related* and *proportional* to the offense, as when a student who cheats on a test is given a failing grade for that test (and only that test), students should *not* be punished by having their grades lowered. Lowering grades as punishment for misbehavior will cause bitter resentment against the teacher, and it may well also harm the student's motivation for studying, "Why should I work if I can't get better than a C?"

Punishment should closely follow the offense if it is to be effective. Again, the student must see that his own behavior has brought on the punishment, that he has no one to blame but himself. If punishment is too far removed from the offense or if it goes on for too long a time, "You'll stay in for a week!" this connection will be lost. The misbehavior that led to the punishment will be all but forgotten, but the punishment itself will remain. So will a lot of anger and resentment.

Punishment should be flexible, so that the student can redeem himself and restore normal status by showing improvement. This gives the student some incentive to improve, and it helps drive home the point that the teacher punishes because he must, not because he wants to. Teachers should strive to avoid (or break) the habit of threatening inflexible punishments, "You'll stay after school for a week . . . get an 'F' in conduct . . . have to get special permission to leave your seat from now on." These threats are inappropriate over-reactions, and they leave the teacher stuck with either following them up or taking them back. Either way he loses. If he follows through and "executes the sentence," he will deepen the student's discouragement and resentment. If he backs off, he will appear inconsistent or wishy-washy, and will "lose face."

Exclusion from the group

Exclusion from the group must be handled properly if it is to be used successfully as a punishment technique. Teachers often misuse it in a way that actually makes it function as a reward instead of a punishment. Ideally, a specific place should be designated for exclusion from the group. It should be located so that a student sent there will be excluded psychologically as well as physically.

He should be placed behind the other students, where he cannot easily disrupt a lesson or distract their attention. To help insure a feeling of exclusion, the student himself should be placed facing a corner or wall, rather than facing the rest of the class. This, in combination with the techniques for explaining the punishment described above, will make it very likely that the exclusion will be experienced as punishment and will have the desired effects on behavior.

Exclusion should be terminated when the student indicates he is ready to behave properly. If he does not say this spontaneously, the teacher should go to him when the opportunity arises and ask if he thinks he is ready to participate in the lesson and behave as expected. The student's stated intention to behave should be accepted when it is given. He should not be subjected to nagging about his earlier behavior or to a "grilling" in which he is required to make specific promises: "You'll stop calling out answers without raising your hand? You'll pay attention and stop talking to your neighbor during the lesson?"

Also, when the student requests readmittance, the teacher should respond in a way that clearly accepts him back into the group. Vague phrases like, "Well, we'll see," should be avoided. The student should be given a brief statement showing him that the teacher has heard and accepted his intention to reform, and then he should be instructed to rejoin the class: "Well, John, I'm glad to hear that. I hate to exclude you or anyone else. Go back to your seat and get ready for our arithmetic lesson."

Sometimes an excluded student may quickly come to the teacher with a half-hearted or tongue-in-cheek pledge to reform. In such cases, especially when there has been a previous history of failure to take exclusion seriously, the teacher may wish to reject the student's gesture and send him back to the place of exclusion. This should be done with caution, since it is better to give the student the benefit of the doubt than to risk undermining his reform efforts.

When the student's plea is rejected, the reasons must be made clear to him. He must see that the teacher is acting on the basis of observing his behavior, and not because he dislikes him or is picking on him: "I'm sorry, Johnny, but I can't accept that. Several times recently you have promised to behave and have broken that promise as soon as you rejoined the group. I don't think you realize how serious a problem this has become. Go back to the corner and stay there until I get a chance to come and talk to you about this some more."

Punishment as a last resort

We cannot stress too strongly that punishment is a measure of last resort that should be used only when absolutely necessary. It is appropriate only when students persist in disruptive behavior despite continued attempts to explain and encourage expected desirable behavior. It is a way to curb misbehavior in students who know what to do, but refuse to do it. It should not be used when the student's misbehavior is not disruptive or when the problem exists because he does not know what to do or how to do it. In these situations punishment will only make the problem worse.

First, punishment places unnecessary attention and emphasis on undesirable behavior, instead of on desirable behavior. Second, it tends to reduce work involvement and raise the level of tension in the room (Kounin, 1970). Thus the use of punishment in handling one control problem may contribute to causing several others. This is part of the reason why teachers who rely on punishment have more, not fewer, control problems. They are attempting to treat their problems through a stop-gap control measure instead of prevention and cure and, meanwhile, are undermining their chances for gaining the admiration and respect required to treat problems successfully.

This does not mean that any behavior that is not disruptive should be allowed to continue. Withdrawal, daydreaming, sleepiness, and other nondisruptive behavior can be serious problems if they are characteristic and continuing. However, punishment is an unnecessary and inappropriate response to such behavior. This is also true for problems such as failure to answer questions or to do assigned work and for all situations in which the student needs instruction about what to do and how to do it. If a student fails to turn in assigned work, he should be made to complete it during free periods in the school day or else kept after school to complete it.

Coping with serious adjustment problems

Most classrooms have one or more students who show serious and continuing disturbances. These students require individualized treatment beyond that so far suggested for the class in general. This section presents suggestions for dealing with these more serious problems.

General considerations

Although different types of serious problems require different treatment, certain general considerations apply to all of them.

1. *Do not isolate the student or label him as a unique case.* Because expectations and labels can act as self-fulfilling prophecies it is important that the disturbed student not be labeled or treated as someone special, someone totally different from the rest of the class. This means, among other things, that interactions with the student concerning his behavior should be as private as possible, and should not be conducted in front of the rest of the class any more than is absolutely necessary. The effect will be to cut down the need for face-saving behavior on his part and also to reduce the possibility that he can use his typical behavior problem to gain attention from teacher or peers.

2. *Stress desired behavior.* This method has been mentioned before, but it is doubly important for students who show continuing behavior problems. Such continuing problems are harder to eliminate once they have become labeled as characteristic of the student. The label places undue attention on his particular form of misbehavior, and it tells him that the teacher expects him to misbehave in this way. To avoid this, the teacher should regularly stress the behavior that he is trying to get the student to learn and not the misbehavior he shows now. Stress on the positive must be more than mere verbal convention, of course. The teacher must not only talk this way, he must think this way and act in a manner that is consistent with the intention of moving the student toward desired behavior.

A positive manner can be used even with things that appear to be almost completely negative, such as stealing or destruction of property. True, it would be awkward to reward a student for not stealing, or not destroying property. However, these problems can be redefined in a more positive way that leads to the desired behavior on the part of the student.

If property destruction is due to impulsivity or carelessness, the teacher can instruct the student about how to handle the property carefully and can praise him when he does so. If stealing results from real need (poverty), the teacher should plan with the student ways that he can borrow the items he's been stealing or earn the right to keep them. Meanwhile, the student can be praised for his progress in "keeping the rules" or in "learning to respect the property rights of others." If the student has been stealing or destroying property to seek attention or group status, or to express anger or frustration, the teacher can work to help him to recognize this and to develop more appropriate ways of meeting these needs. Here again, any positive progress the student shows should be labeled and praised.

By defining problems in a positive way, teachers give students a goal to work for and suggestions about how to work toward it. This tends to energize both the teacher and student, giving them the feeling that they are making progress in solving the problem. In contrast, when the problem is defined purely negatively, "You've got to stop . . . ," both teacher and student are left at an impasse. The student misbehaves and the teacher responds by criticizing his behavior and perhaps by punishing him for it. Both teacher and student are left where they started, and the cycle is likely to repeat itself over and over.

3. *Focus on the student's school-related behavior.* When a student shows seriously disturbed behavior in school, such behavior is usually part of a larger pattern of disturbances. Many different factors may be contributing to causing the problem, including some that the teacher can do little or nothing about (broken home, inadequate or sadistic parent, poor living conditions, etc.). Some teachers give up hope when they hear about such things, feeling that the student will not change unless his home environment changes (Good et al., 1969). Other teachers become uninvited psychotherapists or social workers, attempting to change the home situation as well as to deal with the student in the classroom. This often does more harm than good.

Even though people show reliable individual differences and stable personality traits, most behavior is situational (Mischel, 1968). Teachers, for example, show certain behaviors during the school day that are associated with the teaching role. These behaviors tend to appear only during the school day and are not included in teachers' behavior outside the school in their roles as husband or wife, parent, neighbor, and so forth.

This is also true of students, who learn to play the student role by showing the behavior that teachers expect and reinforce. It is this student role that teachers should be most concerned with in dealing with their classes. No matter what the student's home background, and no matter what personality disturbance he shows, the teacher can and should expect him to behave acceptably as a student. Factors in the home or other out-of-school environments may need to be taken into account, but they should neither be used as an excuse for failing to deal with him nor allowed to become a focal concern that obscures treatment of his school-related misbehavior.

Generally, then, teachers are advised to confine their treatment efforts to the student's school behavior and to aspects of his home environment that are closely related to his school behavior (such as asking parents to see that he goes to bed early enough on nights before school, or that he does his homework). These are appropriate and expected teacher concerns. They are also the areas in which teachers can and should be effective in dealing with the student. Going beyond these areas is risky, unless the teacher has the necessary expertise and a good relationship with both the student and his family.

4. *Build a close relationship with the student, and use it to learn his point of view.* A student's failure to respond to a reasonable and patient teacher's normal behavior signals that some special problem is operating that needs special teacher treatment. Perhaps the student is unwilling to respond because of anger or other negative emotions or is unable to respond because of emotions or impulses he cannot control. Here it is important for the teacher to build a close relationship with the student as an individual (as opposed to an impersonal student in the class), both to develop better understanding of his behavior and to earn the respect and affection that will make him want to respond.

To do this, the teacher needs to take time to talk with the student individually, either after school or at prearranged conferences during school hours. The teacher should make clear his concern for the student's welfare (not merely about his misbehavior) and his willingness to help him improve. He should encourage the student to talk about the problem in his own words, listening carefully and asking questions to help clarify when he does not understand. The best questions are simple and open-ended. They do not put words into the student's mouth or make guesses about what is going on in his mind.

The teacher should make it clear to the student that he wants to hear what he has to say, so that the student doesn't get the impression that the teacher is waiting to hear one thing in particular. The teacher might help by expressing puzzlement over the student's behavior, and perhaps also by pointing out that he is hurting himself in addition to causing problems for the teacher. This should not become a sermon, however, or get in the way of the teacher's main message that he wants the student to tell his story in his own words.

Preferably, the discussion will produce something that suggests treatment procedures. If the teacher has been part of the problem because of his own behavior toward the student (if he has been sarcastic or hostile, for example), he should admit this and promise to change his behavior. If the student makes a suggestion that is reasonable, it should be accepted. For example, a seventh grader may request that he not be asked to read aloud from his seventh-grade history book, since he barely reads at the second-grade level. This request could be granted, provided that a plan is devised to see that the student learns to read better. If the student's suggestion cannot be accepted, the reasons should be explained. The teacher may also wish to offer suggestions. These must be presented as suggestions, however, and not conclusions. The student should feel free to express his opinion about whether or not they will help. In any case, discussion should continue until suggestions for behavioral change are identified and agreed upon.

At times these may be only partial solutions or steps toward solving the problem. This may be appropriate, however, since some problems are serious and deep-rooted enough that they are not going to be solved in one day or with one conference. It is sufficient as a first step if both parties communicate honestly during the conference and come away from it feeling that progress is being made.

Although serious behavioral disturbances require individualized treatment, there are some general principles teachers can follow in working out a treatment plan. Teachers should (1) avoid isolating the student or labeling him as a unique case; (2) stress his progress toward desired behavior rather than nag him about misbehavior; (3) focus primarily on his school-related behavior, even where severe out-of-school problems exist; (4) develop a close relationship with the student so that he will strive to earn teacher affection and respect.

With any serious problem, the teacher should arrange a conference and question the student to discover how he sees the situation. Questions should seek to get the student to explain in his own words or to clarify ambiguities; they should not "put words into his mouth." This questioning phase should be followed by a discussion phase in which agreements about suggested solutions are worked out. Suggestions about individualized treatment of several behavior problems commonly faced by teachers are given in the following sections.

Defiance

Most teachers find defiance to be particularly threatening, or even frightening. What is the teacher to do with a student who vehemently talks back or who loudly refuses to do what he is asked to do?

To begin with, the teacher must remain calm so as not to get drawn into a power struggle with the student. The natural tendency of most adults in this situation is to get angry and strike back with a show of force designed to put down the rebellion and show the student that "he can't get away with it." While such a show of force may succeed in suppressing the immediate defiance, it will probably be harmful in the long run, especially if it involves loss of temper by the teacher or public humiliation of the student.

If the teacher can overcome the tendency to react with immediate anger, he will be in a good position to deal with defiance effectively. Acts of defiance tend to make everyone in the room fearful and uneasy, including the student who rebels. The other students know that the act is serious and may bring serious consequences, and they will be on edge waiting to see what those consequences are going to be. The teacher can gain two advantages by pausing a moment before responding to defiance: (1) he will gain time to control his temper and think about what to do before acting and (2) the mood of the defiant student is likely to change from one of aggression and anger to one of fear and contrition during this time. Thus it is helpful to ponder the situation for a few moments before responding. Meanwhile, the class will wait in silent anticipation to see what is going to happen.

When the teacher does act, he must do so decisively, although with a calm and quiet manner. If possible, he should give a general assignment to the class and then remove the defiant student from the room for a conference. If this is not possible or if the defiant student remains defiant and is unwilling to leave for a conference, he should be told that the matter will be discussed after school. This should be done with a tone and manner that communicates serious concern, but no threats or promises should be made.

The defiant student and his classmates should know that some action will be taken, but they should not be told exactly what it will be.

The following response would be appropriate: "John, I can see that something is seriously wrong here, and I think we better do something about it before it gets worse. Please step out into the hall and wait for me—I'll join you in a minute." An alternative would be "Please sit down and think it over during the rest of the period—I'll discuss it with you later, after class."

It is important that defiance be handled in a private conference. First, the fact that defiance occurred at all is a signal that something is seriously wrong with the student and probably also with the teacher-student relationship. This calls for discussion and resolution. Second, the problem should be dealt with privately instead of in front of the rest of the class. When the teacher's authority has been threatened by an angry outburst, both the teacher and the student will find difficulty in handling the situation in front of the class. Both will be strongly motivated to save face, the teacher by demonstrating his authority and the student by showing his determination to stick with his earlier defiant statements.

The teacher can minimize both of these problems by stating that the matter will be dealt with in a private conference. The statement tells the class that the teacher can and will handle the situation and allows the teacher to deal with the student in a way that does not humiliate him or incite him to further defiance. He can even afford to let the student "get in the last word," since the matter will be taken up again later.

If the student wants to "have it out" publicly, the teacher should flatly refuse. He should say that the matter is between the two of them, and that he does not want to cause embarrassment. He might also wish to add that he is angry and wants to wait until he calms down and thinks about the matter before taking action. If necessary, he should send the student out into the hall or to the principal's office.

Defiant acts are usually the culmination of a buildup of anger and frustration in the student. Difficulties at home or in relationships with peers may be part of the problem. However, the teacher is almost always part of the problem too. Students are unlikely to defy their teacher unless they resent him to some degree or feel that he is picking on them. Therefore, in discussing defiance with the student, the teacher must be prepared to hear him out. There must be discussion, not a lecture or argument. The student will likely accuse the teacher of treating him unfairly, and the teacher must be prepared to entertain the possibility that he is right. If the teacher has made mistakes, he should admit them and promise to change his behavior in the future.

It is usually best to encourage the student to say everything he has on his mind before attempting to respond to one or more of the points he raises. This helps the teacher get the full picture and allows him some time to think about what he is hearing. If he attempts to respond to each separate point as the student raises it, the discussion may turn into a series of accusations and rebuttals. This exchange can leave the student with the feeling that his specific objections have been "answered," but that he still is right in accusing the teacher of general unfairness. Regardless of the specific points raised, the teacher should, therefore, clearly express his concern for the student and his desire to treat him fairly. This reassurance (backed, of course, by appropriate behavior) will be more important to the student than particular responses to particular accusations.

With some defiant students, it may be important also to review the teacher's role. The student should understand that the teacher is primarily interested in teaching him, rather than in ordering him around or playing policeman. He must see that the teacher's exertion of authority is done for good reasons having to do with the education of himself and his classmates.

Even serious cases of defiance can usually be handled with one or two sessions like these, if the teacher is honest in dealing with the student and if he follows up the discussion with appropriate behavior. Although unpleasant, incidents of defiance present the teacher with a blessing in disguise. They bring out into the open problems that have been smoldering for a long time under the surface. The defiant act itself will usually have a cathartic effect on the student, releasing much of the tension that has built up and leaving him in a more receptive mood for developing a more constructive relationship with the teacher. Much good can come from the situation if the teacher takes advantage of it by remaining calm, showing concern for the student and willingness to listen to him and following up with appropriate behavior.

The show-off

Some students continually seek attention from teachers or peers by trying to impress or entertain them. They can be very enjoyable for the teacher if they have talent for the role and if they confine their show-off behavior to times and places that are appropriate. Often, however, they are exasperating or disruptive.

The teacher's basic method of dealing with show-offs should be to give them the attention and approval they seek. However, this attention and approval should be confined as much as possible to appropriate behavior. Inappropriate behavior should be ignored. When it is too disruptive to be ignored, the teacher should be careful not to do or say anything that will either call attention to the misbehavior or make the student feel rejected. Thus a comment like, "We're having our lesson now," would be better than, "Stop acting silly." If the student seeks individual attention at an awkward time, he should be delayed rather than refused. He should be told that the teacher will take up the matter with him at a specified later time.

When praising a show-off, praise only appropriate behaviors and specify what is being praised. This will motivate him to repeat these behaviors to gain teacher approval, and will help to reinforce subtly the idea that he can get approval through appropriate behaviors and will not need to clown or go to elaborate lengths.

In general, show-offs need constant reassurance that they are liked and respected, and teachers should try to fill this need. However, specific praise and rewards should be reserved for appropriate behavior. Inappropriate behavior should go unrewarded and, as much as possible, unacknowledged.

Aggression

One of the basic principles of behavior modification is that desirable behavior should be rewarded and undesirable behavior should be ignored. The second part of this principle often cannot be applied to aggressive students, however, because they may hurt other students or damage classroom equipment. This, of course, should not be ignored or allowed. Whenever such harmful or destructive behavior appears, the teacher should demand an end to it immediately. If the student does not comply, the teacher should not hesitate to physically restrain him (if it is possible for him to do so). If the student responds by straining to get away, making threats, or staging a temper tantrum, he should be held until he regains self-control.

While restraining the student, the teacher should speak to him firmly but quietly, telling him to calm down and get control of himself. The student should be reassured that whatever he is concerned about will be discussed and dealt with, but not until he calms down and no longer needs to be restrained. If he insists that the teacher let go of him, he should be firmly told that the teacher will do so as soon as he stops yelling and squirming. This verbal assurance can be nonverbally reinforced by gradually relaxing the grip on the student as he gradually tones down his resistance. When the teacher is ready to release him completely he should do so quietly and informally. If he does it in a formal fashion, "Are you ready to be quiet now?" the student will likely feel the need to make face-saving gestures after he is released.

Restraint may also be required if two students are fighting and do not respond to demands that they stop. The teacher should not attempt to stop a fight by getting in between two participants and trying to deal with both of them at the same time. This will more than likely result in delay, confusion, or even possibly in the teacher getting hit. Instead, the teacher should restrain one of the participants, preferably the more belligerent one.

The student should not only be restrained, he should be pulled back and away from his opponent so that he is not hit while being held. This will effectively stop the fight, although it may be necessary to turn around and order the other participant to stay away. It is also helpful if the teacher does a lot of talking at this point, generally aimed at getting the students to calm down and explaining that the matter will be dealt with shortly, when they comply. If the teacher does not talk and otherwise generally take over here, the students are likely to exchange threats and other face-saving actions.

Humor is very helpful here, if the teacher has the presence of mind to use it. Threats and face-saving actions are more effective and tend to be reinforced when they are taken seriously. However, if the teacher responds with a smile, or with a little remark to show that he considers them more funny or ridiculous than serious, they are likely to stop quickly: "All right, let's stop blowing off steam."

Once an aggressive student has calmed down, the teacher should remove him from the class and talk with him individually. If two students were fighting, it may be necessary to talk to both together. As usual, the teacher should begin by hearing the student out. It is important to help aggressive students see the distinction between feelings and behavior. Feelings should be accepted as legitimate, or at least as understandable.

Thus if the student states that he hates the teacher or some other student or that he is angry because of unfair treatment, he should be asked to state his reasons for feeling this way. The feeling itself should not be denied, "That's not nice—you must never say that you hate someone," or attacked, "What do you mean? Who do you think you are?" If the student has been are treated unfairly, the teacher should express understanding and sympathy. "I can see why you got angry."

If angry feelings are not justified, the teacher should explain the situation at length in a way that does not deny the reality of the feelings, but at the same time does not legitimize them: "I know that you want to be first, but you've got to remember that the others do, too. They have the same rights as you have. So there's no point in getting angry at someone because they went first. You'll have to learn to get used to waiting your turn. If you try to be first all the time, the others will think you are selfish and won't like you as much."

Although the teacher should accept feelings and sometimes expressly legitimize them, he should not accept *misbehavior*. He should clearly state to the student that he will not be allowed to hit others, destroy property, or otherwise act out angry feelings in destructive ways. The student will be expected to control himself and to confine his responses to acceptable behavior.

Habitually aggressive students require some resocialization in order to teach them new ways of dealing with their frustrations or anger. The student must learn that frustration and anger do not justify aggressive behavior. He should be told that he is expected to express his feelings verbally rather than by acting out, and some specific suggestions or instructions about how to do this should be given.

For example, the student who "hits first and asks questions later" needs instruction on handling frustrations and conflicts. He should be urged to inhibit tendencies to strike out, and he should be taught how to resolve conflict through discussion and more appropriate actions. He should be taught to ask classmates what they are doing or why they are doing it instead of simply assuming they are deliberately provoking him. He should be instructed to express his feelings verbally to whoever has caused him to become angry, since this person may have acted unwittingly and may not even realize that he made someone angry or why.

If the students are old enough to participate meaningfully, role reversals in which each puts himself in the place of the other to reenact the situation are valuable. These should be followed with specific suggestions about how to handle the situation that produced the conflict. If it is already covered by a rule, the students should be reminded of this rule. If not, a rule for the future should be suggested.

In continuing conflicts over who goes first or who gets to use what equipment, for instance, a procedure insuring that everyone has equal turns would be appropriate. For short run or single events, a random method, such as calling the toss of a coin, might be better. Where the situation is complex and the students are old enough, some suggestions for give-and-take bargaining could be made. In a ball game, for example, a player who did not get to play the position he wanted to play could be compensated by being allowed to select his place in the batting order.

Students should be encouraged to settle disputes through discussion and bargaining by themselves as much as possible, but also cautioned to bring unresolved disputes to the teacher rather than allow them to escalate into a fight.

A teacher should also try to help an aggressive student see the consequences of his aggressive behavior, largely by appealing to the Golden Rule. The student can usually see that he will dislike another student who tries to bully him, cheat him, or destroy his property. He will then be in a better position to understand why others will dislike and avoid him for the same reasons. It is also helpful to show by examples that he must learn to verbalize his feelings and seek solutions to problems with the other people involved instead of striking out at them. He must see that others will know why he is angry only if he tells them and that hitting them will only make them angry too.

If the aggression results mostly from the student's failure to deal properly with certain situations (inability to share, inability to wait his turn, tendency to overreact to teasing or to accidental physical contact), the teacher should work specifically on this problem with him. Here the teacher must stress that not only the student's behavior but also his overreactive emotions are a part of the problem. To point out emotionality does not mean to instruct the student to deny his feelings; his anger or resentment are plenty real. However, it does mean that in the future he will be expected to work on controlling his feelings in frustrating situations. He must see that certain frustrations are unavoidable, and that by continuing to overreact to them he succeeds only in making himself unhappy and unpopular.

More serious than the cases where students respond to frustration with aggression are those cases in which the student attacks others for no apparent reason. Unprovoked attacks on others are serious, and students who do this regularly may require professional treatment. Sometimes a brutal or sadistic home environment will produce a child who hates everyone and everything and acts out this hatred frequently. Sometimes too, for a variety of reasons, a child may acquire a self-image of himself as a "tough guy" and may actually want others to fear and dislike him. Even in these very serious cases, however, there are many things that teachers can do.

As with any other aggressive students, of course, the teacher should attempt to talk with this student to understand him better and to clarify and explain behavioral expectations. Also, aggressive acting out will have to be dealt with directly as it occurs, as usual. There are other things, however, that the teacher can do to help deal with the problem indirectly. These things will help both student himself and the others in the class to see him in a more positive light.

First, the teacher should avoid labeling him and avoid reinforcing any negative label he may apply to himself. Thus the teacher should not refer to the student as a bully or announce that he is being separated from his neighbors because he "can't keep his hands to himself." These and similar actions imply that the student is different, that there is something permanently wrong with him, or that he cannot control himself. Such remarks should be avoided in favor of actions that will help express the confidence that he can and will learn to behave acceptably.

The teacher can help the student practice a more positive role by arranging for him to play such a role toward his classmates. It might be helpful for this student to be used as a tutor, for example, or to teach others useful skills that he knows (tying shoes, operating equipment, arts and crafts, music, or other talents). In reading and role-play situations, he should be assigned parts that feature kindness, friendship, and helpfulness toward others; he would be ideal for the part of an ogre that everyone feared and disliked until they found out how good he was underneath.

Cooperative and helpful behavior by the aggressive student should be acknowledged and praised whenever it occurs. Also, potentially serious conflicts should be nipped in the bud if the teacher can spot them early enough. By skillful intervention he can turn a potential fight into a cooperative situation by making specific suggestions about how the students can handle it. For good measure, he can then add that he is very pleased to see that they can cooperate together. These and similar behaviors can help change a negative self-concept and begin to make the student see himself as someone that others will want to get to know and will like as a friend.

So far, we have given suggestions about what teachers *should* do to deal with aggressiveness in students. Before leaving this topic, it is worth discussing one frequently advocated technique that we specifically do *not* recommend. This is the practice of providing substitute methods for expressing aggression, such as telling the student to punch a punching bag instead of another student or instructing him to act out aggression against a doll that he is to pretend is the teacher. Such practices have been recommended by psychoanalytically oriented writers who believe that angry feelings must be acted out in behavior and who see substitutes as a way of doing it harmlessly. The usual rationale given for this recommendation is that the acting-out of angry feelings will have a cathartic effect that will reduce or eliminate the anger. Without such release in behavior, the anger presumably will remain and grow, eventually to be released in harmful fashion.

This suggestion has a wide appeal because it has a certain face validity, especially the notion that expression of feelings leads to a cathartic effect. Most people do experience a catharsis if they "get it off their chest" or "have it out." Expressing angry feelings verbally is probably a good thing. This does not mean, however, that hostile impulses need to be acted out behaviorally.

Encouraging a student to act out his anger against a substitute object can only increase or prolong the problem, not reduce it. Instead of helping him to learn to respond more maturely to frustration and to learn more acceptable ways of acting when frustrated, this method: (1) reinforces the idea that his overreactiveness is expected, approved, and "normal"; (2) reinforces the expectation that whenever he has angry feelings he will need to act these out behaviorally; (3) provides an inappropriate model for the rest of the class, increasing the likelihood that the problem will spread to them, too.

The problem here is that the connection, "I need to act out angry feelings—I can release them through catharsis," is merely the end point of a chain of reactions. The connections "frustration–angry feelings," and "angry feelings–act out" precede a cathartic end point. Every time the end point of the chain is repeated and reinforced, the whole chain that led up to it is repeated and reinforced. Thus the student is reinforced not only for expressing extreme anger harmlessly, but also for building up extreme anger in the first place and for believing that this emotion requires or justifies aggressive behavior.

Thus teachers are not doing students any favors by encouraging them to act out hostility against substitute objects. They are merely prolonging and reinforcing immature emotional control. If kept up long enough, this sort of treatment will produce an adult who is prone to having temper tantrums at the slightest frustration and who spends much of his time building up and then releasing hostile feelings. This sort of person is neither very happy nor very likable and is, in a word, immature.

The teacher should not attempt to get students to act out all emotions. Instead, he should work on helping them to clearly distinguish between emotions and behavior and between appropriate and inappropriate emotions. Inappropriate emotions (unjustified anger or other emotional overreactions) should be labeled as such, and the reasons why they are inappropriate should be explained. Behavior that it is simply unacceptable must not be tolerated, no matter how strong the student's emotions or how strong his impulse to act out. Acceptable (and more effective) alternatives should be explained and insisted upon. All aspects of the teacher's behavior should communicate the expectation that the student can and will achieve mature self-control. There should be no suggestion that he is helpless in the face of uncontrollable emotions or impulses.

Unresponsiveness

Some students lack the self-confidence to participate normally in classroom activities. They do not raise their hands seeking to answer questions, and they will copy from a neighbor, take a guess, or leave an item blank rather than come and see the teacher about their seatwork. When they are called on and do not know an answer, they will stare at the floor silently or perhaps mumble incoherently. Sometimes this "strategy" is successful, since many teachers become uneasy and give the student the answer or call on someone else rather than keep him "on the spot." Observers who see such behavior should communicate it to the teacher, since teachers usually are not aware of it.

In general, fears and inhibitions about classroom participation should be treated with indirect rather than direct methods. Attacking the problem directly by labeling it and urging the student to overcome it can backfire by making him all the more self-conscious and inhibited (much research on stuttering, for example, shows this). Therefore, the teacher should stress what the student should be doing, rather than what he is not doing. When he is called on, he should be questioned in a way that communicates that the teacher wants and expects an answer. Questions should be asked directly. They should not be prefaced with stems like, "Do you think you could . . ." or "Do you want to . . . ," since these suggest uncertainty about the student and make it easy for him to remain silent. Also, questions should be asked in a conversational, informal tone. If asked too formally, the question may sound too much like a test item and may unnecessarily stir up anxiety.

Questions should be accompanied by appropriate gestures and expressions to communicate that the teacher is talking to the student in question and expects an answer from him. He should look at the student expectantly after asking the question. If the student answers, he should respond with praise or with relevant feedback. If he answers too softly, he should be praised and then asked to say it again louder, "Good! Say it loud so everyone can hear." If he appears to be about to answer, but hesitating, the teacher can help by nodding his head, forming the initial sound with his lips, or encouraging him verbally, "Say it." If the student does not respond at all, the teacher can give him the answer and then repeat the question or ask him to repeat the answer. If he mumbles or partially repeats, he should be asked to repeat it again and then praised when he does so. All of these procedures are geared to make clear to the student that he is expected to talk, to give him some practice in doing so, and to reassure him and reward him when he does.

Interactions with such students should be deliberately extended at times, both to give them practice at extended discussions and to help eliminate the idea that they can keep interactions short and infrequent by lying low. Thus if the student answers an initial question correctly, sometimes the teacher should ask him another question or have him elaborate on the response. If he fails the initial question, the follow-up question should be a simpler one that he is likely to be able to handle. In general, questions that require him to explain something in detail will be the most difficult. Progressively simpler demands include factual questions requiring a short answer, choice questions requiring him only to choose among presented alternatives, and questions that require only a yes or no response. If the student does not respond to any level of questioning, he can be asked to repeat things or to imitate actions. Once he begins to respond correctly, the teacher can move back up to more demanding levels as his confidence grows.

The inhibited student needs especially careful treatment in situations where he is not responding. As long as he appears to be trying to answer the question or to begin to make a response, the teacher should wait him out. If he begins to look anxious, however, like he is worrying about being in the spotlight instead of thinking about the question, the teacher should intervene by repeating the question or giving a clue. He should not call on another student, nor allow others to call out the answer.

In these situations the teacher should not allow the child to "practice" resistance or nonresponsiveness (Blank, 1973). Anxiety or resistance should be cut off before it gets a chance to build, and the teacher should be sure to get some kind of response before leaving the student. If he does not respond to any of the questions requiring a verbal answer, he can be asked to make a nonverbal response such as shaking his head or pointing to one of two or more alternatives. With very young children the teacher might ask them to imitate a physical action or even manually guide them in performing a physical action until they begin to do it themselves. In any case, it is important to get some form of positive response from the student before leaving him.

Students at all levels should be instructed to say, "I don't know," rather than remain silent when they cannot respond. This teacher instruction will remove the stigma that some students attach to saying, "I don't know." Many students will hesitate to say this because previous teachers have unwittingly implanted the idea that this is shameful and unacceptable through such comments as, "What do you mean, you don't know? Don't tell me you don't know. Read the material and then you'll know." By legitimizing this response, the teacher can make it possible for the nonresponsive student to answer verbally even when he does not know the answer to the question asked.

These methods are difficult to apply in large group situations with extremely unresponsive students who often do not say anything at all. In these cases, the better course might be for the teacher to temporarily avoid calling on a student while he works with him in individual and small group situations. This type of student needs to be brought along slowly. Usually time is required to get rid of strong inhibitions or fears, and much progress can be undone by attempting to push the student too far too fast. With continued progress and regular success, his confidence will grow and his tolerance for being "on the spot" will increase. The teacher should continue to make sure that he gets a response of some kind from this student every time he deals with him, and he should see that the student does not become regarded as someone who does not answer and who, therefore, is no longer asked to respond.

If this type of inhibition is a widespread problem in a particular teacher's class, the teacher is likely to be causing or contributing to it. Observers should look for signs of overvaluing correct answers and of showing impatience or disgust when a student does not respond correctly. The teacher's handling of seatwork should also be observed to see if he is scaring students off by criticizing them instead of helping them when they come to him with questions.

Failure to complete assignments

Teachers often complain that certain students fail to complete seatwork and homework assignments. This is something that can and should be dealt with, although the method used will depend on the reason why assignments are not turned in.

In some cases the student does not turn in work because he cannot—he has spent time trying to cope with it, but has not been able to figure out how to do it. This is not a motivation problem; it is a teaching problem. What is needed is remedial work to help him make up what he does not understand and to move him to the point where he can do it himself.

Great patience and determination are needed in working with these students, since they will need support and encouragement to keep trying. If the teacher criticizes them, embarrasses them before the group, or shows impatience or frustration, they will likely begin to simply copy from neighbors rather than continue to try to do the work themselves.

The teacher should encourage this student by pointing out the progress he is making relative to where he has been, regardless of where he stands relative to others in the class. The teacher will need to make time for conducting remedial teaching with him or to plan some other remediation arrangement (see Chapter 8). In any case,

slow learners need a teacher's patience, more appropriate assignments, and remediation, not criticism or punishment for failing to do
what they simply are unable to do.

For whatever reasons, there are some who could do the work
but do not do it and, therefore, do not turn it in or do not finish it.
The best way to deal with this problem is to stop it before it gets
started, or at least before it becomes a large problem. From the
beginning of the year, teachers should be very clear about instructions
for seatwork and homework. Their purpose and importance should
be explained to the students, and this explanation should be backed
with appropriate behavior such as collecting it, checking it, and giving
feedback or remedial work when necessary.

Although the teacher may wish to make variable or open-ended
assignments (such as identifying extra problems to do for extra
credit or "to see if you can figure them out"), each student should
have a clear-cut minimum amount of work for which he is accountable. This amount may (and often should) vary from student to
student for instructional reasons, but there should be a clear understanding about what each must turn in and when it is due.

Students involved in seatwork should be monitored closely to
see that they are working productively. Teachers should make very
clear from the beginning of the year that students are expected to
finish their seatwork assignments before doing anything else during
this time. Clear procedures should be established for what a student
should do when he does not understand and, therefore, cannot continue, as well as what he should do if he finishes. The established
policy must then be consistently enforced so that everyone forms
the habit of doing his seatwork when assigned.

Failure to turn in homework is a more difficult problem to
handle, since the teacher cannot monitor the student and intervene
if he is not working properly. He can and should keep a careful
check of homework being turned in, however, so that he can assign
students who did not complete it to do so during free periods at
school (if they are able to do the work). If they do not complete the
job during free periods at school, they should be kept after school
to complete it. Here again, the policy must be established right from
the beginning of the year that assignments are to be completed
and turned in on time. If they are not, completion of the assignment
should be made the top priority item for the student whenever he is
not involved in a lesson or other instructional activity.

Of course, this assumes that homework assignments are relevant
in content and appropriate in level of difficulty. If failure to turn

in homework is a frequent problem in a particular class, the type of homework being assigned and the way homework is monitored when it is turned in should be reviewed and adjusted.

A few students may have a problem completing homework because of pressures from job demands or a poor home situation. Where this appears to be the case, the problem should be discussed at length with the student, and a mutually agreeable solution should be worked out. Schools should be flexible enough to make time and space available to students who realistically cannot do homework at home. Students in such situations need a helping hand, not more trouble.

In some cases the teacher may wish to contact the student's parents regarding his homework. This may not be helpful. The question of whether or not to bring the parents in on problems like this will be discussed in a later section.

Analyzing student behavior

Many forms of student behavior that sometimes cause problems for teachers have not been discussed in this chapter; behavior such as student habits that irritate or disgust the teacher, students who bait the teacher with provocative or embarrassing remarks, and various signs of mental or emotional disorder. These problems are hard to generalize about, since they usually require a specific diagnosis to determine why the student is behaving the way he is and to suggest possible treatment. Suggestions about how teachers can proceed in dealing with these problems are given below.

Should anything be done at all?

As a first step, the teacher might ask whether or not it is wise to do anything about the problem. Certain behavior might be particularly irritating to the teacher but yet be normal or at least accepted in the student's environment. Vulgar language and frequent references to sex, which might be of concern if demonstrated by a middle-class ten-year-old, for example, are perfectly normal in a high school serving students from the slums.

Also, some things the teacher may know about a student may have nothing to do with the student's behavior in the classroom. For example, a teacher may discover that a boy who behaves acceptably in class and who turns in his assignments has been drinking heavily on weekends or has fathered an illegitimate child. Unless the teacher has a close relationship with the boy, he might do more harm than good by involving himself in the situation.

Finding out what the behavior means

To the extent that the relevant behavior problem occurs in the classroom, the teacher should question the student and conduct systematic observations of him. These observations will help the teacher gain a better understanding of the meaning of the student's behavior and the reasons he acts as he does (if the student does not know the reasons or has not divulged them). When a student's behavior is particularly unusual or irritating, a teacher (or anyone) can easily become so concerned that he notices only the behavior and little else. It is important to *remember, then, that the student's behavior may be just a symptom of an underlying problem, and that his symptomatic behavior is not as important as the reasons that are producing it.*

If the behavior seems to be simply a habit and not part of a large complex of problems, it can be handled straightforwardly. The teacher should insist that the student drop the irritating habit and learn more appropriate behavior. This explicit improvement demand should be supported by an appropriate rationale (appeal to school rules, to social convention, or to the Golden Rule).

Where the student's habit is not fundamentally evil or immoral, but is merely a violation of school rules, social convention, tact, good taste, or simply of the teacher's personal preferences, this distinction should be made clear to the student. He should not be made to feel guilty, or to feel that his habit is a sign that something is seriously wrong with him. He should understand that the teacher objects to the timing of the act or the way it was carried out, but not necessarily to· the act itself. Teachers are justified in forbidding habits that are disruptive or irritating enough to interfere with their teaching; however, such habits should not be described as worse than they really are.

If the student's behavior seems to be more serious or complex than a simple habit and if he has not given an adequate explanation for it, careful observation is needed.

Observations should begin by trying to describe the behavior more precisely. Is it a ritual or focal behavior that is repeated pretty much the same way over and over (masturbation, spitting, nose picking) or is it a more general tendency (aggression, suspiciousness, sadistic sense of humor) that is manifested in many different ways? Perhaps the description can be narrowed down more specifically. Does the student show a recognizable pattern? For example, do a student's suspicions center around a belief that others are talking about him behind his back, or does he instead think he is being picked on or cheated? If he does think others are talking about him, what does he think they are saying or accusing him of? If the student laughs inappropriately, what makes him laugh? If this could be discovered, it might provide clues to what his behavior means.

Besides narrowing down the behavior more specifically, observations should establish the conditions under which it occurs. After all, the student does not show this symptomatic behavior all the time. The following are some of the questions the teacher might ask in trying to analyze it. Is it a chronic problem, or is it something that started suddenly in the recent past? Is it more likely to happen at a particular time of day or a particular part of the week? Does it occur more frequently when tests are given, for example, or when a film is shown in the classroom? Are there common elements in the situations in which the behavior has been observed? Such common elements might lead to the identification of the events that trigger off the reaction.

Teachers should also ask themselves what they were doing immediately before the student acted out. This might reveal that the teacher tends to trigger off the behavior himself by treating the student unfairly, or at least in a way that the student thinks is unfair. Analyses of this sort help the teacher place the student's behavior in context as a symptom and may help identify the underlying cause. This, in turn, will enable the teacher to move away from an essentially negative, describe-the-problem-but-don't-do-anything-about-it approach, "How can I get John to stop sulking and refusing to participate?" and to move toward diagnosis and treatment, *"How can I help John see that when I refuse to let him do something he wants to do that I am not angry with him or rejecting him?"*

In summary, teachers should question students and observe them systematically when they show repeated disturbing behavior. Attention should focus more on the meaning of and reasons for the behavior rather than on the behavior itself. Unless the behavior is an isolated, simple habit, detailed observations may be needed to discover the causes and plan appropriate treatment.

Arranging a conference

Often the simplest and best way to understand the student's behavior is to talk to him about it. This can be done in a conference arranged during a free period or after school. The main purpose here, besides seeking information, is to show concern for the student. The teacher should note the observations he has made about the student's behavior, state that he is concerned about this behavior, and ask the student if he will explain it to him. The main thing is to get the student talking and then to hear him out.

The student probably will not be able to state why he acts as he does, and the teacher should not expect him to. If the student had this much insight, he probably would not be behaving symptomatically in the first place. Hopefully, some helpful clues or information will emerge from the discussion. If the conference does produce a breakthrough, fine. If not, at least something will have been accomplished if the student comes away with the knowledge that the teacher is concerned about him and wishes to help. In any case, the conference should be concluded in some way that gives the student a feeling of closure.

If his behavior has been disruptive, the teacher should clarify expectations and limits, as well as reach an agreement with the student about any special action to be taken. If the student's problem requires no special action or if the teacher does not yet know what action to take, he can conclude the conference by telling the student that he is glad to have had a chance to discuss the problem with him and that he will help in any way he can if the student will let him know how.

Bringing in parents and other adults

Teachers should think twice before involving parents, principals, counselors, or other adults in a problem involving their students. This tends to escalate the seriousness of the problem in the minds of all concerned and to label the student as a "problem student." Thus the expected benefits of involving additional adults must be weighed against the possible damage that could result from such labeling.

Usually, the teacher should turn first to a counselor, a school psychologist, or other professional, if such a source is available at the school. By discussing the situation with such a resource person, preferably after the person has observed in the teacher's classroom several times, the teacher might gain a new insight or get some specific suggestions about treatment. A knowledgeable principal, assistant principal, or fellow teacher might also provide this resource.

In seeking advice, the resource person's title is less important than the quality of his observations and suggestions. If he has usually been helpful in providing insight or suggestions about dealing with students' problems, the teacher stands to benefit from talking with him.

Some resource people may be available to deal with the student directly rather than through the teacher. Again, this recourse may or may not be helpful. There is usually little point in having a student tested, for example, unless there is a question of a physical problem. Knowledge of the student's scores on an intelligence or personality test usually contributes little or nothing to the solution of his problem.

Testing may make it worse, in fact, by labeling him in a way that leads to unfortunate self-fulfilling prophecy effects.

Thus there is little point in bringing in other adults to deal with the student directly unless they are capable of treating him in some effective way. Merely sending a student out of the room occasionally to talk to a counselor, vice-principal, or "disciplinarian" almost never does any good over the long run. If the student's behavior problem is in the classroom, it must be dealt with there.

Contacting a student's parents about a behavior problem can also be risky. After all, to the extent that a student has serious general emotional or behavioral problems, his parents are probably the biggest single reason for them. Merely informing the parents of the problem will do no good and probably will do great harm. If the teacher gives parents the impression that he expects them to "do something," they will probably threaten or punish the student and let it go at that. Teachers should be careful not to give parents this impression unless they have specific suggestions to propose to them.

Sometimes specific suggestions can be given, as when the teacher enlists the parents' help in seeing that the student gets enough sleep, does his homework, eats breakfast in the morning, and so forth. In the process of making suggestions, teachers may also need to tell parents many of the things discussed in this book. The need to think of punishment as the last resort and the need to have confidence and positive expectations for their children are two particular points that many, perhaps most, parents violate when their children have problems.

If the parents are called in mostly so that the teacher can get information from them, this should be made clear to them. They should know that the teacher does not intend to simply complain about their child or to demand that they do something about him. The teacher should simply state his observations about their child's behavior and his concern about him and ask the parents if they can add anything that might help him understand their child better or deal with him more effectively.

He should question the parents to see how much they know about the problem, and what their explanation for it is, if they have one. If some plan of action emerges, it should be discussed and agreed upon with the parents. The teacher and parents should also agree on what the parents are going to tell the student about the conference. If no particular parental action is being suggested, the conference should be brought to some form of closure by the teacher, "Well, I'm glad we have had a chance to talk about George today. I think you've given me a better understanding of him. I can't think of anything special or unusual that you or I should try to do with him. I'll keep working with him in the classroom, and let you know about his progress. Meanwhile, if something comes up that I ought to know, give me a call." With this approach, the parents should emerge from the conference knowing what to tell their child about it and what, if anything, the teacher is requesting them to do.

Bearing the unbearable

Teachers are often in the uncomfortable position of being forced to try to cope with problems that simply cannot be resolved satisfactorily under the circumstances. If enough seriously disturbed students are in a single classroom, a single teacher is not going to be able to deal with all of the serious problems successfully and teach the curriculum at the same time to the whole class. When things get unbearable, something has to give; either the problem has to be whittled down some, or the teacher needs help from outside resources. Unfortunately, resources adequate to do the job usually are not available.

The resources that are available are usually not successful. Parents and school disciplinarians are usually armed only with pep talks, threats, and punishment. Suspension from school merely deepens the student's alienation and makes it harder for him to cope when he comes back (*if* he comes back). Placement in a class for the mentally retarded, a class for the emotionally disturbed, or a reform school, although well meant and usually referred to as "treatment," usually represents the first step on a one-way ladder going down.

Genuinely therapeutic treatment is available, but unless the student's family is wealthy and willing to pay high professional fees, the student will likely have to go on a waiting list. If he is lucky he may get treated a year or two later, but not now.

Thus in the vast majority of cases involving disturbed students, the only effective treatment the student will get must come from his classroom teacher (with the help of counselors, school psychologists, or other professionals who might be available as resources). If the student is almost old enough to drop out of school or if he is in danger of being thrown out, this may be his last real chance to head off a pattern of lifelong failure and misery. It is for this reason that teachers must push themselves to their limit before giving up on any student, and even then they should do so only for the sake of the rest of the class.

Summary

The key to successful classroom management lies in using the preventive techniques described in the previous chapter. Consistent use of these techniques will eliminate most classroom problems. Those problems that remain, however, should be handled with the techniques described in the present chapter. Since many major disruptions start as minor misbehavior, teachers should know how to stop minor problems quickly and nondisruptively. To be able to do this, they must form the habit of monitoring the classroom regularly so that they always know what is going on.

Much misbehavior can be simply ignored. When it is not disruptive, and when the students involved quickly return their attention to the lesson or assignment, it is best for the teacher to let the matter go without interrupting the activity or calling attention to the misbehavior. If the misbehavior is prolonged or begins to become disruptive, direct intervention will be needed. When the students know what they are supposed to be doing, and when the nature of their misbehavior is obvious to the teacher, there is no need for the teacher to question them or conduct an investigation. His goal here is to return them to productive activity as quickly and nondisruptively as possible. Ideally, this should be done in a way that does not even call attention to the misbehavior. This can be done through eye contact, touch or gesture, moving closer to the students involved, calling on an inattentive student, or praising the appropriate behavior of a student seated near the one who is misbehaving.

When it is not possible or advisable to use these nondisruptive direct intervention techniques, the teacher should call the students' names and correct their behavior by telling them what they are supposed to be doing or by reminding them of the rules. Intervention here should be brief and direct, and it should focus on the expected desirable behavior rather than on the misbehavior. Questions, flaunting of authority through threats or harshness, and nagging should be avoided.

It will be necessary for the teacher to question students when the misbehavior has been serious or disruptive and when the teacher is unclear about the facts. Such investigations should be conducted privately, to minimize the need for face-saving. The teacher should assure all students involved that they will be heard, but he must insist that each student wait his turn while he deals with one student at a time. Questions asked during these investigations should be confined to those seriously intended to elicit relevant factual information.

The teacher should not make any decisions or attempt to settle the issue until he has heard everyone out. After the teacher has gathered as many relevant facts as he can, he should take positive action aimed at both resolving the problem as it presently stands and preventing its return in the future. This will mean clarification of expected behavior, and perhaps the establishment of a new rule or agreement. Ordinarily there will be no need for punishment, which should be reserved as a measure of last resort to use with students who repeatedly persist in the same kinds of misbehavior.

Because punishment is a stop-gap control measure rather than a solution, and because it involves many undesirable side effects on both the student being punished and on his classmates, it should be used only as a last resort. It should be clear to everyone involved that the offending student has brought punishment upon himself through repeated misbehavior, so that he has left the teacher with no other choice. Appropriate forms of punishment include withdrawal or restriction of privileges, exclusion from the group, and assignments that force the student to reflect upon the importance of the behavioral norms he has violated and the rationale for them. To be more effective, punishment should be related to the offense, should be as brief and mild as possible, and should be flexible enough so that the student can redeem himself by correcting his behavior.

Most teachers will have a few students with long standing and severe disturbances that will require extraordinary corrective measures. Suggestions for dealing with some of the more common types of disturbances are given in the chapter. Such serious problems require careful observation and diagnosis followed by individualized prescription and treatment. However, there are a few general principles teachers should bear in mind when planning their approach to these problem students. First, teachers should treat such students just like they treat other students as much as possible, so that these students do not become thought of as "special cases." Second, teachers should continually stress the positive with such students, indicating the desirable behavior they expect from them and communicating their expectation that the student will improve. Third, teachers will usually have to form close individual relationships with such students, so that the students will like and respect them enough to want to earn their respect and affection in return. Fourth, teachers should concentrate on the in-school behavior of problem students; teachers' attempts to become the student's psychotherapist or the family's social case worker often do more harm than good.

Although it is almost always useful to gather information and to solicit advice, teachers should think carefully before involving anyone else in their relationship with a problem student. This step may escalate the problem in the minds of everyone involved and could lead to undesirable self-fulfilling prophecy effects. Most relevant information can be gotten by observing and questioning the student himself, and most beneficial changes will come as a result of time spent establishing and using a good relationship with the student. Thus, unless they are lucky enough to have access to an intervention expert who has built up a generally successful record, teachers are likely to get more from observing and talking with problem students than from talking about the students with their parents or with school personnel. Most classroom problems must be solved in the classroom, regardless of whatever additional problems may exist on the outside.

SUGGESTED ACTIVITIES AND QUESTIONS

1. Reread the case presented in Chapter 1 and pinpoint the management errors that the teacher made. Then, using the content of this chapter and your own ideas, specify how the teacher could have behaved more profitably.

2. Ask your instructor or in-service leader to find films or video tapes of teaching behavior, and use the rating scales that accompany this chapter to rate the teacher's managerial ability. Try to identify as many good and poor techniques as you can. Whenever you spot an ineffective technique, try to suggest alternative techniques that the teacher could have utilized.

3. Summarize in five brief paragraphs the guidelines that a teacher can use to deal with the five classroom-adjustment problems that were discussed in this chapter (defiance, show-off behavior, aggression, unresponsiveness, and failure to complete assignments). Practice your ability to deal with these problems in role-play situations with a few other people. Specify a hypothetical problem, select someone to be a student and someone to be the teacher, and allow other participants to provide feedback. Did the teacher deal with the problem effectively? Did he seem sincere? What alternatives could have been used?

4. Review or construct your list of student behaviors or characteristics that are most likely to embarrass you or to make you anxious. Practice how you will deal with these situations in your classroom. For example, if students who threaten your authority are an especially vulnerable or sensitive area for you, list student statements that are likely to touch you off and practice how you would this situation:

TEACHER: You're right, Frank, what I told you yesterday was incorrect. Thank you for looking this up and bringing it to my attention.

HERB: *(gleefully bellowing from the back of the room):* You're always wrong! We never know when to believe you.

5. Describe five techniques that a teacher can use to eliminate minor student misbehavior relatively quickly and nondisruptively. (See also Exercise 8 in Chapter 6, Suggested Activities and Questions.)

6. Why should teachers avoid threats and appeals to authority when stopping misbehavior through direct intervention?

7. Why do the authors not recommend the use of physical punishment in school settings?

8. In general what steps can a teacher follow to make exclusion from the group an effective punishment (student misbehavior is markedly reduced or eliminated)? In particular, how does the teacher behave when excluding or readmitting students to group activities?

9. Why in most cases should teachers focus their attention on the student's school related behavior rather than on the student's out of school behavior?

10. When is punishment necessary, and what is the most appropriate way to administer punishment?

11. A ninth-grade history teacher sees Bill Thomas grab (without apparent provocation) Tim Grant's comb and throw it on the floor. Bill and Tim begin to push each other. What should the teacher do? Be specific. Write out or role-play the actual words that you would use. As a teacher, would you behave differently if you had not seen what preceded the pushing?

12. Ruth Burden, who teaches eleventh-grade English, has noticed that Ed James has slept through her class for a week. Should she arrange a conference with the student? If not, what should she do? If so, specifically what should Miss Burden do and say at the conference? Assume that Ed relates that he cannot sleep at night because his parents fight nightly and that even after their argument ends he is so upset that he cannot sleep? Should Miss Burden talk to the parents and, if so, what should she say?

FORM 7.1. Teacher's Reaction to Inattention and Misbehavior

USE: When the teacher is faced with problems of inattention or misbehavior
PURPOSE: To see if teacher handles these situations appropriately
    Code the following information concerning teacher's response to mis-
behavior or to inattentiveness. Code only when teacher seems to be aware of
the problem; do not code minor problems that teacher doesn't even notice.

BEHAVIOR CATEGORIES   CODES

	A	B	C
A. TYPE OF SITUATION			
1. Total class, lesson, or discussion	1. 3	3	4
2. Small group activity—problem in group	2. 3	3	46
3. Small group activity—problem out of group	3. 1	2	2
4. Seatwork checking or study period	4. 1	3	4
5. Other (specify)	5. 4	3	2

6. __ __ __
7. __ __ __

B. TYPE OF MISBEHAVIOR
   1. Brief, nondisruptive, should be ignored
   2. Minor, but extended or repeated. Should
      be stopped nondisruptively
   3. Disruptive, should be stopped quickly. No
      questions needed
   4. Disruptive, questions needed or advisable
   5. Other (specify)

8. __ __ __
9. __ __ __
10. __ __ __
11. __ __ __
12. __ __ __
13. __ __ __
14. __ __ __
15. __ __ __

C. TEACHER'S RESPONSE(S)
   1. Ignores (deliberately)
   2. Nonverbal; uses eye contact, gestures or
      touch, or moves near offender
   3. Praises someone else's good behavior
   4. Calls offender's name; calls for attention or
      work; gives rule reminder. No overdwelling
   5. Overdwells on misbehavior, nags
   6. Asks rhetorical or meaningless questions
   7. Asks appropriate questions—investigates publicly
   8. Investigates privately, now or later
   9. Threatens punishment if behavior is repeated
  10. Punishes (note type)
  11. Other (specify)

16. __ __ __
17. __ __ __
18. __ __ __
19. __ __ __
20. __ __ __
21. __ __ __
22. __ __ __
23. __ __ __
24. __ __ __
25. __ __ __

CHECK IF APPLICABLE
_____ 1. Teacher delays too long before acting, so problems escalate
_____ 2. Teacher identifies wrong student or fails to include all involved
_____ 3. Teacher fails to specify appropriate behavior (when this is not
        clear)
_____ 4. Teacher fails to specify rationale behind demands (when this is
        clear)
_____ 5. Teacher attributes misbehavior to ill will, evil motives
_____ 6. Teacher describes misbehavior as a typical or unchangeable trait;
        labels student

NOTES: *#1, 2, and 4 were all for student #12 (he seems*
to be the only consistent problem as far as
management goes).

FORM 7.2. Case Study

USE: *To do concentrated observations on one or a few students who are*
     problems for the teacher
PURPOSE: *To systematically gather information needed to understand the*
     student's behavior and to make recommendations to the teacher
     Use the codes on this page to record the student's behavior and link
it to antecedent causes when possible.

A. STUDENT BEHAVIOR

	Behavior	TIME		CODES A	CODES B
1.	Pays attention or actively works at assignment		1.		
2.	Stares in space or closes eyes	8:15	1.	1	
3.	Fidgets, taps, amuses self	8:23	2.	6	1
4.	Distracts others—entertains, jokes	8:24	3.	1	
5.	Distracts others—questions, seeks help, investigates	8:29	4.	11	10
		8:30	5.	1	
6.	Distracts others—attacks or teases	8:38	6.	6	4
7.	Leaves seat—goes to teacher	8:40	7.	1	
8.	Leaves seat—wanders, runs, plays	8:47	8.	2	2
9.	Leaves seat—does approved action (what?)	8:49	9.	1	7
10.	Leaves seat—does forbidden action (what?)	8:51	10.	5	2
11.	Calls out answer	8:53	11.	1	6
12.	Calls out irrelevant comment (what?)	9:00	12.	9	
13.	Calls out comment about teacher (what?)	9:27	13.	15	1
14.	Calls out comment about classmate (what?)	9:28	14.	1	9
15.	Deliberately causes disruption	9:34	15.	6	1
16.	Destroys property (whose? what?)	9:36	16.	1	7
17.	Leaves room without permission	9:45	17.	9	
18.	Other (specify)	:	18.		
		:	19.		

B. APPARENT CAUSE
   What set off the behavior?
   1. No observable cause—suddenly began acting out
   2. Appeared stumped by work, gave up
   3. Finished work, had nothing to do
   4. Distracted by classmate (who?)
   5. Asked to respond or perform by teacher
   6. Teacher checks or asks about progress on assigned work
   7. Teacher calls for attention or return to work
   8. Teacher praise (for what?)
   9. Teacher criticism (for what?)
   10. Teacher praises or rewards another student
   11. Teacher criticizes or punishes another student
   12. Teacher refuses or delays permission request
   13. Other (specify)

TIME	#	A	B
:	20.		
:	21.		
:	22.		
:	23.		
:	24.		
:	25.		
:	26.		
:	27.		
:	28.		
:	39.		
:	30.		
:	31.		
:	32.		
:	33.		
:	34.		
:	35.		
:	36.		
:	37.		
:	38.		
:	39.		
:	40.		

NOTES:
   9:45 Recess.

Note any information relevant to the following points:

STUDENT'S EMOTIONAL RESPONSE

1. Complaints (He is disliked, picked on, left out, not getting share, unjustly blamed, ridiculed, asked to do what he can't do or he's already done):

2. Posturing Behavior (threats, obscenities, challenging or denying teacher's authority):

3. Defense Mechanisms (silence, pouting, mocking politeness or agreement, appears ashamed or angry, talks back or laughs, says "I don't care," rationalizes, blames others, tries to cajole or change subject)

   Grins while being "talked to", blames student #7 ("He hit me first").

Check if applicable:

   ✓ 1. Teacher tends to overreact to student's misbehavior
   ___ 2. Student's misbehavior usually ultimately leads to affection or reward from the teacher
   ___ 3. Student usually acts out for no apparent reason
   ✓ 4. Student usually acts out when idle or unable to do assignments
   ___ 5. Student usually acts out when distracted by another child
   ___ 6. Student usually acts out in response to the teacher's behavior.

POSITIVE BEHAVIOR

1. Note the student's changes in behavior over time. When is he most attentive? What topics or situations seem to interest him?

   Attentive throughout reading group.

2. What questions does he raise his hand to answer?

   Seeks to respond in all situations — whenever he thinks he can answer.

3. What work assignments does he diligently try to do well?

4. What activities does he select if given a choice?

CHAPTER 8

Classroom grouping

Previous chapters have identified a variety of teaching behaviors that can be used to exert desirable effects upon student behavior. For the most part, the suggestions advanced in this book have dealt with teaching behavior and classroom interaction. In this chapter we will focus on a different aspect of classroom life by examining how teachers arrange the classroom environment for learning. In particular, we will review the literature on ability grouping in order to see if grouping students for instruction, on the basis of student aptitude or achievement, is a sound instructional strategy.

In addition, the chapter will describe ways in which the classroom teacher can organize the classroom in order to have more time to work with certain students on special learning problems, while other students are allowed to pursue topics of individual interest. Finally, we will describe peer tutoring (letting students teach one another), review relevant literature on this topic, and provide practical guidelines for teachers who would like to utilize peer-tutoring techniques in their own classroom.

Ability grouping: little positive value

The notion of ability grouping is a very appealing one; logic would seem to dictate that teachers could do a better job if differences in student ability were not so great. The teacher often goes too slow for the high achiever, and too fast for the low achiever. Thus, ability grouping is an attempt to reduce the range of student ability so the teacher can instruct more effectively. However, several authoritative reviews of ability grouping, when viewed in combination, suggest that ability grouping *per se* is likely to have little positive effect on student achievement. Furthermore, such grouping is often found to reduce the achievement of low-achieving students and to fail in preparing students effectively for life in a pluralistic society (Borg, 1966; Findley and Bryan, 1971; Goodlad, 1960; Heathers, 1969; Johnson, 1970; Tuckman, 1970). In fact, most recent studies have suggested that when ability grouping does affect student achievement, the effect is usually negative: students placed into the lower ability levels, relative to other students, suffer an educational decline (Findley and Bryan, 1971). Findley and Bryan summarize the findings of their own report thusly:

> *Grouping practices based on standardized measures of achievement not only tend to restrict the quality of the instructional experience of children with respect to academic and social learning, but also, as a result of ethnic and socioeconomic separation, tend to restrict the overall range of experiences and learning opportunities available in the classroom.*

The reader should understand that these references to ability grouping refer to situations in which students were assigned to rooms on the basis of IQ and achievement levels. They do not refer to ability grouping within the classroom. For example, sixth graders could be assigned to rooms on the basis of achievement levels (Room A = 5.5 or below, Room B = 5.5 to 6.5, and Room C = 6.5 and above) or IQ scores (students in Room A = 100 or below; Room B = 100 to 115, and Room C = 115 or above). Once the teachers in classrooms A, B, and C meet their students, they can assign them to ability groups within the classroom.

These studies did not refer to ability assignments within the classroom but to grouping by assigning students to separate classrooms. In such ability groupings, high- and low-achievement students are completely separated from one another and have no chance to interact. Such groups are often called *homogeneous groupings*, because an attempt is made to substantially reduce the range in IQ or achievement among students in the same class. The students are then similar in aptitude or ability, hence the term homogeneous.

In contrast, when children are assigned at random (e.g., all fifth-grade students' names are on a sheet in alphabetical order and the principal assigns every third name to classroom A, B, C), there is more mixture. Random selection results in a greater range of student ability or aptitude, and thus the term *heterogeneous* is often applied. The reviews indicate that when students are assigned to special homogeneous groups, they do not systematically achieve at higher levels than students who are heterogeneously grouped, and in fact homogeneously grouped students, especially those in low ability groups, have frequently been found to make smaller achievement gains than similar students in heterogeneous groups.

An example

The reader should know how these comparisons are made. Let us look at some fictitious data. Although procedures vary somewhat from study to study, typical features of ability group studies are (1) similar schools are selected, some practicing homogeneous grouping and others grouping heterogeneously; (2) students are tested at the beginning of the year on an IQ or achievement test and then assigned randomly to classes in some schools and by test score in other schools—for purposes of discussion, let us assume that sixth-grade students in ability-grouping schools are assigned to classes on the basis of an IQ test (100 or below, low group; 100 to 115, middle group; 115 or above, high group); (3) at the end of the year children in both types of schools are tested. The data in Table 1 are typical of the results such studies show at the *end* of the school year. The reader should note that the two groups were equal at the beginning of the year. As shown in Table 1, there is little difference in this pseudo data between ability grouped and nongrouped classes. What differences do exist favor the students in the schools that utilized heterogeneous grouping. An investigator finding such differences would conclude that grouping children by ability levels made little difference on achievement and aptitude scores.

Numerous studies similar to our fictitious example have been conducted. Sometimes students in low ability, homogeneous groupings are found to benefit, while students of high ability suffer in heterogeneous groupings. Other studies find just the opposite results. Still other studies indicate that heterogeneous grouping benefits children at all ability levels, and yet other studies report that homogeneous grouping benefits children from all ability levels. Hence, one might reasonably conclude that ability grouping *per se* has no effect of its own, and that the relationship between grouping patterns and student achievement depends upon the ways in which teachers adapt to ability-grouping procedures. However, the reader should note that reviewers who have spent a great deal of time analyzing the results from numerous studies conclude that there is a strong tendency for ability-grouping procedures to penalize the low achiever without

TABLE 1

FICTITIOUS DATA COMPARING THE EFFECTS OF ABILITY GROUPING ON STUDENT PERFORMANCE

	LOW IQ	MIDDLE IQ	HIGH IQ
Homogeneous Schools			
Math: Grade Level	5.8	6.8	7.7
Reading: Grade Level	5.6	7.0	8.0
IQ	99	108	119
Heterogeneous Schools			
Math: Grade Level	5.9	6.7	7.7
Reading: Grade Level	5.7	7.3	8.4
IQ	104	110	121

adding any compensatory gain for high achievers. Furthermore, studies suggest that the affective development of students (how students feel about themselves and school) has not been enhanced by ability grouping. In general, lows are found to lose, educationally, under homogeneous grouping policies, and no group of students consistently benefits from such grouping practices.

Why has ability grouping not worked?

Why then has ability grouping failed? Johnson (1970) suggests that few attempts have been made to change teachers' behavior to enable them to take advantage of new situations. Teachers in schools that practiced ability grouping were not provided with new skills or curriculum materials that were aimed specifically for different levels of students. Goldberg et al. (1966) suggest that teachers did not adjust their content to meet the special needs of students at different achievement levels, but they note that some teachers of the low-ability groups taught less content to low-level pupils and set lower achievement goals for lower-ability students.

Pfeiffer (1967) provides experimental data showing that there were no differences in teacher-student interactions (using the Flanders system, an observation instrument used to code the type and relative frequency of teacher and student talk) in homogeneously and heterogeneously grouped classes. Not surprisingly, he also found no differences in effects on student achievement. Certainly, if students are treated in the same way they will respond similarly. Pfeiffer also reported that most teachers who taught low-ability groups expected their groups to make little progress. Heathers (1969) also asserts that the quality of instruction in the low-ability groups tends to be inferior.

Thus there is some literature suggesting that teachers do not change their behavior substantially to take advantage of being able to work with special levels of students, and that when they do change their behavior, the likely result is that *low-ability sections will receive a poorer quality of instruction.* Poorer instruction in these circumstances can probably be explained as follows. First, teachers underestimate the ability of students in low groups because the label "low ability" creates a rigid stereotype of student incompetence in the teacher's mind (Tillman and Hull, 1964). Second, the quality of instruction in the low-ability sections sometimes suffers because teachers do not enjoy teaching low-ability students.

Teachers who instruct high-ability students or who teach in heterogeneous classes are more often challenged and motivated by incisive student comments or questions. Such student behaviors, which do much to make the teachers' task an enjoyable one, are less frequent in low-ability classes. If teachers do not like to instruct low-achievement students, the small, steady gains they register may go unnoticed and the teachers may come to view their job as a dull, boring routine. In fact, as was discussed in Chapter 4, teachers in low-ability sections who have no confidence in students' ability to learn may do more than simply model apathetic neutrality. They may engender feelings of defeat and incompetence in the students, thus assuring that they will make minimal progress at best.

That teachers do, indeed, prefer not to teach low-ability students can be seen in Table 2. The data in this table are taken from a poll conducted by the National Educational Association in 1968 (as reported in Findley and Bryan, 1971). Teachers were asked to respond to this question: What types of pupils would you prefer to teach, so far as ability is concerned? Obviously, few teachers prefer to work with low-ability students. Table 2 also shows that secondary teachers, in particular, prefer to teach homogeneous classes (of high or average ability). Other researchers have also noted teachers' preferences for teaching homogeneous classes (Rock, 1929; Otto, 1941).

Group placement is relatively permanent

We have seen that students assigned to low-ability sections often receive inferior educational opportunities and achieve less than similar students who are enrolled in heterogeneous classrooms. There is a tendency for two additional things to occur: (1) students assigned to low sections are typically students who come from low socio-economic backgrounds and (2) once a student is placed into a low group he tends to stay there. Johnson (1970) writes about both of these points:

TABLE 2

TEACHERS' PREFERENCE FOR TEACHING
CHILDREN OF VARYING ACHIEVEMENT LEVELS

	ELEMENTARY	SECONDARY	TOTAL
High	18.4%	34.6%	26.0
Average	44.7	38.9	42.1
Low	4.3	1.9	3.1
Mixed	21.3	15.2	18.4
No preference	11.3	9.4	10.4

Not only are the procedures used to assign students to ability
levels unreliable and the probability of a student who is
misplaced being reassigned is very low, but the system seems
to discriminate against the lower class so that they are most
often placed in lower ability tracks no matter what their true
ability is.

That ability groupings are rigid has been shown by Jackson (1964),
who noted that transfer into new ability sections at the end of
the year averaged only from one to five percent. In a three-year
longitudinal study, the annual transfer rate from one stream to
another stream was 2.3 percent (Douglas, 1964).

Mackler (1969) concluded from data collected in a longitudinal
study of more than one thousand children in a Harlem ghetto school
that placement into a low-ability group has permanent effects upon
the student. He suggests that the process works like this: school
teachers reward students who are polite, who listen passively, and
who follow rules; pupils who regularly behave in desirable ways in
kindergarten are placed in the top first-grade classrooms; other
kindergarten students are assigned to average first-grade classrooms;
and children who did not attend kindergarten are assigned to the
bottom first-grade section.

If a capable student is assigned to a bottom section, the road
to the top is a very steep, demanding journey. As Mackler points
out, bottom first-grade classes are filled with immature students who
cannot learn as quickly as students in top classes, and much teacher
time is spent in dealing with student needs and problems rather than
with instruction. A student will find it difficult to succeed under such
circumstances, but if he does he might make the next-to-the-top
group in the second grade and, if he does especially well, the top

group by the third grade. Mackler's data show that no student made it to the top group after the third grade. Thus if a child is placed in a bottom group in first grade, the odds are that he will stay there and fall further behind students in the better ability classes every year he remains in school. Those few who move from the bottom have to do so quickly, because pathways to higher groups are seemingly more difficult to find at higher grade levels.

Husen and Svensson (1960) have shown that lower-class students, even when their achievement merited it, did not move into higher tracks as early or as frequently as did students from higher socioeconomic levels. Similar conclusions have been reached by other investigators (McCandless, 1967; Kennedy et al., 1963). Capable students who come from lower-class homes sometimes are handicapped by unnecessary placement in lower ability groups, perhaps because some teachers accept the label of the student's ability level as fact and do not seek confirmatory information. Therefore, in spite of procedures for allowing students to move freely from group to group at certain times in the year, few students actually move because teachers are so heavily influenced by the ability labels and IQ scores.

Students are often misclassified and suffer because of low placement

We have seen that students can be misplaced (every time students are assigned to ability groups with even the best instruments, at least 10 percent will be misclassified), and that when they are misplaced downward they are penalized. What happens when students are placed into higher groups than their scores justify? Douglas (1964) reports a study in which a group of high-ability students were assigned, at age eight, to different sections. Some were assigned to groups higher than their ability suggested, some to groups lower than suggested by their ability. Also, a group of low-ability students were similarly misplaced. Some were placed into higher sections than their score justified and others were placed into lower sections. Three years later, at age eleven, the effects of ability grouping on these students were observed. The results were clear, and the same results were observed for both high- and low-ability students: those students who were placed into higher sections improved; those students who were placed into lower groups deteriorated. These results are striking. The placement of students into ability sections has a profound effect upon students. Students benefit from high placement and are penalized for low placement.

Tuckman and Bierman (1971) report a study that also shows gain for students who are misplaced upward. They studied the effects of upward placement on 805 black junior and senior high students who, on the basis of their performance, had been designated as medium- and low-ability students. Half of these students were assigned to high or medium groups (low-ability students to medium groups and medium-ability students to high groups). The other half of the students stayed in their previously assigned medium and low groups, thus allowing for a direct comparison of how assignment to a particular ability group affects student performance.

Tuckman and Bierman report that on standardized achievement tests given at the end of the year, the students who had been placed in higher groups outperformed those students who remained in their original assignment group. This finding did not hold for all students, but it did occur with enough regularity to demonstrate that placement of students in higher ability groups raises the performance of many students on standardized tests of achievement.

At the end of the year, teachers made recommendations for assigning students to ability groups for the next year. Interestingly, 54 percent of the students who had been placed into a higher group were nominated by the teachers to stay in the higher group; in contrast, only one percent of the control students were nominated to move up. Thus in this study of the effects of placement in higher groups, student performance improved and many students were able to stay in the higher group. Apparently there is a tendency for students to stay in a higher group once they get there.

As we have seen, the self-perpetuating phenomenon operates in both directions. Placement in a particular group, regardless of student ability, influences placement the following year. Apparently, teachers' expectations for student performance are heavily influenced by the grouping label. The teacher sees the student as a good student because he is in a good group, and this tautology, in part, guarantees that once a student is placed in a particular group he will stay there.

Why does higher placement help students?

If placing students in a higher group than their present level of achievement would dictate has a generally desirable effect on achievement, why is this so? For example, in the Tuckman and Bierman study, one could argue that student improvement was explained by (1) exposure to teachers who treated them differently because the teachers expected good performance; (2) opportunity to mix with brighter peers who model better skills and attitudinal adjustment to school demands; and (3) placement in a higher group helped the student to perceive himself more favorably and motivated him to try harder.

What produces the effects? Let us examine the labeling effect of ability grouping a bit further. Experimental data collected by Schrank (1968, 1970) suggest that the teacher's knowledge of and belief in the validity of pupil assignment into ability levels is a critical point. First, he studied the effects of group labeling on 100 enlisted airmen who were studying at the United States Air Force Academy Preparatory School. This school normally grouped its students for instructional purposes on the basis of demonstrated ability, so that instructors and students accepted grouping as a normal procedure.

Schrank decided *not* to group students by ability, according to the typical practice, but instead to assign students *randomly* to the sections. *The sections still had ability labels, but neither the students nor the instructors knew that these ability labels had no validity.* After seven months of instruction in mathematics and English, the class performance (midterms and final exams, etc.) of the airmen were analyzed. The findings were strikingly clear. Each section achieved a higher mean grade than the next lower section. Schrank concluded that any student who is placed in a low-ability group suffers an academic handicap for as long as he is in that class, and that students placed in high-ability groups receive an unfair advantage.

However, in a second study conducted at the United States Air Force Academy with 420 cadets, Schrank found that the ability-group label did *not* influence student performance as it had in the first study. Schrank writes:

> *The procedures for the two labeling effect experiments were almost identical except for one major difference. While the instructors involved in the first experiment were not informed that the grouping was random, the instructors participating in the second experiment knew from the start that ability grouping was only being simulated.*

In combination, these two studies suggest that the effect of the ability label is, in part, dependent upon the teachers' belief in the ability groupings. That is, the ability label influences student behavior because it influences teacher attitude and behavior. In any case, all four studies (Douglas, 1964; Tuckman and Bierman, 1971; Schrank, 1968, 1970) strongly suggest that students of relatively low ability can achieve in classes where the workload and teacher demand for academic success are high. Similar conclusions have been reached elsewhere (Little, 1968; Coleman et al., 1966).

We agree with the conclusion of Findley and Bryan (1971): ". . . the evidence simply indicates that ability grouping per se tends to be ineffective and do more harm than good." This is not to suggest that ability grouping in and of itself is bad or that it cannot work successfully. It does show that ability grouping has been found to be ineffective in practice and that schools or school districts using it would do well to examine their implementation procedures to see if grouping is really working to maximize the potential of all learners.

In many situations, ability-grouping procedures operate so as to undermine the confidence and ability of students who happen to be placed in low-ability sections, either correctly or incorrectly. Johnson (1970) expresses it this way:

> *There is growing evidence that under the conditions with which ability grouping is usually used it affects attitudes toward other students in ways that are detrimental to a democratic, pluralistic society. There are indications that ability grouping results in an intellectual snobbery where students designated as high ability avoid associating with students designated as low ability.*

Some educators approve of ability grouping

Despite the lack of data to support ability grouping, it is still a favored school practice. A somewhat dated (1961) research poll by the National Education Association (reported in Findley and Bryan, 1971) indicates that teachers of the 60s favored ability grouping, according to their responses to this question: "Considering all the advantages of ability grouping according to IQ or achievement scores, do you favor such grouping into separate classes . . . ?"

	ELEMENTARY	SECONDARY
Approve	57.6%	87.3%
Disapprove	33.1	8.6
Don't know	9.3	4.1

Again we see that secondary teachers are especially predisposed to homogeneous grouping practices. Of course, the reader should note that the range of student ability (and previous experience) in randomly assigned classes at the secondary level is much greater than in elementary schools. For example, in second-grade classes in a middle-class school, perhaps 70 to 90 percent of the students would fall into the same one-third of the distribution (high, middle, or low) in mathematics and reading; this figure might fall to 50 to 60 percent in a seventh-grade, middle-class school. This is to say that student differences accumulate with age and schooling, so that the same group of students is more heterogeneous in secondary than elementary grades.

More recent data (Findley and Bryan, 1971) suggest that ability grouping in one form or another is practiced in roughly 77 percent of the nation's public schools. However, only slightly more than 20 percent of the schools use grouping at all grade levels, with grouping being more frequent at secondary levels than elementary. Also, although roughly 80 percent of schools used test scores for assigning students to ability groups, only 13 percent used test scores exclusively.

Not surprisingly, the questionnaire data indicate that school districts practicing ability grouping see it as a useful way to provide for individual differences in students and to make teaching easier. Correspondingly, school districts not practicing ability grouping see it as stereotyping students too early, reducing the possibilities of movement into higher groups as they mature cognitively and become more capable students, and lowering both teacher and student motivation. Findley and Bryan caution that many school districts did not respond to some questions on the questionnaire, and that these generalizations might be affected in some nonrandom way. Nevertheless, the data indicate that ability grouping is still a prevalent practice, especially in large school systems and at the secondary level.

Most readers of this book will not have direct opportunities to decide whether or not schools or teachers will utilize ability grouping. The teacher accepts a job, and the school policy is already set. However, perhaps this chapter will encourage you to question the assumption and actual implementation of ability grouping in your particular school. Again, our intent is not to suggest that every ability-grouping system is categorically bad, but rather to suggest that many ability grouping plans do waste human talent and that any plan that segregates students on the basis of ability needs to be carefully scrutinized. If you are asked to teach a low-ability group, guard against the tendency to underestimate the ability of these students. Research has shown that these students do learn when they are properly taught.

Grouping within classrooms

Regardless of whether or not schools separate students into classes by ability, many teachers will group students *within* their classes by ability levels. Here again, this grouping should be carefully considered. For example, teachers can profit from grouping students who read at the same level into reading groups. However, *this selection opens the door for teaching the students as a group rather than as individual learners. This sort of group teaching must be avoided.*

Previously, we noted that even high-ability students who are appropriately placed into high-ability groups do not consistently outperform and, in fact, are often outperformed by high-ability students who remain in heterogeneously grouped classrooms. This kind of performance occurs for two interrelated reasons: (1) teachers do not develop materials or methods suited to the unique demands of the student ability level they work with and (2) teachers tend to view students within an ability group as similar and treat them alike without acknowledging the differential needs of each student. Consequently, in some circumstances, a student may be more likely to receive individualized instruction in rooms that are heterogeneously grouped.

We have argued that homogeneous grouping typically does not have a favorable influence on student development, and we have suggested that grouping in a heterogeneous classroom *may* have desirable effects. The reader may feel that the same arguments (both positive and negative) apply to grouping at all levels. However, there is one major difference that justifies the practice of grouping within heterogeneously grouped classrooms. Remember heterogeneous grouping leaves students from varying achievement levels in the same room, so it is possible for low- and high-ability students to be grouped together when it is advantageous to do so. Also, a single teacher is much more *flexible* to regroup as new needs arise than when grouping is systemwide, and this flexibility may make it easier for the teacher to treat students as individual learners rather than as group members.

The point here is a simple one. All students in a reading circle should not be treated in the same way. Some of them will have more difficulty than others and should be formed into a separate group when their performance demands more direct assistance from the teacher. Correspondingly, some will make progress more readily and should not have to remain in the same circle. If a student shows the ability to move to a different group (for example, a group that does relatively more silent reading and discussion and relatively less oral reading), he should move to that higher group. Similarly, there is no restriction on the number of reading groups or mathematics groups. For example, a class may need five reading groups (two in silent reading practice and phonetic drill, one in heavy oral reading and working

on verbal expression, two in independent reading, filling out work-
book questions and discussing, etc.) but only two math groups or
vice versa.

Teachers need to be flexible

The teacher should ask himself: How mobile are my groupings?
How frequently do I change my groups? Do I do it twice a month or
twice a year? Classroom grouping assignments should be reviewed
regularly and routinely with an eye toward forming new groups
whenever possible. A group should exist in the classroom for only
one legitimate purpose: to facilitate teaching and learning by placing
together students who have similar learning needs. When a student
masters phonetics, he no longer needs to be in a group that spends
half its time on phonetics drill. Too often groups are convenient
devices that keep teachers from thinking and prevent them from
effectively dealing with problems. Teachers place children into high,
middle, or low groups and then do not think about them again;
but they have to think about them. Grouping can be a powerful
tool if teachers use it as an effective way of organizing students for
learning specific skills, and if the teachers disband groups once their
usefulness ceases and form new groups as new needs become apparent.

Teachers also need to evaluate, regularly, the similarity of the
grouping patterns. Are the high, low, and middle groups of students
identical for both reading and mathematics? If so, students have
been misclassified. In general the younger the student, the more
similar are his abilities in different areas. In a first- or second-grade
classroom, there may be considerable overlap in the ability place-
ments of students across different subject areas. However, even here,
grouping would not ordinarily be identical. As students grow older,
their skills will become progressively differentiated, so that it is not
uncommon for some sixth-grade students to be top readers but
relatively low performers in math. Teachers need to be alert to the
tendency to label a student as high in reading and then automatically
classify him on the same basis for mathematics or social science.
Teachers should examine the correspondence of the ability group
assignments across subjects and determine if such classifications are
indeed valid.

Students who needlessly find themselves in the bottom group
in every phase of classroom life may come to view themselves as
incompetent, and in time they may give up in the classroom and
accept the idea that they are inferior. When this happens, students

begin to mobilize their efforts to avoid potentially humiliating experiences (shy away from the teacher, fail to volunteer, etc.) rather than try to learn new skills or to improve existing ones.

This tendency to cover, to protect oneself, is especially strong when classmates are excessively harsh to these students when they do perform inadequately. If students do, in fact, develop the label of slow learner and accept that role definition, they have a difficult time changing their self-image. For example, even when such a student moves into a new classroom and is met by a teacher who has high expectations for him, he may constantly be reminded by his classmates that he is a poor student. The teacher calls on him, for instance, and after a pause a student says, "He doesn't know. He never does." Similarly, when he is asked to place his homework on the board, a couple of students may be heard to snicker.

Rigid groups may create unhealthy learning environments

Teachers must prevent the emergence of caste systems in their classrooms, especially where certain students are placed in low groups in several different areas. Caste systems can and do develop, particularly if teachers help give the impression that slower students are inferior. Obviously, no respectable teacher would do such a thing consciously, but there is some literature to suggest that some teachers inadvertently behave in such a way as to engender or perpetuate classroom feelings of elitism.

Rist (1970) provides a gripping example of how powerful an effect teachers can exert on students. He followed a group of students from kindergarten through the second grade, and showed how powerful the influence of the first grouping was on their educational lives. After a few days in class the kindergarten teacher began to call consistently on the same students to lead the class to the bathroom, to be in charge of playground equipment, to take attendance and carry messages to the office, and so on. On the eighth day of class, this teacher made permanent seating assignments.

At table 1, the table physically closest to the teacher's desk, the teacher placed those children who were highly verbal, the same ones who tended to approach the teacher without apprehension, who were free of body odor, and who came from relatively higher socioeconomic backgrounds. Interviews with the teacher suggested that these groupings were based on the teacher's expectations of students' success or failure. On the eighth day of class the teacher spontaneously verbalized low expectations for the performance of children at tables 2 and 3. Interestingly, children who were shy and had trouble communicating with the teacher were placed furthest away from the teacher, adding another barrier to their achieving contact with the teacher.

The kindergarten teacher's differential expectations for the children were observed in differential teacher behavior toward the children at table 1 and those at tables 2 and 3. In Show-and-Tell and similar activities, the teacher showed more attention and interest in the experiences of higher status children. Also the teacher conversed more with the children at table 1 but directed more criticism toward students at tables 2 and 3. Students at tables 2 and 3 received less contact with the teacher and less instruction and hence were less involved in classroom activities. Not surprisingly, Rist reports that, in response to this teacher behavior, attempts by those students to get teacher attention declined as the year progressed.

Particularly damaging was the fact that the favored students picked up the teacher's low esteem toward the others, so that they also turned against them. As the year progressed, children at table 1 more frequently ridiculed children at tables 2 and 3. Of interest was the fact that students at tables 2 and 3 directed hostile comments toward one another and received them from students at table 1, but the students at tables 2 and 3 typically did not express hostility toward those at table 1, and those at table 1 did not express hostility toward one another. Apparently, the children had internalized the pecking order and had learned to direct derogatory remarks only at the "inferior" students.

Rist followed 18 of these 30 children when they were placed into the same first-grade classroom, and he noted that all children who had been placed at table 1 in kindergarten were placed at table A (the best group) in the first-grade classroom. No student who had been placed at table 2 or 3 in kindergarten was placed at table A. Those students who had been at tables 2 and 3 were placed at table B, (with the exception of one placed at table C). The students at table C, the low group, were primarily children who were repeating the first grade from the previous year.

Subsequent follow-up data in the second grade revealed the same pattern. There the teacher termed the best group the Tigers, the middle group the Cardinals and, *unbelievably*, labeled the low group the Clowns. No student who had not been at table A in the first grade moved up to the Tigers. Students from tables B and C formed the Cardinals, and students repeating second grade from the previous year were the Clowns. Rist suggests that this teacher, instead of forming groups on the basis of *expected* child performance, formed groups according to how children had performed in school previously. Rist explains the rigidity of the grouping system this way:

> *No matter how well a child in the lower reading groups might*
> *have read, he was destined to remain in the same reading*
> *group. This is, in a sense, another manifestation of the*
> *self-fulfilling prophecy in that a "slow learner" had no*
> *option but to continue to be a slow learner, regardless*
> *of performance or potential.* [Italics in original.]

Again we see how grouping students can lead the teacher to treat the group as a group and can result in classrooms where high-achieving students feel superior and act in a derogatory manner toward low- and middle-achieving students.

Grouping: some positive suggestions

We have reviewed a number of ways in which grouping may affect students in a negative fashion. We will now discuss ways in which teachers may group students to facilitate the development of positive sociopsychological classroom environments. To begin, let's describe a way in which schools that do use ability grouping can more effectively assign students to classrooms. The Findley and Bryan plan combines the strength of both homogeneous and heterogeneous groupings. Remember, the claimed advantage of homogeneous grouping is that it reduces the spread of student ability within a classroom, making teaching of the class easier. The disadvantages are that the lack of diversity does not allow students to learn empathy for others who differ from themselves, and that the technique often results in less individualized instruction because teachers come to treat the group as a group. Findley and Bryan (1971) present a plan that successfully reduces the range of student ability in a class but still leaves a moderate range, so that the advantages of diversification can take hold. Their plan follows.

> *An important part of what children learn is obtained*
> *directly from other children who know things they do not*
> *know. This may be furthered by planned heterogeneous*
> *grouping which involves the bringing together of students*
> *who deviate extensively on a given variable. For example,*
> *in an elementary school social science class a topic for*
> *discussion might be the State of California. The student's*
> *knowledge of the state is the variable. Some student might*

have lived or visited in the state and observed a great amount
of realistic information pertaining to the state. A group is
formed consisting of those knowledgeable students and those
desiring to learn about the state. In this instance we have an
"ad hoc" heterogeneous group. The knowledgeable members
have an opportunity to gain in leadership and communication
skills through instruction of the others. The others, with
guidance, are motivated to learn what their peers know.

Heterogeneous grouping of this nature is practiced in
the non-graded school. Children assigned in a non-graded school
vary considerably in age, experience, and knowledge. The
heterogeneity is planned so that the children can learn from
each other.

Heterogeneous grouping of the more common variety,
putting together children in unselective fashion, may achieve
the same effect if the teacher remains alert to opportunities
to promote exchange of ideas, information, and skills in
diverse groups. The key is to stimulate the desire to share
novel information, rather than to promote headlong competition.

STRATIFIED HETEROGENEOUS GROUPING

The illustration just cited presents a clear case for the
values of heterogenous grouping. But let us consider another
situation commonly faced in elementary schools in which it
has been customary to teach classes of 30 or so children in
self-contained classrooms where they stay with the same
teacher in the same room for practically the entire day. Suppose
we accept the criticism of those who argue for homogeneous
ability grouping to reduce the span of ability in each classroom,
yet are even more attentive to the criticism of those who argue
against homogeneous grouping of whole classrooms because
of the stigma this places on those in the low groups while
giving the high groups an unwholesome feeling of general
superiority. Can these views be accepted in a classroom
organization plan that has its own peculiar advantages? It has
been done.

A fundamental plan of organization recommended as
an alternative that meets these requirements has been developed
in Baltimore. The plan may be called "stratified heterogeneous
grouping." Under this plan, if three classes of 30 are to be
formed from 90 children ready to start fifth grade, the
children would be ranked in order of excellence on some
composite—say, a standardized test battery—and then be

subdivided into nine groups of ten each. Teacher A would be given a class consisting of the highest or first ten, the fourth ten, and the seventh ten; Teacher B would have the second, fifth, and eighth tens; Teacher C would then be given the third, the sixth, and the ninth (lowest tens), as shown below.

Teacher A	Teacher B	Teacher C
Group 1 (1–10)	Group 2 (11–20)	Group 3 (21–30)
Group 4 (31–40)	Group 5 (41–50)	Group 6 (51–60)
Group 7 (61–70)	Group 8 (71–80)	Group 9 (81–90)

Note the several merits of this scheme. First, there is no top or bottom section; the sections overlap, so invidious comparisons between groups are minimized. Second, each class has a narrower range than the full 90 have: Teacher A has the top ten, but none of the bottom 20; Teacher B has neither the top nor the bottom ten. Third, teachers can give special attention where it is needed without feeling unable to meet the needs of the opposite extreme: Teacher A can give a little special attention to the top ten because the bottom 20 are not in the class; Teacher C can concentrate on the bottom ten, without fear of "losing" the top 20. Fourth, each class has leaders of appropriate capability to stimulate each other in a fair, competitive way while giving leadership to lower groups; note particularly that in Teacher C's class, the top group is the third ten, a group that has probably always had to play second fiddle to some in the first or second ten. Finally, no teacher has to teach the bottom group of a homogeneous plan, that mixture of disruptive, leaderless children who lack motivation and capability and make teachers like homogeneous grouping, but dislike to teach the slow groups.

Such a method of grouping is not offered as a complete answer by itself, but as a constructive step in the right direction. It is, moreover, compatible with other special teaching arrangements, like team teaching, peer tutoring, and early education. *

The plan described above is one way to achieve a wider mix of students at different achievement levels in the same room without forcing a teacher to prepare instructional material for the full range

*From Warren G. Findley and Miriam M. Bryan, *Ability Grouping 1970: Status, Impact and Alternatives* (Athens, Ga.: Center for Educational Improvement, University of Georgia, 1971).

of student learning needs. We feel that the plan discussed by Findley and Bryan is an interesting, workable strategy. However, three important points should be considered when the plan is evaluated.

1. The groups do overlap, but they are different. Group A, for example, is still the highest group since it has the highest students from each third. Group C, in a relative sense, is the lowest group. Although Group C has many extremely capable students, in the minds of the teacher (and the students or parents) this group may become the "difficult" group to teach. Obviously, the strength of this grouping plan is that it minimizes group differences; however, sometimes slight differences in ability become exaggerated in daily practice. When this plan is implemented, it would be important to see if any tendency exists for allowing Group C to become a "low" group. Our statement here is not a criticism of the plan but rather a reminder that the potential weakness of any grouping plan is that the low group often becomes "unteachable."

The Findley and Bryan plan is designed to eliminate or reduce the possibility that any group will be assigned an "unteachable" label. We suspect that the plan will eliminate invidious comparisons, but if the plan is utilized it is mandatory to check for possible undesirable effects, for no grouping plan can guarantee *ipso facto* that low expectations will not develop.

2. It is also important that teachers expect good performance from their low-achievement students. While we do not deny the fact that some teachers do not enjoy teaching low-ability students, we do insist that these students are capable of good performance when they receive enthusiastic instruction that is appropriately matched with their aptitudes and interests. Also, it should be realized that there are teachers who do enjoy teaching low-ability students and who find their teaching efforts to be important and very rewarding. If the primary motivation for grouping students is to avoid working with large numbers of low-achievement students, the plan will probably not work. Again we suggest that if teachers do not feel that low-ability students can learn and if teachers are unwilling to engage in remedial activities with these students, no grouping pattern will be successful.

3. A real strength of the plan discussed by Findley and Bryan is that it allows for students of differing ability to mix without leaving the teacher with the time-consuming task of preparing instructional activities for every achievement level. Thus, their plan reduces the range of ability level that a given teacher will instruct. However, it should be pointed out that the range of ability in all classes is sufficiently wide to require teachers to treat students as individual learners and not as group members. (We shall return to this point later in the chapter.) When a teacher considers *any* grouping plan, he should ask himself "Does this plan help me to deal more adequately with idiosyncratic learning needs of individual students?"

Although the Findley and Bryan plan offers numerous advantages, many schools and teachers may prefer to assign students to classes randomly and then to group them for instruction within classes. Still, teachers may group in ways other than just within each classroom. For example, three first-grade teachers known to the authors devised their own grouping plan. Originally, students had been randomly assigned to each class. Each teacher taught and carefully observed the students in her class for a period of six weeks. Then the teachers divided the students in their classrooms into high, middle, and low groups for mathematics and for reading (*the groups were not the same in each subject area*), and one teacher took the high readers, another the middle readers, and the third the low readers. However, in mathematics, the teacher who had taken the low readers took the high mathematics students and the teacher who had taken the high readers took the low mathematics students.

Separate teacher assignments were undertaken so that students did not come to view one classroom as the dummy room, another as the brain trust room, and so forth. This plan also widened the students' experience by enabling them to come into contact with different teachers and learning to cope with different classroom tempos, for example. The students remained with their regular teacher for all other activities (science, social studies, art, music, lunch, and recess) and went to their special rooms only for reading and mathematics. Thus, many students were working with three different teachers. An extra advantage to this plan was that when a student experienced academic difficulty, all three teachers frequently had pertinent knowledge of him and, therefore, could help analyze their mutual teaching behavior and collectively answer the question, "What can we do differently to help him?"

These teachers were careful not to treat students as a group, even though they had been assigned together because of similar aptitude. The teachers were using groups not as a convenient way to forget about individual students but as a way to organize for meeting specific and mutual learning needs. Some weeks there were four mathematics groups, and other weeks only two, depending upon progress during the previous week. In addition, the teachers made ample use of peer tutoring, allowing students to assist one another so that the teacher could spend more time with those who needed remedial or enriched work.

In addition to changing the number of groups, the three teachers also frequently changed the composition of groups within classrooms and met weekly to change groups across classrooms. At those meetings, the teachers also compared students and exchanged suggestions on how to facilitate the growth of those who were not making satisfactory progress. The teachers, all outstanding, were notable in their capacity for blaming themselves, *not students*, when learning progress was not satisfactory. They continually looked for ways to improve instruction. They shared information about student behavior with one another as well as with parents. Furthermore, they looked for progress, especially in the lows, so that they could move a student into an advanced group as fast as his progress allowed.

Finally, by moving students to other classrooms and by rotating the ability levels in different subjects to different teachers, the teachers were able to reduce the stigma of being in a particular learning group, especially the low group, and communicate to the students that learning is an enjoyable process wherein each student compares his progress with himself. They showed that grouping is a useful way for students to *learn* together and not, as students often learn, a way to prevent the slow ones from interfering with the progress of brighter ones. The possibility exists for teachers in the same grades (or even across grade levels) to work out arrangements so that in some subjects students are working closely with others of similar ability and in other subjects with peers who are both faster and slower than they are, thus exposing them to a wide variety of learning experiences, both social and academic.

Individualization within groups

As a teacher, you may find yourself unable to ability group with other teachers at your grade level for a variety of reasons. For instance, your teaching methods may vary widely from those of the other teachers, or the principal may forbid the transfer of students to different rooms. You may still choose to use ability grouping within your classroom to obtain groups of students who at the time of grouping have similar learning needs. The same rules apply. If you regroup students frequently, if you recognize individual differences and needs within each group by using materials as necessary, and if you do not attach undesirable labels or treat some groups in inferior ways, then ability grouping is a tool that will help you to teach more effectively in the classroom.

By now you are probably raising some important questions. What is meant by *individualized instruction within groups?* How do I find time to do this? The first question is much easier to answer: if some students continue to have trouble even though most group members have mastered the material, then the teacher must deal with those who continue to have difficulty. There is no reason to continue with the entire group. Students who have mastered the material need not be held back. They should be allowed to go on to another meaningful activity. Those who do not master the material need to learn it. Sometimes this simply means to repeat and/or reteach the material. However, reteaching may frequently mean that the teacher will have to present the concept in a different way with fresh, new examples. If the students did not learn it the first time, they are unlikely to learn it the second time unless the teacher presents it in a new way.

Often teachers will repeat the same example several times, so that finally the student will give the "right answer." When teaching is just a series of repetitions the student may learn nothing but be able to give the right answer because the teacher has repeated it so frequently. The student, like a parrot in a cage, is able to say the right things, but attaches no meaning to what he says. Teachers, then, would do well to use different techniques and examples if the student does not learn after a couple of presentations. Varying the method maximizes the chance that students will learn the key concepts.

What we mean by individualization within groups is that students who need remedial work within a group should get it, and students who know the material should be allowed to forge ahead. For example, if three students in a group of seven have mastered story vocabulary on Monday, they should not have to review the story vocabulary on Tuesday and Wednesday. The teacher need not meet with the entire group for all 30 minutes on both days. Instead, he might work with four students reviewing the story words for 20 minutes, and then work with the other students for 10 minutes reviewing their answers to questions about the story.

Teachers too often are tied to time limits and groupings. If a group is scheduled to meet for 30 minutes, they meet for 30 minutes, regardless of their performance. This rigidity in classroom time often is wasteful. One way the teacher can meet individual needs within groups is to break the group down into even smaller units when the need or opportunity arises, releasing students who have learned and concentrating on those who need more work. Still, this practice does not provide enough extra time for reaching students who need remedial or enrichment teaching. What other alternatives does the classroom teacher have?

Peer tutoring

Peer tutoring, allowing students to help one another, is a very useful strategy that can help the teacher to individualize instruction. In a variety of situations, teachers and schools are allowing students to become responsible for assisting and guiding the academic growth of fellow students. In some situations students within the same classroom are tutoring one another, while in other situations fifth- and sixth-grade students are tutoring second and third graders. In still other settings, adults and college students are tutoring pupils from all age levels. The purpose of this section of the chapter is to introduce the concept of peer tutoring and discuss some of the research that has been conducted in this area.

The increased interest in the use of students as tutors has stemmed in part from the realization that, for many students, school life guarantees their failure. Deutsch (1964) writes that when students fall behind other students (or when they enter school already behind) they do not catch up, and, in fact, the difference in school performance between these students and the rest of the class becomes wider each year. The wide differences in ability and interest among those who do perform well in school also creates the need for teachers to personalize instruction if students are to progress optimally. Teachers in self-contained classrooms with thirty or more pupils seldom have enough time to individualize their instruction as fully as they would prefer.

Some advantages

Thus one possible advantage to using student tutors is that the teacher could be free to work with fewer students in face-to-face situations and would have more time to work with students having very difficult learning problems. There are, of course, other potential advantages in allowing older students to assume partial responsibility for managing the academic progress of younger students. Young children who are aided by older students might learn to trust and to seek information from older students and other authority figures (such as teachers) instead of avoiding them or feigning competency. That is, in direct tutorial situations, students may learn that much may be gained by seeking information when they are confused or need facts. If the descriptive analysis of Holt (1964) is accurate, students, when confronted with the "unknown" in classroom activities, normally evoke self-defeating strategies that allow the student to "look good" but which interfere with their learning.

Certain gains might also occur for the older student who tutors younger ones. For example, he may develop interpersonal skills for relating to other persons more fully, and he may also learn to care more deeply and honestly about the progress of others. Students helping others in reading or math, for example, may develop more interest in improving their own competency in the subject matter, and they may develop more empathy for the plight of their own classroom teacher.

Some students may learn more from one another than they learn from a teacher. Thomas (1970) makes this point when he writes, "Intuitively, many teachers know or suspect that they cannot communicate with some of their students." Consequently, another potential reason for using students as tutors is that the teacher may be unable to reach some pupils. For teaching some children, tutors may be more effective (perhaps because tutors use simple, direct language and examples that are more easily understood than those of the classroom teacher or because they have gone through the same learning problems fairly recently). Peer tutoring, then, has been advocated as a tool for helping both tutors and tutees to make progress in mastering subject matter as well as to increase interpersonal communication skills.

Let us consider some of the questions about the utility of peer tutoring. Does peer tutoring really work? If so, under what circumstances? Is the best strategy to let students in the same room tutor one another, or is it more efficient to let fifth- and sixth-grade students tutor younger students? Can all students be tutors? The number of adequate studies related to these questions does not justify firm conclusions at present; however, most of the data that do exist suggest that peer tutoring has some positive learning influence on both tutor and tutee and, at the same time, frees the teacher to work with students who need special help.

Cloward (1967) reports an experiment in which tenth- and eleventh-grade students who were at least two years below their age norm in reading were paid $1.35 per hour to tutor fourth and fifth graders who were having reading difficulties. Before the actual tutoring program began, the tutors were paid for attending planning sessions, and they were paid also for attending two hours of in-service training each week during the experiment. The students then tutored the younger children four hours a week for 26 weeks. Tests given five months apart showed that on the average the tutees gained six months, while the control children gained three and one-half months. Experimental students who did the tutoring gained 3.4 grades, while control students gained 1.7. Students who did the tutoring gained 1.7 grades more than comparable senior high students who did not tutor. Thus, students who had experienced much failure and frustration themselves were able to sympathetically aid others and gain new confidence or new interest in their own reading ability in the process.

Such spectacular results have not always been replicated, and some research has shown very little change in tutee performance. However, in general, the literature is promising. Among the most important comprehensive sources available on peer-tutoring research are two dissertations completed at the University of Texas (Thomas, 1970; and Snapp, 1970). Students interested in a complete review of the literature are referred to these two sources. (A selective review of the literature is provided in Appendix B (p. 379), and the teacher who is interested in gaining more information should review these practical sources.)

Thomas' (1970) study is particularly interesting. He examined the relative effectiveness of fifth- and sixth-grade tutors and college tutors for tutoring second-grade students in reading. He found, in general, that the elementary-school tutors were just as effective in tutoring second graders as were college students. Interestingly, the college students were seniors enrolled in a reading methods course who had almost completed their undergraduate teacher education.

Thomas describes some notable differences in the tutoring behavior of the college- and elementary-school tutors. Although the college and elementary tutors were equally successful in producing gains, they interacted differently with the younger students. Thomas (1970) stated it this way:

> *In analyzing the different groups of tutors, one is struck by the differences in their approach to the tutees. The college age tutors seemed to be attempting to coax the tutees into liking them, into enjoying the reading materials, and into practicing the reading skills. The elementary age tutors, for the most part, were more direct and businesslike. They seemed to accept the fact that the tutees had problems in their school work, and seemed to feel that the tutoring sessions were for teaching those materials in front of them, not for going off in tangents and discussing matters outside the lesson.*

Snapp (1970) reports that Ellson (1970) has examined the tutoring behaviors of various age groups (college students, trained teachers, adult potential dropouts, etc.). Ellson concludes that programmed (clearly specified format) tutoring can be carried out effectively by fifth and sixth graders, and he notes that tutors gain at least as much as tutees. Perhaps the most striking conclusion Ellson advances is that college graduates and professional teachers were relatively unsuccessful as programmed tutors.

Thus, in different ways, Thomas' and Ellson's observations suggest that college students or professional teachers are not necessarily good tutors. Their lack of effectiveness may be due to a number of factors, such as (1) successful tutoring may demand direct instruction, whereas adults tend to be indirect; (2) the vocabulary and examples of an adult may be too complex for younger children; (3) tutors who are close in age to the tutee may remember their own difficulty and frustration with the material and tend to keep a lesson-focus orientation longer than adults. The preceding statements are, of course, only hypotheses. However, although many adults are effective tutors, there is some reason to believe that the behaviors involved in effective individual tutoring may be different from teacher behaviors that are effective for working with groups of students.

There is also reason to believe that students *may be* more effective tutors if they are trained for their tutorial role. Niedermeyer (1970) presents data showing that fifth-grade students who were trained to tutor did, in fact, tutor differently untrained tutors. Unfortunately, Niedermeyer did not determine whether trained tutors obtained more achievement from tutees than the untrained tutors. Thus, we know that college students tutor differently than do elementary-school students, and that trained and untrained fifth-grade tutors behave differently in tutoring situations. However, no data indicate the specific behaviors of effective tutors. Although Thomas (personal communication) has related that training may be desirable in certain situations, his own experience has convinced him that even first-grade students can effectively work with classmates without elaborate training.

Some practical suggestions

Thus peer tutoring has been tried in a variety of settings, and it frequently results in increased achievement by students who do the tutoring as well as by students who are tutored. Although some reports suggest that peer tutoring has not increased achievement, there are no reports indicating that students were harmed by the process. Also, even where no achievement gains result, teachers gain more time to work with students who need individual help. However, it should be noted that the largely favorable results of peer tutoring experiments may be due, in part, to the fact that they have been conducted mostly by innovative school districts or teachers who have been careful to create a positive set toward tutoring for both the students being tutored and those doing the tutoring. That is, peer tutoring, like ability grouping, can be effective or not, depending upon how it is implemented. The following guidelines can be used to create peer-tutoring opportunities.

1. To begin with, the teacher should create the mental set that *we all learn from one another.* This is more readily believed by students when the teacher consistently models and points out to students how he learns from them. Again, the teacher can help reduce unnecessary competition in the classroom by stressing that the goal for all students is to learn as much as they can about essential school topics and about topics that are meaningful to them as individuals. Such behaviors help students to learn that the yardstick of success is how we compare to our past performance and not how much smarter or faster we are than someone else.

2. The second essential step in implementing peer-tutoring programs is to work out the procedural details. There are several essential procedural matters that should be noted. We suggest that the students be requested to help plan the program from the beginning. In general, these procedural matters need to be agreed upon:

(a) Definite times of the day should be set up for tutoring, so that students quickly learn that there are specific class times for helping one another (to avoid continuous disruption in class).

(b) Specific assignments need to be outlined. The teacher should mimeograph the directions each tutor is to follow each week. For example, "Johnny, this week from 8:00– 9:00 you will work with Gay and Terry. On Monday you will use the flash cards and review with them the 7, 8, and 9 multiplication tables. Repeat the tables twice for each of them and then get individual responses from each of them. The last time, write down the mistakes that each makes and return the sheet to me. On Tuesday, you will find audio tape number 16. Play it for Gay and Terry and listen with them to the rhyming words. Then go to the word box and find the rhyming words sheet. Read the material sentence-by-sentence, and get Gay and Terry to identify the rhyming words."

(c) Allow a tutor to work with one or two tutees for a week or two weeks so that you can make sequential assignments and so that learning exercises are not constantly starting anew. However, tutors in the same room should not work with any student or group for longer than a couple of weeks. This will prevent "I'm your teacher" attitudes from developing. Of course, these attitudes are much less likely to occur if older students or students from other classes at the same grade level are used as tutors. But since this is often impossible, the guidelines suggested here are presented for the teacher who is using student tutors within his own classroom.

(d) Tutors should not be asked to administer real tests to tutees. One purpose of peer tutoring is to develop a cooperative sharing between students. Asking tutors to quiz their tutees often defeats this purpose.

(e) All students in the room should, at times, be tutors, and all children in the room should be tutees. Slower students can help faster ones in the lower grades by listening to their spelling words or by checking their drill recitations in math. Teachers should see that students have the appropriate answer keys to perform this role adequately. In this way, students learn that they all need help and can benefit from one another.

(f) Teachers need not keep to the tutor model (one child flashes cards, the other responds) but can expand, when appropriate, to small work-team assignments (from two to eight students on a team). Shy students can be assigned to work with friendly, nonaggressive extroverts. Students with art talents can be paired with bright but artistically barren students in teams to gather facts and then graphically represent them (e.g., to chart the major battles of the Civil War). These combinations allow students to work together and gain interpersonal skills as well as to master selected content. While the students are so paired, the teacher is free to meet with a reading group for a second time on the same day to give them needed extra oral practice; hold an enrichment discussion, bringing in new content with a fast group; move from team to team, listening to their ideas and conversing with children informally; and work with individual students who require special attention.

(g) Both learning teams and peer tutoring will take a substantial amount of teacher time to get off to a good start, especially where students have not participated in these activities before. However, these are important techniques to free the teacher for other instructional tasks and for allowing students to assume responsibility for helping others and constructively exchanging ideas in the classroom. Take your time, at first, and be sure that all students understand what they are to do.

The first week you ask students to tutor, you should model the behaviors you want. For example, pass out the mimeographed instructions and have all the students read them. Then select an individual student and sit with him in the middle of the room while you tutor him in accordance with the directions. Do not just describe what to do. Actually do it, modeling the appropriate behaviors.

After this demonstration, you might select another two students, and have them model the next set of directions. Then you might wish to break everyone into pairs and go around listening and answering questions. After a couple of practice sessions like this, most students will be able to assist others, at least in repetitious drill-like activities.

The first week you implement a peer-tutoring program you may have a loud, somewhat disorganized room as students argue over where to go, and so forth. Remember that learning does not necessarily require passive, quiet students, and that any teacher trying a new exercise will have minor adjustment problems as students learn new roles.

(h) Pairing of best friends is often unwise, for several reasons: friends tend to drift away from the learning exercises; the number of classmates that a given student interacts with in the classroom is reduced; and friends, in a moment of anger, are more likely to "play teacher" by becoming excessively critical or indulging in ridicule. Although many friends can work well together, many cannot, and the teacher should use caution in such groupings.

(i) Communicate to parents that all students will be

tutored by classmates and will in turn tutor classmates during the year. This is especially important in high socioeconomic status areas where some parents may be upset upon learning that their daughter is being tutored by their neighbors' son and may immediately begin to fear that their neighbors will feel they are inadequate parents. Needless concern can be eliminated if you communicate to parents the purpose of the tutor program in a letter or visit and point out that this occurs for one or two hours during the day. List these times and invite them to visit whenever they want to do so.

3. The third essential skill needed to establish peer tutoring, in addition to creating a positive set and establishing clear operating procedures for the students, is creative organization. Although peer tutoring will give you more time in the classroom, it takes a great deal of planning time outside the classroom. Organization is the key. Tutors need clear directions, but they also need variety. You cannot program a spelling drill week after week. You have to plan so that the tutors and tutees receive an interesting mix of topics (e.g., one week drill review, the next week mutual library research, the next week writing stories, and the next spending money in a simulated grocery store or calculating batting averages).

In addition to tutoring assignments, at times allow the students to work as learning teams. Sometimes students of similar aptitude should work on a problem-solving task. At other times, combine students whose weaknesses and strengths facilitate one another in useful ways.

Independent work and learning centers

Teachers can save much time for working with specific students by carefully structuring time for students to engage in interesting, creative tasks of their own choosing. Teachers often find that some students, particularly bright high achievers, finish their work sooner than others. These students are too often punished indirectly (given more of the same work to do, etc.) for rapid work. If anything, students in these circumstances should be rewarded. Biehler (1971) suggests a particularly good idea for older elementary students: an open-ended, personal yearbook in which the student is allowed to write stories and illustrate or embellish them, whenever he finishes his assigned work. What each student puts in the book is completely left up to him.

Other age-worn but, nevertheless, acceptable ideas include allowing students to work on book reviews on some aspect of a curriculum topic (e.g., American Indians) or to act as a resource specialist or to tutor other students. However, book reports, if overly structured, may do little to encourage reading for enjoyment and interest. Often it is useful for the teacher and the student to discuss the book not only for plot but also in terms of why the student liked or disliked the book. Occasionally, teachers should carefully structure long periods of independent work for all students (not just those who finish quickly) and thereby systematically save time for remedial, enrichment, and informal conversations with individuals.

To facilitate independent study, the classroom can be arranged in more optimal ways. Figure 6 shows how one teacher arranged her first-grade classroom. This diagram of the classroom was made as the teacher instructed a reading group. By looking at Figure 6 you can see how the teacher's room arrangement allows for both group work and independent student activities. Six students are in the reading group with the teacher and two students are reading at the independent reading table. The reading center, separated by bookcases from the rest of the room, provides students with a place where they can read their favorite books in comfortable privacy. Thus, as students finish their work properly the teacher can allow some of them to go to the reading center and read a book of special interest in a quiet, relaxed way. The teacher may, at times, choose to use the reading center for independent but structured learning activity. For example, the student may be asked to write a book report on a book he chooses or one that is assigned.

We can see that eight children are working at the listening center, which is a portable tape recorder with eight earphones that can be wheeled from table to table. One student has passed out pencils and accompanying exercise sheets, while another student is in charge of turning on the tape recorder and turning it off when the taped exercise is completed. All students in the class have been taught how to operate the recorder, and student helpers are assigned and rotated on a regular basis by the teacher. Similarly, four students are viewing filmstrips without direct teacher supervision. Again, all students have been taught how to operate the machine. The teacher allows "today's teacher" to run the machine and to call on students, in turn, to read the story which accompanies the pictures. When the students finish watching the filmstrip and complete the written exercises, they move to another activity at their seats.

When the arrangement shown in Figure 6 was made, nine children were working independently at their seats and three children were working at the social studies center. The observer noted that

FIGURE 6. Physical Arrangement of a First-Grade Classroom

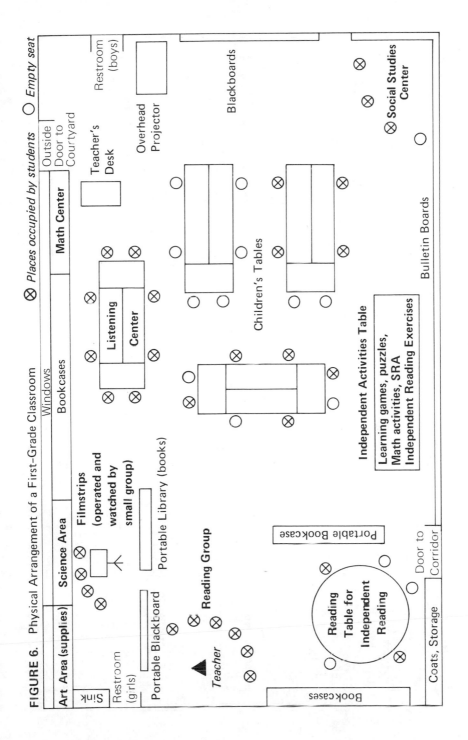

⊗ *Places occupied by students* ○ *Empty seat*

FIGURE 7. A Classroom Divided into Learning Centers

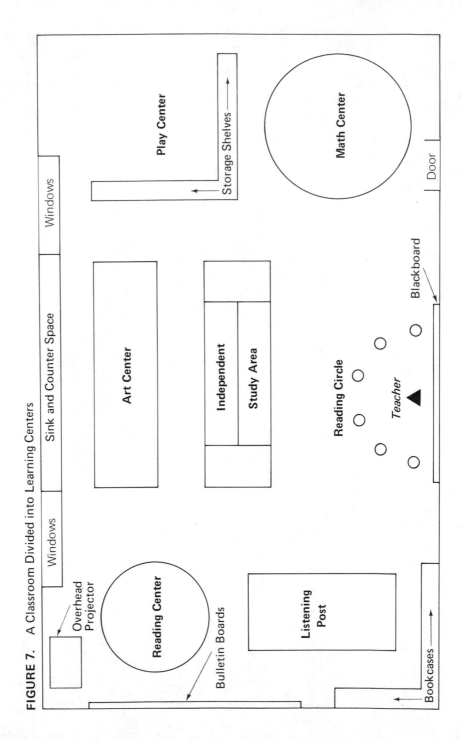

two of the students were "buddy reading" stories printed by their fellow classmates about the social studies unit, while the other student was busily painting a picture of a recent social studies field trip for the class mural. When he finished his painting he crossed off his name on the social studies blackboard and another student began painting his picture. When the teacher terminates the reading group, all students will rotate to a new activity and, as we have pointed out previously, with careful teacher planning these shifts can be made quickly and effortlessly.

There are countless ways in which a teacher's classroom can be organized. Dollar (1972) suggests a room arrangement similar to the one depicted in Figure 7. As can be seen in this diagram, the traditional rectangular seating arrangement has been done away with, allowing the room to be filled with a number of potentially exciting learning centers. A teacher, if he so desires, could program most of a student's day around learning-center activities. Here is one student's schedule for an entire day. Although there would be a few others with the same schedule, there would be many different schedules within the room. For example, another student might begin his day reading with the teacher in a reading group and end it at the listening post.

JOHNNY'S SCHEDULE

8:30– 9:15	*Math corner*
9:15– 9:30	*Math with his group*
9:30–10:00	*Reading with his group*
10:00–10:15	*Morning recess*
10:15–10:30	*Social studies with entire class*
10:30–11:15	*Social studies in small project group*
11:15–11:45	*Lunch*
11:45–12:15	*Story center*
12:15– 1:00	*Free selection*
1:00– 1:30	*Math instruction with entire class*
1:30– 2:00	*Art center*
2:00– 2:15	*Recess*
2:15– 2:30	*Listening post*
2:30– 3:00	*Reading instruction—independent work at the study area*

The teacher, through careful scheduling, would allow students to be at different learning centers or working in different project groups; the teacher would then have time free for instructional work with a small group or for remedial work. Although many teachers may prefer not to use center arrangements this heavily, such arrangements provide excellent independent study areas, and most teachers who set them up will find that they add greatly to classroom flexibility by providing a wider repertory of assignments.

Teachers in some classrooms may not be able to set up five or six different learning centers at a given time. Physical limitations (e.g., chairs that are bolted to the floor) may allow room for only two learning centers. In such cases, teachers may provide variety by setting up a science and an explorer center for two weeks, and then setting up for another two weeks a creative writing and mystery reading center, and then music and historical centers. The list of possible centers is limited only by the teacher's imagination. The reader should have realized by now that learning centers are exciting educational alternatives, but if they are to be run successfully, teachers must spend a great deal of time organizing them properly. For example, the reader may properly ask, "Where does the teacher find time to make out all those schedules in addition to the time required to prepare for each student's individual instruction?" It is true that much advanced teacher planning is needed. However, teachers typically can plan a student's schedule for one- to two-week time periods, so that planning of new schedules is not necessary for each student each day.

In addition, many school districts now provide teachers time to plan instructional activities with other teachers at the same grade level. Although teachers will have to make schedules for their own individual pupils, great use of planning time can be made by sharing ideas about the content of learning centers and by preparing different activities for different learning centers, thus reducing the amount of planning time necessary for any one teacher. (More will be said about this sharing of planning time later in the chapter.)

Students need to know how to use learning centers. Like all classroom assignments, tasks at learning centers need to be clearly specified if students are expected to work on their own with a minimum of teacher guidance. Rules for using the equipment and handing in assignments must be clearly established. Rules, and the activities that take place in learning centers, of course, vary with the age and aptitude of students. However, the following material from Dollar (1972) illustrates the general need for establishing rules and guidelines for academic assignments.

SOCIAL STUDIES
1. Choose a card and find the book to go with it.
2. Read the book or pages listed on the card and then answer the questions on your own paper.

3. Put your papers in the yellow basket and write your name on the back of the card.
4. You may answer the questions at your own desk or in the social studies corner.

READING CENTER
1. Pick a book from the shelf with a card in it.
2. Read the book.
3. Answer the questions on the card at your desk.
4. On a piece of paper put the title of the book and the number of the card. Number the questions as you answer them on your paper.
5. When you have finished, put your name on the back of the card and check your name on the chart.

PLAY CENTER
1. Only one person may hammer or saw at the same time.
2. You may only use the hammer or saw between 8:00 and 8:30.
3. Leave the erector set, hammer, saw, nails, or boards in the center.
4. Clean up when you have finished.

MATH CORNER
1. There should be only three people playing math games at one time.
2. You may:
    a. play a game quietly
    b. work problems on the blackboard
    c. use the flannel board
    d. pick out what you like and return to your desk to work on it
3. To use the math cards in the box you must:
    a. pick out any card you want
    b. work the problems on your own paper at your desk
    c. when you finish put your paper in the basket, and sign the card on the back

LISTENING POST
1. Sit down at the table—no more than seven people at a time.
2. Pick a record to listen to. Only one person should work the record player.

3. Put on the headphones.

4. Turn on the record player and listen to a story.*

It may be useful to have "operational" rules such as those Dollar lists posted at each learning center. Such procedural guidelines allow students to function quasi-independently of the teacher. Teachers can use learning centers to expose students to a variety of interesting educational tasks. Young students, for example, might be asked to do independent work by listening to a story and then responding to questions about it. The questions can be simple, "Were there three bears in the story?" or complex, "Listen to the story for four minutes. Can you write your own ending?" The point here is that in creating learning centers, you are free to use your own imagination and to create your own material. Although companies do make filmstrips, tapes, and other materials that can be used for independent classroom work, some of the best assignments will come from spontaneous events that occur in the classroom.

For example, one day during a seventh-grade English class, the principal makes one of his frequent PA announcements. At the end of it, Joe Jordan says, loudly enough to be heard by half the class, including the teacher, "What in the world would it be like if one day he kept his mouth shut!" After the class snickering dies down, Miss Thornton's appeal to logic, "But what would happen if he made no announcements?" leads the class to the general conclusion that nothing significant would be lost if the principal never spoke over the PA again, because teachers could make the announcements. She then decides to give the following assignment for independent work. "Assume there was no television, radio, or newspaper communication for two weeks. Write a theme on one of the following topics: (1) how would your life be affected; (2) how would attendance at a national sports event be affected; (3) how would someone wanting to buy a house be affected; (4) how could supermarkets advertise their 'Thursday-thru-Saturday' specials; (5) think of your own topic and have me approve it."

If the class is interested in a topic and wants to pursue it, success is guaranteed. Although many commercially produced units are good, not all students will respond favorably to them. In working with older students, the best approach is to allow the students to choose among alternatives if their interest is to be captured. Let us look at a few assignments that teachers can and have used in the classroom.

*From Barry Dollar, *Humanizing Classroom Discipline* (New York: Harper & Row, 1972). Copyright © 1972 by Barry Dollar. By permission of the publishers.

Some examples

The listening post is a popular learning place in the first- and second-grade classrooms. At a table in a corner of the room are several earphones that plug into a tape recorder. A group of six to eight students work at the table at a time. The tapes are stories (taken from supplementary information in teachers' editions of the textbooks; Science Research Associates' commercially produced products; *Weekly Reader;* or stories especially recorded by the teacher, based on special interests or incidents that have emerged in the classroom). Eight to ten Yes or No questions about the story come after it, followed by answers to the questions so students can evaluate their own work. At the listening post are a stack of ditto sheets with ten spaces where the student can circle either Yes or No, a can of pencils, six to eight earphones, and the tape recorder.

To avoid confusion, one student can be designated as leader. The others quietly sit down and put on the earphones. The leader starts the tape recorder, stops it at the signal given on the tape, passes out paper and pencils for the questions, starts the tape recorder again, stops it at the end, collects the papers and pencils, and sees that the table is ready to be used by the next group. To enhance the learning activity by making it more autonomous, teachers can also put the correct answers at the end of the tape and thereby provide students with immediate and direct feedback. After a few drills on procedure, the group at the listening post will be able to function quite independently. The teacher merely rewinds the tape and signals the next group. Thus, even first graders can independently engage in carefully structured learning tasks.

In addition to tapes and filmstrips, learning centers can be filled with hundreds of mimeographed learning sheets. The complexity of the tasks, of course, vary with the age and aptitude of the learners. For example, in the math corner on April Fool's Day, the second-grade teacher might give students the sheet in Figure 8 and ask them to find the mistakes by circling all errors that appear on the calendar. (Students could be asked to make their own calendars and see if their classmates can find the errors they purposefully make.)

Many teachers have found special-feature learning centers to be useful. For example, the teacher may write an introduction to a mystery story (three to fifteen pages, the length varying with the age and aptitude of the readers). Younger students are requested to tape record their own ending to the story, while older ones may be requested to write their own endings and compare them to those of others. At other times in the special-feature corner, the teacher

FIGURE 8. An Independent Work Sheet

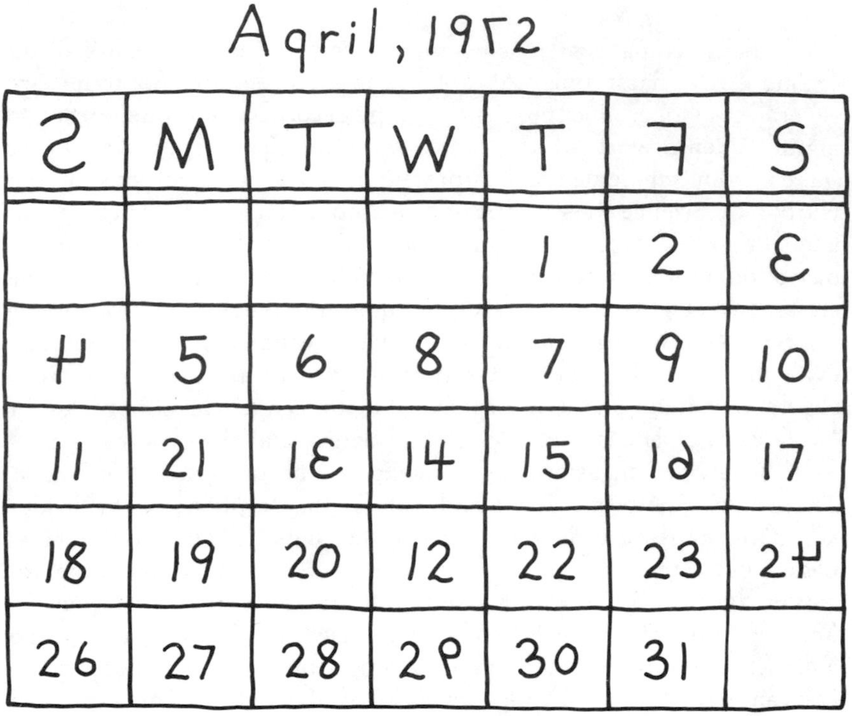

Aqril, 19Г2

Ƨ	M	T	W	T	Ⅎ	S
				1	2	Ɛ
Ʉ	5	6	8	7	9	10
11	21	1Ɛ	14	15	1ð	17
18	19	20	12	22	23	2Ⅎ
26	27	28	2Ҁ	30	31	

may simply have students respond to interesting questions. "On one page respond to this question: How would you spend a million dollars? Think! Tell *why*, as well as *what* you would buy." "Relate in 200 words or less how you would feel if you (dropped, caught) the winning pass in a championship football game." "Assume that when you woke up today, it was the year 2025. Describe what you will actually be doing in the year 2025. How old will you be then? What job do you expect to hold? Will there still be jobs in the year 2025?" The ideas presented here are but suggestive of the many things that teachers can create in the classroom.

However, the really good things will probably be the exercises you prepare especially for a class or a smaller group of learners, based upon a special interest that you have observed. A good idea would be for teachers at the same grade level in in-service meetings to share ideas for independent learning centers. In fact, one teacher could put together several weeks of math work, while another makes multiple copies of listening tapes and assignment sheets and a third works on language arts units. Such sharing reduces the amount of preparation time for each teacher and enables teachers to produce high-quality units. Naturally, once created, the learning centers are valuable resources that the teacher can use year after year with only minor modifications (most modifications simply being the addition of new units to match spontaneous interests of students).

Similarly, a good project for preservice teachers in a college course would be to form work teams, dividing the class into four project groups (e.g., math, social studies, reading, and science) with each group preparing from five to ten projects. In this way teachers would have the chance to swap ideas and to learn how to implement the learning-center concept by actually planning sequential units and writing them into operational form. In addition, students could keep copies of all class materials and thus would be able to begin teaching with a number of concrete ideas that could be used in their own classroom learning centers.

Independent work for secondary students

The learning-center notion as discussed so far has much more relevance for the elementary-school teacher than for the secondary teacher who teaches but one subject and sees students for only about one hour each day. However, certain subjects at the secondary level are well suited to independent study or independent group projects.

In addition to allowing students to learn from one another, the independent group project method allows the secondary teacher time to meet many of his students as individuals and works in a way similar to that already described for elementary schools. While students work in project teams, the secondary teacher is free to pass from group to group, sharing ideas and talking informally. The guidelines here are similar to those suggested for younger students working in project teams, except that students in secondary classrooms are able to work for longer periods of time without direct teacher assistance. Students may be assigned to one- or even two-week projects. Again, the assignments should be interesting, enjoyable activities that allow students to think about topics of interest and to cooperatively share ideas as they attempt to solve a problem.

Topics can be traditional assignments, such as all groups first do basic research on four political candidates who are seeking the presidential nomination, summarizing the basic stance of each candidate on selected issues; separate groups decide how their candidate would respond to a list of questions asked at a press conference in the South, North, East, and West; and then role-playing these press conferences.

The key points to note in such assignments are (1) students begin by having a common reading assignment, so that they share at least a minimum amount of information and have clear, specific knowledge that they can use to solve problems, (2) students are then placed into a position where they can summarize their information and apply it to a particular situation and, typically, are given a choice regarding which specialty group they want to work in, and (3) they are given an opportunity to share information with other groups by presenting the views of their candidate in a general classroom discussion, where (4) they have the opportunity to receive evaluative feedback (correcting factual errors or conflicts in their position) from the teacher and fellow students.

Most students enjoy the opportunity to work independently to gather facts on a concrete problem and use the information in simulated situations. Again, organization is the key. Teachers need to provide some structure to the learning task, identify pertinent resources, and let the students know how they will be held accountable. Of course, teachers need not structure all assignments. After students have been through the process once, the teacher can solicit and use student ideas in creating learning tasks. The more important elements of group work are that the assignment has a clear focus (whether teacher defined or group defined), that each student is held accountable for at least a part of the discussion, and that group tasks are enjoyable.

Topics need not always be traditional, content-centered assignments. Attitudes and awareness may be stimulated by combining factual knowledge with student impressions and values. For example, the above exercise would largely involve students describing and reciting what political journalists had written. Other assignments may begin with content and end with expressions of feelings. For example, tenth-grade males in a world history class might be divided into four independent groups. Each group would be presented with summary descriptions of the desirable physical and personality characteristics of women in four different countries in the 1850s, and they would then be asked to speculate about the cultural factors that led to and perpetuated the characteristics of the ideal woman in each of these countries. Female students in the class could be divided into four groups and asked to respond to such questions as: "What were the roles of women in each of these countries and to what extent were women satisfied with their respective roles?"

Later, group discussion could center on the frustrations that led to the women's rights vote in the United States and on why some countries and cultural milieus allowed women to assume more responsibility earlier than did others. When and under what circumstances did women become activists? How did men respond to the emerging independence of women? What is male chauvinism? Can a woman become President? What is the woman's role in contemporary American life?

Teachers who prefer not to use large amounts of class time for independent group work can still make efficient use of brief group assignments in the classroom. Teachers who lecture daily or who involve the entire class in daily discussion will be surprised at how effectively group assignments can enhance group discussion. Although the process can work in countless ways, the most basic procedure is as follows: (1) the previous night, the entire class is assigned certain pages to read in their texts, (2) at the beginning of the period, the teacher breaks the class into five small groups and gives each group two or three different questions to answer, (3) he allows each group 10 to 15 minutes to discuss their answers, look up information in textbooks, and so forth, (4) the class is brought back together and the teacher *randomly* calls on a particular group member to answer a question. He then encourages students from *other groups* to react to the adequacy of the answer and allows students who were in the original group to embellish the answer, defend it with logical argument, and so on.

If the teacher regularly assigns students to different groups, several good things occur. First, students are regularly interacting with many other members of the class, and in discussing interesting questions about course material, students have the chance to learn from one another. Students in small groups also have a greater chance to talk than they do in large groups, and the shy student, in particular, feels more comfortable in expressing his ideas in safer surroundings (when these students learn that they can express themselves and that others are interested in what they have to say, it will be possible for them to speak more freely in front of the whole class). Students are task oriented in these sessions because they know that any one of them may be called on to answer one of the group's questions, and they know that the teacher or a student in another group may ask them for a clearer answer or more information. Perhaps most importantly, this procedure mobilizes the student's attention, forces him to focus his thoughts on relevant questions, and helps to provoke learning. Finally, students, after listening and practicing their own responses, are interested in sharing their ideas and getting feedback from others. If the teacher conducts such sessions with interest in the students' answers and responds to their comments constructively, the students will learn that the teacher is genuinely interested in their learning, not just quizzing them about the reading assignment.

Of course, this approach, like any activity, can be overdone. Too much of even a good thing can become boring and trite. What we have tried to do in this chapter is to present a variety of ways in which the teacher can group for instruction. No one way is preferred.

The particular learning goals and the idiosyncratic nature of a given class or pupil, as well as the particular teacher, dictate the most appropriate instructional patterns. Clearly, there are many times when teacher lecturing with little or no student comment is desirable (e.g., when a new unit is beginning and the students have read little related material). There are also times when oral student reports, peer tutoring, learning-center work, individual work, and project groups are appropriate. In fact, the effective teacher will probably engage in all of these activities at one time or another during the year, presenting the students with a variety of stimulating learning experiences.

Summary

We have suggested in this chapter that grouping students on the basis of their achievement level is often an undesirable instructional decision. Too often students lose their individual identities when they are placed in an ability group. That is, teachers sometimes treat students on the basis of their group placement. Students who learn more quickly or more slowly than other group members receive *group* assignments rather than individual assignments that are geared to the specific errors that the student made on his last work assignment. A group assignment is not likely to be geared to the student's unique special interests.

In addition to teachers' tendencies to treat students as group members rather than as individual learners, there are other disadvantages to ability grouping. For example, too often under rigid grouping plans students tend to stay in the same group year after year regardless of their progress. Also, rigid grouping plans make it likely that students will seldom receive sustained contact with high-achievement students. There is reason to believe that both high- and low-achievement students *can* learn from one another when they are placed together in learning situations.

Stress has been placed on organizing the classroom so that the teacher will have time to conduct remedial or enrichment work with individual students. Chapter 4 made the point that teachers too often act as referees, telling students what they do incorrectly but frequently failing to provide them with information or skills for correcting their *error set*, the predisposition to repeat the same mistake.

We suspect that teachers often act this way because they feel that they do not have time to perform remedial work, and/or because the time to do this would take away too much time from other students. To help with this problem, a plan was advanced in this chapter for allowing students to pursue independent work in the classroom. Such techniques, when tailored to the specific demands of a particular classroom and teacher, will provide teachers with the necessary time for remedial work, while allowing students to develop increased capacity for organizing, directing, and evaluating their own learning.

Finally, the concept of peer tutoring has been discussed. The use of students to teach other students is certainly a strategy that teachers should consider and perhaps experiment with. Certainly, like any other teaching technique, peer tutoring will be more useful to some teachers than others. Also, it should be noted that a teacher is not necessarily a good teacher if he uses peer-tutoring strategies or a bad one if he decides not to use them. Like any other classroom behavior, the usefulness of peer tutoring depends upon the effect it has upon students. If the technique helps students to learn more efficiently and involves them more directly in classroom life, it should be continued.

SUGGESTED ACTIVITIES AND QUESTIONS

1. As a classroom teacher, if you use or plan to use ability grouping as an instructional pattern, state the criteria that you will use to assign students to groups and to rotate students from group to group.

2. Describe two or three types of learning centers (that were not discussed) and indicate the types of materials and activities that would be utilized at the centers.

3. With a group of teachers or fellow students who share a similar interest in teaching the same subject, prepare actual instructional material that could be used in a learning center.

4. Outline a plan (please use your own ideas as well as those presented in the book) that will allow students to spend a major portion of their days at learning centers. Design the room arrangement for your classroom, specify the learning centers that are created, and make schedules for individual students.

5. Read several of the articles on peer tutoring listed in Appendix B (p. 379).

6. When and under what circumstances might it be effective to group students for instruction?

7. Why has ability grouping been relatively ineffective?

8. In general what types of students do teachers prefer to teach and why?

9. Why might placing students in a higher group than their achievement levels suggest have a positive effect on their subsequent achievement?

10. Why do students usually remain in low groups once they are placed there?

11. Why do teachers need to reevaluate their grouping patterns and frequently rotate students from one group to another?

12. What are some of the possible advantages that might occur when peer tutoring and individualized learning programs are utilized?

13. What proactive behaviors can teachers engage in to make peer tutoring programs effective?

FORM 8.1. Student-Managed Learning Experiences

USE: When teacher has been observed frequently enough so that reliable information can be coded
PURPOSE: To see if teacher is providing opportunities for students to make choices and manage their own learning experience

Record any information relevant to the following points:

PROVIDING CHOICES
Does the teacher include time periods or types of activities in which students can select from a variety of choices in deciding what to do or how to do it?
Only when (if) they finish seatwork. They can color or use supplementary readers.

Can you see places where provision for choice could easily be included?
Several learning centers could be created with available equipment, including some with audio-visual self-teaching equipment.

COOPERATIVE LEARNING
Does the teacher encourage students to work cooperatively in groups at times? *Top reading group (only) reads on their own at times.*

Can you see places where provision for cooperative learning could easily be included? *Other reading groups could read alone, too, or at least do flashcard drills. Teacher often has children color a picture or do some other small activity related to topics studied that day. She could plan larger, cooperative projects just as easily.*

PEER TUTORING
Does the teacher ever ask students to tutor or otherwise assist their peers?
Occasionally, if a child has been absent for a few days.

Can you see ways the teacher could arrange to do this (if he does not)?
Flashcard drills in both language arts and math.

CHAPTER

9

Additional suggestions about looking in classrooms

Previous chapters have stressed four major aspects of teacher behavior, and classroom observers or teachers who analyze their own behavior should carefully look at the teacher's ability to use these very special skills: (1) skill in communicating respect and belief in children's ability to perform academically; (2) skill in modeling desirable language, social skills, and problem-solving abilities; (3) managerial skill in organizing and maintaining effective learning environments; and (4) skill in grouping students, enabling students to learn from each other, and allowing the teacher time for both remedial and enrichment activities. We believe these skills are the heart of good teaching.

There are other important things to look for in the classroom, however, and the plan for this chapter is to discuss some additional teacher and student behaviors and to provide the reader with rating skills to measure the presence or absence of these behaviors. Many points to be discussed have been found to relate to student achievement or interest in schoolwork and should be of special interest to teachers and observers alike. Other points included are based upon the authors' observation of effective teachers and discussion with them. Some of the topics presented in this chapter flow directly from research; however, many topics represent only what is thought to be the best of conventional wisdom and practice.

Let us point out that there is no such thing as a single concept of the "good teacher." We know too much about teaching and teachers to present any such simple, unsatisfactory definition. Many students suggest that different teachers have different effects on students. An achievement-oriented, introverted teacher, for instance, may have better interactions with certain types of learners, while a social-oriented, extroverted teacher may have more facilitative interaction with other students. We suspect that different patterns of instruction may, at times, be necessary for disadvantaged versus advantaged students or for fast versus slow readers.

Thus no specific formula exists for determining a good teacher. Earlier material stressed that teachers must show their respect for their students. However, teachers have unique styles, and there are many ways in which different teachers can show respect. One teacher may make it a point to visit with each student a couple of minutes each day in order to discuss topics that are especially important to him. Another may take the time to visit each student's home and urge parents to visit the classroom. Yet another teacher may use much class time dealing with student problems (e.g., two students claim the same pencil) rather than always arbitrarily avoiding them through the use of a convenient rule (e.g., pencils with two owners become teacher's property). Similarly, we have stressed the significance of the teacher's role as a model in the classroom, but there is no one correct way to "model" how to solve a problem. Some teachers may prefer to show the entire class, while others may wish to show small groups or to have a pupil model the solution for his classmates.

Although it is neither possible nor desirable to specify with complete detail how teachers should behave in the classroom, it is possible to note things that should occur regularly in the classroom. That is, we can look for the presence or absence of certain teacher behavior. Whether or not teachers model their thinking for their students is easy to note on the presence-absence basis: the teacher does model or he does not. Most of the measures we will talk about in this chapter are presence-absence variables. We can say that these things should take place, but the frequency of their occurrence and the way in which one performs the behavior depends upon his style as a teacher and upon the particular situation. Teachers are decision makers, and they have to decide upon appropriate ways in which to intervene with their own students.

For example, in principle, it is important for teachers to help students deal with misunderstandings and express their feelings openly, but discussing the motivation underlying the behavior of two students who were fussing in line while twenty-five others waited for lunch would not be a smart decision. Because of the management considerations involved here, it would be better to simply remind the students of the rules or, if the problem is serious, to defer dealing with it until the rest of the class is settled down for lunch. Thus we cannot say that certain general principles hold for all situations, without qualifications. We can say, however, that teachers should frequently model their thinking and problem-solving skills so that their students can learn that classroom problems have definable cause-effect relationships and are potentially solvable. Now let's review some of the important events that should be occurring in the classroom.

Child attention

Little is known about how children learn, but one fundamental fact we do know is that one must attend to and think about most learning tasks if he is to master them. A useful focal point for teachers and observers is to identify the number of students who attend to their learning tasks. Given all we know about the attention span, it is not reasonable to expect students to be attentive at all times. Of course, we would expect more than 20 percent, for example, to be attending to the learning task. Teachers should be able to create learning environments in which 80 percent to 90 percent of the students are attending to the learning task at a given time. There will always be reasons that certain students do not attend to the learning task. Pencils have to be sharpened, resource books have to be returned, and so forth. There are other typical, but less overt, factors that also might reduce a given student's attentiveness (e.g., students are frequently hungry, need to go to the bathroom, or hear students outside). The question we try to answer about student attention is, simply, what percentage of the students are actively paying attention or involved in assigned or independent work?

The students need not be sitting quietly at their desks. They can be reading their books in the middle of the floor, drawing at the easel in the art corner, or talking with other students about a group project. The only important consideration is whether or not they are actively involved in assigned or self-selected work.

Older students might possibly be listening attentively or thinking about a work problem although they appear to be gazing out the window or staring blankly at the floor. Young children are more typically doing what they seem to be doing. It is possible, however, for first graders to squirm and still pay attention. In early elementary-school grades, an especially good way of looking in classrooms, then, is to determine what percentage of students are involved in learning tasks.

1. When the teacher gives directions, how many students watch him?
2. When he finishes giving directions, how many students start work?
3. When students are working at their desks, how many are writing or reading?
4. When the teacher works with a reading group or a subgroup of students, what percentage of the remainder of the class remains involved in work?

Interpretations of classroom attention have to be made with reasonable care. For example, a reflective student may spend time organizing and thinking before he begins to respond in writing. However, if large numbers of students do not begin work within a reasonable period of time, it is a signal that something has gone wrong (unclear directions, lack of student interest, etc.).

The authors have been in some classrooms where 70 percent to 80 percent of the students were in *neutral* (sitting, doing nothing productive) for long periods of time; this is, of course, a waste of time. No wonder students explode with exuberant joy when the school bell rings if they spend much of the day in neutral! Situations where so many students are disengaged from school activity occur most frequently when teachers who are strict disciplinarians conduct small group lessons. The teacher's assignment of seatwork may be inadequate; typically, the faster students finish and sit with no new assignment and the slower students give up on what, for them, is a difficult assignment. The teacher with strict disciplinary tactics has taught them not to make noise or get out of their seats, so they sit there with nothing to do. Some teachers who control less rigidly, but who also fail to plan appropriate seatwork assignments, typically have 20 percent to 30 percent of the class misbehaving (talking to other students who are trying to work, walking around the room aimlessly, pinching a neighbor) and a high percentage in neutral.

Thus we can safely say that, in general, good teachers will have a high percentage of their students "tuned-in" to the learning task most of the time. Teachers who regularly have high percentages of inattentive students are advised to examine their teaching behavior and to seek ways to improve. Teachers often accept inattention. They describe and label it but do nothing to change it. For example, a teacher explaining an assignment to the class says, "I notice that several of you are not paying attention, and when we start our homework four or five of you will be at my desk, asking for directions."

The teacher then continues to explain the homework. When he stops, several students do appear at his desk to seek more information.

Teachers must intervene when students are inattentive. A good way to look at teachers' attention-demanding behavior is to observe what happens when students continually call out the answer without really listening to the question—even before the teacher finishes asking the question. Other ways to gauge this behavior are to see how often students answer a different question from the one asked by the teacher or have their hand up before the teacher asks a question. In these situations, does the teacher recognize and deal with the problem, or does he appear oblivious to it? Does he remind the class of the appropriate rule (i.e., listen to the question)? If not, what does he do?

Many teachers and observers are unaware of the vast amounts of time that some students daily spend in neutral. Teachers need to be alert to this idleness and determine how they can reduce the amount of time that students have to sit in their seats, bored, with nothing to do. Certainly, the fact that students appear to be doing their assigned task does not guarantee that they are engaged in *purposeful activity*. We can say, however, that when students seem to be involved that the minimal condition for learning has been met and that it is possible for learning to take place. Some research has demonstrated that student attention is measurable and associated with student achievement (Lahaderne, 1968; Cobb, 1972). Now that we have identified student attention to and active involvement in work as a key to learning, we can ask, "What can a teacher do to increase student involvement in work?"

Teacher enthusiasm

In understanding why a student works enthusiastically at some tasks, it is useful to ask yourself such questions as "What do I really get into and why?" "When do I really enjoy a task?" "Why do I stop some work after just a few moments but work at other tasks endlessly?" There are many exceptions, but basically we are more likely to try things or to want to do what we see others enjoying. The 16-month-old girl curls up on the couch and reads her book because she has seen her father do that. There's a bit of Tom Sawyer in all of us. Children are especially susceptible to "interest created by others." Often we see young children become interested in a puzzle only after another child picks it up. Children, then, are especially interested in what others are doing, and young children are especially interested in doing what adults enjoy doing. To the list of skills that were mentioned in the modeling chapter we should add: the teacher should model enthusiasm and a genuine interest in the subject under study. (If the teacher does not like to paint fences, why should the students?)

Although we have been emphasizing the fact that young children respond favorably to enthusiasm, the same is true for older students. College students, in describing instructors, frequently stress teacher enthusiasm as an important, vital aspect of teaching behavior (Costin, Greenough, and Menges, 1971).

Several research studies suggest that teacher enthusiasm influences students' achievement (Rosenshine, 1970). Although it is impossible to specify the behaviors of an enthusiastic teacher with precision, certainly these terms are important predictors: alertness, vigor, interest, movement, and voice inflection. The key aspect is that teachers are alive in the room; they move from place to place and come into close contact with more students; they show surprise, suspense, joy, and other feelings in their voices; and they make the subject interesting to the student by relating it to their own experiences and show that they themselves are interested in the subject.

Alexander Mood (1970) in the provocative book *Do Teachers Make a Difference?* indicates his belief that teachers of today's students must have the dramatic qualities of an actor:

> *Showmanship is for all teachers. There was a time, now long past, when school may have been something of a relief to children burdened with arduous chores at home or on the farm. Nowadays, they mostly watch television at home. In comparison with that, school is usually a drag, strictly from dullsville . . . a humdrum performance simply will not hold the attention of our children; they will switch to another channel. . . .*

In the past few years, the authors have frequently heard teachers complain that their efforts to prepare for students are often met with a chorus of, "but we've done that before," or "we've seen that before." Interestingly, basic research concerning the eye patterns of children watching Sesame Street has yielded some gripping data. It was found that children did not attend to an adult voice with an adult picture on the screen for any length of time. However, children did pay attention to an adult voice when accompanied by an animated figure (a bouncing chart, puppets, etc.). Apparently, some children, even before they enter school, are learning to tune out an adult who stands relatively motionless before giving information.

Thus, in looking in classrooms, it is very important to assess the extent to which the teacher projects a genuine, enthusiastic regard for the subjects he teaches. Tom Sawyer-like characteristics have always been an important dimension of teacher behavior, and if TV and kindergarten experience are truly making the traditional elementary school experience more staid and insipid, then it will become even more important for the teacher to be able to generate enthusiasm for classroom activity. In particular, teachers may have to do a convincingly good job of explaining the fun of repeating and trying to do better the things one has done in the past. However, many teachers do this and do it well. Bereiter et al. (1969) provides this account of how a teacher generated a performance from her students.

> *When a good teacher pointed to a picture and said, "What's this?" she expected all children to respond. If they didn't respond, she would perhaps smile and say, "I didn't hear you. What's this?" By now all of the children were responding. She would smile, cock her head and say, "I didn't hear you." Now the children let out with a veritable roar. The teacher would acknowledge, "Now I hear you." and proceed with the next task. It was quite noticeable that the children performed well on the next task, with virtually 100 percent of them responding. Basically her approach was to stop and introduce some kind of gimmick if the children—all of them—were not responding or paying attention. She did not bludgeon the children, she "conned" them. It seemed obvious that they understood her rules; she would not go on until they performed. It seemed that they liked performing, because when they performed well she acted pleased.*

Enthusiasm is an important teacher behavior for capturing and maintaining student interest. Apparently, there are at least two major aspects of enthusiasm. The first is the teacher's ability to convey his sincere interest in the subject. This is an aspect of modeling, and even shy teachers should be able to demonstrate this behavior. The other aspect is vigor and dynamics. Here, the teacher who has difficulty projecting excitement and enthusiasm in his voice can utilize other techniques to dramatize school events. Three days in advance, the teacher may begin to tell his students that they will soon be summarizing a fascinating unit on explorers, a mystery novel, or other subject and thus let the suspense build up.

Of course giving advance notice does not imply that the intervening three days will be boring by contrast. Just the opposite is true. If handled properly by the teacher, the intervening days before the "big event" can be made more enjoyable and interesting by occasionally stressing the long-run goals or payoff that the short-run work is building toward. As a case in point, an American history teacher's announcement that, "Three days from now we will role-play the 'Scopes trial,' " can be followed by techniques that build interest and suspense for the role-play exercise and also maximize the satisfaction of daily learning. The teacher might build suspense and interest by asking students to imagine themselves in the place of a historical person. "Put yourself in the place of William Jennings Bryan and analyze the feelings, values, and attitudes of people in this Tennessee town." What arguments would you advance? What types of witnesses (pastors, medical experts, etc.) would you want to use? Students' independent reading or homework might become more useful if the teacher stated, "On Thursday we will be selecting jurors for the trial Now before doing this we need to find out on what basis prosecution and defense attorneys can reject witnesses. . . ."

Similarly, teachers can make a field trip especially important by having students bring in their travel permission forms from their parents several days in advance and responding with appropriate concern when someone fails to bring the slip back: "Timmy, be sure and bring that slip in tomorrow. I would hate for you to miss the trip. It is really going to be fun. We will. . . ." In contrast, the less effective teacher responds with indifference to the student's failure to bring in the permission form: "Well, get it here tomorrow." Of course, the teacher has to be enthusiastic about mathematics, spelling, and other basic subjects as well as story time. He must generate enthusiasm for the basic content that the students deal with and not restrict his enthusiasm to special events. Teacher enthusiasm for the learning task will do much to obtain and keep student interest.

The match

If students are to work at school tasks with vigor and enthusiasm, they must be able to do the tasks they are asked to perform. Few of us work very long if we do not enjoy successes in the process. In fact, we have long known that persistence on tasks is largely determined by how successful one has been on similar tasks in the past (Sears, 1940). Students' ability to do school assignments determines to a large degree whether they form the belief that they can learn independently. One way of looking in classrooms is to assess the match between what the teacher asks the student to do and what the student is capable of doing. We know that a major factor determining how well a student learns a particular lesson is its relationship to what he already knows (Ausubel, 1963). Hunt (1960) has argued that the teacher's task is to provide the student with a progressively more difficult task than the work he has been doing but not so difficult as to frustrate him or erode his confidence. Thus, the ideal task presents a new challenge but has the potential of being solved independently by the student.

Unless you observe in the classroom for several visits or closely monitor the work of several students, it may be difficult to determine if the match between student and task is being achieved in the room. However, a quick assessment of the teacher's ability to do this is simply to observe the number of differential books and materials that are being used in the classroom. Even students who are homogeneously grouped will still have different interests and different academic difficulties. It is particularly discouraging to enter a classroom and see that students are treated strictly as groups with the entire day's assignments on the board: "Bluebirds reading from 8:30–9:00; 9:00–9:30, write the ten sentences on the board; math, do pages 61-64 . . ." This is not to suggest that teachers should not write assignments on the board; it is probably good to write assignments on the board as a way to cut down confusion and needs to bother the teacher. The point here is that no student should be treated as a group member for the entire day. Certainly there are reasons for group assignments, but students also need to be able to work on their own problems.

Let's assume that Robin Miller, a Bluebird, does poorly on today's math work. Tomorrow she does not need to work pages 65–70 with the Bluebirds. Instead, she needs to correct the error set that interfered with her work on pages 61 to 64. Classes are busy places and, obviously, every student cannot have individualized pacing for every subject. However, to the extent that it is possible, teachers should recognize students' individual strengths, weaknesses, and interests, and provide them with assignments related to their own (not just their group's) development. In classrooms of good teachers there will be evidence of such differential assignments.

Another way to determine if teachers are matching tasks to student ability is to observe how often slow students finish their assignments. In many classrooms, the slow or low-achieving students never finish their assignments. Often this failure to finish assignments prevents them from doing things that the other students get to do simply because they work faster. For example, some teachers in early elementary school hold Show-and-Tell classes right before noon, and participation in Show-and-Tell often depends upon finishing assigned work. Sometimes the work itself is involved in the Show-and-Tell. For example, the students have been working on art pictures related to a reading story, and upon completion of the pictures they show the class their art work and describe what they were doing. However, low achievers often have great difficulty in finishing their independent reading, so that many of them do not get to start on their pictures, and those who do not get through in time do not get to share them with the rest of the class.

It is very important that the slow students finish their work and get into the habit of completing work rather than giving up. The teacher may have to reduce the amount of work that he assigns the slow students for a while, to get them into the habit of getting feedback and to teach them that they can finish their work with a positive feeling and without a sense of being overwhelmed. The teacher who matches the amount and difficulty level of work with the time and ability of the student has done much to help the student gain some feeling that he can achieve in the classroom.

Remedial teaching

Remedial teaching is closely related to "the match." In both cases, the teacher must recognize that a problem exists, that learning is not as effective as it could be, and that intervention is needed. Too many teachers are concerned with moving the class as a group as fast as possible, and they neglect, often without awareness, the student who cannot keep up. Even the best teachers often feel guilty about the time they spend with low students because during that time they are not challenging the bright students. As we have seen in the preceding chapter, there are ways in which teachers can increase the amount of time they spend with low-achievement students, while at the same time allowing faster students to develop skills for relatively autonomous, self-guided learning.

Remedial teaching is something we see too little of in schools. Students who enter the third grade without a good phonics background seldom learn phonics. More typically, they will start with the same reading material that other students receive, and then struggle the entire year with the first seventy pages while other students complete the book and several others to boot.

A basic aspect of remedial teaching is teacher commitment to the belief that every student can and will learn. Bereiter et al. (1969) describes what this attitude looks like in the classroom.

> *The good teacher apparently tended to overteach. She hesitated to move on to another task until all of the children in her group were performing adequately. The teacher who was not as good did not get as much feedback from the*

*children. She did not seem to have the burning desire to teach
every child. She let the children get by with performances
that would not be acceptable to the good teacher. In one
sense, the good teachers reminded one of Helen Keller's
teacher, as she was portrayed in* The Miracle Worker. *They
felt that the children could perform and should perform if the
teacher knew how to reach them. The teacher who was not so
good seemed to have a more mechanical view of the teaching
process. It did not seem to bother her if the children did
not perform well.*

In looking in classrooms, we would suggest noting the relative
concern and time that the teacher focuses on the task of remedial
teaching. Observers should look for evidence of remedial teaching.
Does the teacher meet with students who are having trouble with
homework assignments or are experiencing other study difficulties?
All too frequently, the teacher's method of remedial teaching is to
assign the student the same reading that the other students do, but
then ask him to answer only half of the questions. Seldom do teachers
with sixth-grade students who read at the second-grade level secure
books written at the lower level that cover roughly the same material
other students in the same class are reading. Valuable, indeed, are
books in the classroom on famous persons and history, for example,
that are written with different vocabularies so that all students can
at times read successfully about the same topic.

Clearly, when we talk about remedial teaching, we mean adjust-
ing the curriculum to the student and not vice versa. If students can
read at only the second-grade level, they should not have to read
a fifth-grade or sixth-grade text and continuously be subjected to
failure. Rather, the teacher, as best he can, should attempt to start
where the student is and advance him to more complex tasks as
rapidly as possible. When teachers deviate from the curriculum or
abandon a textbook in order to more appropriately deal with a
student's learning problem, they may wish to consult their school
principal. The principal, as the instructional leader of the school,
is often able to suggest ways to obtain appropriate remedial materials.

In many ways, remedial teaching is closely tied to what some
investigators (Husen, 1967; Rosenshine, 1968; Shutes, 1969) call
"opportunity to learn." These investigators have found, not surprisingly, that students' opportunities to learn the criterion materials
relate positively to the amount they do learn. Obviously, if students
are not exposed to material, they cannot deal with it and cannot learn
it. Remedial teaching forces the slower student to deal actively with

more content and thereby provides him with more opportunity to learn the material. It also allows him to learn the material at an appropriate pace. Carroll (1965) has noted that slow learners are capable of learning whatever most fast learners achieve, but he suggests that slow learners pace themselves so that they may take four to five times as long as the fast learner to master the same material.

Other gains probably occur from the remedial process. For example, many unsuccessful students characteristically do not think about or attack their work in a goal-oriented, problem-solving manner. Typically, they jot down the first things that occur to them and hand their papers in as quickly as possible because they are too afraid to look back over their work (Holt, 1964). Students who behave in this way long enough ultimately learn that the classroom is not a place where serious, exciting business occurs, but is rather a place where things occur for mysterious reasons.

The teacher can do a great deal to enhance the slower student's sense of control, his belief in his own ability to think, if he helps him to see the relationship between teacher questions and concrete strategies for finding the answers. This means that if a student cannot respond, the teacher will show him how he could have found the answer. He reminds the student by giving directions to the appropriate page or explaining the process involved so that the student learns that answering classroom questions is a rational process.

Students who are afraid to look back typically cope with classroom assignments by "guess and look" techniques. They never adopt active learner roles simply because they do not have any control over the learning situation. Remedial teaching coupled with the appropriate match of students with material they can master is the first step in helping students to become active self-evaluators. This remedial matching has to be one of the central goals of schools if the continual academic regression of slow students is to be reversed. We know all too well that the low achiever falls further behind each year he remains in school. Perhaps disadvantaged students suffer most from this lack of remedial teaching in that they do not possess many of the necessary beginning skills and, as a consequence, quickly fall even further behind. Certainly, good teachers attach much value to their remedial and diagnostic role.

Too many school teachers fail to leave time in their schedule for the reteaching of a lesson not learned by students. Lessons that are not grasped may need to be *changed*, not merely retaught. If students do not learn the material the first time, repetition alone does not always guarantee that they will learn it the second time through.

Teachers should revise lessons when necessary, by breaking them down into smaller steps and adding new examples and exercises. Learning theorist Robert Gagné (1962) has noted that the design of instruction (sequencing of subtasks leading to the concept, principle, or other training goal) is more important in advancing learning than are some of the better known psychological principles such as reinforcement or distribution of practice. The revision of lessons, then, is a vitally important teacher task. Teachers, we feel, should spend at least 20 percent to 50 percent of their day in recycling work with low achievers and enrichment work with high achievers. These figures increase as the age of the students and their capacity for independent work increases.

The needs of faster students are also important. Robinson (1962) writes: "We are quite right in insisting that the demands of the school should not go beyond the child's capacity to perform. We are quite wrong if we do not add that the demands of the school should not be *below* the child's capacity. . . ." No teacher will be able to predict consistently which tasks will challenge, but not overwhelm, students. Thus, if teachers are to achieve the appropriate match for students, they will need to engage regularly in remedial and recycling activities for both their fast and slow learners. The teacher's ability to generate student enthusiasm for "something old"—a review topic— is an especially important skill, and if we observe a class over several days, we should see signs of review work being enthusiastically pursued by teacher and students alike. There is no reason to apologize for remedial work and every reason to engage in it. Also, if fast learners are to engage enthusiastically in learning activities, they must be allowed to move on to new tasks when they master present instructional goals.

Adapting material to student interest

Student interest is also closely related to the topic of the match of material to student. Just as *ability* to perform and be challenged by assigned work is important, so also is *interest* in the work. Each person's day-to-day behavior confirms this fact. If we try to play bridge and enjoy it we will soon master the complicated set of rules that must be memorized if we are to play the game well; however, we often fail to memorize phone numbers that we frequently dial or other tasks for which we have little special enthusiasm. Our interest, our drive to learn, will focus our attention, and we will persist in learning complex material *if we want to do so.*

Earlier, in discussing teacher enthusiasm, we noted that students are more likely to be interested in something if they see others enjoying it. Obviously, initial interest in the learning task is more likely to be sustained if the task is related to students' interests. For example, fourth-grade students may catch the teacher's spark of interest for collecting information and using library books just by listening to the teacher talk. However, such interest may be dampened by a few tranquilizing assignments: name the state bird for each state, find the birthdays of each President's wife, list the date for each state's admission to the Union, and collect all the information you can about a famous explorer. Now some children may enjoy looking up the Presidents' wives' birthdates. Just as importantly, some children would find such exercises patently boring. These students, if continually asked to use the library to find answers to boring questions, will learn that the library is a boring place where they find the answers to someone else's questions, not their own.

If, in this example, the teacher's goal is to teach the students that systematically collecting accurate information is an important, exciting activity, the teacher will fail with a number of his students. To begin with, why must every student have the same assignment? Several choices could be listed; for example: (1) In which World Series in the last ten years were the most home runs hit? (2) How are the sites for World Fairs selected? (3) Name the state bird for each state. (4) What are the causes of pollution? (5) Write your own question, get it approved, and then answer it. This set of questions will appeal to a wider range of student interest, and student interest determines the value of such questions. If the student is really interested in finding the answer, then the question is useful in helping him to develop appropriate attitudes toward resource books and skills for using them. Students' interests vary widely, and few topics will appeal to every student. Thus a teacher increases the chance that students will find a task inherently interesting if he allows for student selection of study topics whenever this is consistent with instructional objectives.

Obviously, there are some questions students should work on independent of their interests, but not many. When possible, give students alternative ways of fulfilling classroom exercises. Students should enjoy learning, and little effort is required to inject more meaningful problems among the many mathematical problems that ask students to compute the latitude of London or the air time from Denver to Chicago. For example, boys who work only five minutes on long division have been observed to work several hours computing the batting averages of their favorite baseball stars; girls have been observed to work diligently attempting to determine how many records or clothing items they can buy for a specific amount of money.

Similarly, students respond favorably when school lessons are related to one another, as opposed to when they are presented as unrelated and often meaningless activities. For example, in writing expression and practice periods, students can use that week's list of 19 new spelling words to write his own story. In this way students learn to use new words in a meaningful context in addition to learning how to spell the words correctly.

This is not to say that students should do whatever they please. Schools exist for learning and school activities should be designed to teach students to use information, to process it, and to make decisions. We agree with Wingo (1950) who writes:

> *Research and theory seem to show one thing clearly. Reflective thought is called into play* only in the presence of problems which are of genuine concern to the learner. *The failure of most schools to stimulate reflective thought very likely can be accounted for by their failure to organize instruction so that children encounter concrete problems with which they have great concern to deal.*

We also concur with Johnson's (1946) statement: "Human energy is never more extravagantly wasted than in the persistent effort to answer conclusively questions that are vague and meaningless."

It is important for teachers to consider why and in what ways the questions they raise are important to students. Most curriculum content can be related to student interests, and by pointing out that relation students can be led to answer their own questions and, at the same time, fulfill the curriculum requirements. Much of the curriculum focuses on vitally important basic skills that students must master. However, whenever possible, teachers should provide students with reasons why they are answering questions and why they should seek information, choices for completing academic units in their assignments, and relationships of material ideas in books to the things that are relevant in everyday living. Learning is fun, and instances of the teacher's effort to relate materials to student interests will be evident in the effective teacher's classroom. Too many teachers feel guilty when students enjoy learning, because they see schoolwork as a tedious chore. *Learning should be fun.*

Providing for self-evaluation
Closely related to the importance of using student interest, whenever appropriate, is the idea that students must be taught skills for self-evaluation—the ability to evaluate their own academic output.

If students are to become independent, autonomous learners, they must have opportunities for self-evaluation. Today's information explosion has rendered invalid the notion of the teacher who can present the "important facts" to students. There are too many important facts, and few facts are so dependably important that they need to be committed to memory. Perhaps most important for twentieth and twenty-first century life, students need to acquire a respect for knowledge, skills for acquiring and assessing needed information, and abilities to identify problems that need to be solved. We live in an age when computers can help us solve problems, but the human agent still is needed to identify the problem and gather the relevant information. Schools and teachers need to develop students' capacities for evaluating their own work, assessing their own inadequacies, and determining what they need to do to correct such inadequacies (i.e., to define problems).

Sexton (1969) has written that schools are especially hard on male learners, pressing them to conform to docile patterns of behavior and to accept passive roles. Silberman (1970) in his chapter, "Education for Society," points out that schools are obsessed with keeping students silent and immobile. Students that are 11 and 12 years old have to get permission to go to the bathroom, are constantly told what to do, and then are told how well they have performed when they finish.

Although some rules are necessary, teachers should, in every possible way, increase the student's capacity and *power* for regulating his own classroom behavior and evaluating his own academic work. Much research indicates that students feel relatively powerless in schools. This is true, no doubt, because they see teachers make the rules, evaluate performance, call on students, terminate activities, and otherwise control the classroom. Jackson (1968) clearly shows that the teacher defines the "good life" and rewards those students who lead the good life. The student's job is to find what the teacher wants and perform accordingly. Not surprisingly, then, students see themselves with only limited classroom decision-making power (Wolfson and Nash, 1968).

Not only does the student have to contend with "teacher power," but he has to overcome the coercive aspects of group life if he is to become an independent, autonomous learner. The crowd places certain demands on the learner. One major aspect of crowding is that students are so busily involved in life that they have little time to look at it (Plant, 1930). They must constantly respond to immediate demands and have little time to think about or evaluate what they are doing. Classrooms, in most situations, are places for action, not reflection, and may favor the student with the impulsive cognitive style to the relative neglect of the reflective thinker.

In observing classrooms, one should look for indications that say, "These students have a chance to further their intellectual and behavioral independence." A few ways this process can be manifested are as follows:

1. Students can go to the restroom when they care to do so, even though they might have minor restrictions such as no more than two out of the classroom at a time, and no one can be gone longer than five minutes.

2. Students are asked to explain their thinking, even when their answers are correct. Too often teachers ask students to explain their thinking only when they have responded incorrectly. At the incidental level, when the teacher questions only incorrect answers the students learn that the teacher is interested only in *right answers*. Teachers can show students that they are interested in the thinking behind an answer by asking for more information when the response is correct. "Yes, the cube would be white, but why? Why would it be white?"

3. Students are asked to evaluate their own work, or the work of other students occasionally. This can, of course, be done in a variety of ways. When a student answers a question, the teacher, instead of reacting immediately, may ask other students to react. The teacher may hand back to students their own papers and ask them to look at their work and pick out the strongest part and to explain why it is particularly good, or to pick out the weakest part and explain why it is weak and how it can be improved. Similarly, the teacher can have students exchange papers and ask each student to make the paper he looks at better by adding ideas or arguments that the original author had not considered.

Of course, allowing students to react to the papers of other students has to be handled carefully. Teachers should delay the exchange of student papers until after students have had regular practice in critiquing their own papers. Even then, teachers would be advised to restrict the scope of evaluation to something simple such as, "List two ideas that might make the paper a better one." Asking students to limit their suggestions would minimize situations in which students are overwhelmed by numerous "helpful comments" and would not frustrate students unduly when they cannot generate several helpful comments.

Such assignments are useful for teaching students the fun of sharing information and for demonstrating that in many situations there is no one right way to prepare a paper. Of course, such procedures help the student to develop an ability to look at and to think about his work rather than to do assignment after assignment without ever thinking. An especially effective technique for helping first- or second-grade students to understand their progress and improvement is to let them see and compare a handwriting exercise they did in October with one done in December.

4. Students are allowed to make decisions. They may be simple, "Do we do math first today, or would you prefer to read?" or intermediate, "This afternoon and tomorrow afternoon you will have time to write a story about your favorite American. He can be a politician, baseball player, or whatever. Anything goes as long as the paper is factual. Use the resource books in the back of the room whenever you need them." Or student decisions can be important in class planning, "During the next four weeks I have three major objectives for us to cover. How do you want to go about learning this material, and what other topics do you want to learn during this time period?"

Teachers must give students real opportunities to make decisions. If decisions are called for, even simple ones, teachers must allow students to make them. Nothing convinces students that they are powerless more than teachers who bombard them with: "Do you want to read the *Weekly Reader* now? *(Students boo in chorus.)* Well, you're going to read it anyway." For young children or for older students who have not been trained in self-evaluation, the teacher may have to ask simple questions, accept the students where they are, and help them to develop skills for self-evaluation as rapidly as possible. The ability to criticize one's self openly and undefensively is a learned skill. Obviously, teachers are the ultimate decision makers in classrooms, and they have responsibility for evaluating student performance. But if teacher evaluation is the only type of evaluation in the classroom, students are not being stimulated to think about their own work.

5. The teacher responds when students ask questions relevant to the subject discussion at hand. Earlier, we emphasized the importance of the teacher responding to students' questions, particularly those questions that are at least in some way related to the subject matter discussion. When students ask questions, they are signaling their interest in the subject matter and their desire to really learn. At these times, teachers can significantly influence student learning by taking time to deal with their questions in depth, giving not only the information students ask for, but frequently providing them with resources and ways in which to continue pursuit of the question.

6. The teacher allows students to question his behavior and to question subject content. In many classrooms, the students go about learning the curriculum blindly without questioning any interpretations made in the book. An important lesson for students to learn is that just because a statement is in a book does not necessarily mean it is true. It is essential for the student to know that much of what is in a book is an author's hypothesis, his best guess at present. While his hypothesis may be an intelligent guess based upon long, extended periods of study, nevertheless, the student should realize that much of what appears in a textbook is conjecture.

Unfortunately, students in many classrooms learn the curriculum, the book at hand, without question. Much is lost when students are not taught to deal with the subject matter, to play with it and consider it from different points of view. Teachers exert a powerful, positive influence on students if they model appropriate reactions toward the curriculum. They should occasionally ask students to question certain points and may occasionally disagree with a point in the book. Obviously, it does not make a great deal of sense for the teacher to continually criticize and disagree with the textbook. However, such expressions are useful if the teacher does have honest disagreement with a point in the book. When the teacher is dealing with his own hypotheses he should inform the students that his statements are his best guess and that they can question his opinion.

Using a variety of teaching methods

Trump and Baynham (1961) found that it was very difficult to motivate even the most able students to do creative work, because they were so used to doing only precisely what teachers assigned, and the assignments seldom make the student exert much initiative. Teachers can play a valuable role in increasing students' capacities for self-evaluation and autonomous learning and should view this activity as one of their primary duties.

In addition to encouraging students to develop their capacity for self-evaluation, teachers should structure learning situations so that students can develop skills in expressing themselves orally and in working with other students on joint projects. Trump (1966) summarized the need this way:

> Students need to learn how to orally express ideas effectively, to listen to the ideas of others, and to identify areas of disagreement and consensus and to respect each other in the process. These skills have to be taught and they have to be practiced. I am sorry to say . . . that these skills are not practiced in today's classrooms. What is called classroom discussion is little more than an oral quiz conducted by the teacher.

During part of each instructional week, students should be allowed to work in small (five to fifteen members) groups in order to practice communicative skills as well as to apply academic content to solve problems. The small group makes possible student participation in problem-centered discussion, and many students feel more comfortable expressing themselves in small groups than they do in larger groups or in whole-class activities. Also, when students are broken into small groups many more students are able to practice communicative skills than is possible in large group activities.

Student motivation and interest is often positively affected when teachers involve them in small group activities, provide them with interesting projects, and supply them with clear procedural guidelines for accomplishing those project goals. The previous chapter described a variety of ways in which the teacher can divide the class into smaller instructional groups. The point here is to suggest that small group work, if it is *well planned*, can be a vital part of life in both elementary and secondary classrooms.

Teachers can benefit from using a wide variety of instructional techniques. In keeping with the theme of this chapter, it is useful to point out that, just as there is no such thing as a single type of "good teacher," there is no such thing as the "correct method." One good teacher may utilize three-fourths of his class time in small-group activities, while another may spend but two-fifths or less of his class time in this way.

In *secondary schools*, the value of teacher lecturing and presenting facts versus the desirability of teachers using discovery approaches (allowing students to solve problems quasi-independently of the teacher) has been hotly debated. No evidence consistently demonstrates the superiority of either approach. In recent years it has become quite fashionable in educational circles to criticize the lecture approach categorically. Much of this criticism is undoubtedly deserved, for many teachers have been excessively tied to a lecture approach (and probably to a decaying set of lectures). Most of us have had too many experiences with teachers who were dull and ineffective, but frequent, lecturers. Some of the major charges that critics have leveled at lecture procedure are as follows:

1. Lecture presentations deny students the opportunity to practice social skills.
2. The lecture presentation makes the implicit suggestion that all learners need the same information, and this assumption is typically incorrect.
3. Lectures often are longer than the attention span of the student, so students often "tune out" the information.
4. Essentially, the lecture method conveys only information and does not affect attitudes or skill development.
5. Students can read factual material on their own. Why waste their time with lectures?

However, Ausubel (1963), among others, has pointed out that effective lectures can provide students with information that it would take hours for them to collect. Those who argue the value of lectures raise a simple question: why force the student to search hours for information when a lecture will allow them to obtain information quickly that they can then utilize to solve problems? This point obviously has merit. Thus, lectures are neither all good nor all bad. The important question is not, "Should we lecture?" but instead is, "When should we lecture?"

Hoover (1968) provides some useful guidelines outlining situations in which it may be appropriate for the teacher to make lecture presentations:

1. When the needed background information is not readily accessible to students
2. When the facts or problems are of a conflicting nature
3. When the unique experiences of an individual (teacher, student, or resource person) enable him to give a lecture that substantially contributes to the clarification of issues
4. When time is of the essence and the sources of data are widely scattered
5. When a change of pace, or variety, is needed (many oral reports and demonstrations fall into this category)
6. When the presentation of data is more likely to result in greater understanding than would otherwise be possible

We feel that several major types of instructional approaches have valid purposes. Teachers who use a variety of approaches will probably obtain a more effective response from their students. For one thing, a variety of instructional methods (assuming they are carefully planned and implemented) will stimulate student interest. Teacher lectures mixed with small-group work, panel discussions, an occasional debate, and other devices add more spice to classroom life. Second, teachers using both small-group and large-group techniques can gain the benefits of both if they carefully sequence activities.

For example, criticisms of lecture methods include the charge that they do not allow for student involvement in the learning activity or allow for students to develop social skills. A teacher may, therefore, choose to make a short, fifteen-minute lecture to structure a problem and to provide students with necessary information and then to break the class into small, problem-solving groups.

If the teacher can lecture in an interesting, enthusiastic fashion that crystallizes issues and helps the student to raise questions that he can eventually answer, then lectures are a valuable learning device. Teachers using lectures should view them not only as a convenient device for presenting information but also as a way to stimulate student interest and to raise interesting questions that students will want to answer in small-group or independent activities that follow the lecture. If the teacher lectures in a manner that bores or irritates the students, then the lecture method is nothing but a waste of time.

One argument for team-taught classrooms is that teachers with good lecturing styles can perform those chores while small-group specialists might pick up in areas where the lecturer is less capable.

Above all, if teachers are to make extended use of lecture techniques in secondary schools, they must be able to express themselves clearly and succinctly. The need for clarity will be discussed briefly in the following section.

Clarity

If students are to become involved in their work, they must clearly understand what they are to do. This is especially true when they are given independent work assignments. They must know exactly what their options are, and in those rare instances when they have total freedom to do what they please, they must understand this also. Does the teacher clearly communicate to students the objectives of the lesson? How long does it take for the objective to be clear to the students? Often lectures begin without introductions and end without clear summaries. Such behavior makes it extremely difficult for students to listen for main points, and unlikely that they will maintain interest in what the teacher talks about. Ausubel (1963) has discussed the usefulness of "advance organizers" (information that describes what students are to learn before instruction begins).

For example, a physical education instructor before listing and describing twenty different penalties that might occur during a hockey game could provide his students with some way to organize the information they are about to receive. "Today we are going to discuss a variety of penalties that might be called during a hockey game. We will discuss in detail ten minor penalties and ten major penalties; we will also discuss the differences between major and minor penalties. At the end of the period I will show you twenty slides and ask you to name the penalty and tell me whether or not it is a major or minor penalty."

Advance organizers provide the student with a mental map so that when he listens to the teacher talk, or when he reads, he can fill in and expand as he identifies relevant concepts and information. When students do not have advance information about the purpose of a lecture or reading assignment, their thinking is often disorganized and ineffective. A clear explanation of the assignment helps the student to focus on the main ideas and to order his thoughts effectively.

The point here is, of course, a simple one: we are much more likely to find something if we know what we are searching for. However, many teachers, when engaging in expository teaching, violate this simple rule by failing to tell students the purpose of the lecture in advance. Before lecturing, teachers should tell students what they are expected to learn in the lecture and why it is useful or important for students to know this information. At the conclusion of lectures, teachers should summarize the main points in a few simple sentences. Providing a clear introduction and a strong summary takes but little planning and presentation time on the teacher's part and will greatly facilitate students' ability to learn the material, because such structuring helps the student to see essential facts and concepts more clearly.

Vague or difficult language and ambiguous questions make it difficult for students to respond in question-answer or recitation periods. There is some experimental evidence to suggest that teachers who use clear and appropriate language (i.e., that all students in the class can understand) obtain higher achievement from their students (Rosenshine and Furst, 1971). Although the dimensions of clarity have not been fully determined, the following terms indicate the general meaning of the concept: the points the teacher makes are clear and easy to understand; the teacher spends little time answering student questions about what he means (i.e., questions are phrased so that they are answered the first time without additional information); the teacher uses few vague expressions such as "a little" and "many."

Although ratings of clarity require the observer to make some inferences, an observer can fairly easily judge, along global dimensions, the clarity of a teacher's presentation (see scales at end of chapter). However, in order to add specificity to our discussion, we will describe more fully certain aspects of clarity. Perhaps the most important dimension of clarity is an ability to ask oral questions effectively. This topic will be discussed in the next section.

Effective oral questions

The appropriateness of a question depends upon the purpose of the classroom exercise and the characteristics of the students. For example, the teacher may ask questions to see if students are ready for the impending discussion, determine if students have achieved learning objectives, arouse student interest, or stimulate critical thinking. A "good" question for arousing student interest in the discussion may not be a good question for assessing student learning.

Although the definition of a good question depends on its context, certain guidelines can be applied to most questions. Groisser (1964) indicates that a good question is (1) clear, (2) purposeful, (3) brief, (4) natural and adapted to the level of the class, and (5) thought provoking. Some elaboration of these descriptions follows.

1. *Clear questions* are questions that precisely describe the specific points to which a student is to respond. Vague questions can be responded to in a variety of ways and their ambiguous nature confuses students. For example, Groisser writes: "If a teacher of Spanish wished to call attention to the tense of a verb in a sentence on the board and asked, 'What do you see here?' the student would not know exactly what was being called for. Better to ask, 'What tense is used in this clause?' " Vague questions often result in wasted time as the student asks the teacher to repeat or rephrase the question. Furthermore, vague questions fail to identify the specific attack point for the student (e.g., "What's wrong with football?" vs. "Why do many college football players never receive a degree?" or, "What about beer?" vs. "What ingredients are used to make beer?" or "Should sixteen-year-olds be allowed to buy beer?") In addition to lack of specificity, questions are unclear when asked as part of a series. Groisser writes:

A third-grade teacher, in discussing the War of 1812 asks, in one continuous statement, "Why did we go to war? As a merchant how would you feel? How was our trade hurt by the Napoleonic war?" The teacher is trying to clarify his first question and to focus thinking upon an economic cause of the war. In his attempt to help, he actually confuses.

The teacher in this case would have been more effective if he had asked a clear, straightforward question to begin with "What was the cause of the War of 1812?" waited for the student to respond, and then probed for economic causes if the student failed to mention this area in his answer. Teachers often ask students two or three questions in one or rephrase their original question a number of times. When faced with such a series of questions, pupils do not know precisely what the teacher is asking. Even if students do respond correctly in such situations, many students will not gain from the answer because they were confused or distracted by the teacher's question.

The usefulness of clear and specific (highly focused) questions as well as clear teacher language has been demonstrated in some experimental situations (Wright and Nuthall, 1970; Rosenshine, 1968). Teachers should strive to ask students questions that *clearly cue the students to respond along specific lines.* This, of course, does *not* mean that the teacher cues the answer, but rather that the teacher does clearly communicate the question to which the student is to respond.

2. Most of us would agree that, at a logical level, questions need to be *purposeful.* That is, teacher questions should lead toward a clear achievement of the lesson's intent. Question series that are not planned in advance are seldom purposeful. (It is useful to write out questions that will be asked during class discussion.) Teachers who ask most of their questions "off the cuff" will ask many questions that are irrelevant or confusing and which work against achievement of the goal of the lesson by the students.

Questions should be asked in carefully *planned* sequences, however, or else teacher-directed discussion periods are meaningless. The teacher should not ask a series of questions of the pupil before he has a chance to respond. Young students, especially, will have a difficult time responding when the teacher asks him five separate questions at the same time. Questions should be asked in carefully planned sequences but should be asked one at a time. Questions should not be asked randomly, but in integrated series, so that the activity is a learning experience, not just a check to see if students have learned the material. Thus teachers should attempt to plan (write out) question sequences that will lead students first to identify and/or review essential facts, then to refine their understanding of the information, and finally to apply their knowledge to real or hypothetical problems ("Now that we have identified the properties of these six pieces of wood, which would you use to build a canoe, . . . a huge sailboat?"). Such planning will help insure an orderly progression through the various objectives involved. Of course, the teacher should not let a prepared sequence of questions shackle him to a fixed course. Legitimate and worthwhile side roads may be opened by pupil questions, and these should be pursued.

3. Questions should be *brief*. Long questions are often unclear. The longer a question is, the more difficult it is to understand, and this is especially true for young students. Although long questions are not always unclear, they often are, and teachers would do well to ask questions of elementary-school children in short, specific language.

4. Using *natural, simple language* (as opposed to pedantic, textbook statements) and adapting the question to the level of the class are two ways to prevent language from interfering with teacher-pupil discussion. Does the teacher use words that the students understand? Can all the students in the classroom understand the teacher or only the brighter half of the class? All the students, at all times, must be able to understand the teacher. Otherwise there is no way for them to be able to do the sorts of things the teacher wants done.

This does not mean that the teacher should not use big words. In fact, students benefit greatly from being with a teacher who introduces new, big, unfamiliar words with precision. The verbal facility of the teacher, the clarity of his language, does much to help them learn and use more appropriate, more precise language in their daily lives. However, a teacher needs to be very aware of the vocabulary level of the students in his class, so that when he introduces a new word he can immediately clarify it and help them make that word their own word.

5. Good questions are thought provoking. In general, good discussion questions should arouse a strong, thoughtful response from students, "I never thought of that before," or "I want to find the answer to that question." Questions or discussion sessions should force students to think about the facts that they possess and to integrate or to apply them. Earlier, stress was placed on the use of probing questions (Chapter 1), to help students to clarify their ideas, and on the importance of conducting discussions that center on topics that are important to students so that they are motivated to share their ideas with other students and to seek additional information. The use of probing questions and discussion topics that have high interest value to students are two ways to increase the probability that students will think about the discussion topic. However, it is still essential for the teacher to plan questions that ask students to analyze or synthesize facts rather than to merely list them.

Although it may be necessary to ask factual questions to see if students possess the factual information necessary for a purposeful discussion, most questions should be asked in such a way as to make students use information, rather than just recite, and to want to respond. It should be noted that the criterion that good questions should be thought provoking is probably more applicable to older elementary and secondary school students than to young elementary school students who often benefit from discussions that are fact oriented.

Questions to avoid

Groisser (1964) points out that certain question-asking habits of teachers often lead to unproductive student responses. He describes four types as being particularly misused: (1) yes-no questions, (2) tugging questions, (3) guessing questions, and (4) leading questions.

1. Groisser advises against the excessive use of yes-no questions because they are typically asked only as a warm-up for another question. For example, the teacher asks, "Was Hannibal a clever soldier?" After the student answers, the teacher says, "Why?" or "Explain your reason." Teachers hoping to get responses from other students will often ask yes-no questions such as, "Do you agree with Jane's answer?" These yes-no questions confuse the lesson focus and waste time. The teacher would do better to ask the real question, "Why do you agree or disagree with Jane's answer?" without the preceding artificial yes-no question.

We see two additional dangers in yes-no or other choice questions, "Was it Hamilton or Jackson?" These dangers are enhanced when teachers do not follow up choice questions after the student makes his response. In the first place, choice questions encourage guessing (even when they have no idea how to respond, students will be right 50 percent of the time in such cases). Holt (1964) describes vividly how students read teachers like traffic lights in such situations, and how quickly they change their answers at the slightest teacher frown. Thus students are apt to develop devious strategies for getting the teacher to cue the answer in these situations rather than to concentrate on the question itself.

The other disadvantage to yes-no and choice questions is that they have *rather low diagnostic power*. One value of any student's response (whether it is correct or incorrect) is that it cues the teacher as to the most appropriate way to proceed. Unfortunately, responses to choice questions provide a poor basis for deciding whether students know the material, because they often involve guesswork. *Choice and yes-no questions should seldom be asked*. Choice questions are sometimes useful for low-achieving and/or sensitive students who have a difficult time responding in general class discussion. Such questions are relatively simple to answer, and for these students this type of warm-up is often useful before asking a more substantive question. However, for most instructional purposes, choice and yes-no questions should be avoided.

2. Tugging questions or statements often follow a partial or incomplete student response, "Well, come on," "Yes . . .?" Tugging questions essentially say to the student "Tell me more." However, these questions are often *vague* and are not effective in obtaining additional student response. When students are stuck for a response, they need a clue, not teacher nagging. After a student has responded to the initial question, the teacher will be more likely to get additional information from the pupil if he asks a new, more specific question than if he continues to ask, "What else," "What's another reason," and so forth. For example, the teacher asks, "Why did the Pilgrims build and live in a fort?" A student responds, "They built a fort to protect themselves from the Indians and from animals." The teacher, if he wants the student to focus upon the advantages of community living, might then ask, "What advantages did the Pilgrims have living in a group?"

3. Guessing questions require students *to guess or to reason* about a question either because they do not have the factual knowledge to answer more precisely—for example, "How far is it from New York to Wichita, Kansas?" "Why does the same facial expression have different meanings in different cultures?" "How many business firms have offices on Wall Street?" or because the question has no correct answer, "In the song 'Houston,' why do you expect Dean Martin wanted to go there?"

"How many games will a football team in the National Football League have to win to be a conference champion?" Guessing questions are often a useful way to capture student imagination and to actively involve them in the discussion. However, if overused or used inappropriately, guessing questions encourage students to guess or respond thoughtlessly rather than to think.

The value of guessing questions depends upon how the teacher uses them. If he is asking for a guess, then such questions are pointless; however, if the teacher is really asking students to formulate hypotheses and encouraging them to make realistic estimates on the basis of limited information, then such questions can be valuable. The game Twenty Questions is an excellent case in point for young elementary students. If the teacher allows aimless guessing, the game is of no value. If, however, the teacher models by playing the game himself and demonstrating appropriate problem-solving behavior, it can be a valuable learning experience.

Similarly, in secondary mathematics classrooms students may learn to enjoy working and reasoning with subjects such as abstract formulas when they are introduced with questions like, "How many games will the Cardinals have to win if they are to win the pennant? Let's see, the last ten years the range has been . . . ," or "How could we figure the formula? They have a six-game lead with twenty-two games remaining to be played."

Guessing questions are useful if they are tied to teacher strategies that help the student to think rationally and systematically and are designed to arrive ultimately at a thoughtful response. Guessing questions that are used to encourage impulsive, irrational thought are pointless and self-defeating. The momentary enthusiasm such questions may generate is not worth the possible risk of teaching children inappropriate attitudes about classroom life.

4. Leading questions such as, "Don't you agree?" and other rhetorical questions should be avoided because they reinforce student dependency upon the teacher and tend to undermine independent student thought. *Questions should be asked only if the teacher wants a real response.* Remember, if you take the time to ask a question, it should be a genuine question. Questions such as the following should be avoided: "Johnny, you do very much like to read about the exciting Pilgrims, don't you?" The teacher nods his head as Johnny looks at him and says, "Yes." The avoidance of rhetorical questions and meaningless questions helps students develop the expectation that when the teacher asks the question, something important, something interesting, is happening in the classroom.

Good questioning procedure

The techniques for asking questions effectively as discussed here are largely adapted from Loughlin (1961) and Groisser (1964). Many educators have written about the topic of classroom questions. Unfortunately, however, few data have been collected to confirm or to deny the various contentions that have been made. However, common sense, logical thinking, and some empirical data suggest that the following guidelines are reasonable. Before proceeding further, the reader may prefer to pause and to consider his personal strategy for asking questions in the classroom—what criteria have you utilized (or will you utilize) to guide your behavior in asking questions in the classroom?

Grossier suggests that the following procedures will help teachers to improve the quality of their classroom questioning. He writes that questions should be planned, should be logical and sequential, should be addressed to the class, should allow pupils time to think, should be balanced between fact and thought questions, should be distributed widely, should be asked conversationally, should not be repeated, and should sometimes get pupils to respond to other pupils' answers.

The first two points are already familiar to us and the efficacy of such action is apparent. However, the usefulness of addressing most questions to the entire class (and then to an individual) is not as apparent at first glance. Groisser suggests that teachers will get better attention from their students if they wait to call on a student until after they ask the question. He suggests that the teacher ask the question, delay and allow the students time to think, and then ask a student to respond. This way, everyone in the class is responsible for the answer. Everyone is not held responsible for an answer if the teacher names a student before he asks a question or if he calls upon a student as soon as he finishes asking the question.

In general, it seems desirable to call upon a student to respond only after the question had been asked and only after the teacher has paused, allowing the students time to think. Obviously, there are exceptions to this general strategy, and Groisser cites at least three situations where it makes more sense to call upon the student before asking the questions: (1) the teacher notices an inattentive student and wants to draw him back into the lesson, (2) the teacher wants to ask a follow-up question of a student who has just responded, or (3) the teacher is calling on a shy student who may be "shocked" if called upon without advance warning.

All of us doubtlessly agree that pupils need to have time to think, but how much time is optimal for a given student or a particular class? Groisser's implicit hypothesis is that if teachers delay before naming a student after they ask a question, then more students will think about the question and become involved in the discussion. There is no definitive research to show that students actually use this time to think. However, Rowe (1969) presents data suggesting that teachers who manage to prolong their waiting time for five seconds get longer student responses than teachers who quickly ask another question or call on another student when their questions are not immediately answered. Perhaps if the teacher delayed too long, pupil attention might wander. However, it does seem reasonable that a short pause before asking a student to respond is likely to heighten student interest in the question.

In addition, we believe it equally important that the teacher be prepared to wait for a student's response after calling on him. Rowe (1969) reports that teachers in one experiment were found to wait longer for a response from their more capable students than for slower students. Less capable students, then, had to answer more rapidly than bright students. Teachers need to be careful that *low expectations* for a student do not cause them to give up prematurely on him when he fails to answer immediately.

In general, if the teacher asks a question, he should never answer the question himself. If he asks a low-achieving student a question, for example, he should be prepared to wait until the student makes some sort of response. It may be useful for the teacher to rephrase, to repeat, or to give clues. However, it is very important that the teacher develop the expectation on the part of the students that when he asks a question, he expects a verbal answer, even if that answer is, "I don't know," or "I'm not sure."

That questions should be balanced between fact and thought questions is probably self-evident. However, although a variety of questions is an important dimension in the classroom (especially since textbook questions and writing are mainly directed at memory questions) teachers should not consider fact questions unimportant. *Such questions for young students are especially important, as those students learn best if the material to be learned is highly structured. Many of the questions asked in elementary school classrooms should be fact questions.* Some research has suggested that young children from disadvantaged backgrounds may learn more effectively when factual questions are stressed (Ragosta et al., 1971). In any case, students at all levels are likely to learn more when fact and thought questions are organized in series to emphasize points and lead to a goal.

Groisser and Loughlin both suggest that teachers should distribute their questions widely rather than allow only a few students to answer most of them. The implicit hypothesis here is that students will learn more if they are actively involved in classroom discussions than if they sit passively in the room day after day, without participating. There is, of course, no direct research to support this notion, and each reader can surely recall a reticent student who rarely participated in classroom discussions, but who had excellent grades. However, it seems especially true that the low achiever with a short attention span needs to be called on occasionally to keep him from tuning out the lesson. Although no research supports this suggestion, logic would seem to dictate that if you want to hold students responsible for the questions asked, you will have to call on them occasionally. Thus, it would seem desirable that teachers call on a wide number of students in order to increase student attention and to provide more students with a chance to practice oral communication skills.

Another point advanced by both Groisser and Loughlin is that teacher questions and student answers normally should not be repeated immediately. This, of course, assumes that the teacher's original statement is audible and clearly expressed. Teachers who continually repeat and rephrase their own questions communicate to the students that they need not pay attention to the teacher, that he will always repeat the question if he calls on them. This is also a sign of poor preparation or disorganized thinking.

Similarly, many teachers get into the habit of repeating student responses, "John has told us that in his opinion there were three fundamental reasons that account for the Civil War. First he suggested . . ." This practice wastes time and teaches students that they need not pay attention to what a classmate says, because the teacher will always repeat it. Such behavior often lessens the value of pupil response and fails to hold students responsible for what others say.

However, like all rules, there are exceptions. One exception to not repeating the answer comes when working with young children in drill-like recitation activities. In such situations, "Yes, two-plus-two equals four," "The tallest block is the red one," "Yes, we call this figure a circle," the teacher can conveniently repeat the child's answer to let him know that he is correct, while at the same time modeling speaking in complete sentences. When teachers are dealing with rote material (factual, one-word answers) and working with young children, it is often desirable to repeat the child's answer.

An exception to the rule about repeating student responses occurs when the teacher repeats the response but rephrases it somewhat in order to summarize and pull together important material that has come out in the discussion. Still, the teacher should respond this way only periodically and when it is important to do so (i.e., not after every student response), or else he may indirectly teach students that "the teacher can always say it better than we can." Teacher summaries are important in classroom discussion, but teachers should not always perform this role. They should encourage students to summarize points made previously in the discussion and to describe how other students' comments fit in with the discussion.

Students should receive information about the correctness or incorrectness of their responses. This acknowledgment is especially important for low-achieving students, who may have no idea about the appropriateness of their responses. Teacher feedback on student responses is also one of the easiest ways for a teacher to maintain interest. A great deal of research on motivation consistently shows that students at all age levels benefit from frequent feedback about their work. Earlier, we discussed the importance of giving the students a goal, letting them know why they were participating in the particular lesson. It is equally important to let them know how they are doing in the lesson, how much progress they have made. The easiest way for teachers to give students feedback is after individual responses. Yet, research has shown that teachers sometimes do not give feedback, especially with certain types of students. Teachers should make sure they give some sort of response every time the student makes an answer in the class. Feedback does not have to be long and elaborate, although sometimes this is necessary and appropriate. Frequently, short comments such as, "right" "okay," are all that is necessary to tell the student that he is on the right track or that his answer is completely adequate. Interestingly enough, the students that often receive no feedback after they have responded in the classrooms are low-achieving students (Brophy and Good, 1970*b*; Good, Sikes, and Brophy, 1972). This is especially inefficient, of course, since these students are those who are least likely to know if the answer they have given is correct or incorrect. Without teacher feedback, such students often do not know if they have adequate information or not.

Teachers, of course, do not have to physically provide this information themselves at all times. For instance, teachers can provide feedback sheets so that students can assess the quality of their own work. The importance of allowing students to check their own work was stressed earlier in this chapter. Ways in which teachers can be assisted by students in instructing and providing feedback to other students have also been discussed previously.

Often teacher behavior tells students that the teacher is more interested in quizzing them than in sharing or discussing information. Does the teacher present questions as a challenge or as a threat? Teachers who question students in harsh terms are likely to threaten them and make it difficult for them to share their thinking with the teacher. When the teacher asks a question, the situation should be simply an exchange of information. The teacher is trying to assess the knowledge that a student possesses in that particular subject. A student's answer, whether it is completely correct or completely wrong, conveys the same amount of information to the teacher. It allows him to make a decision: Does the student need more work? Can he go to the next exercise? Does he need to review? Therefore, teachers should be very sure that when they ask questions, they present the question as an interesting challenge to the student or as a friendly exchange of information in order to get maximum motivation and productivity from him in his answer. That is, questions should be honest questions asked because the teacher seeks to see if the student understands the material. Too often questions are aggressive, asked in the spirit of, "Say something and then I'll tell you why you're wrong."

Teacher questions should be asked conversationally. Groisser suggests that allowing students to respond to each other is another way that teachers can demonstrate their interest in obtaining student discussion. Groisser writes:

> *Many teachers seize upon the first answer given and react to it at once with a comment or with another question. . . .*
> *It is more desirable, where possible, to ask a question, accept two or three answers, and then proceed. This pattern tends to produce sustaining responses, variety, and enrichment. It encourages volunteering, contributes to group cooperation, and approaches a more realistic social situation.*

Such a technique is useful for *modeling* the teacher's interest in the exchange of information rather than pressing for the one right answer, for indicating that there may not always be one right answer, and for showing that the teacher is interested in information about the area as well as the answer. Teachers will get students to listen more carefully to the responses of fellow students if they occasionally call on them to respond to one another's answers. Wright and Nuthall (1970) present research data showing that teachers (teaching an experimental elementary science lesson) who obtained good achievement from their students frequently redirected questions to several students. Apparently, then, having pupils reacting to other pupil responses is a valuable teacher behavior in some situations, especially in older elementary school levels and in secondary classrooms. Teachers who teach very young children (preschool through second grade) should realize that this procedure is often very time consuming and that for many activities dyadic (teacher-to-pupil) teaching is much more desirable.

Teacher organization, teacher awareness

Past research (Ryans, 1960) has reported that efficient, well-prepared teachers are more effective than disorganized ones. More recently (Kounin, 1970), some research has suggested that teachers who are aware of student behavior and interests maintain more effective learning environments than teachers who are not aware of what goes on in classrooms. Preparation time is necessary, for example, to explain special remediation sessions with students, to divide students into new mathematics groups, to grade papers immediately so they can be returned the very next day, or to prepare assignments that interest both male and female learners. Similarly, much time is required to be aware of student interests (hold private conversations with them at recess, visit their homes, etc.) so that such information can be used to instructional advantage.

Awareness and organization for the most part involve *proactive* behavior that occurs before the teaching act. However, in addition to spending time, the teacher has to *demonstrate* his awareness to students if it is to have maximum effect. For example, the sixth-grade teacher shows his concern for students by commenting upon book reports and returning them to students the next day. Although another conscientious teacher may spend more time and write more comments, by waiting several days he may also lose student confidence in his view of their work as important. Similarly, students may benefit if the teacher explains fully how he has organized the week's work in the way that he has. Teachers would do well to show their knowledge of students at each available opportunity. Teachers rarely engage in personal discussions with students; they seldom talk to pupils privately about such things as student hobbies, and they seldom use such information when they do have it.

Knowledge about students is not enough; concern for student interests must be communicated to them. We feel that effective teachers will spend much time in planning instruction for enrichment and remediation purposes and will spend time acquiring more information about students. Such behaviors as clipping out newspaper articles because they are of special interest to a student, checking out library books and telling the students that certain books have been chosen for them, and writing down students' errors in order to remember to call attention to their progress on future work when these errors are eliminated will do much to communicate concern for students and increase their personal involvement in classroom life.

Many teachers function under the mistaken belief that to talk to students, to know them, is to weaken classroom discipline. Common sense tells us that the opposite is true. We strive to cooperate with people who care about us and talk with us. Special stress must be placed on the communication of concern, as research by Hoyt (1955) has shown that the mere possession of information about pupils does not in itself produce increased student achievement, although it was associated with better student attitudes toward teachers.

It is the active process of seeking and using information about students that improves classroom communication and ultimately classroom learning. Teachers need to take the time to talk with students, to acquire information about their needs and interests, and to use such information actively in designing instructional goals. Unfortunately, the university teacher-training program, the school principal, and the school system have set a bad example for teachers in this respect. Teachers in their training program or in their classroom have seldom been consulted about things that are important to them. Thus, it is sometimes difficult for the teacher to see the need for consulting students about their school needs when he was seldom consulted about his own school needs. However, students who are occasionally consulted about their needs and who frequently work on problems that are especially meaningful to them will respond with much enthusiasm and respect for the classroom.

SUGGESTED ACTIVITIES AND QUESTIONS

1. Several different and important teaching behaviors were presented in this chapter; however, a summary synthesizing this information was not provided at the end of the chapter. Show your mastery of the important aspects of the chapter by writing *your own* summary in a couple of typewritten pages. You may wish to compare your summary with the summaries made by classmates or fellow teachers.

2. What are some of the advantages and disadvantages involved when students are asked to summarize material on their own?

3. Plan a brief fifteen-minute teaching lesson (a discussion), and write out the sequence of oral questions that you will use to advance the discussion fruitfully. Try to apply the criteria suggested in this chapter for asking effective oral questions. Role-play your discussion if you have the opportunity to do so.

4. The criteria on question asking that were presented in this chapter were designed to aid teachers in asking *oral* questions effectively. In general, these criteria apply to written questions as well, but there are some exceptions. For example, why might a *series* of written questions that are all related to the same question be an effective procedure? For example, "What were the major causes of the war? Were economic factors or diplomatic breakdowns more important?" Try to identify other guidelines or criteria that are applicable only to written questions.

5. As a teacher, how can you adapt lesson content to student interest? Be realistic and specific when you respond.

6. Review and revise (as necessary) your statements that you made after reading Chapter 1 when you attempted to identify those teaching behaviors and characteristics that are signs of effective teaching. How much has your view of effective teaching changed?

7. You have now completed reading the substantive chapters of this book that describe effective classroom behaviors. What important aspects of teacher and student behavior have been neglected in this book? Why do you feel that these behaviors are important? Compare your list with ones made by others.

8. Role-play the process of introducing and ending lessons enthusiastically. Define the situation (age of students, etc.) so that others may provide you with appropriate feedback.

9. Why do some teachers feel uncomfortable when students perceive learning as fun?

10. Why should students be allowed to talk freely about opinions that differ from the teacher's or the book's opinion?

11. Select some of the forms at the end of the chapter and use them in observing real or simulated teaching.

12. Discuss (with classmates or fellow teachers) specific ways in which you as a teacher can increase opportunities for your students to engage in self-evaluation.

13. Why is it important that students assume responsibility for evaluating their own learning?

14. What does the term *match* refer to?

15. Give concrete instances when lecturing might be desirable teacher behavior.

16. Why is it impossible to give a precise definition of the *effective teacher?*

FORM 9.1. Variety of Teaching Methods

USE: Whenever the class is involved in curriculum-related activities
PURPOSE: To see if teacher uses a variety of methods in teaching the cur-
riculum
*   Each time the teacher changes activities, code the time and the type of*
activity.

BEHAVIOR CATEGORIES A. OBJECTIVES		START TIME	CODES A	B	ELAPSED TIME
What is teacher doing?					
1. Introduce new material	1.	8:30	2	5	10
2. Review old material	2.	8:40	1	1	10
3. Give or review test	3.	8:50	4	1,3	5
4. Preview or directions for next	4.	8:55	transition		5
assignment	5.	9:00	2	5	8
5. Checking seatwork in progress	6.	9:08	1	1	11
6. Other (specify)	7.	9:19	4	1,3	5
	8.	9:24	transition		6
B. METHODS	9.	9:30	2	5	10
What methods are used to	10.	9:50	1	1	12
accomplish objectives	11.	10:02	4	1,3	8
1. Demonstration or diagram at	12.	10:10	transition		5
blackboard	13.	10:15	Recess		15
2. Lecture	14.	10:30	transition		3
3. Prepared handouts (diagrams or	15.	10:33	1	7	27
teaching aids)	16.	11:00	2	10,14	25
4. Media (filmstrip, slides, tape,	17.	11:25	transition		5
record, etc.)	18.	11:30	Lunch		
5. Questioning students to check	19.	:			
understanding	20.	:			
6. Inviting and responding to	21.	:			
student questions	22.	:			
7. Focused discussion (prepared,	23.	:			
sequenced questions)	24.	:			
8. Unfocused discussion (rambling,	25.	:			
no specific objective)	26.	:			
9. Students take turns reading or	27.	:			
reciting	28.	:			
10. Drill (flashcards, math tables,	29.	:			
chorus questions)	30.	:			
11. Practical exercise or experiment	31.	:			
12. Seatwork or homework assign-	32.	:			
ment	33.	:			
13. Field trip, visit	34.	:			
14. Game, contest	35.	:			
15. Other (specify)	36.	:			
	37.	:			
NOTES:	38.	:			
	39.	:			
	40.	:			

NOTES:

1—11: Reading groups
15: Social studies
16: Spelling (Went around
room twice, then had
spelling bee)

FORM 9.2. Seatwork

USE: *Whenever part or all of the class is doing assigned seatwork*
PURPOSE: *To see if seatwork appears appropriate to students' needs and interests*

WORK INVOLVEMENT
At fixed intervals (every 3 minutes, for example), scan the group and note the number of students working productively, in neutral, or misbehaving.

	WORKING	NEUTRAL	DISRUPTIVE				
1.	13	2	1	21.			
2.	14	2	0	22.			
3.	13	1	2	23.			
4.	9	7	0	24.			
5.	7	9	0	25.			
6.	6	10	0	26.			
7.	7	9	0	27.			
8.	8	4	4	28.			
9.	8	0	8	29.			
10.	7	1	8	30.			
11.				31.			
12.				32.			
13.				33.			
14.				34.			
15.				35.			
16.				36.			
17.				37.			
18.				38.			
19.				39.			
20.				40.			

During this 30-minute period the teacher was working with one reading group. The work-involvement coding refers to the other 16 students who were working independently.

APPROPRIATENESS OF ASSIGNMENTS
What seems to be the problem with students who are not productively involved? (Check statements that apply.)

_____ 1. Assignment is too short or too easy—students finish quickly and do not have other work to do.
_____ 2. Assignment is boring, repetitive, monotonous.
__✓__ 3. Assignment is too hard—students can't get started or continually need help.
_____ 4. All of the above—assignments are not differentiated to match student needs.

The Stars seemed too confused to get started.

DISTRACTIONS
What distracts students from seatwork? What do they attend to or do when not working?

Disruptions, especially by #12

STUDENT ATTITUDES
What clues to student attitudes are observable during seatwork periods? When students can't get an answer do they concentrate or seek help, or do they merely copy from a neighbor? How do they act when the teacher's back is turned? Do they notice? Do they make noises and gestures? Do they seem to be amused by the teacher? Fear him? Respect him?

#12 "passes licks" when he thinks he can get away with it. Problems occur when others strike back and disruption spreads.
Other kids mostly concentrate on work.

FORM 9.3. Discussions

USE: When the teacher conducts a class discussion
PURPOSE: To see if teacher uses principles for conducting effective discussions
    Use this scale when the teacher is leading a discussion (or what is intended to be a discussion), to interpret current events or to review and integrate or apply earlier learning.

PURPOSE
Code teacher's apparent intent
   ✓ 1. Clear focus—teacher has specific objectives in mind
       2. Unfocused—no attempt to confine discussion to a narrow set of questions

PARTICIPATION
Tally the number of times the teacher *answers his own questions*
1. Only after repeated attempts to get students to answer   *III*
2. After only a single attempt to get a student to answer   *I*
3. Without any attempt to get a student to answer   *o*
Tally the number of *different* students who participate *Htt Htt I (of 24)*

Tally the number of times the teacher asked a student to react to another student's statement   *o*

STUDENT COMMENTS AND QUESTIONS
When a student made a relevant comment or question, what happened?
Tally the frequency of each of the following:
1. Teacher ignored student   *o*

2. Teacher gave a brief, half-hearted, or unsatisfactory response   *I*

3. Teacher gave good response and/or integrated the student's comment or question into the discussion   *III*

4. Teacher referred comment or question back to class   *o*

NOTES:
    Teacher was obviously following outline in manual. Seemed mostly intent on getting across content, but did try to deal with relevant questions. Brushed off questions to be covered next week.

FORM 9.4. Feedback to Correct Answers

USE: In discussion and recitation situations when students are answering
*   questions*
PURPOSE: To see if teacher is giving appropriate feedback to students
*   about the adequacy of their responses*
*   When a student answers correctly, code as many categories as apply to*
the teacher's feedback response.

BEHAVIOR CATEGORIES
1. Praises
2. Nods, repeats answer, says "Yes," "That's right,"
   "Okay," etc.
3. No feedback—goes on to something else
4. Ambiguous—doesn't indicate whether or not answer is
   acceptable
5. Asks a student or the class whether answer is correct
6. Asks someone else to answer the same question
7. New question—asks same student another question
8. Other (specify)

NOTES:

Both praised answers were called out
by # 19, a high-achieving student.

CODES

1.	2	26.	__
2.	2	27.	__
3.	2	28.	__
4.	2	29.	__
5.	3	30.	__
6.	2	31.	__
7.	7	32.	__
8.	2	33.	__
9.	2	34.	__
10.	3	35.	__
11.	2	36.	__
12.	2	37.	__
13.	1	38.	__
14.	2	39.	__
15.	2	40.	__
16.	1	41.	__
17.	2	42.	__
18.	2	43.	__
19.	2	44.	__
20.	__	45.	__
21.	__	46.	__
22.	__	47.	__
23.	__	48.	__
24.	__	49.	__
25.	__	50.	__

FORM 9.5. Feedback When Student Fails to Answer Correctly

USE: In discussion and recitation situations when students are answering questions
PURPOSE: To see if teacher is giving appropriate feedback to students about the adequacy of their responses
When a student is unable to answer a question, or answers it incorrectly, code as many categories as apply to the teacher's feedback response.

BEHAVIOR CATEGORIES
1. Criticizes
2. Says "No," "That's not right," etc.
3. No feedback—goes on to something else
4. Ambiguous—doesn't indicate whether or not answer is acceptable
5. Asks a student or the class whether answer is correct
6. Asks someone else to answer the question
7. Repeats question to same student, prompts (Well?" "Do you know?" etc.)
8. Gives a clue or rephrases question to make it easier
9. Asks same student an entirely new question
10. Answers question for the student
11. Answers question and also gives explanation or rationale for answer
12. Gives explanation or rationale for why student's answer was not correct
13. Praises student for good attempt or guess
14. Other (specify)

CODES

1.	2	26.	___
2.	2,6	27.	___
3.	2,8	28.	___
4.	2,10	29.	___
5.	2,10	30.	___
6.	2,12	31.	___
7.	___	32.	___
8.	___	33.	___
9.	___	34.	___
10.	___	35.	___
11.	___	36.	___
12.	___	37.	___
13.	___	38.	___
14.	___	39.	___
15.	___	40.	___
16.	___	41.	___
17.	___	42.	___
18.	___	43.	___
19.	___	44.	___
20.	___	45.	___
21.	___	46.	___
22.	___	47.	___
23.	___	48.	___
24.	___	49.	___
25.	___	50.	___

FORM 9.6. Assigning Seatwork and Homework

USE: When teacher presents a seatwork or homework assignment
PURPOSE: To see if teacher's instructions are clear and complete
    Each time teacher presents seatwork or homework, code as many behavior categories as apply.

BEHAVIOR CATEGORIES   CODES

A. *DEMONSTRATIONS AND EXAMPLE PROBLEMS*

	A	B	C	D
1.	3,5	2	1	
2.	3,5	2	1	
3.	3,5	2	1	
4.				
5.				
6.				
7.				
8.				
9.				
10.				
11.				
12.				
13.				
14.				
15.				
16.				
17.				
18.				
19.				
20.				
21.				
22.				
23.				
24.				
25.				
26.				
27.				
28.				
29.				
30.				
31.				
32.				
33.				
34.				
35.				
36.				
37.				
38.				
39.				
40.				

A. *DEMONSTRATIONS AND EXAMPLE PROBLEMS*
  1. No demonstration was needed or given
  2. No demonstration was given, although one was needed
  3. Teacher demonstrated or called on students to do so. Activity was demonstrated in proper sequence, with no steps left out
  4. Demonstration was poorly sequenced, or steps were left out
  5. Each step was verbally described while being demonstrated
  6. More verbal description should have accompanied the demonstration
  7. Demonstration too long or complex; should have been broken into parts

B. *CHECKING FOR UNDERSTANDING*
  1. The teacher never asked whether directions were understood
  2. The teacher asked if the students understood, and no one said they didn't
  3. The teacher called on one or more volunteers to demonstrate understanding
  4. The teacher called on one or more non-volunteers to demonstrate understanding
  5. The teacher failed to call on any low achievers (bottom 1/3 of group) to see if they understood

C. *DEALING WITH CONFUSION*
How did the teacher respond if one or more students was confused?
  1. No one was confused
  2. The teacher repeated directions and demonstrations, made sure everyone understood
  3. The teacher repeated directions and demonstrations, but didn't make sure everyone understood
  4. The teacher promised individual help to those who needed it before starting work
  5. The teacher delayed giving help ("Try to do it yourself first")
  6. The teacher told students to get help from other students
  7. The teacher failed to deal with the problem directly, student remained confused, teacher never specifically told him what to do about it

D. *CLARITY ABOUT SPECIFICS OF ASSIGNMENT*
  1. Students were not clear about which problem or pages were assigned
  2. Students were not clear about what was required or optional
  3. Students were not clear about what to do if they needed help
  4. Students were not clear about what was allowed if they finished

FORM 9.7. Questioning Techniques

USE: *When teacher is asking class or group questions*
PURPOSE: *To see if teacher is following principles for good questioning practices*
 For each question, code the following categories:

BEHAVIOR CATEGORIES

CODES

A. *TYPE OF QUESTION ASKED*
 1. Academic: Factual. Seeks specific correct response
 2. Academic: Opinion. Seeks opinion on a complex issue where there is no clear-cut response
 3. Nonacademic: Question deals with personal, procedural, or disciplinary matters rather than curriculum

B. *TYPE OF RESPONSE REQUIRED*
 1. Thought question. Student must reason through to a conclusion or explain something at length
 2. Fact question. Student must provide fact(s) from memory
 3. Choice question. Requires only a yes-no or either-or response

C. *SELECTION OF RESPONDENT*
 1. Names child before asking question
 2. Calls on volunteer (after asking question)
 3. Calls on nonvolunteer (after asking question)

D. *PAUSE (AFTER ASKING QUESTION)*
 1. Paused a few seconds before calling on student
 2. Failed to pause before calling on student
 3. Not applicable; teacher named student before asking question

E. *TONE AND MANNER IN PRESENTING QUESTION*
 1. Question presented as challenge or stimulation
 2. Question presented matter-of-factly
 3. Question presented as threat or test

	A	B	C	D	E
1.	1	2	2	1	2
2.	1	2	2	1	2
3.	1	3	2	1	2
4.	1	2	2	1	2
5.	1	2	2	1	2
6.	1	3	2	1	2
7.	1	2	2	1	2
8.	2	1	1	1	1
9.	1	2	2	1	2
10.	1	2	2	1	2
11.	1	2	2	1	2
12.	1	2	2	1	2
13.					
14.					
15.					
16.					
17.					
18.					
19.					
20.					
21.					
22.					
23.					
24.					
25.					
26.					
27.					
28.					
29.					
30.					
31.					
32.					
33.					
34.					
35.					
36.					
37.					
38.					
39.					
40.					

 Record any information relevant to the following:
Multiple Questions. Tally the number of times the teacher:
1. Repeats or rephrases question before calling on anyone __//__
2. Asks two or more questions at the same time __0__

Sequence. Were questions integrated into an orderly sequence, or did they seem to be random or unrelated?
 Teacher seemed to be following sequence given in manual (led up to next history unit).
Did students themselves pose questions? *No*

Was there student-student interaction? How much? *None*

When appropriate, did the teacher redirect questions to several students, or ask students to evaluate their own or other's responses? *No*

CHAPTER 10

Improving classroom teaching

Our purpose has been to present and to describe a variety of behaviors that should appear in the classroom, and to provide ways of measuring the presence or absence of these teacher and student behaviors. We hope that teachers have been stimulated to look at their behavior and to make plans for improving their teaching effectiveness. In this last chapter we will present some guidelines that may facilitate your thinking about in-service training and self-improvement.

Remember, the perfect teacher does not exist. All of us who attempt to influence student learning can refine existing teaching skills, discard ineffective techniques, and develop new tactics. Some teachers, for example, may be excellent lecturers and classroom managers, but only average in stimulating independent student work and in leading class discussion. None of us will ever be perfect teachers, few will even be excellent in all dimensions of teacher behavior, but all of us can become better teachers than we presently are. And this, the continuous process of improving our teaching skills, is the essence of professional teaching.

Teachers, like everyone else, are sometimes unwilling to examine their own behavior and engage in self-evaluation. Is this because teachers are not committed to their profession or are unwilling to engage in the extra work necessary to improve their existing skills? Is it because they feel that they are already functioning at optimum effectiveness? We doubt it. We think teachers will seek opportunities to evaluate and improve their teaching, if acceptable and useful methods are available. The very fact that we have written this book attests to our belief in teachers' willingness to participate in self-evaluation and benefit from it. However, certain obstacles minimize self-improvement in some teachers and these must be successfully removed if consistent and continual development is to take place.

The socialization process

We feel that teachers are hindered in their efforts to improve their teaching skills for several basic reasons. Perhaps the most fundamental obstacle that reduces our ability to engage in self-evaluation is the socialization process we have gone through. Most of us have seldom engaged in self-criticism or self-evaluation that was designed not only to uncover existing weaknesses but also to improve and eventually eliminate such weaknesses. Most of us have occasionally engaged in destructive self-criticism; however, we seldom link criticism with constructive plans designed to improve our skills.

In part, we act this way because our past socialization (and especially our experiences in schools) has not helped us to develop the needed skills. For example, has a teacher ever returned an "A" paper to you with these instructions: "Basically your paper is very sound; however, I have identified a few flaws, and I am sure you will find additional ways to improve the paper upon rereading it yourself. For your next writing assignment I want you to rewrite this paper, eliminating the weaknesses that I have indicated and building upon the paper in new ways that you discover by *thinking* about it again." Certainly, most of us have had to rewrite papers, but seldom "A" papers, and seldom have we been asked to rethink a paper and incorporate new ideas of our own into it.

Typically, when we redo assignments it is because they are "inferior," and when we repeat them we do so only to incorporate someone else's criticism of our work. Indeed, for most of us school seldom allowed us time to *think* about what we were doing. We were simply too busy finishing assignments to think about them. John Holt's (1964) observation that students hurry to finish assignments so that they do not have to think, to worry, was true at certain times in most of our lives. Remember the feeling of relief when major tasks or final exams were completed? No matter how well or how poorly we think we have performed, we feel relieved when we hand in the paper because we are finished. We no longer have any control over the paper, and we do not have to think about it any more.

Socialization in schools tends to emphasize: do not look back, keep moving forward. Although the advice to move forward is sound, only by examining our past and present performance can we monitor our progress and determine if in fact we are moving forward or merely traveling in circles. Relatively little of this is done in most schools.

A second source of difficulty is that school experience has often emphasized analytical thinking at the expense of synthesis. For example, we might regard the following behavior in a tenth-grade social studies classroom as an example of analytical thinking:

TEACHER: "Now what's wrong with having congressmen elected every two years? John, you answer this question."

JOHN: *(hesitatingly and in a soft tone)* "Well, ah, I think that they spend too much time trying to be reelected. *(John notices the teacher beaming and nodding, so he begins to speak more confidently and loudly.)* Since they come up for reelection every two years, they have to immediately begin getting money for reelection. Since they seek funds to build their campaign chest primarily from the same people who financed their original candidacy, they owe these men a double debt. So it is hard for them to be their own man."

TEACHER: "Good answer, John. Carol, what does John imply when he says 'be their own man'?"

CAROL: "Well, he's suggesting that the candidate's debt to these men and his continual dependency upon them, ah, since they have to be elected every two years, puts him in such a position that he may feel he has to cater to their needs. But even if he is a strong man, the two-year election procedure is bad because the congressman continues to run, makes speeches, raises money and has little time to do the job he was elected to do."

Although such discussions are vitally important in the classroom, they seldom go beyond an analysis stage that criticizes or defines the problem. For example, the teacher might continue this discussion by pointing out the desirability of controlling campaign spending and making the source of contributions public knowledge—commonly talked about solutions that *others* have suggested. Seldom do classes attempt to develop their own unique solutions to problems. Yet this is the meaning of synthesis: taking the facts and readdressing the problem in a different fashion.

For example, the social studies teacher might "playfully" suggest to the class that senators, even though they are elected for six-year terms, spend vast amounts of time running for reelection, and that a majority of their decisions are made on the basis of "how does it affect my reelection chances?" He might even suggest that politicians, because of their basic nature, even if given ten years in office would still spend more time on running for office than running the office. The teacher could also call for students to suggest ways in which elected federal representatives could be held accountable for their local and national constituency: "Should daily logs of their time expenditures be kept? What are the pros and cons? Should they hold regular office hours for the public? Should they spend a designated number of days in the local state?"

This example was presented to suggest that even in school situations calling for critical thinking, demands are seldom made for original, practical suggestions that might improve the problem situation. There are many teachers, of course, who do stimulate this type of thinking from their students, but most teaching emphasizes analyses *per se*. Fortunately in recent years there has been increased emphasis upon process approaches and problem-solving activity, but most who presently teach were socialized in schools that demanded and rewarded analytical thinking. This heavy emphasis on criticizing gave most of us plenty of practice in pinpointing weaknesses but comparatively little practice in attempting to find ways to make the subject of criticism better.

Not only was most evaluation external and nonconstructive, evaluation time (report cards, returned papers, class discussions) taught most of us to perceive evaluation as an arbitrary threat. The way it was handled told us "where we stood," not "how we could improve." Thus we tended to avoid evaluation. (For example, in Spanish class, if we had time to thoroughly translate the first two pages we waved our hands vigorously when the teacher asked for volunteers at the beginning of a lesson. However, we slumped in our chairs and hid behind our neighbor's head late in the period unless we knew the material thoroughly and were prepared to perform.) Since evaluation was so strongly associated with negative consequences it evoked the attitude of "I'm going to be exposed," not "I'm going to receive new information," evaluation, even self-evaluation, still tends to make us somewhat anxious.

Our past socialization in schools has given most of us very little training in or inclination for conducting self-evaluation. (Our hurried assignments that upon completion we never had to think about again, emphasis on critical thinking that was seldom connected with a call for new ideas and new solutions, and our negative expectations about evaluation functioned to stifle reflection.)

Experimenting and growing

Teachers are unique individuals with different strengths and weaknesses. You will have to develop routines and teaching tactics that allow you to express yourself and stimulate students in ways that are most effective for you.

Of course, this means that you have to *search* and experiment with different teaching methods before you reach a style that is comfortable and right for you. We have stressed the desirability of using a variety of teaching methods in the classroom, because students have different learning needs and are often stimulated by different learning techniques. However, even though you should provide time for students to work in small groups, for example, you still have to set up the system that will work best for you. Perhaps you are not comfortable with peer-tutoring techniques but are particularly adept at setting up small learning teams. Then continue to work up new ways to use learning teams in meaningful assignments, and do not attempt peer-tutoring techniques (although you will want to study the literature and consult with other teachers who use the technique before discarding the notion completely). Similarly, you may like the idea of setting up learning centers in your classroom but not for mathematics or reading, because you like to monitor student progress personally in these subjects. If that is your feeling, then do not set up learning centers in these two subjects. Your comfort with a technique, and student response to the technique, are the key indicators of success. Teachers sometimes reject their own feelings or the reactions of their students when they plan lessons. The teacher is a decision maker in the classroom and must use his own reaction to the situation and that of his pupils, if instruction is to be improved.

Teaching techniques are justified if, and only if, they work in the classroom. They work when you feel comfortable using them and when students respond by learning and enjoying classroom assignments. If you systematically try an approach for a reasonable amount of time and it does not work for you in your classroom, *then discard the approach and develop techniques that do work for you.* There is no need to teach the way your cooperating teacher did (he may have been a poor model) or the way you think you "should" teach, without regard to your own feelings or to the responses of your students.

If you are to improve your teaching, you must be willing to critically examine the classroom behavior of yourself and your students and be willing to try new ways of teaching when the present ones are not working. Even when you become comfortable with all your teaching behaviors, you should still continue to experiment with new behaviors and grow more resourceful as a teacher in order to have greater impact on your students. A good teacher continually tries to find new ways to relate the subject matter to students.

Teaching is difficult

Few teachers will be excellent in all aspects of teaching. Too often teachers enter the classroom with unrealistically high expectations (I will capture the interest of every student at every moment, and every lesson I teach will be completely successful), so that when their success does not match their expectations they become depressed and disappointed. When this occurs, there is a tendency to rationalize or to blame the student for one's own inability to spark student response. If difficulty continues the teacher may withdraw and begin to justify and rationalize his present behavior rather than to search for new styles of teaching. This occurs in part because teachers do not realize that other teachers have had and continue to have difficulties. Every teacher who teaches for any length of time will teach lessons that go sour, will say the wrong things to students, and so forth. Teaching is difficult! We must not become complacent about our mistakes, but we must readily accept them as our own errors and begin efforts to eliminate them.

Like everyone else, teachers tend to talk about their successes, not their failures. Thus some teachers, especially young teachers, may become anxious and discouraged when they have trouble because they hear nothing but the good or interesting things that other teachers are doing. The authors have known some beginners who fully expected to be accomplished teachers by October of the first year! These same teachers have described their feelings of disappointment and ineptness when they did not meet with easy success and have stated that they felt reluctant to approach veteran teachers because they thought it would be an admission of failure and disgrace.

If you have thoughts like this, dismiss them because they are nonsense. Teaching is difficult, challenging, and exciting work, but it takes time to develop and refine teaching skills. Most experienced teachers are sympathetic to the problems of beginning teachers and will be glad to try to help. However, few of us like to be approached by someone who says, "Tell me what to do." It is much better to approach other teachers by telling them that you have a teaching problem and would like to exchange ideas with them and benefit from their experience. Remember that all teachers, even veteran teachers, have classroom problems from time to time, and that the appropriate strategy is not to hide mistakes (like we learned to do as classroom students) but to seek help from other teachers and to strive to solve the problem.

How do I identify good behaviors?

We have stressed that the teacher must decide what is "good" behavior by observing the effects of his behavior upon students. (Do tests reveal appropriate learning? Do lectures lead students to raise their own questions? Do students appear to enjoy activities? Do anonymously administered questionnaires show student satisfaction?) There is no concrete formula for specifying good teaching, because research examining teacher behavior has not yielded a definite set of teaching behaviors that are always clearly related to student growth (Dunkin and Biddle, 1973; Rosenshine and Furst, 1971). As stated previously, the advice given in this book has been stimulated by available research, but we have often gone beyond these data in order to supply easily applicable, prescriptive suggestions. These statements about what should be occurring in the classroom will help provide teachers with a map, a way of looking at classroom life.

There are many other materials that teachers can use effectively in in-service programs that are specifically geared to the improvement of instruction. It is impossible to list all books that could be used, but we can list types of books that refer to relevant concerns of teachers, and provide a few specific examples of each type. We have attempted to present specific advice suggested by available research and by the practice of good teachers. We make explicit statements about behaviors with which teachers can experiment. (Other authors have also prepared books that suggest specific behaviors or skills that teachers might practice in their efforts to become better teachers: Borg et al., 1970; Dollar, 1972; Emmer and Millett, 1970; Mager, 1962; McNeil, 1971; Popham and Baker, 1970a, 1970b, and 1970c.)

Others have also provided realistic descriptions of classroom problems and teacher-student dialogue (Greenwood, Good, and Siegel, 1971; Amidon and Hunter, 1967). These materials may be especially useful in obtaining teacher participation in the formative stages of in-service training programs. Teachers may initially be more comfortable in talking about classroom problems *per se* rather than their personal problems. However, such materials should be used to facilitate discussions about personal teaching problems and not used to *avoid* such discussion. That is, eventually the discussion focus should move from "How can that teacher deal with that problem?" to "How can we deal with our problems?"

In addition to reading about teaching behavior, teachers may also benefit from reading about other teachers' feelings about students and about being evaluated. Books by Greenberg (1969) and by Jersild (1955) are especially useful in dispelling such myths as "I will love all students at all times." In this same vein, teachers may benefit more from knowledge about how other teachers react to the teaching task. For example, how do teachers know when they are doing a good job? Revealing interviews with experienced teachers are found in Jackson (1968).

There are a number of critical books that attack the present educational system and/or teaching-training institutions as ineffective or self-defeating. In stimulating thinking, especially the search for alternative modes of instruction, these books are quite effective (Holt, 1964; Kohl, 1967; Smith, 1969; Silberman, 1970).

Two reviews of research on teaching are extremely valuable because they critically question what is known about teaching and call for more research on explicit questions. The reviews show that very few teaching behaviors are invariably related to student achievement (Dunkin and Biddle, 1973; Rosenshine and Furst, 1971). These materials are especially useful to teachers who want to engage in self-study programs, because they underline the fact that while empirical data can provide some direction, teachers themselves have to assume the responsibility for evaluating the effectiveness of their own classroom behavior.

Teachers can use these sources to begin thinking about their classroom behavior and to develop plans for experimenting in the classroom. However, we are perhaps putting the horse before the cart. Before changing, the teacher needs to assess his present behavior. It is useful to ask, "Where am I?" before "Where am I going?" Teachers are too busy for much self-observation and most operate in self-contained classrooms. Not all will have the benefit of video tape recording or regular supervision. For these reasons, we have provided a number of forms at the end of each chapter to help you think about your own teaching. You can use many of the forms yourself, but they can be used more effectively by a fellow teacher or supervisor who visits your room. Take advantage of this resource whenever possible.

How to start self-evaluation

The starting point is to find out where you presently are, and to make definite plans (changing certain behaviors, trying new instructional styles) for the future. Go back through the text of this book and list, on three separate pages: (1) behaviors that you think you perform capably at present, (2) those that you need to work on or that you have not tried, and (3) those which you are not sure how capably you perform. Take the first list and store it in your desk. This list represents progress that you have made as a teacher.

For example, you may note on this list that you already ask a variety of factual and higher order questions and that you ask questions before calling on students. On your list for Needs Work, you may note your tendency not to follow through on warnings to students, your basic inconsistency as a classroom manager. After a few hours of work in which you list your strong and weak points, you will have a rough map of your ability as a teacher. Now you are ready to begin work on the list of needed improvements. Make plans for remediation so that you can move one or more items from the Needs Work list to the Okay list in the near future.

Some of the areas mentioned in this book may be blurred to you, in the sense that you do not know how well you behave in these categories. Perhaps you are not sure if you emphasize the intrinsic interest that lessons hold for the student rather than threatening "Pay attention or you'll fail the exam." Monitor your behavior as best you can, and begin to assign these areas to the Okay or Needs Work sheets as soon as you can.

In other words, take some time to carefully assess yourself and begin to draw a map of your strengths and weaknesses. Naturally, your map of yourself will differ somewhat from the map that your students would draw of you or one that an observer would draw after spending two weeks in your class. Which one of these maps is the most objective is a question that cannot be answered. In some situations the students' map might be a truer picture. However, even where you can use only your own map, it will be a useful guide for making classroom decisions if you look at yourself openly and undefensively. The next step is to use the map for making plans for improvement.

Make explicit plans

Teachers who attempt to improve their classroom teaching must be able to explicitly decide what they want to do and how they can tell if their plan is working. Too often our half-hearted New Year's resolutions are never acted upon because they are too unclear. Statements such as "I want to be a better driver," "I want to help the community more," or "I want to be a more enthusiastic teacher," are seldom accomplished, simply because they are not concrete suggestions that guide behavior.

The following statements are much more likely to result in behavior change, because they specify the desired change: "On long trips I plan to stop and relax for ten minutes every two hours," "I want to keep my speed under 70 at all times," "I plan to devote ten hours a week from September through November working on the community chest drive," "I want to tell students why a lesson is important before the lesson begins," and "I want to model my sincere interest in the lesson."

These statements clearly indicate *how* the individual is to behave if he is to reach his goal. If he stops for ten minutes after driving for two hours, he has met the goal; thus, in the above examples self-evaluation is very easy. Similarly, self-evaluation is relatively simple in a number of teaching situations. However, certain aspects of teacher behavior are more difficult to evaluate. For instance, teachers frequently set goals for students as well as for themselves. The teacher may say, "I want to tell students why a lesson is important before the lesson begins, and I want to model my sincere interest in the lesson so more students will pay attention to the lesson and will not engage in long private conversations with their neighbors during the lesson." In this case, teachers need to evaluate both their own behavior and the behavior of their students.

In judging the behavior of students, the teacher can see if students do appear to pay attention and if they refrain from extended private conversations during the lesson. However, if the teacher's goals become more complex and the evaluation more demanding, he will need to watch video tapes or seek the assistance of observers to help him assess his progress. These topics will be discussed later in the chapter.

The message here is simple. If you do not know where you are going, you are unlikely to get there. Teachers need to state goals in explicit language. Careful statement of the goal accomplishes two objectives: (1) the teacher knows exactly what behavior he is trying to effect and (2) the teacher can easily assess his progress by examining his actual behavior in comparison with the behavioral goal. The key is to state goals in terms of explicit, observable behaviors. Detailed accounts of how to state goals in behavioral terms may be found in Popham and Baker (1970a) and Mager (1962).

Action

After taking a look at yourself and stating explicit behavioral goals, the next step is to choose two or three old behaviors that you want to change or new instructional procedures you want to try out. Be careful in your zeal to try new things that you do not attempt to change too many things at once. Changing behavior, even our own, takes careful work, and it is easy to become overwhelmed and discouraged when we attempt to change too much too rapidly. Therefore, take a few things at a time and carefully monitor your progress.

For example, if you attempt to call on students randomly, you may have to write out the names of students in advance on flash cards so you can shuffle through the stack. Always calling on students who have their hands up is a difficult habit to break. Changing our behavior on certain dimensions is so difficult and demands so much concentration that we will not succeed if we dilute our efforts by trying to change several things at the same time. Most people make more progress in the long run by changing only one or a few behaviors at a time, moving to new ones only when the newly acquired behaviors become firmly established habits.

After you decide upon concrete goals and after implementing your change for a couple of days, start to monitor the class for feedback about its effectiveness. For example, after you try to introduce lessons that make it explicitly clear to the students why the lesson they are about to study will be important to them, determine, to your satisfaction, whether more students follow the directions or seem interested. Similarly, if you start to call on other students to react to fellow students' responses, note if students seem to pay greater attention to the discussion topic.

Remember, the strategies listed in this book are not always appropriate; their effectiveness depends upon stimulating desirable student responses. Strategies that you invent yourself should be evaluated in the same way: what effect do they have on student behavior and attitudes?

You are not alone

Teachers may wish to begin their evaluation and continue it for a while, operating independently of feedback from other sources. However, all teachers will benefit from interacting with others and sharing ideas about classroom teaching and should begin to do this at some point.

Many school districts now have video tape equipment. If you are fortunate enough to have access to such equipment, arrange to have one or two of your typical lessons video taped. Do not attempt to construct special units or to review old material. Teach your regularly scheduled lessons in your normal fashion. Then, when you start your assessment program, you can not only rely on memory but also can view yourself on tape as you assess your weak and strong points. After a couple of weeks, make arrangements to retape your behavior in similar lessons so you can watch for signs of progress in your behavior and in the responses of students.

If your school does not have video equipment, check with your principal and see if arrangements can be made to bring it in from the central office. In many school districts equipment is available for loan but often goes unused. Central school officials are usually delighted when a school or individual teacher requests use of the video equipment. If a school makes repeated requests, it is sometimes possible for equipment to be assigned to it permanently. If it is impossible to secure video equipment, cassette audio recorders are readily available and can be used to provide useful information about the verbal behavior of teachers and students.

Where video tape equipment is not available, teachers can use other sources to get relevant feedback information. For example, many elementary school teachers work in team teaching or nongraded situations where it is easy to arrange for another teacher to watch them for a half hour or so. Similarly, teachers can use student teachers, student observers, and parents, on occasion. Secondary teachers can make arrangements to trade weekly visits during free periods with other teachers.

In these arrangements that are not a part of a regular in-service training program, it is usually best to tell the observer what to look for specifically. Prepare an observation form for him to use if possible. There is so much to see in the classroom that an observer may not notice the things that the teacher would like to receive feedback about. The teacher is a decision maker, and in planning his professional development he should be deciding upon which weaknesses to work on first; therefore, teachers should request rather specific feedback when they invite an observer into their room. The observer, of course, can always volunteer additional information besides that requested.

Curriculum supervisors can also be used to provide teachers with relevant feedback. Most supervisors are delighted when teachers make explicit observation requests. Often supervisory visits are as frustrating for the supervisor as for the teacher. Since the supervisor may not know the goals of a particular lesson or how it fits into a unit, it is difficult for him to provide helpful feedback to a teacher. However, armed with a specific request, supervisors can provide relevant feedback about areas of interest to the teacher.

Students, of course, are another source teachers can tap for relevant information about their teaching behavior. Informal conversations and anonymously administered questionnaires will provide the teacher with useful information. Teachers who have never solicited student comment may be dismayed at first when they see the variety of comment. Students have unique perspectives, and different students may label the same behavior as a weakness or a strength. However, if you carefully look over their responses, you can usually identify several items that most students label as good or bad. Then you can take action on these points of agreement.

We have found that student feedback is most useful if it is delivered anonymously. Also, rather than ask for global comments or ratings, it is usually more useful to ask for specific reactions. One method is to request three or more positive statements about strengths and three or more criticisms of weaknesses from each student. This forces each student to be specific and to provide a more balanced critique than more global, free-response methods.

In-service education

Teachers can often use regularly scheduled in-service time for work in small self-improvement groups. This is especially useful when in-service meeting time is devoted to small group work with teachers who share common problems. In elementary schools, for instance, teachers at each grade level can meet in separate small groups. In secondary schools, teachers can also be subdivided into smaller groups according to the subject taught (social studies, mathematics, English, etc.) so that they may discuss common problems. Small groups provide an excellent chance for teachers to receive feedback and suggestions from their professional peers.

Teachers in small self-improvement teams may wish to regularly view and provide feedback about one another's tapes. In particular, teachers can use this opportunity to have peers provide information about those aspects of teaching behavior that they want to have evaluated. This procedure is in marked contrast to the typical in-service program or consultation activity that provides teachers with training, information, or evaluative feedback that the consultant wishes to talk about. Teachers are not always interested in these topics. Teachers meeting in small study groups have the opportunity to structure in-service programs that have personal meaning and value for them.

Most principals will be delighted to allow teachers to spend in-service time functioning as self-study teams. Usually, teachers who want such a program need only to contact the principal and communicate the seriousness of their intent and their willingness to work out a strong in-service training experience.

In general, participation in self-study groups should be voluntary, and plans should be made so that participants can join a self-study team when they are ready to do so. The desirability of a voluntary program is probably self-evident. Nothing hurts a program that involves the sharing of information and the search for new alternatives more than someone who participates solely because he has to do so. Consideration should be given, however, to those teachers who want to benefit from study-group activities at some point in time but who are not ready to do so at the beginning of the year. It is a perfectly reasonable and understandable desire for the teacher to want to assess his own behavior and develop his own goals before joining a self-improvement group. Initially, in-service study groups should only attempt to help teachers develop the new behaviors and new interaction styles that *they* want to learn.

Three rules should be kept in mind when such in-service groups begin to function. The first one we have mentioned previously—group structure and feedback exist to provide teachers with information that augments their personal self-development. The group provides a unique set of eyes and resources to give teacher information regarding behaviors that he wants to receive feedback about. Thus, *the teacher functions as a decision maker, planning his own developmental goals.* The group functions as a barometer, telling the teacher how he looks to them and suggesting alternative ways in which he might reach the goals that he himself has set. Teachers in the group will, of course, have their own viewpoints and each will react to a certain extent in terms of his own strength, weaknesses, and preferences.

The teacher, then, should create reality for the group by telling them what his current goals are and specifically outlining what behaviors and techniques they should examine when they view his video tape or when they come into his room to observe. Also, as previously mentioned, when a teacher or a group of teachers begins to engage in self-development activities there is a tendency to do too much at once. Initially the individual teacher should limit improvement areas to only a few, so that full attention can be directed toward work on these new skills. Correspondingly, the group should help the teacher by restricting their comments to these designated behaviors. After the group has functioned as a group for a few weeks, then the "video teacher of the week" may begin to ask the group to focus on all dimensions of teaching that were exhibited in the film. When the teacher is ready for such feedback, the group can help the teacher to learn more about how others react to his teaching.

The second rule to follow, then, especially in the group's formative weeks, is *do not overwhelm the teacher with information.* Restricting discussion to a few areas will help, and it may be useful to limit the number of comments that each group member makes about each behavior being discussed. When first experiencing the process of sharing critical comment, it is easy for the teacher to become overwhelmed. We can profit from only so much information at a given time, particularly if much of the feedback is negative. No matter how competent and resilient a teacher may be, if he receives notice of fifty things that he did wrong, there is a strong tendency to give up (at least psychologically) and accept his failure as permanent. When we receive a plethora of negative comment we do not know where to begin; we tend to be immobilized.

We mentioned before that when in-service groups first begin to function, it is generally more useful if group members restrict their feedback to those skills that the teacher has selected. However, even when teachers begin to seek more general feedback, it is still important that group members do not overload the teacher with more information than he can comprehend. In-service groups may benefit from such an artificial rule as: each participant writes out his reaction to the two or three major strengths and the two or three major weaknesses of the presentation. This guideline limits the amount of information that a teacher receives initially, but it does focus the teacher's attention on a small, manageable list of "points to consider." The guideline also allows the teacher to have in writing (for future review) the basic reactions of each participant to his lesson.

Useful feedback should not only provide the teacher with a rough assessment of his strengths and weaknesses but also should focus on specific ways to improve teaching. Ensuing discussions should focus on alternative procedures that the teacher might have used to provoke a more desirable student response. Effective in-service sessions allow the teacher to receive both a realistic reaction (both positive and negative) to his performance on the behaviors in question and to receive direct assistance in the form of information about alternative behaviors to use in the future. In-service self-study groups should not only evaluate present teaching but also provide some direction for subsequent teaching.

A third rule to bear in mind is to *be honest.* Self-study groups lose their effectiveness when individuals engage in either of two participatory styles: Pollyanna and Get-the-Guest. Too many teachers are unwilling to say what they feel about another teacher's behavior, perhaps because they are afraid that openness and frankness will lead other teachers to respond in kind when they are being evaluated, or because they feel that the teacher will be hurt by an honest reaction. Such masking of reactions to behavior is self-defeating. Teachers can grow only if they get honest, objective feedback about their behavior. Criticism followed by new ideas or approaches that may improve upon present practice is the best way the group can assist a teacher in his self-development efforts. To be sure, we should reinforce the good things that a teacher does. We all like to know when we have done well, and it is especially important that we receive praise and encouragement when we improve upon a skill that has taken us several weeks to develop. If a teacher has been working on a technique for a few weeks and shows improvement, let him know about the improvement he has made as well as the ways in which he can still improve. But in all cases do pinpoint the major weaknesses (being careful not to *overdwell* on minor issues or provide more feedback than the teacher can benefit from) and suggest ways in which the teacher can attempt to improve. If there is no critical comment, there is no impetus or direction for growth.

The other undesirable participant role is the carping critic who criticizes excessively and thoughtlessly. Perhaps such behavior is motivated by the need for self-protection (if everybody looks bad, I'll be okay). Perhaps such teachers are just insensitive to the needs of others. At any rate, such behavior rarely does any good, and participants who cannot deliver criticism tactfully and who cannot link criticism with positive suggestions should be encouraged and helped by other group members to develop these skills. When participants are not willing to temper their excessive criticism, they should not continue in the group, for their presence generally generates a great deal of hostility and prevents the development of an atmosphere that is marked by the sharing of information and positive planning to improve classroom instruction.

The principal as facilitator

The school principal and other auxiliary school personnel (e.g., the school psychologist) can rotate from group to group and serve as other participants willing to share ideas with teachers. Of course, the principal can play a valuable role in the in-service development of teachers by soliciting funds to buy appropriate video equipment and by scheduling video taping so that optimum use can be made of the video equipment. For example, it may be necessary for first- and second-grade teachers to have different in-service training days from the third-, fourth-, fifth-, and sixth-grade groups, so that all groups will have video equipment available to replay their tapes or the tapes of other teachers.

In general, the principal can create the conditions needed for suitable self-improvement groups. When video equipment is not available in the short run, the principal can help teachers arrange to visit other teachers in the school to observe their teaching and supply helpful feedback. As we pointed out earlier, a major obstacle to improvement in the classroom is that most teachers teach in self-contained classrooms and do not receive *systematic* feedback from responsible sources about teaching aspects that they are really interested in. Thus principals are valuable instructional leaders when they take the time to create opportunities for teachers to aid other teachers to improve their teaching skills by observing their behavior and providing them with systematic feedback.

In addition, films of teaching behavior that lend themselves to critical analysis are now available. Principals with teachers who want to develop their teaching skills may obtain these films and show them in small groups, allowing teachers to rate film behavior and to suggest alternative teaching methods. Although this procedure will help teachers to develop skills for objectively examining behavior, the principal should not force teachers to stay at this level for very long. If he cannot obtain video equipment immediately, it is important that he arrange for teaching pairs to visit one another for at least a half hour each week. The sooner teachers receive feedback, the sooner they can begin to plan strategies for improving their teaching.

To the extent that teachers have found in-service training programs boring and a waste of their time in the past, to that extent the programs were unrelated to their needs as teachers. Much time and effort is currently being placed on developing curricula that are inherently more interesting for students and that allow students more opportunity for pursuing topics independently. Perhaps corresponding emphasis should be placed on developing ways to allow teachers to become more active in the development of in-service training programs that meet their needs and interests rather than subjecting them to a passive role. We feel that allowing teachers to use part of regular in-service time to engage in independent self-improvement activities, either as individuals or in groups, would be a valuable addition to the in-service program.

After teachers begin to work on self-improvement, they will be in a position to advise the principal as to the type of university consultant that would facilitate their own in-service program. Teachers given the freedom and responsibility for planning their own in-service training typically view the task quite seriously and work earnestly to develop useful programs. As a resource specialist and general facilitator, the principal can aid immeasurably by supplying teachers with copies of the books mentioned earlier in this chapter and other books that the teachers request or that the principal feels are useful for stimulating teacher thought and experimentation. Of course, the best way the principal can influence and encourage the development of his teachers is to have a genuine interest in their self-development and respect for their efforts in that direction and to model his own search and experimentation with ways of becoming a better principal.

Do look back

Clearly the intent of this chapter is to encourage teachers to look at their classroom behavior and to plan ways to make their classrooms more meaningful and exciting for students. Stress has been placed upon the fact that objective, improvement-oriented self-evaluation is difficult for many of us to engage in, simply because we have not been trained to do it. Any significant new experience is always a challenge, and self-evaluation is no exception. Your first efforts to look at your own behavior openly will be difficult and perhaps frustrating. However, such analysis, if it is tackled one step at a time and linked to prescriptive strategies for improving behavior, will lead to self-growth and the accompanying joy of becoming more effective.

This book has been an effort to encourage you to look at your behavior and to assume responsibility for your own development as a teacher. Certain scales and materials are included in the book to help you assess your behavior and plan new instructional strategies, but ultimately you and only you can evaluate the effects of your teaching. Do not avoid your responsibility by uncritically accepting someone else's advice on teaching philosophy.

Remember, a teaching strategy is good when two basic conditions are satisfied: (1) students learn the material that they are supposed to master and (2) students are interested and find the learning process enjoyable so that they initiate learning efforts of their own and can progressively assume more responsibility for planning and evaluating their own work.

It is up to you to identify teaching behaviors that meet these criteria and to weave them into a teaching style that you feel comfortable in using, so that you look forward to class and to teaching generally. You are the teacher, and you must assume responsibility for establishing a learning atmosphere that is stimulating and exciting for yourself as well as for the students. If you do not enjoy class, your students probably will not either!

SUGGESTED ACTIVITIES AND QUESTIONS

1. Make a list of all the books and ideas that you want to explore in the near future. Please do not limit your selection to materials listed in this text. Rank the three things you most want to learn. This will serve as your in-service map. Compare your notes with other teachers, and if you have similar interests, share material and collectively urge the principal to design in-service programs that will satisfy these needs.

2. Make a list of your teaching strengths and weaknesses. Make specific plans for improving your two weakest areas.

3. Read the cases in Appendix A and see if you can pinpoint the teaching strengths and weaknesses that appear there. Compare your ratings with those made by others.

4. What are the possible advantages and disadvantages of using parents or retired but capable adults as observation sources to supply teachers with feedback about their behavior?

5. Why is it difficult for most of us to engage in self-evaluation?

6. Why do teachers benefit more from critical but prescriptive feedback than they do from vague positive feedback?

7. How can the school principal help to facilitate the development of effective in-service programs?

8. How can teachers initiate self-improvement programs?

9. Should young teachers seek advice from veteran teachers? If so, under what circumstances and in what manner?

10. As a teacher, how can you help your students to develop the skills and attitudes for examining their own work nondefensively?

11. We have stressed the need for you to seek evaluative comment and to analyze your behavior if you are to grow and to improve. We seek your evaluative comment. We would like to know how useful the book is from your perspective, and we would like to know if deficiencies exist so that future editions of this book can be improved. We encourage you to write us with your feedback and suggestions. (What was your general reaction to the book? Is it relevant to teachers and future teachers? What topics were omitted that you feel should be in future editions? What advice or suggestions in this book did you disagree with and why? Did we communicate negative expectations or provide contradictory advice, and if so, where and how? Were there sections of the book that you found especially helpful and why?) We will be delighted to receive your suggestions and criticisms, and your comments will be given serious consideration when a new edition of this book is written.

Appendix A
practice
examples

This appendix includes five brief examples of classroom life in elementary school and junior and senior high schools. These case materials will give you an opportunity to apply the material you have mastered in this book. Try to identify the teaching strengths and weaknesses that appear in the case teaching episodes that follow and to suggest alternative ways in which the teacher could have behaved differently to improve the classroom discussion. Then compare your insights with those of your classmates.

Case 1
Charles Kerr had done his student teaching on the secondary level with majors in social studies and PE. Since there was a surplus of teachers seeking positions in his field at the high schools in his area, he accepted a position as a sixth-grade teacher temporarily while waiting for an opening on the coaching staff of one of the athletic programs in the high schools. He teaches in an all-white middle-class school and he has good social rapport with his students.

TEACHER: Class, today we are going to talk about the upcoming presidential elections. The actual election is not for a whole year, but some men, senators mainly, have already announced themselves as candidates. Tom, tell me why men

Note: We acknowledge the capable assistance of Kathey Paredes in preparing the first draft version of some of the examples.

like the senators from Maine and Ohio have said they are
going to run for President this soon?

TOM: Because they don't want the President to stay in office
anymore.

TEACHER: A lot of people don't want that, but they aren't
running; there's a good reason you haven't thought of yet;
try again.

TOM: I don't know; I don't care much about the election.

TEACHER: Well, you should care; it won't be too long before you
can vote and you need to be aware. Susanne, what reason
can you come up with?

SUSANNE: Maybe people don't know them very well.

TEACHER: That's right. They need the advance publicity. Brian,
what kind of elections are held in each individual state
before the general election?

BRIAN: Preliminary?

TEACHER: The word's primary—but that was close enough. Craig,
who can run in the primary?

CRAIG: Republicans and Democrats.

TEACHER: And that's it? Suppose I wanted to run and I'm neither
one of those mentioned, then what?

BRIAN: You couldn't do it.

TEACHER: (*impatiently*) Jane, stop shuffling your feet that way—
do you think I could run for President if I wanted?

JANE: I suppose so.

TEACHER: You don't sound very definite in your opinion; be de-
cisive and tell me yes or no.

JANE: Yes!

TEACHER: All right—don't be wishy-washy in your opinions.
Now, Tony, who would you like to see run for President?

TONY: The mayor of New York.

TEACHER: How about you, Janette?

JANETTE: The honorable senator from Texas.

TEACHER: Why?

JANETTE: Because he's attractive and colorful.

TEACHER: (*sarcastically*) Girls don't think logically sometimes.
Bobby, could you give me a more intelligent reason than
Janette?

BOBBY: Because he has had lots of experience.

TEACHER: In my opinion, I don't think that counts for much, but
at least you are thinking along the right lines. Danny, what
will be a major issue in this campaign?

DANNY: Crime.

TEACHER: (*with a loud, urgent voice*) Crime is always an issue; there's something else you should concern yourself about as an issue; I'll give you another chance.

BARBARA: (*calling out*) Won't the economy be an issue?

TEACHER: I'll ask the questions, Barbara, and you be thinking of some good answers! Danny, have you thought of it yet?

DANNY: Probably the economy and foreign policy.

TEACHER: Certainly. Rob, since you have been doing so much commenting to everyone around you back there, tell me, should we fight other people's wars? What should our foreign policy be with respect to small wars?

ROB: If they need the help and can't defend themselves.

TEACHER: Does that really sound sensible to you? Do you want to go to some distant part of the world and get killed?

ROB: No, but I don't think we should let other powers move in and take what they want either.

TEACHER: Of course not, but I don't think we should get involved in foreign affairs to the point of war and you shouldn't listen to anybody who tells you we should. Back to the issues; we decided war should be over and that we should get out no matter what the costs; there are a few more issues you might hear a lot about. Yes, Margaret?

MARGARET: Don't you think the war is just about over now and will be by the election?

TEACHER: No, I don't; if I did think so, I wouldn't have brought it up here; pay attention! We only have eight minutes more before the bell rings and then you can do what you want to do. Pay attention to the discussion and quit moving around. Now let's get back to my question. Tim?

TIM: There aren't enough jobs for everyone.

TEACHER: No, there aren't. I wanted to teach high school, but there are already too many of those teachers; so don't decide to be a high-school teacher because there may not be a job for you.

CONNIE: You mean I shouldn't become a teacher?

TEACHER: I would consider something else where there might be more job openings. What I would like you to do is find some resource material that will tell you more about the elections and what we can expect in the way of candidates and issues. John, when we go to the library what might you look for to find this information?

JOHN: Magazines.

TEACHER: Yes, which ones?

JOHN: *Time, Newsweek.*

TEACHER: Good. Where else, Leslie?

LESLIE: Newspapers.

TEACHER: Which ones?

LESLIE: Local newspapers.

TEACHER: You had better go further than that. Why should you look at more than one newspaper, Mike?

MIKE: Our paper might not have anything in it about elections.

TEACHER: No. The reason is that different papers have different views of the candidates. I want you to have two different viewpoints in your papers. Now, I want you to write a good paper on what we have discussed today using reliable resources. If you have forgotten the style you are to use, get out the instruction sheet I gave you a few weeks ago and follow it point by point. Tomorrow you are going to defend your positions to the class. The class will attempt to tear apart your papers. So write them carefully or else your poor logic will embarrass you.

Case 2

Linda Law is teaching for her second year at Thornton Junior High School. The students at Thornton come from upper middle-class homes and Linda teaches social studies to the brightest ability group of ninth-grade students. Today she is deviating from her normal lesson plans in order to discuss the Tasadays tribe that resides in the Philippines Rain Forest.

TEACHER: Class, yesterday I told you that we would postpone our scheduled small group work so that we could discuss the Tasadays. Two or three days ago Charles mentioned the Tasadays as an example of persons who were alienated from society. Most of you had never heard of the Tasadays but were anxious to have more information, so yesterday I gave you a basic fact sheet and a few review questions to think about. I'm interested in discussing this material with you and discussing the questions that you want to raise. It's amazing! Just think, a stone age tribe in today's world. What an exciting opportunity to learn about the way man used to live! Joan, I want you to start the discussion by sharing with the class what you thought was the most intriguing fact uncovered.

JOAN: (*in a shy, shaky voice*) Oh, that they had never fought with other tribes or among themselves. Here we are, modern man, and we fight continuously and often for silly reasons.

SID: *(breaking in)* Yeah, I agree with Joannie, that is remarkable. You know, we have talked about man's aggressive nature, and this finding suggests that perhaps it isn't so.

SALLY: *(calling out)* You know, Sid, that is an interesting point!

TEACHER: Why is that an interesting point, Sally?

SALLY: *(looks at the floor and remains silent)*

TEACHER: Why do you think these people don't fight, Sally?

SALLY: *(remains silent)*

TEACHER: Sally, do they have any reason to fight?

SALLY: No, I guess not. All their needs . . . you know, food and clothing, can be found in the forest and they can make their own tools.

TEACHER: Yes, Sally, I think those are good reasons. Class, does anyone else want to add anything on this particular point? *(She calls on Ron who has his hand up.)*

RON: You know what I think it is that makes the difference, well, my dad says it is money. He said that if these Tasadays find out about money, there will be greed, corruption, and war all in short order.

TEACHER: Ron, can you explain in more detail why money would lead to deterioration in life there?

RON: *(with enthusiasm)* Well, because now there's no direct competition of man against man. It's man and man against nature and what one man does is no loss to another man.

TONY: *(calling out)* Not if food or something is in short supply!

TEACHER: Tony, that's a good point, but please wait until Ron finishes his remarks. Go ahead, Ron.

RON: Well, money might lead to specialization and some men would build huts and others would hunt and exchange their wares for money and eventually men would want more money to buy more things and competition would lead to aggressive behavior.

TEACHER: Thank you, Ron, that's an interesting answer. Now, Tony, do you want to add anything else?

TONY: No, nothing except that Ron's making a lot of generalizations that aren't supported. You know, the Tasadays might have specialized labor forces. Now there's nothing in the article I read about this.

TEACHER: That's good thinking, Tony. Class, how could we find out if the Tasadays have a specialized labor force?

MARY: *(called on by the teacher)* Well, we could write a letter to

Dr. Fox, the chief anthropologist at the National Museum, and ask him.

TEACHER: Excellent. Mary, would you write a letter tonight and tomorrow read it to the class and then we'll send it.

MARY: Okay.

(*The teacher notices Bill and Sandra whispering in the back corner of the room and as she asks the next question, she walks half-way down the aisle. They stop talking.*)

TEACHER: What dangers do the Tasadays face now that they have been discovered by modern man?

TOM: (*calling out*) I think the biggest problem they face will be the threat of loggers who are clearing the forest and the less primitive tribes who have been driven further into the forest by the loggers.

TEACHER: Why is this a problem, Tom?

TOM: Well, they might destroy. You know, these less primitive tribes might attack or enslave the Tasadays.

TEACHER: Okay, Tom. Let's see if there are other opinions. Sam, what do you think about Tom's answer?

SAM: Well, I do think that those other natives and loggers are a threat, but personally I feel that the Tasadays' real danger is sickness. Remember how, I think it was on Easter Island, natives were wiped out by diseases that they had no immunity to. I think they might be wiped out in an epidemic.

TEACHER: What kind of an epidemic, Sam?

SAM: Well, it could be anything, TB, you know, anything.

TEACHER: Class, what do you think? If an epidemic occurred, what disease would be most likely involved?

CLASS: (*no response*)

TEACHER: Okay, class, let's write this question down in our notebooks and find an answer tomorrow. I'm stumped, too, so I'll look for the answer tonight as part of my homework. I'm going to allow ten minutes more for this discussion, and then we'll have to stop for lunch. I wish we had more time to discuss this topic; perhaps we can spend more time tomorrow. In the last ten minutes, I'd like to discuss your questions. What are they? Call them out and I'll write them on the board.

ARLENE: I was surprised that the oldest of these people were in their middle forties and the average height was only five feet. It looks like living an active outdoor life, they would be healthy and big. What's wrong with their diet?

MARY JANE: I'm interested in a lot of their superstitious behavior. For example, why do they feel that to have white teeth is to be like an animal? . . .

Case 3

Mrs. Jackson taught school for two years in the 1950s then retired to raise a family. Now that her children are grown, she decided to return to the classroom and has received a teaching position in a large city school. Her third-grade class is composed of equal numbers of black, Oriental, Mexican-American, and white children whose parents work but are still very involved in the school's activities. Previously, Mrs. Jackson had taught in an upper middle-class school, and although she had adapted her lesson plans to the changes in curriculum, she had not expected to have to change her approach to teaching since children, their behavior, and their needs remain pretty much the same over the years. Today, she is reviewing multiplication tables with the class, working with everyone the first twenty minutes and then dividing the children into four groups to complete their assigned independent work. The teacher sits with one group and helps them with their lesson.

TEACHER: Today, children, let's review our 8 and 9 times tables; whichever group can give me all the answers perfectly will be able to use the math games during independent work instead of having to do the exercises in the book. John, what is 8 x 9?

JOHN: 72.

TEACHER: Tim, 8 x 0.

TIM: 8.

TEACHER: Wrong, tell me what 8 x 1 is?

TIM: 8.

TEACHER: Yes, now you should know what 8 x 0 is.

TIM: (*no response*)

TEACHER: Tim lost the contest for group 3.

JAN: (*calls out*) Why didn't you ask me, I know the answer!

TEACHER: I'm glad that you do, so you can teach Tim and your group will win next time. I'm going to ask Terri what 8 x 2 is?

TERRI: 16.

TEACHER: Mark, what is 8 x 4?

MARK: 32.

TEACHER: Lynn, 8 x 6?

LYNN: 48.

TEACHER: Judy, 8 x 10?

JUDY: 56, no. Wait a minute. (*Teacher pauses and gives her time to come up with another answer.*) It's 80, isn't it?

TEACHER: Yes, it is. Jeff, give me the correct answer to this one, and your group will have a perfect score; what is 8 x 11?

JEFF: (*Thinks a minute and Carrie, from another group, calls out.*)

CARRIE: 88!

TEACHER: Carrie, it was not your turn and now I'm not going to give your group a chance to win. I'm sure Jeff knew the answer and so his group has done the best so far. Now, Linda, let's see how well your group will do; what is 9 x 3?

LINDA: 28; no! 27.

TEACHER: Are you sure?

LINDA: I think so.

TEACHER: You must be positive; either it is 27 or it isn't. Class?

CLASS: Yes!

TEACHER: All right. Chuck, you don't seem to be listening so I will ask you the next one. What is 9 x 6?

CHUCK: (*counting on his fingers silently*)

TEACHER: We haven't got time to wait for you to get the answer that way and that's not the way I taught you to do multiplication. Let's see if your friend Bobby can do better.

BOBBY: (*looks at Marilyn without giving any response*)

TEACHER: Marilyn is not going to give you the answer; this was something you were supposed to learn for homework last night. Did you do it?

BOBBY: Yes.

TEACHER: Well, since you did the work you should be able to answer my question. Again, what is 9 x 6?

BOBBY: I can't remember.

TEACHER: Marilyn, do you know?

MARILYN: 56?

TEACHER: (*exasperated*) For as many times as we have done these tables, I don't know why you can't learn them. I think this group will have to go back and do some work in the second-grade math book until they are ready to learn what everybody else is doing. (*Class laughs.*) Now, let's look at our chart here and everyone together will recite the tables twice. (*Class reads down the chart.*)

TEACHER: I have written the pages and directions for each group on the board. Terri, your group may get the games out because you know your tables. Matthew, read me what your group is to do.

MATTHEW: "Find the products (*Matt falters on word, teacher gives it to him*) and factors" (*doesn't know word*).

TEACHER: How can you expect to do the work if you can't read the directions? I guess I had better read it. Now does everyone understand? (*No comment from group.*) All right, go to work and I don't want any interruptions while I'm working with Tim's group. Chuck, you get out the second-grade books and start on the pages that I have written up here. I'm sure you understand what all of you have to do.

TEACHER: Will the monitors pass out paper? John, if you don't think you can do the job without chatting with your friends, you had better give the papers to someone else. Elaine and Mike, I like the way you are sitting—ready to go to work! Let's see how quietly we can all do our work today.

(*with group 3*)

TEACHER: Carrie, you're a good thinker, do this problem on the board for me.

(*Carrie does it correctly.*)

TEACHER: That's good. Darryl, you try this one—(2 x 3) x 6.

(*Darryl works it out.*)

TEACHER: There's another way; could you do that, too?

(*Darryl starts, but can't finish.*)

TEACHER: I'll finish it for you and then tell me what I did to get the answer. (*Writes (2 x 6) x 3.*)

DARRYL: You just changed the brackets.

TEACHER: Will I get the same answer? (*Chorus: yes!*) Paula, you make up a problem of your own and Ted will figure it out. (*She does.*)

TED: What is 7 x 4?

TEACHER: Ted, we just went all through this; now do the best you can.

(*Ted does and gets the wrong answer.*)

TEACHER: I guess Paula will have to do it herself. Tonight I'm going to give you extra homework so that you will know this type of problem perfectly.

Case 4

Matt Davidson teaches American literature at an all-white middle-class high school. The seniors in his class at Windsor Hills have been doing some concentrated study in the field of Mark Twain's writings. They are of above average intelligence and have previously read two other novels by Twain.

> TEACHER: Class, I know I didn't give you as much time to read *The Adventures of Huckleberry Finn* as we might ordinarily take; however, since you are familiar with Twain's style, his settings and characters, I knew you would be able to grasp the content and motives in the story without much trouble. *Huckleberry Finn* is considered to be a classic today, a real artistic work of fiction.
>
> TEACHER: Stylistically, why is this book considered to be a masterpiece, John?
>
> JOHN: He used a setting in Missouri and adapted the narrative to the dialects common to that place and time.
>
> TEACHER: Good. Was there one dialect only?
>
> JOHN: No, I think maybe there were two.
>
> TEACHER: Actually, there were several—Huck's and Tom's, Jim's, Aunt Sally's and others. Dialect here was a necessary ingredient to the fiction of the time. What sets the mood, what gives the structure to the story?
>
> TERRI: (*calling out*) The time.
>
> TEACHER: Could be to a small extent, but not what I had in mind, Terri. Where is the setting?
>
> TERRI: St. Petersburg, Mo.
>
> (*Teacher notices Matt drawing on a piece of paper and looks at him as Terri responds. When Matt looks up the teacher catches his eye and Matt puts away his paper.*)
>
> TEACHER: All right. Could Twain have taken Huck to Phoenix, Arizona and related the story exactly the same? How about that, Tim?
>
> TIM: I guess not, there's no Mississippi River in Phoenix.
>
> TEACHER: Exactly. Develop that thought further, Tim—keep in mind the author himself.
>
> TIM: Twain grew up in Hannibal and he probably saw much of what he wrote about.
>
> TEACHER: You're right there. Did you want to add something, Melissa?
>
> MELISSA: The story is probably semiautobiographical, then, with a few names and places changed.
>
> TEACHER: Yes, I think so too.
>
> MARK: (*calling out*) There probably weren't any slaves in Phoenix, either, so Jim might have not been in the story.

LARRY: (*calling out*) There might have been.

TEACHER: I think Mark is pretty close to the truth in what he said, Larry, but that's something for you to look into. So, locale is important. Now, what is the book about—is it just about a boy going down the river? Lynne?

LYNNE: It's an adventure story.

TEACHER: Could you lend a little more depth of thought to your answer? Is it just a comedy?

LYNNE: A thoughtful one.

ED: (*calling out*) It has a more serious element—satire.

TEACHER: I don't think we've discussed satire and I'm glad you brought it up. What is your definition of satire?

ED: Well, for instance, Aunt Sally and Aunt Polly always pretended to be so virtuous and Christian-like, but they were willing to sell Jim back into slavery. Huck wanted to get away from all the hypocrisy and fraud.

TEACHER: Very good! But, Huck had a hard time coping with this. What one particular quality or emotion did Huck have, as opposed to say, Tom, Linda? (*reading her book*)

LINDA: He was smarter?

TEACHER: That's not so much a quality—this is something he feels.

DUANE: (*calling out*) Sad, about the way people treat each other.

TEACHER: That's more what I was looking for, Linda. He was sensitive. Whom was he most sensitive about, Carol?

CAROL: Tom, I guess.

TEACHER: Oh no. He accepted Tom for what he was—a foolish little kid. The story revolves around Huck and one other person. Who, Bobby?

BOBBY: It was Jim. Huck knew slavery was wrong and was disturbed by it. Mr. Davidson, was slavery over yet?

TEACHER: No, this takes place in 1850 and slaves were not emancipated until the end of the Civil War in 1865. Your answer is correct. The way Tom treated Jim—always hurt his feelings; that hurt Huck, too. Chris, did Jim reciprocate this treatment toward the boys by being cruel in some manner?

CHRIS: I think he did.

TEACHER: Give me an instance when.

CHRIS: (*no response*)

TEACHER: Can you remember anything Jim did on the raft?

CHRIS: (*no response*)

TEACHER: Did you read the book?

CHRIS: No.

TEACHER: I think it's important you read it and I'm sure you will find it very captivating. Susann, who is the most admirable character?

SUSANN: Jim, because he was always loyal and dedicated to Huck no matter what.

GERRY: (*calling out*) No, I think it was Huck because he was always wrestling with his conscience and knew things were wrong.

TEACHER: Both answers are correct and show good reasoning. There is never one necessarily right answer when discussing literature—it's a matter of your interpretation as you read it and see it. Who are the villains? Kevin?

KEVIN: The most obvious are the Duke and the Dauphin.

TEACHER: Why, Leslie?

LESLIE: (*rustling through the pages*)

TEACHER: You don't need to look it up; just give me your impression of their characters.

LESLIE: They pretended to be royalty and Shakespearean actors, but they really lied and cheated people out of their money.

TEACHER: Right, Huck's father was something of a villain, and the Grangerfords and Shepherdsons were certainly not the most upstanding citizens. Turn to page 254 and read this short passage with me. I think this pretty well summarizes Huck's feelings:

"But I reckon I got to light out for the territory ahead of the rest, because Aunt Sally she's going to adopt me and civilize me, and I can't stand it. I been there before."

TEACHER: A very important concept is contained here. Who can discover what it is? Yes, Marilyn?

MARILYN: He doesn't want to have any part of fancy clothing, going to school or church, or eating off a plate.

TEACHER: Yes, he wants his freedom. Let's do a little deeper analysis of Huck's character. I'm going to put some questions on the board and you tell me as best you can what Huck really thought about the Grangerfords, about slavery, about the Duke and Dauphin, and so forth. How did he confront and deal with these people?

Case 5

Joan Maxwell has been teaching the first grade for seven years in a small rural community school. Her students are children of primarily farm and ranch workers of lower middle-class background. Joan and her husband both received their degrees from a large university and now operate a lucrative business in the area. Joan is introducing a science lesson today; it's late fall and the children have been asked to bring in some leaves to show changes in leaf colors from season to season. The class has previously discussed seasonal changes and what weather patterns occur during these times.

TEACHER: Boys and girls, let's first review what we talked about last week when we were writing our stories about different seasons.

SHARI: (*calling out*) Do we have to do this? Why can't we do something fun instead of doing something we don't like?

TEACHER: We can't always do things we enjoy. Carol, do you remember how many seasons we have in a year?

CAROL: Three.

TEACHER: No, we wrote more stories than just three—think for a minute.

CAROL: Four!

TEACHER: All right, now can you name them for me?

CAROL: Fall, winter, summer . . .

TEACHER: Didn't you write four stories?

CAROL: I don't remember.

TEACHER: (*forcefully, but with some irritation*) You may have to go back and write them again. Who knows the fourth season? Can somebody in my special Cardinal group respond? John, you answer.

JOHN: Fall, winter, spring, and summer.

TEACHER: Good thinking! It helps us to remember seasons sometimes if we think about important holidays that come then. Tim, in what season does Christmas come?

TIM: (*no response*)

TEACHER: You weren't listening. I want you to put those leaves in your desk and not touch them again till it's time. Cory, when does Christmas come?

CORY: In the winter.

TEACHER: How do you know it's winter, Mark?

MARK: Because of the snow and ice and rain . . .

TEACHER: Does it snow here?

MARK: No.

TEACHER: How do you know it's winter, then?

MARK: (*no response*)

MARY: (*calling out*) It snows at Christmas where I used to live.

TEACHER: Mary, if you have something to say, will you please raise your hand? (*She does.*) Now, what did you say?

MARY: Where I used to live it did snow, but not anymore.

TEACHER: Right! In some places it does snow and not others. Clarence, why wouldn't it snow here?

CLARENCE: Because it's too warm?

TEACHER: It's not warm here! I told you this before a couple of times. *(turns to Tim)* I asked you once before to put those away and you can't seem to keep your hands on the desk, so I'm going to take them away from you and when we do our project you will have to sit and watch! Don't anyone else do what Tim does. Now, let's talk more about the fall season and get some good ideas for our story. What is another word for the fall season? Lynne?

LYNNE: Halloween.

TEACHER: I didn't ask you to give me a holiday, a word.

LYNNE: I can't think of it.

TEACHER: I'm going to write it on the board and see if Bobby can pronounce it for me.

BOBBY: *(no response)*

TEACHER: This is a big word, Bobby. I'll help you.

JUDY: *(calling out)* Autumn!

TEACHER: *(turns to Judy)* Is your name Bobby?

JUDY: No.

TEACHER: Then don't take other children's turns. Now, Bobby, say the word. *(He does.)* I think this is a good word to write in your dictionaries. Get them out and let's do it now.

JANE: I don't have a pencil.

TEACHER: That is something you are supposed to take care of yourself. Borrow one or stay in at recess and write it then. Let's look at these pictures of leaves as they look in the fall and spring. Mary Kay, can you tell me one thing that is different about these two pictures?

MARY KAY: The leaves are different colors.

TEACHER: Good. Tell me some of the colors.

MARY KAY: In spring, they are a bright green.

TEACHER: Right. Joe, how about the other ones?

JOE: They are brown and orange and purple.

TEACHER: I don't see any purple—you've got your colors mixed up. Tony?

TONY: It's more red.

TEACHER: Yes. Steve, we are finished writing in our dictionaries; put it away. You can finish at recess with Jane. Some people in our class are very slow writers. Take out your leaves now. Mark, how does that leaf feel in your hand?

MARK: It feels dry and rough like old bread. *(Class laughs.)*

TEACHER: Don't be silly! How did it get so dry? Marilyn?

MARILYN: It fell off the tree.

TEACHER: Yes, a leaf needs the tree to stay alive, is that right, Dave?

DAVE: You could put it in water and it would stay alive.

TEACHER: Not for long. Martha, what else can you tell me about these leaves.

MARTHA: I don't have one.

TEACHER: I don't know what to do about children who can't remember their homework assignments. You will never be good students if you don't think about these things. Mike, what do you see in the leaves?

MIKE: Lines running through.

TEACHER: We call those lines veins. Are all leaves the same shape?

MIKE: No, my leaf came from a sycamore tree and it has soft corners, not sharp ones.

TEACHER: That's good. I think you will be able to write an interesting story. Two holidays come during the fall; who can name one? Terri?

TERRI: Halloween.

TEACHER: That's one; Jeff do you know another?

JEFF: *(no response)*

TEACHER: It comes in November and we have a school holiday.

JEFF: Easter?

TEACHER: No, that is in the spring; we have turkey for dinner this day.

CHORUS: Thanksgiving.

TEACHER: Now do you remember, Jeff? I would like you to write about Thanksgiving in your story, then you won't forget again. Now we are ready to put our vocabulary words on the board that we will use for our story and pictures.

(Teacher notices Shari, Jim, and Rick exchanging their books but she ignores their misbehavior.)

TEACHER: Ed, you come up here and Sally come up here and help me print our vocabulary words on the board. Ed, you print these four words *(hands him a list)* and Sally, you print these four.

TEACHER: What are you kids doing in that corner? Shari, Rick, Jim, Terri, Kim, stop fighting over those books. *(All the children in the class turn to look at them.)*

RICK: Mrs. Maxwell, it's all Kim's fault.

KIM: It is not. I wasn't doing anything. Shari, Rick, and Jim have been fooling around but I've been trying to listen.

TEACHER: Quiet down, all of you. You all stay in for recess and
we'll discuss it then.

KIM: Not me!

TEACHER: Yes, all of you.

KIM: *(mutters to her friend)* It's not fair.

TEACHER: Kim, what did you say?

KIM: Nothing.

TEACHER: That's more like it.

TEACHER: Okay, Ed, put your words up.

ED: I've lost the list . . . *(Class roars with laughter.)*

Appendix B
peer
tutoring:
a
selective
bibliography

Asbell, B. Let the children teach—child to child tutoring. *Redbook*, 1966, *126*, 52–53.

Barrett-Lennard, G. Significant aspects of a helping relationship. *Mental Hygiene*, 1963, *47*, 223–227.

Baun, E. Washington University campus Y tutoring project. *Peabody Journal of Education*, 1965, *43*, 161–168.

Bell, S., Garlock, N., and Colella, S. Students as tutors: high schoolers aid elementary pupils. *Clearinghouse*, 1969, *44*, 242–244.

Bender, K. Using brighter students in a tutorial approach to individualization. *Peabody Journal of Education*, 1967, *45*, 156–157.

Briggs, D. Older children teaching youngsters. *Journal of the California Teachers Association*, 1967, *63*, 24–26.

Caditz, R. Using student tutors in high school mathematics: weak students profit from volunteer assistance. *Chicago School Journal*, 1963, *44*, 323–325.

Chesler, M. Tutors for disadvantaged youth. *Educational Leadership*, 1965, *22*, 559–563, 605–607.

Cloward, R. Non-professionals in education. *Educational Leadership*, 1967, *24*, 604–606.

———. Studies in tutoring. *Journal of Experimental Education*, 1967, *36*, 14–25.

Cowen, E. Mothers in the classroom. *Psychology Today*, 1969, *3* (7), 36–39.

Criscuolo, N. Developing effective reading tutors. *Educational Horizons*, 1970, *49*, 63–64.

Delaney, A. Good students help deficient pupils. *School Activities*, 1963, *35*, 36.

Dembo, M. and Good, T. Team learning: implications for the classroom teacher and school psychologist. *Journal of School Psychology*, 1970, *8*, 57–59.

Deutsch, M. The disadvantaged child and the learning process. In A. Passow (ed.), *Education in Depressed Areas*. New York: Columbia University Press, 1963.

Deutsch, M. Early social environment: its influence on school adaptation. In D. Schreibner (ed.), *The School Dropout*. Washington, D.C.: National Education Association, 1964.

Ellson, D., Barber, L., Engle, T., and Kampwerth, L. Programmed tutoring: a teaching aid and a research tool. *Reading Research Quarterly*, 1965, *1*, 77–127.

Ellson, D., Harris, P., and Barber, L. A field test of programmed aid and directed tutoring. *Reading Research Quarterly*, 1968, *3*, 307–367.

Fleming, J. Pupil tutors and tutees learn together. *Today's Education*, 1969, *58*, 22–24.

Frager, S. and Stern, C. Learning by teaching. *Reading Teacher*, 1970, *23*, 403–409.

Gartner, A., Kohler, M., and Riessman, F. *Children Teach Children: Learning by Teaching*. New York: Harper & Row, 1971.

Geiser, R. Some of our worst students teach! Report of a unique tutoring system. *Catholic School Journal*, 1969, *69*, 18–20.

Hamilton, A. Here come the tutors! *PTA Magazine*, 1965, *60*, 7–9.

Harris, M. Learning by tutoring others. *Today's Education*, 1971, *60*, 48–49.

Hassinger, J. and Via, M. How much does a tutor learn through teaching reading? *Journal of Secondary Education*, 1969, *44*, 42–44.

Hawkins, T. Utilizing the services of academically talented students. *Journal of Negro Education*, 1965, *34*, 93–95.

Hunter, E. A cross-age tutoring program encourages the study of teaching in a college methods course. *Journal of Teacher Education*, 1968, *19*, 447–451.

Karowe, H. How volunteers can help disadvantaged children. *Children*, 1967, *14*, 151–155.

Klemm, E. Appropriate school programs. *Education*, 1965, *85*, 486–489.

Kuppel, H. Student tutors for floundering classmates. *School Activities*, 1964, *35*, 255–256.

Landrum, J. and Martin, M. When students teach each other. *Educational Leadership*, 1970, *27*, 446–448.

Lippitt, P. and Lohman, J. Cross-age relationships: an educational resource. *Children*, 1965, *12*, 113–117.

Little, D. and Walker, B. Tutor-pupil relationship and academic progress. *Personality and Guidance Journal*, 1968, *47*, 324–328.

Lucas, J., Gaither, G., and Montgomery, J. Evaluating a tutorial program containing volunteer subjects. *Journal of Experimental Education*, 1968, *36*, 78–81.

Luke, Sister Mary. Project tutoring—it worked! *Catholic School Journal*, 1966, *66*, 64–65.

Mallery, D. Something more: student teachers. *Saturday Review*, 1966, *49*, 40–41.

Maurer, D. Pair learning techniques in high school. *Phi Delta Kappan*, 1968, *49*, 609–610.

McCoy, C. Effects of three styles of tutoring on tutor attitude change, tutee attitude change differences and tutee grade changes. Unpublished master's thesis, University of Texas, 1968.

McCracken, R., Leaf, B., and Johnson, L. Individualizing reading with pupil teachers. *Education,* 1965, *86,* 174–176.

McWhorter, G. and Levy, J. Influence of a tutorial program upon tutors. *Journal of Reading,* 1971, *14,* 221–224.

Melaragno, R. and Newmark, G. A study to develop a tutorial community in the elementary schools. TM 4203/000/00, Santa Monica: System Development Corporation, 1969.

Nations Schools. Students assist each other at tutorial project school. Pacoima Public Schools, Los Angeles, 1969, *84,* 44.

Newman, J. Grad students make great tutors. *Instructor,* 1970, *79,* 45–46.

Niedermeyer, F. Effects of training on the instructional behaviors of student tutors. *Journal of Educational Research,* 1970, *64,* 119–123.

Niedermeyer, F. and Ellis, P. Remedial reading instruction by trained pupil tutors. *Elementary School Journal,* 1971, *7,* 400–405.

Payne, W. Organizing tutoring: new dimensions for increasing skills. *Journal of Secondary Education,* 1967, *42,* 21–24.

Reading Newsreport. Who teaches best, teachers or kids? 1969, *3,* 10–15.

Rime, L. and Ham, J. Sixth-grade tutors. *The Instructor,* 1968, *77,* 104–105.

Shapiro, A. and Hopkins, L. Pupil-teachers. *Reading Teacher,* 1967, *21,* 128–129.

Shaver, J. and Nuhn, D. Underachievers in reading and writing respond to a tutoring program. *Clearing House,* 1968, *43,* 236–239.

Snapp, M. A study of the effects of tutoring by fifth and sixth graders on the reading achievement scores of first, second, and third graders. Unpublished doctoral dissertation, University of Texas, 1970.

Squires, M. Youth tutoring youth. *School and Community,* 1971, *57,* 20–21.

Stouffer, R. and Groff, P. Should you use pupil tutors? *Instructor,* 1967, *77,* 35.

Surratt, P., Ulrich, R., and Hawkins, R. An elementary student as a behavioral engineer. *Journal of Applied Behavioral Analysis,* 1969, *2,* 85–92.

Tannenbaum, A. An evaluation of STAR: a non-professional tutoring program. *Record,* 1968, *69,* 433–448.

Thelan, H. Tutoring by students. *School Review,* 1969, *77,* 229–244.

Thomas, J. Tutoring strategies and effectiveness: a comparison of elementary age tutors and college age tutors. Unpublished doctoral dissertation, University of Texas, 1970.

Trasin, W. Can learners teach? *Clearing House,* 1960, *34,* 263–265.

Truher, H. Who shall be tutored? *Education,* 1959, *79,* 580–582.

Weitzman, D. Effects of tutoring on performance and motivation ratings in secondary school students. *California Journal of Educational Research,* 1965, *16,* 108–115.

Wright, B. Should children teach? *Elementary School Journal,* 1960, *60,* 353–369.

Wright, E. Upper graders learn by teaching. *Instructor,* 1969, *78,* 102–103.

General
references

Adams, R. and Biddle, B. *Realities of Teaching: Explorations with Video Tape*. New York: Holt, Rinehart and Winston, 1970.

Almy, M. *Ways of Studying Children*. New York: Teachers College Press, Columbia University, 1969.

Amidon, E. and Hunter, E. *Improving Teaching: The Analysis of Classroom Verbal Interaction*. New York: Holt, Rinehart and Winston, 1966.

Anderson, H. H. and Brewer, H. M. Studies of teachers' classroom personalities I: dominative and socially integrative behavior of kindergarten teachers. *Applied Psychological Monographs*, 1945.

Ausubel, D. *The Psychology of Meaningful Verbal Learning: An Introduction to School Learning*. New York: Grune and Stratton, 1963.

Baker, H. *Film and Videotape Feedback: A Review of the Literature*. Report Series No. 53, Research and Development Center for Teacher Education. Austin: University of Texas, 1970.

Bandura, A. *Principles of Behavior Modification*. New York: Holt, Rinehart and Winston, 1969.

Beez, W. Influence of biased psychological reports on teacher behavior and pupil performance. *Proceedings of the 76th Annual Convention of the American Psychological Association*, 1968, 605–606.

Bereiter, C., Washington, E., Englemann, S., and Osborn, J. *Research and Development Programs on Preschool Disadvantaged Children*. Final Report, OE Contract 6–10–235, Project #5–1181. Washington, D.C.: U.S. Department of Health, Education, and Welfare, Office of Education, Bureau of Research, 1969.

Biehler, R. *Psychology Applied to Teaching*. Boston: Houghton Mifflin, 1971.

Blank, M. *Teaching Learning in the Preschool: A Dialogue Approach*. Columbus, Ohio: Charles Merrill, 1973.

Borg, W. *Ability Grouping in the Public Schools: A Field Study* (2nd ed.). Madison, Wisconsin: Dumbar Educational Research Services, 1966.

Borg, W., Kelley, M., Langer, P., and Gall, M. *The Mini-Course: A Microteaching Approach to Teacher Education.* Beverly Hills, Calif.: MacMillan Educational Services, 1970.

Brophy, J. and Good, T. Brophy-Good system (teacher-child dyadic interaction). In A. Simon and E. Boyer (eds.), *Mirrors for Behavior: An Anthology of Observation Instruments Continued, 1970 Supplement.* Vol. A. Philadelphia: Research for Better Schools, 1970 (a).

————. *Individual Differences: Toward an Understanding of Classroom Life.* New York: Holt, Rinehart and Winston, 1973.

————. Teachers' communications of differential expectations for children's classroom performance: some behavioral data. *Journal of Educational Psychology,* 1970, *61,* 365–374 (b).

Brubaker, H. Are you making the best use of cumulative records? *Grade Teacher,* 1968, *86,* 96–97, 222.

Bryan, J. and Walbek, N. Preaching and practicing generosity: children's actions and reactions. *Child Development,* 1970, *41,* 329–353.

Burkhart, R. (ed.). *The Assessment Revolution: New Viewpoints for Teacher Evaluation.* (National symposium on evaluation in education.) Buffalo, N.Y.: New York State Education Department and Buffalo State University College, 1969.

Burnham, J. *Effects of experimenters' expectancies on children's ability to learn to swim.* Unpublished master's thesis, Purdue University, 1968.

Carroll, J. School learning over the long haul. In J. Krumboltz (ed.), *Learning and the Educational Process.* Skokie, Ill.: Rand McNally and Company, 1965.

Channon, G. *Homework.* New York: Outerbridge and Dienstfrey, 1970.

Chase, C. The impact of some obvious variables on essay test scores. *Journal of Educational Measurement,* 1968, *5,* 315–318.

Claiborn, W. Expectancy effects in the classroom: a failure to replicate. *Journal of Educational Psychology,* 1969, *60,* 377–383.

Cloward, R. Studies in tutoring. *Journal of Experimental Education,* 1967, *36,* 14–25.

Cobb, J. Relationship of discrete classroom behavior to fourth-grade academic achievement. *Journal of Educational Psychology,* 1972, *63,* 74–80.

Coleman, J., Campbell, E., Hobson, C., McPartland, J., Mood, A., Weinfield, F., and York, R. *Equality of Educational Opportunity.* Washington, D.C.: U.S. Office of Health, Education, and Welfare, 1966.

Costin, F., Greenough, W., and Menges, R. Student ratings of college teaching: reliability, validity, and usefulness. *Review of Educational Research,* 1971, *41,* 511–535.

Davis, O., Jr. and Tinsley, D. Cognitive objectives revealed by classroom questions asked of social studies student teachers. *Peabody Journal of Education,* 1967, *45,* 21–26.

Deutsch, M. Early social environment: its influence on school adaptation. In D. Schreibner (ed.), *The School Dropout.* Washington, D.C.: National Education Association, 1964.

Dollar, B. *Humanizing Classroom Discipline: A Behavioral Approach.* New York: Harper & Row, 1972.

Douglas, J. *The Home and the School: A Study of Ability and Attainment in the Primary School.* London: MacGibbon and Kee, 1964.

Doyle, W., Hancock, G., and Kifer, E. Teachers' perceptions: Do they make a difference? Paper presented at the annual meeting of the American Educational Research Association, 1971.

Dunkin, M. and Biddle, B. *The Study of Teaching.* New York: Holt, Rinehart and Winston, 1973.

Ehman, L. A comparison of three sources of classroom data: Teachers, students, and systematic observation. Paper presented at the annual meeting of the American Educational Research Association, 1970.

Emmer, E. *The effect of teacher use of student ideas on student verbal initiation.* Unpublished doctoral dissertation, University of Michigan, 1967.

Emmer, E. and Millett, G. *Improving Teaching Through Experimentation: A Laboratory Approach.* Englewood Cliffs, N.J.: Prentice-Hall, 1970.

Findley, W. and Bryan, M. *Ability Grouping, 1970 Status: Impact and Alternatives.* Athens, Ga.: Center for Educational Improvement, University of Georgia, 1971.

Flavell, J., Botkin, P., Fry, C., Wright, J., and Jarvis, P. *The Development of Role-Taking and Communication Skills in Children.* New York: Wiley, 1968.

Fleming, E. and Anttonen, R. Teacher expectancy or My Fair Lady. *American Educational Research Journal,* 1971, *8,* 241–252.

Gagne, R. Military training and the principles of learning. *American Psychologist,* 1962, *17,* 83–91.

Gallagher, J. Expressive thought by gifted children in the classroom. *Elementary English,* 1965, *42,* 559–568.

Goldberg, M., Passow, A., and Justman, J. *The Effects of Ability Grouping.* New York: Teachers College Press, 1966.

Good, T. Which pupils do teachers call on? *Elementary School Journal,* 1970, *70,* 190–198.

Good, T. and Brophy, J. Changing teacher behavior: an empirical investigation. Unpublished manuscript, 1972.

Good, T., Schmidt, L., Peck, R., and Williams, D. Listening to Teachers. Report Series No. 34, Research and Development Center for Teacher Education, Austin: University of Texas, 1969.

Good, T., Sikes, J., and Brophy, J. Effects of teacher sex, student sex, and student achievement on classroom interaction. Technical Report No. 61, Center for Research in Social Behavior. Columbia: University of Missouri, 1972.

Goodlad, J. Classroom organization. In C. Harris (ed.), *Encyclopedia of Educational Research.* (3rd ed.). New York: Macmillan, 1960.

Gordon, I. *Studying the Child in School.* New York: Wiley, 1966.

Greenberg, H. *Teaching with Feeling.* New York: Macmillan, 1969.

Greenwood, G., Good, T., and Siegel, B. *Problem Situations in Teaching.* New York: Harper & Row, 1971.

Groisser, P. *How to Use the Fine Art of Questioning.* New York: Teachers' Practical Press, 1964.

Guszak, F. Teacher questioning and reading. *Reading Teacher,* 1967, *21,* 227–234.

Haynes, H. Relation of teacher intelligence, teacher experience and type of school to types of questions. Unpublished doctoral dissertation, Nashville, Tenn.: George Peabody College for Teachers, 1935.

Heathers, G. Grouping. In R. Ebel (ed.), *Encyclopedia of Educational Research*, 4th ed. New York: Macmillan, 1969.

Henry, J. Attitude organization in elementary school classrooms. *American Journal of Orthopsychiatry*, 1957, *27*, 117–133.

Hess, R. Social class and ethnic influences on socialization. In P. Mussen (ed.), *Carmichael's Manual of Child Psychology*, 3rd ed., Vol. 2. New York: Wiley, 1970.

Hess, R., Shipman, V., Brophy, J., and Bear, R. Mother-child interaction. In I. Gordon (ed.), *Readings in Research in Developmental Psychology*. Glenview, Ill.: Scott-Foresman, 1971.

Hoffman, M. Moral development. In P. Mussen (ed.), *Carmichael's Manual of Child Psychology*, 3rd ed., Vol. 2. New York: Wiley, 1970.

Holt, J. *How Children Fail*. New York: Pitman, 1964.

Hoover, K. *Learning and Teaching in the Secondary School: Improved Instructional Practice*. Boston: Allyn and Bacon, 1968.

Horn, E. *Distribution of Opportunity for Participation among the Various Pupils in Classroom Recitations*. New York: Teachers College Press, 1914.

Hoyt, K. A study of the effects of teacher knowledge of pupil characteristics on pupil achievement and attitudes toward classwork. *Journal of Educational Psychology*, 1955, *46*, 302–310.

Hudgins, B. and Ahlbrand, W., Jr. *A Study of Classroom Interaction and Thinking*. Technical Report Series No. 8. St. Ann, Mo.: Central Midwestern Regional Educational Laboratory, 1969.

Hunt, J. Experience and the development of motivation: some reinterpretations. *Child Development*, 1960, *31*, 489–504.

Husen, T. (ed.). *International Study of Achievement in Mathematics: A Comparison of Twelve Countries*, Vol. 2. New York: Wiley, 1967.

Husen, T. and Svensson, N. Pedagogic milieu and development of intellectual skills. *School Review*, 1960, *68*, 36–51.

Jackson, B. *Streaming: An Educational System in Miniature*. London: Routledge and Kegan Paul, 1964.

Jackson, P. *Life in Classrooms*. New York: Holt, Rinehart and Winston, 1968.

Jackson, P. and Lahaderne, H. Inequalities of teacher-pupil contacts. *Psychology in the Schools*, 1967, *4*, 204–208.

Jackson, P. and Wolfson, B. Varieties of constraint in a nursery school. *Young Children*, 1968, *23*, 358–367.

Jersild, A. *When Teachers Face Themselves*. New York: Teachers College Press, 1955.

Johnson, D. *The Social Psychology of Education*. New York: Holt, Rinehart and Winston, 1970.

Johnson, W. *People in Quandaries: The Semantics of Personal Adjustment*. New York: Harper & Row, 1946.

Jones, V. *The influence of teacher-student introversion, achievement, and similarity on teacher-student dyadic classroom interactions*. Unpublished doctoral dissertation. Austin: University of Texas, 1971.

Kennedy, W., Van deRiet, V., and White, J. A normative sample of intelligence and achievement of Negro elementary school children in the southeastern United States. *Monographs of the Society for Research in Child Development*, 1963, *28*, 6.

Kleinfeld, J. Instructional style and the intellectual performance of Indian and Eskimo students. Final Report No. 1-J-027. Washington, D.C.: U.S. Department of Health, Education, and Welfare, 1972.

Klinger, R. and Dollar, B., 1972. (Personal communication.)

Kohl, H. *36 Children*. New York: New American Library, 1967.

Kounin, J. *Discipline and Group Management in Classrooms*. New York: Holt, Rinehart and Winston, 1970.

Kozol, J. *Death at an Early Age*. Boston: Houghton Mifflin Co., 1967.

Kranz, P., Weber, W., and Fishell, K. The relationships between teacher perception of pupils and teacher behavior toward those pupils. Paper delivered at the annual meeting of the American Educational Research Association, 1970.

Lahaderne, H. Attitudinal and intellectual correlates of attention: a study of four sixth grade classrooms. *Journal of Educational Psychology*, 1968, *59*, 320–324.

Little, R. Basic education and youth socialization in the armed forces. *American Journal of Orthopsychiatry*, 1968, *38*, 869–876.

Lippitt, R. and Gold, M. Classroom social structure as a mental health problem. *Journal of Social Issues*, 1959, *15*, 40–49.

Loughlin, R. On questioning. *Educational Forum*, 1961, *25*, 481–482.

Mackler, B. Grouping in the ghetto. *Education and Urban Society*, 1969, *2*, 80–95.

Mager, R. *Preparing Instructional Objectives*. Palo Alto, Calif.: Fearon Publishers, 1962.

McCandless, B. *Children: Behavior and Development*. New York: Holt, Rinehart and Winston, 1967.

McNeil, J. *Toward Accountable Teachers: Their Appraisal and Improvement*. New York: Holt, Rinehart and Winston, 1971.

Mendoza, S., Good, T., and Brophy, J. *Who Talks in Junior High Classrooms? Report* Series No. 68, Research and Development Center for Teacher Education. Austin: University of Texas, 1972.

Meyer, W. and Thompson, G. Sex differences in the distribution of teacher approval and disapproval among sixth-grade children. *Journal of Educational Psychology*, 1956, *47*, 385–396.

Mischel, W. *Personality and Assessment*. New York: Wiley, 1968.

Mood, A. *Do Teachers Make a Difference? A Report on Recent Research on Pupil Achievement*. U.S. Office of Education-58042, Washington, D.C.: U.S. Government Printing Office, 1970.

Niedermeyer, F. Effects of training on the instructional behavior of student tutors. *Journal of Educational Research*, 1970, *64*, 119–123.

Otto, H. Elementary education—II, organization and administration. In W. Monroe (ed.), *Encyclopedia of Educational Research*, 1st ed. New York: Macmillan, 1941.

Palardy, J. What teachers believe—what children achieve. *Elementary School Journal*, 1969, *69*, 370–374.

Peck, R. Promoting self-disciplined learning: a researchable revolution. In B. Smith (ed.), *Research in Teacher Education*. Englewood Cliffs, N.J.: Prentice-Hall, 1971.

Perkins, H. *Human Development and Learning.* Belmont, Calif.: Wadsworth, 1969.

Pfeiffer, I. Teaching in ability grouped English classes: a study of verbal interaction and cognitive goals. *Journal of Experimental Education,* 1967, *36,* 33-38.

Piaget, J. Piaget's theory. In P. Mussen (ed.), *Carmichael's Manual of Child Psychology,* 3rd edition, Vol. 1. New York: Wiley, 1970.

Plant, J. Some psychiatric aspects of crowded living conditions. *American Journal of Psychiatry,* 1930, *9,* 849-860.

Popham, W. and Baker, E. *Establishing Instructional Goals.* Englewood Cliffs, N.J.: Prentice-Hall, 1970 (*a*).

————. *Planning an Instructional Sequence.* Englewood Cliffs, N.J.: Prentice-Hall, 1970 (*b*).

————. *Systematic Instruction.* Englewood Cliffs, N.J.: Prentice-Hall, 1970 (*c*).

Quirk, T. An experimental investigation of the teacher's attribution of the locus of causality of student performance. *Dissertation Abstracts,* 1967, *28,* 2565A.

Ragosta, M., Soar, R. S., Soar, R. M., and Stebbins, L. Sign vs. category: two instruments for observing levels of thinking. Paper presented at the annual meeting of the American Educational Research Association, 1971.

Rist, R. Student social class and teacher expectations: the self-fulfilling prophecy in ghetto education. *Harvard Educational Review,* 1970, *40,* 411-451.

Robinson, D. Scraps from a teacher's notebook. *Phi Delta Kappan,* 1962, *43,* 44.

Rock, R. A critical study of current practices in ability grouping. *Educational Research Bulletin,* Catholic University of America, Nos. 5 and 6, 1929.

Rosenshine, B. Enthusiastic teaching: a research review. *School Review,* 1970, *78,* 499-514.

————. Objectively measured behavioral predictors of effectiveness in explaining. In N. Gage, M. Belgard, D. Dell, J. Hiller, B. Rosenshine, and W. Unruh, *Explorations of the Teacher's Effectiveness in Explaining.* Technical Report No. 4, Research and Development Center in Teaching. Stanford, Calif.: Stanford University, 1968.

Rosenshine, B. and Furst, N. Current and future research on teacher performance criteria. In B. Smith (ed.), *Research on Teacher Education: A Symposium.* Englewood Cliffs, N.J.: Prentice-Hall, 1971.

Rosenthal, R. and Jacobson, L. *Pygmalion in the Classroom: Teacher Expectation and Pupils' Intellectual Development.* New York: Holt, Rinehart and Winston, 1968.

Rotter, J. Generalized expectancies for internal versus external control of reinforcement. *Psychological Monographs,* 1966, *80,* No. 1.

Rowe, M. Science, silence, and sanctions. *Science and Children,* 1969, *6,* 11-13.

Ryans, D. *Characteristics of Teachers: Their Description, Comparison, and Appraisal: A Research Study.* Washington, D.C.: American Council on Education, 1960.

Sanders, N. *Classroom Questions: What Kinds?* New York: Harper & Row, 1966.

Schachter, S. The interaction of cognitive and physiological determinants of emotional state. In L. Berkowitz (ed.), *Advances in Experimental Social Psychology*, Vol. 1. New York: Academic Press, 1964.

Schrank, W. A further study of the labeling effect of ability grouping. *The Journal of Educational Research*, 1970, *63*, 358–360.

Schrank, W. The labeling effect of ability grouping. *Journal of Educational Research*, 1968, *62*, 51–52.

Sears, P. Level of aspiration in academically successful and unsuccessful children. *Journal of Abnormal and Social Psychology*, 1940, *35*, 498–536.

Sexton, P. *The Feminized Male: Classrooms, White Collars, and the Decline of Manliness.* New York: Vintage Books, 1969.

Shaffer, L. and Shoben, E., Jr. *The Psychology of Adjustment: A Dynamic and Experimental Approach to Personality and Mental Hygiene.* Boston: Houghton Mifflin, 1956.

Shutes, R. *Verbal behaviors and instructional effectiveness.* Unpublished doctoral dissertation, Stanford University, 1969.

Silberman, C. *Crisis in the Classroom: The Remaking of American Education.* New York: Random House, 1970.

Smith, B. *Teachers for the Real World.* Washington, D.C.: The American Association of Colleges for Teacher Education, 1969.

Snapp, M. *A study of the effects of tutoring by fifth and sixth graders on the reading achievement scores of first, second, and third graders.* Unpublished doctoral dissertation, University of Texas, 1970.

Snow, R. Unfinished Pygmalion. *Contemporary Psychology*, 1969, *14*, 197–199.

Stevans, R. The question as a measure of efficiency in instruction. *Teachers College Contributions to Education*, No. 48. New York: Teachers College, Columbia University, 1912.

Sullivan, H. *The interpersonal theory of psychiatry.* New York: Norton, 1953.

Susskind, E. The role of question-asking in the elementary school classroom. In *The Psycho-Educational Clinic*, Massachusetts Department of Mental Health Monograph, No. 4, n.d.

Taylor, C. The expectations of Pygmalion's creators. *Educational Leadership*, 1970, *28*, 161–164.

Thomas, J. *Tutoring strategies and effectiveness: A comparison of elementary age tutors and college tutors.* Unpublished doctoral dissertation, University of Texas at Austin, 1970.

Tillman, R. and Hull, J. Is ability grouping taking schools in the wrong direction? *Nation's Schools*, 1964, *73*, 70–71, 128–129.

Trump, J. Secondary education tomorrow: Four imperatives for improvement. *Bulletin of the National Association of Secondary School Principals*, 1966, *50*, 87–95.

Trump, J. and Baynham, D. *Guide to Better Schools.* Chicago: Rand McNally, 1961.

Tuckman, B. *A Study of Curriculums for Occupational Preparation and Education.* Scope Program, Phase I, Final Report, Project No. 8-0334. Washington D.C.: U. S. Office of Education, 1970.

Tuckman, B. and Bierman, M. Beyond Pygmalion: Galatea in the schools. Paper presented at the annual meeting of the American Educational Research Association, 1971.

Tuckman, B. and Oliver, W. Effectiveness of feedback to teachers as a function of source. *Journal of Educational Psychology*, 1968, *59*, 297–301.

Willis, S. *Formation of teachers' expectations of students' academic performance.* Unpublished doctoral dissertation, University of Texas, 1972.

Wingo, G. Implications for improving instruction in the upper elementary grades. In N. Henry (ed.), *Learning and Instruction.* 49th yearbook, National Society for the Study of Education, Part I. Chicago: University of Chicago Press, 1950.

Wolfson, B. and Nash, S. Perceptions of decision-making in elementary school classrooms. *Elementary School Journal*, 1968, *69*, 89–93.

Wright, C. and Nuthall, G. The relationships between teacher behaviors and pupil achievement in three experimental elementary science lessons. *American Educational Research Journal*, 1970, *7*, 477-492.

Name index

Subject
index

76 77 78 9 8 7